New York
Employment Law:
The Essential Guide

Editors

Louis P. DiLorenzo, Esq.
Jeffrey A. Kehl, Esq.

Bond, Schoeneck & King PLLC

NEW YORK STATE BAR ASSOCIATION

New York State Bar Association publications are intended to provide current and accurate information to help attorneys maintain their professional competence. Publications are distributed with the understanding that NYSBA does not render any legal, accounting or other professional service. Attorneys using publications or orally conveyed information in dealing with a specific client's or their own legal matters should also research original sources of authority.

We consider the publication of any NYSBA practice book as the beginning of a dialogue with our readers. Periodic updates to this book will give us the opportunity to incorporate your suggestions regarding additions or corrections. Please send your comments to: Publications Director, New York State Bar Association, One Elk Street, Albany, NY 12207.

SUMMARY
TABLE OF CONTENTS*

---

*   A detailed table of contents, which sets forth the specific questions considered in each chapter, follows at p. xi.

- Construction workers
- Out-of-state employers
- Workers' compensation insurance
- Workers' compensation benefits
- Covered and non-covered activities
- Occupational diseases
- Psychological and psychiatric conditions
- Light or modified duty
- Workplace safety agencies in New York State
- Alcohol, tobacco and weapons in the workplace

- Short-term disability benefits requirements
  - What employees are covered?
  - What employers are covered?
  - Eligibility, filing and reporting requirements
- Long-term disability coverage
- Health insurance requirements (New York State)
- Life insurance
- Overview of federal benefits

- What the law covers
  - What employees are covered?
  - What employers are covered?
  - The relationship between New York and federal requirements
- How the unemployment insurance program is funded
  - Employer "contributions"
  - Employer "payments in lieu of contributions
  - Penalties for non-compliance

- Prohibited types of discrimination
- Who can assert a claim for discrimination
- Damages available for unlawful discrimination
- Who can be liable for unlawful discrimination
- "Disparate treatment" discrimination; "implicit bias"; "cat's paw" discrimination; "mixed motive" discrimination; "adverse impact" discrimination; compensation discrimination
- Sexual harassment and other prohibited forms of harassment
- Disabilities and reasonable accommodation
- Genetic characteristics
- Age
- Pregnancy
- Sexual orientation
- Transgender status
- Religion
- Marital, familial and domestic violence status
- Arrests and convictions
- Retaliation
- Procedural issues

- Employees v. independent contractors (*see also* Chapter 2)
- Interns
- Representation at disciplinary meetings
- Personnel files
- Payments at the end of employment
- Leaving the workplace during work breaks
- Undocumented workers
- Use of employee names and likenesses
- Monitoring e-mail, Internet use and telephone calls

- "Biometric" time clocks

- Computation of time limits

DETAILED
TABLE OF CONTENTS

Chapter 1   The Hiring Process
Christopher T. Kurtz
Hilary L. Moreira
Jacqueline A. Smith
Edited by Jessica C. Moller

Chapter 3   Wages and Salary

Katherine S. McClung
Andrew D. Bobrek
Dennis A. Lalli
Edited by Jeffrey A. Kehl

Chapter 4   Employee Time Off
Caroline M. Westover
Kerry W. Langan
Jessica C. Moller
Louis P. DiLorenzo
Mallory A. Campbell
Edited by Kseniya Premo

Chapter 5   Workers' Compensation and Workplace Safety
Patrick V. Melfi

I.   Workers' Compensation

Chapter 6   Disability, Health, And Life Insurance Benefits

Daniel J. Nugent
Stephen C. Daley
Thaddeus J. Lewkowicz
Edited by Thomas G. Eron

I.   Short-Term Disability Benefits

Chapter 7   Unemployment Insurance
Mark A. Moldenhauer
Edited by John Gaal

Chapter 9   Protecting the Employer's Business
Howard M. Miller
Candace J. Gomez
Edited by Jeffrey A. Kehl

Chapter 10 Discipline
Louis P. DiLorenzo
Edited by Jeffrey A. Kehl

Chapter 11 Discrimination, Harassment and Retaliation
Robert A. LaBerge
Christa Richer Cook
Nicholas P. Jacobson
Edited by John Gaal

I.   General Principles and Background

II. Hiring, Continued Employment, and Post-Employment Issues

III. Liability For Wrongful Acts

IV. Overview Of Discrimination Theories and Concepts

Chapter 12 Miscellaneous Topics of Interest
James J. Rooney
Erin S. Torcello
Mary E. Aldridge
Edited by R. Daniel Bordoni

INTRODUCTION TO THE FIRST EDITION

This book represents a labor of love by the Bond, Schoeneck & King Labor and Employment, Employee Benefits and Immigration Group. Our goal was to take the collective experience of our current practitioners—ranging from junior associates to retirees and building on the legacy of the Firm's previous four generations of labor and employment lawyers—in order to create an accessible reference for questions about New York employment law.

New York employment law is important for historical as well as practical reasons. New York is home to important financial and other markets; contains one of the largest cities in the United States; and has been a leader in addressing workplace issues and problems since long before the terrible Triangle Shirtwaist Factory fire of 1911. It is our hope this book will earn its title and be considered an essential guide to New York employment law for those who need to function in this sphere.

To create this guide, we identified authors within our Firm who could address such wide-ranging issues as contract law, tort law, discrimination law, employee benefits law, worker's compensation law, unemployment insurance law, New York State Department of Labor regulations, wage and hour requirements, litigation, arbitration, mediation and other procedural and substantive areas which bear on the workplace. Although federal statutes (such as the National Labor Relations Act, immigration laws, and federal wage and hour laws) are not directly addressed here, knowledge and familiarity with them was necessary in order to allow appropriate cross-references when required.

Bond's labor and employment lawyers work in our eight New York State offices which cover the length and breadth of the State and represent and counsel clients in virtually every industry. They recognize and appreciate that employment law governs the ongoing relationships in the workplace. Workplace problems are not like car accidents between strangers or malpractice claims. In some ways, employment law bears more resemblance to family law, as it deals with the ongoing relationships among employees, their employers, and their co-workers; and employment law necessarily addresses the issues and events which arise in the entire continuum of the workplace environment. Decisions in the workplace are rarely binary in their impact: rather, they more often involve, and affect, multiple other factors and stakeholders.

Further, each workplace has a unique culture which defines and manages the workforce. The law does not create a workplace culture: it is the relationship between the employer and the employees that determines the culture and is created by people rather than by statutes or the common law. The "correct" legal answer in one workplace culture may not necessarily be the right answer for other cultures. Hopefully, this book will provide the legal rules of the road for those who are responsible for shaping, changing, or maintaining the culture as they deal with the many episodes and events that affect them.

The Bond, Schoeneck & King lawyers who made the prodigious effort required to create this book are listed at the end of the book. A special thank you goes to the authors whose names also appear at the beginning of each chapter for which they made special contributions. Jeff Kehl's editorial work on this book was the "but for" cause for its existence. His knowledge, editorial skills and work ethic are responsible for a cohesive and practical volume. This book has also benefited from the extraordinary efforts of two of the best writers the Bond firm ever enjoyed, John Gaal and Dan Bordoni. Their efforts, as special editors, were invaluable.

We all hope you enjoy this first edition, find it an essential guide and will welcome our later editions.

Lou DiLorenzo

CHAPTER ONE

THE HIRING PROCESS

Christopher T. Kurtz
Hilary L. Moreira
Jacqueline A. Smith

Edited by Jessica C. Moller

INTRODUCTION

The hiring process is of critical importance to employers for three reasons: (1) employers want to attract the best candidates for open positions; (2) there are statutes that regulate both recruitment and hiring; and (3) employers need to avoid legal exposure for discriminatory hiring practices.

In this chapter, we discuss what employers may do, and should avoid, while advertising for, recruiting, interviewing, and hiring new staff. Because compliance with anti-discrimination laws is a critical aspect of the hiring process, there is significant overlap with Chapter 11 of this book,[1] and while some information appears in both chapters, we highly recommend that both be read together.

Specific topics addressed in this chapter are as follows:

I. WHO CAN BE EMPLOYED

[1.1] Who is eligible for employment?

II. JOB ADVERTISEMENTS

[1.2] What information may an employer lawfully include in a job advertisement?

[1.3] What may *not* be lawfully included in a job advertisement?
[1.3.1] New York City Additional Restrictions

[1.4] May a job advertisement include a requirement that the applicant submit to a background check, or that the applicant "must have a 'clean record'"?
[1.4.1] New York City Additional Restrictions
[1.4.2] Other Counties and Municipalities

[1.5] How may employers publicize open positions?

[1.6] For how long should employers maintain copies of job postings and advertisements?

III. EMPLOYMENT APPLICATIONS

[1.7] What kinds of questions are *appropriate* to include on an employment application?
[1.7.1] Questions about prior work history
[1.7.2] Questions about educational background
[1.7.3] Questions about lawful work status

---

1   *See* §§ 11.10–11.25.

[1.8] What questions are *inappropriate* and should *not* be asked on an employment application?

[1.9] What inquiries may be made about arrests and convictions?

[1.10] What is "Ban the Box" legislation?

[1.11] Is there a difference between asking about prior arrests and asking about pending criminal charges?

[1.12] What can an employer do if an applicant has a prior conviction or is the subject of pending criminal charges?

[1.13] May an employer ask about an applicant's current salary?

[1.14] May an employment application include a provision requiring an applicant to submit to a background check?

[1.15] May an employer require job applicants to provide references from prior employers as part of a job application?

[1.16] May an employer require applicants to submit photographs of themselves in connection with an employment application?

[1.17] May an employer use artificial intelligence programs to screen employment applications?

[1.18] For how long should employers keep job applications and other submissions from applicants?

IV. EMPLOYMENT INTERVIEWS AND DECISIONS

[1.19] What questions may be asked during a job interview?

[1.20] What questions may *not* be asked during a job interview?

[1.21] Are there special rules for safety-sensitive positions?

[1.22] May an employer ask if an applicant has medical conditions which might affect his or her ability to do the job?

[1.23] What if an applicant has a visible impairment, or volunteers information about a medical condition, or indicates that he or she needs a workplace accommodation?

[1.24] What information can be collected in a background check of an applicant?
[1.24.1] Federal restrictions
[1.24.2] New York State restrictions
[1.24.3] New York City restrictions

[1.25] May an employer run a criminal history check on a job applicant?

[1.26] What are the additional local restrictions on criminal history checks?

[1.27] How and when is an applicant disqualified by reason of a criminal record?

[1.28] May an employer reject an applicant based on a credit check?

I.   WHO CAN BE EMPLOYED

[1.1]   Who is eligible for employment?

In New York State, a person who is 18 years of age or older, and who qualifies for employment under federal law,[2] may be employed in any capacity.

---

2   Under federal law, a person must either be a United States citizen, hold a "green card" authorizing him or her to work in the United States, or hold a visa which specifically qualifies him or her for employment.

While there are certain occupations in which minors may be employed, either with or without an employment certificate ("working papers"),[3] some occupations are *prohibited* by Labor Law § 133:

- **No minor under 18 may be employed** (other than in a recognized training capacity[4]): to operate a manual elevator; in connection with explosives; to buff or polish metals in manufacturing; at a correctional institution related to the care or custody of inmates; to pack paints or paint components; to operate steam boilers; in construction, demolition or excavation; where there is exposure to radiation, silica or harmful dust; in logging or wood milling; in a mine or quarry; in power-driven woodworking, metal-forming or shearing, in bakeries, or in paper products operations; in the operation of circular saws, band saws, or guillotine shears; in a slaughterhouse or meat-packing plant; in the operation of power-driven hoisting equipment; in the manufacture of brick, tile and "kindred products"; as a helper on a motor vehicle; or as an exotic dancer.[5]

- **No minor under 16 may be employed** in painting or exterior cleaning as part of building maintenance; in a factory (except for delivery and clerical functions); in the operation of washing, grinding, cutting; slicing, pressing or mixing machinery; and in certain capacities in programs operated by the New York State Department of Mental Hygiene.[6]

- **No minor may be employed** "in or in connection with any trade, business, or service" when required to be in school or in violations of the provisions of his or her employment certificate "working papers."[7]

Pursuant to Labor Law §§ 130, 131 and 132, persons under 18 years of age may be employed *without* working papers as follows:

---

3   Regular working papers are issued by the public school district in which a minor resides.

4   The exceptions apply to registered apprentices, student learners in vocational training programs, trainees in approved on-the-job training programs, and minors who have completed one of those programs and are thereafter employed in the same occupation. Labor Law § 133(3).

5   Labor Law § 133(2).

6   Labor Law § 133(1).

7   Labor Law §§ 131(1) and 132(1).

Under 14 years old	Child performer;[a] child model[b]	§ 130(2)(a)-(b)
11 years old or older	Newspaper carrier[c]	§ 130(2)(c)
12–13 years old	Working for a parent or guardian on a home farm or outdoors[d]	§ 130(2)(d)
12–17 years old	With a farm work permit, in a hand harvest of berries, fruits and vegetables[e]	§ 130(2)(e)
Under 18 years old	Performing restitution ordered by a Family Court	§ 130(2)(f)[f]
12–13 years old	Assisting a family member selling produce from the family farm, at a farm stand, or at a farmer's market[g]	§ 130(2)(g)
12–13 years old	As a bridge caddie at a bridge tournament[h]	§ 130(2)(h)
14–15 years old	As a golf caddy; as a baby-sitter; for casual yard work not involving power-driven machinery; and as otherwise permitted above	§ 131(3)
16–17 years old	Farm work; for casual yard work and household chores (including power equipment customarily used in such activities); outdoor work for his or her family not connected with a trade or business; for employment by a non-profit college, fraternity, sorority or student or faculty association; for "the rendering of services for the public good"; and as otherwise permitted above.	§ 132(3)

a.   Subject to additional requirements in N.Y. Arts & Cultural Affairs Law § 35.01 and additional requirements of the Labor Law, including a child performer permit, discussed below.

b.   Subject to additional requirements in N.Y. Arts & Cultural Affairs Law § 35.05.

c.   Subject to additional requirements in N.Y. Educ. Law § 3228.

d.   As long as they are not working in a trade or business, and not at times when they are required to be in school.

e.   As long as for not more than four hours per day (and not at times when required to be in school); between 9:00 a.m. and 4:00 p.m. only between Labor Day and June 20; and 7:00 a.m. and 7:00 p.m. only during the rest of the year.

f.   *See also* Family Court Act §§ 353.6 and 758-a.

g.   But not at times when required to be in school.

h.   But not at times when required to be in school.

With working papers, minors 14 or 15 years old may work (while not required to be in school) in any non-prohibited occupation other than in or in connection with a factory (but *may* work in delivery and clerical functions).[8] *With* working papers, minors 16 or 17 years old may work (while not required to be in school) in any non-prohibited occupation.[9] Restrictions on the permitted hours of work for minors are found in Labor Law §§ 142 and 143. The work of child performers is extensively regulated by Labor Law §§ 150–154-a. Among other things, a special child performer permit is required; there must be compliance with restrictions on spending the child performer's wages; and the child performer must be provided with an education.

II.   JOB ADVERTISEMENTS

[1.2]   What information may an employer lawfully include in a job advertisement?

Job advertisements or postings should include an accurate job description that sets forth the essential functions of the position and any *bona fide* occupational qualifications.[10] For example, if a position requires an individual to have the ability to lift a certain amount of weight, that requirement should be listed in the job advertisement. In addition, any minimum experience/training that is required, any educational qualifications that must be completed, or licenses or certificates that are required for the job, may (and should) be included in a job advertisement.

[1.3]   What may *not* be lawfully included in a job advertisement?

Employers are prohibited from creating job postings or advertisements that express a preference for, or discourage an applicant from applying for, a position because of a protected characteristic (e.g., race, color, religion, sex, age, disability, etc.).[11]

The Equal Employment Opportunity Commission (the EEOC, the agency charged with enforcement of federal discrimination laws) has stated that "help-wanted ad[s] that seek 'females' or 'recent college graduates' may discourage men, or people over 40, from applying."[12] Accordingly, such

---

8   Labor Law §§ 131(1)–(2) and 133(1).

9   Labor Law § 132(1)–(2).

10   *See* § 1.3 below for a discussion of what is meant by a *"bona fide* occupational qualification."

11   Exec. Law § 296(1)(d).

12   U.S. Equal Employment Opportunity Commission, *Prohibited Employment Policies/Practices*, https://www.eeoc.gov/prohibited-employment-policiespractices.

statements in job advertisements may form the basis for a discrimination claim. Similarly, the New York State Division of Human Rights has prevailed in court on its position that "[i]t is an unlawful discriminatory practice for any employer or employment agency to circulate an advertisement which expresses an employment preference based upon sex unless that preference represents a bona fide occupational qualification."[13]

In those rare cases where a person's gender, age, religion, or national origin is a *bona fide* occupational qualification (BFOQ) which is reasonably necessary to the normal operation of a particular business, federal law[14] and New York State law[15] permit an employer to advertise a preference for such limitations.

To establish a defense for a BFOQ, the employer has the burden of proving that a particular class of applicants would be unable to perform the job as required because those applicants do not have a qualification essential to the position. For example, an advertisement for a piano moving position may contain a statement on the order of "must have robust upper-body strength." Although a person with a spinal condition that prevents her from lifting weights of more than 10 pounds is, as a person with a disability, protected against discrimination (and entitled to "reasonable accommodation" in the workplace), she does not have an essential qualification to get a job as a piano mover, because she cannot move a piano even with accommodation.

The above said, employers may not rely on "stereotyped characterizations" as a basis for making a BFOQ determination, and courts interpret the exception to federal and state discrimination laws very narrowly. For example, in *New York State Division of Human Rights v. New York-Pennsylvania Professional Baseball League*,[16] it was ruled in 1971 that being of the male sex was not a *bona fide* occupational qualification for a professional baseball umpire.[17]

---

13   *State Div. of Human Rights v. Binghamton Press Corp.*, 67 A.D.2d 231, 415 N.Y.S.2d 523 (4th Dep't 1979).

14   42 U.S.C. § 2000e-2(e).

15   Exec. Law § 296(1)(d).

16   36 A.D.2d 364, 320 N.Y.S.2d 788 (4th Dep't 1971), *aff'd sub nom N.Y. Div. of Human Rights ex rel. Gera v. New York-Pennsylvania Prof'l Baseball League*, 29 N.Y.2d 921, 329 N.Y.S.2d 99 (1972).

17   *See* Chapter 11 of this book, § 11.12, for a further discussion of *bona fide* occupational qualifications.

While employers generally have the burden of proving a lawful BFOQ, Exec. Law § 296(11) specifically permits *religious organizations* to limit employment or give preference to persons of the same religion or denomination "to promote the religious principles for which it is established or maintained."[18]

[1.3.1]   *New York City Additional Restrictions*

Pursuant to the New York City Administrative Code (N.Y.C. Admin. Code), New York City employers may not circulate any advertisement

> which expresses, directly or indirectly, any limitation, specification or discrimination as to age, race, creed, color, national origin, gender, disability, marital status, partnership status, caregiver status, sexual and reproductive health decisions, sexual orientation, uniformed service or alienage or citizenship status, or any intent to make any such limitation, specification or discrimination.[19]

In addition, New York City employers may not state in an advertisement that being currently employed is a requirement or qualification for the job or that an employer or employment agency will not consider individuals for employment based on their unemployment.[20]

[1.4]   May a job advertisement include a requirement that the applicant submit to a background check, or that the applicant "must have a 'clean record'"?[21]

Inquiries about prospective employees' prior criminal histories, including both prior arrests and prior convictions, are subject to important restrictions. In this section, we address job postings and advertisements; in §§ 1.9–1.12 below, we address the broader topic of pre-employment inquiries about arrests and convictions.[22]

---

18   *See* Chapter 11 of this book, § 11.6, for a further discussion of religiously affiliated employers.

19   N.Y.C. Admin. Code § 8-107(31)(c)(1)(d).

20   N.Y.C. Admin. Code § 8-107(31)(c)(21)(2)(a).

21   For a more general discussion of what types of information may permissibly be included in a background check, see § 1.24 below.

22   *See* Chapter 11 of this book, §§ 11.13 and §§ 11.60–11.64.

While it will be repeated later in this chapter and is also discussed in Chapter 11 of this book,[23] it is important to note that *under no circumstances may an employer ask a job applicant about a prior arrest record.*

Furthermore, there are significant restrictions on asking about, or making employment decisions based upon, prior *convictions* for crimes.

Pursuant to N.Y. Correction Law § 752, employers are prohibited from discriminating against or taking any adverse employment action against an applicant/employee who has been convicted of one or more offenses (or due to a lack of good moral character when that finding is based upon a criminal conviction) unless: (1) there is a direct relationship between one or more of the previous criminal offenses and the employment sought or held; *or* (2) granting or continuing employment would involve an unreasonable risk to property or the safety of welfare of specific individuals or the general public. (For specific procedural requirements which employers must follow in evaluating prior convictions, see § 1.12 below.)

While the above prohibition does not explicitly prevent an employer from including a reference to a "clean record" or "background checks required" in job advertisements/postings, the inclusion of such phrases in a job posting can be used as a basis to claim discriminatory hiring practices based on an applicant's criminal history. Accordingly, it is recommended that such language be avoided unless it is absolutely necessary.[24] In addition to the prohibitions in Correction Law § 752 discussed above, some local jurisdictions have specifically passed legislation that makes it illegal to include such references to background checks or criminal convictions in job postings/advertisements (*see* §§ 1.4.1 and 1.4.2 immediately below).

[1.4.1] *New York City Additional Restrictions*

Pursuant to Title 47, Section 2-04(a)(1) of the R.C.N.Y., the New York City Fair Chance Act,[25] it is a *per se* violation of the law for most employers to include *any* references to background checks or criminal records in a job advertisement or posting, including but not limited to the following phrases: "no felonies," "background check required," or "must have a clean record."

---

23   *Id.*

24   As almost any New York management labor lawyer will confirm, there are "professional" plaintiffs who review job advertisements for the express purpose of asserting discrimination claims based on past criminal history.

25   Title 47 of the Official Compilation of the Rules of the City of New York.

However, pursuant to § 2-04(g), the following positions are exempt from such requirement:

- Positions for which federal, state or local law *requires* criminal background checks.[26]

- Positions for which federal, state or local law *bars* employment of individuals based on criminal history.[27]

- Positions regulated by "self-regulatory" organizations defined in § 3(a)(26) of the Securities Exchange Act of 1934, as amended, 15 U.S.C. § 78a–78qq, where the rules or regulations promulgated by such organization require criminal background checks or bar employment based on criminal history.

- Positions as police and peace officers, or others working for law enforcement agencies and other exempted city agencies, including but not limited to the City Police Department, Fire Department, Department of Correction, Department of Investigation, Department of Probation, the Division of Youth and Family Services, the Business Integrity Commission, and the District Attorney's offices in each borough, or as otherwise determined to be exempt by the Commissioner of Citywide Administrative Services.

[1.4.2]   *Other Counties and Municipalities*

The following counties and municipalities have passed their own local restrictions on criminal history inquiries, and there is every reason to believe that the list below will expand over time:

---

26   This exemption applies only in situations where the employer *must* make the inquiry, and it does not exempt an employer from the general anti-discrimination requirements of § 8-107(10) of the Human Rights Law.

27   Again, this exemption applies only where the employer has no discretion in making the hiring decision, and applies to particular positions where the federal, state or local law bars employment with respect to a particular type of conviction. In such cases, an employer or agent thereof may (1) notify applicants of the specific mandatory bar to employment prior to a conditional offer; (2) inquire at any time during the application process whether an applicant has been convicted of the specific crime that is subject to the mandatory bar to employment; and (3) disqualify any applicant or employee with such criminal history without following the Fair Chance Process. The fact that a position requires a licensure or approval by a government agency does not by itself exempt the employer, employment agency, or agent thereof from the Fair Chance Process. When hiring for such a position, if the exemption in subdivision 2-04g(1)(i) or 2-04g(1)(ii)(A) does not apply, before making a conditional offer, the employer may only ask whether the applicant has the necessary license or approval or whether they can obtain it within a reasonable period of time.

- Albany County

- Dutchess County

- Tompkins County

- Ulster County

- Westchester County

- City of Buffalo

- City of Ithaca

- City of Kingston

- City of Newburgh

- City of Rochester

- City of Syracuse

- Town of Woodstock

- City of Yonkers

[1.5]   How may employers publicize open positions?

Employers may advertise for open positions in a variety of places and mediums, including but not limited to newspapers, job fairs, internet, social media, and "word of mouth."

However, "word of mouth" hiring involves definite risks, which are illustrated by a 1974 decision from New York State's highest court.[28] There, an employer was found to have discriminatory recruitment practices in violation of the New York State Human Rights Law where the majority of the people hired were from "word of mouth" recommendations, and after 50 years of business, the employer had never employed a Black or Hispanic person. On those facts, the State Division of Human Rights determined that such "word-of-mouth" recruitment perpetuated "an all-white work force." Reliance on word-of-mount recruitment was found to have

---

28   *State Div. of Human Rights v. Kilian Mfg. Corp.*, 35 N.Y.2d 201, 360 N.Y.S.2d 603 (1974).

had the effect, even if unintentional, of permitting invidious discrimination, and the employer was ordered to advertise via a method and means that would broaden its scope of recruitment.

[1.6]   How long should employers maintain copies of job postings and advertisements?

The EEOC recommends that employers maintain employment records for one year. However, because the statute of limitations for bringing a discrimination/harassment claim pursuant to the New York State Human Rights Law is three years, we recommend that employers should maintain copies of all job postings/advertisements for at least three years.

III. EMPLOYMENT APPLICATIONS

[1.7]   What kinds of questions are *appropriate* to include on an employment application?

Employers should limit the questions on an employment application to those that specifically relate to the position for which the applicant is applying. Applications should *not* contain questions that (a) are specifically prohibited by law, or (b) could be used to weed out applicants for discriminatory reasons.

Examples of questions that may be asked in an employment application include, but are not limited to, the following:

- General Information (name, address).

- Is the applicant lawfully permitted to work in the United States of America? (*see* § 1.7.3 below for more details)

- The names of any relatives of the applicant already employed by the employer.

- Is the applicant 18 years of age or older? (If the applicant is *not* 18 or older, the applicant may be asked to state his or her age, but the application may not ask anything else about age.)

- Does the applicant hold a valid driver's license? (but only if a driver's license is necessary for the position in question).

- Identification of outside memberships/organizations or activities that the applicant believes are relevant to his or her ability to perform the essential functions of the position in question.[29]

- The applicant's educational history (but not dates of graduation; *see* § 1.7.2 below for more details).

- The applicant's prior work experience (*but see* §§ 1.13 and 1.15 below for more details).

- Whether the applicant has any *pending* (open) arrests. (No employer may ask about *prior* arrests which have been resolved other than by convictions; even questions about pending arrests are not permitted in some jurisdictions; *see* §§ 1.8–1.10 below for more details).

- Whether the applicant has been convicted of a crime (felony or misdemeanor).[30]

- Whether the applicant can perform the essential functions of the job with or without reasonable accommodations.[31]

- The hours of the days/days of the week that the applicant is available to work.

It is good practice for employers to require the applicant to sign and date the application certifying that all the information provided in the application is true and accurate. This is helpful as a basis for discipline or discharge if it is later discovered that the applicant falsified information on the employment application.

---

29   It should be left to the applicant to determine what information he or she wishes to volunteer in response to this question. A question such as "Do you belong to a church, synagogue or mosque?" would suggest a predisposing religious bias on the part of the employer, which would clearly be improper unless the employer is a religiously affiliated employer hiring for a position as to which being a co-religionist is a BFOQ.

30   *But see* § 1.12 below for more details—this question is not permitted in some jurisdictions. Where this question is permitted, it is strongly recommended that any question about prior convictions be followed by: "A 'yes' answer will not in and of itself disqualify you from consideration but may be a reason for further inquiry."

31   This is as far as an employment application can go consistent with federal and state laws prohibiting discrimination on the basis of disability. For a more detailed discussion of "reasonable accommodation," *see* Chapter 11 of this book at §§ 11.35–11.46.

[1.7.1]   *Questions about prior work history*

Employers are permitted to ask about an applicant's prior work history. However, employers should be careful about asking applicants about gaps in their employment history, as that may reveal information about familial status, a serious illness or disability, or another protected characteristic.

In addition, employers should refrain from rejecting job applicants because of their "unemployed status," as this could disadvantage people of a particular race, color, national origin, religion, sex, or other protected class. "Unemployed status" includes any "current or past periods of unemployment."[32]

[1.7.2]   *Questions about educational background*

Employers are permitted to inquire about an applicant's "academic, vocational or professional education and the public and private schools attended."[33] In other words, employers may ask applicants to identify whether they have graduated from high school/college and/or how many years were completed and what, if any, type of degree/course of study was attained or completed.

However, it is generally accepted that employers should *not* ask the dates of graduation or the years of the applicant's attendance, as such inquiries may reveal an applicant's age and could form the basis of an age-discrimination claim.

Of course, an applicant is free to divulge information about his or her age, graduation dates, etc., if he or she chooses to do so.

[1.7.3]   *Questions about lawful work status*

Pursuant to federal law, it is generally unlawful for employers to hire an individual who is not lawfully permitted to work in the United States of America.[34] Accordingly, asking whether an applicant is lawfully permitted to work in the United States is appropriate, and, indeed, should be included in an employment application.

---

32   *See* U.S. Equal Opportunity Commission, Pre-Employment Inquiries and Unemployment Status, https://www.eeoc.gov/laws/practices/unemployed_status.cfm.

33   N.Y. Division of Human Rights, *Recommendations on Employment Inquiries* (2004).

34   *See* 8 U.S.C. § 1324a (Unlawful Employment of Aliens).

However, employers should not include questions about whether the applicant is a "U.S. citizen" or ask applicant to identify a country of origin. A non-U.S. citizen may still be lawfully permitted to work in the United States, and other questions about national origin could be viewed as evidence of discrimination.

Employers should also consider adding the following caution to their employment applications:

> In compliance with federal law, all persons hired will be required to verify identity and eligibility to work in the United State and to complete the required employment eligibility form upon hire.

Employers should remember that at the time of actual employment, all employers must complete U.S. Customs and Immigration Services Form I-9.

[1.8] What questions are *inappropriate* and should *not* be asked on an employment application?

Employers may not include questions designed to elicit answers that yield information that would be unlawful to consider in the hiring decision, such as an individual's race, religion, age, familial/marital status, national origin, disability, veteran status or other protected characteristic that is covered by the New York State Human Rights Law, Title VII of the Civil Rights Act of 1964, the Americans with Disability Act, or the Age Discrimination in Employment Act.[35]

In addition, Labor Law § 201-d prohibits employers from discriminating against applicants for lawful off-duty, off-premises conduct that is performed without the use of employer's equipment or property. This includes, but is not limited to, an individual's political activities, lawful use of consumable products (such as smoking or drinking alcohol), or lawful recreational activities.[36] The only exception to Labor Law § 201-d applies if the otherwise lawful outside conduct: (1) creates a material conflict of interest related to an employer's proprietary or business interests; (2) knowingly violates statutory or contractual conflict of interest provision applicable to state and local government employees; (3) violates a collective bargaining agreement; or (4) violates a contract entered into by

---

35   *See* Chapter 11 of this book, *passim.*

36   *See also* Chapter 8 of this book at §§ 8.22–8.28.

a certified or licensed professional, provided the person's annual compensation is equivalent to at least $50,000 in 1992 dollars.[37] Accordingly, employers should not include questions on a job application that may require an applicant to disclose lawful outside conduct (e.g., associations of which they are members, whether they smoke or drink, what political party the person belongs to, etc.) that is not related to the specific job for which the applicant is applying.

Finally, Labor Law § 194-a prohibits employers from relying on the wage or salary history of an applicant in determining whether to offer employment or in determining the wages or salary for such individual. Section 194-a further prohibits employers from requesting or requiring applications to include their salary history as a condition of being interviewed or considered for an offer of employment.

In addition to the prohibitions of Labor Law § 194-a, various localities (including New York City, Albany County, Suffolk County, Westchester County) have enacted their own prohibitions related to salary inquiries to applicants on job applications or during the interview process, and again, this list is likely to grow. As a result, employers are advised to eliminate any questions related to an applicant's prior salary from a job application.[38]

Examples of *impermissible* questions include, but are not limited to:

- Are you a U.S. citizen?

- Are you married? (This includes asking for an applicant's maiden name or including check boxes for prefixes such as Miss, Mrs., or Ms.)

- What does your husband/wife/partner do?

- What is your age (or date of birth)?

- What is your height and weight?

- What year did you graduate from high school (or college)?

---

37   *Id.* Equivalent to about $93,656.05 in Feb. 2020 (figure from https://www.bls.gov/data/inflation_calculator.htm).

38   The rationale for this prohibition is that it tends to perpetuate salary disparities that have previously impacted applicants who belong to categories of applicants (such as minorities and women) who have been disfavored in compensation.

- Do you have a disability?

- Do you have any impairments—physical, mental or medical—that would interfere with reasonable job performance?

- Do you have children (or how many children do you have)?

- Are you pregnant (or planning to have children)?

- What is your current salary? What was your starting and ending salary in your prior position?

- Have you ever been arrested?

- Where were you born?

- What is your native language?[39]

- Any questions about the applicant's sex, race, national origin, disability, or religion.

- Asking the applicant to identify clubs and organizations he or she is associated with, unless this is actually relevant to the position the applicant is seeking.

- Asking about how much sick leave the applicant has taken in the past, or whether the applicant has taken leave pursuant to the Family Medical Leave Act or has been out of work on a worker's compensation illness or injury.

- Inquiring about an applicant's health history, medications, or physical or mental impairments is also impermissible, except as noted below.

The Americans with Disabilities Act generally prohibits employers from asking disability-related questions or requiring applicants to be subjected to a medical examination until *after* a conditional offer of employment has been made.[40] Employers should limit their pre-offer questions to whether the individual is able to perform the essential functions of the position that he or she is seeking.

---

39   If it is a legitimate qualification for the position, as, for example, where the job involves teaching English as a Second Language to immigrants from the Balkans, it would be permissible to ask a question such as, "Do you speak Albanian?"

40   *See* § 1.40 below for the definition of "conditional offer of employment."

However, if an applicant has a *visible impairment* that the employer believes may require an accommodation, or if the applicant *voluntarily* discloses a disability, the employer is permitted (even *before* making a conditional offer of employment) to ask limited follow-up questions about what type of reasonable accommodation the applicant may need to perform a specific job duty.[41]

[1.9]   What inquiries may be made about arrests and convictions?

Executive Law § 296(16) prohibits employers from asking job applicants about prior arrests (or criminal accusations) that are not *currently pending* against the individual, or which have been resolved in favor of the individual, resolved by a youthful offender adjudication, or which resulted in a sealed conviction.

In general, New York law does not prohibit employers from asking whether an applicant has been *convicted* of a crime or if the applicant has a *pending* (open and unresolved) arrest.

However, various localities have enacted additional prohibitions relating to an employer's ability to ask applicants whether they have any *pending* arrests or if they have been convicted of a crime; *see* § 1.10 below.

[1.10]   What is "Ban the Box" legislation?

Some localities have enacted so-called "Ban the Box" legislation, which refers to a check-off box on an employment application in which the applicant is asked to answer "Yes" or "No" to an inquiry whether he or she has been convicted of a crime.[42] The following jurisdictions are among those which have enacted specific laws prohibiting employers from including a question on an application that inquires about an applicant's prior criminal record and/or pending arrests:

- Buffalo (Buffalo Code §§ 154-24 to 154-29)

- Rochester (R.M.C. §§ 63-12 to 63-16)

- Westchester County (W.C.L. § 700.03(a)(10))

---

41   U.S. Equal Opportunity Commission, *Pre-Employment Inquiries and Disability*, https://www.eeoc.gov/laws/practices/inquiries_disability.cfm; *see also* Chapter 11 of this book at § 11.38.

42   *See also* § 1.7 above.

- New York City (N.Y.C. Admin. Code §§ 8-102, 8-107(10), 8-107(11), 8-107(11-a))

As noted in § 1.4.2 above, similar legislation has been enacted in Albany County, Dutchess County, Tompkins County, Ulster County, City of Ithaca, City of Kingston, City of Newburgh, City of Syracuse, Town of Woodstock and City of Yonkers, and this list is expected to expand.

[1.11] **Is there a difference between asking about prior arrests and asking about pending criminal charges?**

Yes. Exec. Law § 296(16) prohibits employers from asking job applicants about *prior* arrests or criminal accusations that are no longer open, that were resolved in favor of the individual, that were resolved by a youthful offender adjudication, or that resulted in a sealed conviction. The Executive Law does not prohibit questions about *pending* prosecutions.

However, in New York City, the "Fair Chance Act" prohibits an employer from asking about *both pending arrests and prior convictions* until after a conditional offer of employment has been made.[43] In fact, employers in New York City are affirmatively required to notify job applicants that they should not disclose information about any pending criminal cases for which the applicant received an order adjourning the action in contemplation of dismissal that has not been revoked.[44]

[1.12] **What can an employer do if an applicant has a prior conviction or is the subject of pending criminal charges?**

Even if it is permissible to ask about prior criminal convictions or pending arrests, employers may not automatically disqualify an applicant on that basis alone. Article 23-A of the N.Y. Correction Law provides that employers may only deny employment based on an employee's conviction history if: (1) there is a direct relationship between the crime(s) and the specific employment sought; *or* (2) the grant or continuation of employment would involve an unreasonable risk to property or the safety or welfare of specific individuals or the general public.[45]

---

43   N.Y.C. Admin. Code § 8-107(11-a)(3).

44   2019 N.Y. Laws ch. 55, pt. II, subpart O, § 2. An Adjournment in Contemplation of Dismissal (ACD) is a mechanism authorized by New York State Criminal Procedure Law § 170.55 which authorizes a judge to adjourn a prosecution for a relatively low-level offense for a period of six months (or in some cases one year), after which, if the defendant has had no further encounters with the criminal justice system, the charges are dismissed and the record is sealed.

45   Corr. Law § 752.

In determining whether there is a "direct relationship" or "unreasonable risk" employers *must specifically consider* the following eight factors:

1. the state's public policy of encouraging the employment of persons previously convicted of one or more offenses;

2. the specific duties and responsibilities necessarily related to the employment sought;

3. the bearing, if any, that the criminal offense committed has on the applicant's fitness to perform one or more of the duties or responsibilities of the job;

4. the time elapsed since the offense was committed;

5. the age of the individual at the time the offense was committed;

6. the seriousness of the offense;

7. any information produced by the applicant on his or her behalf regarding rehabilitation and good conduct; and

8. the legitimate interest of the employer in protecting property and the safety and welfare of others and the general public.[46]

The law also provides that the employer must take into consideration any certificates of relief from disabilities or certificates of good conduct the applicant may have been granted, as these certificates create a presumption of rehabilitation with respect to the offense committed.[47]

If an applicant is refused employment due to a criminal conviction, the applicant has the right to request and receive a written statement from the employer within 30 days of the denial, explaining the reasons why the applicant was denied employment.[48] When denying employment for this reason, employers should keep a written record which reflects consideration of the above factors.[49]

---

46   Corr. Law § 753(1).

47   Corr. Law § 753(2).

48   Corr. Law § 754. This record should be retained for at least three years.

49   The law does not require any specific "score" on the above factors, but it does require a showing that they have been considered. Again, there are "professional" plaintiffs who bring actions for damages based upon the failure to meet the Correction Law requirements.

[1.13] May an employer ask about an applicant's current salary?

No. Labor Law § 194-a prohibits employers from relying on the wage or salary history of an applicant in determining whether to offer employment *or* in determining the wages or salary for such individual. Section 194-a also prohibits employers from requesting or requiring applicants to include their salary history as a condition of being interviewed or considered for an offer of employment. However, the law does not prevent an applicant from voluntarily (and without prompting) disclosing or verifying wage or salary history.

In addition to Labor Law § 194-a, various localities (including New York City, Albany County, Suffolk County, and Westchester County) have enacted their own prohibitions related to salary inquiries of applicants on a job application or during the interview process. Accordingly, we recommend that employers eliminate any questions related to an applicant's prior salary from a job application.

[1.14] May an employment application include a provision requiring an applicant to submit to a background check?

An employer is permitted, without notice to, or approval from, the applicant to check references and make inquiries into an applicant's background so long as the employer makes these inquiries itself.

However, if an employer uses a third-party (outside) service to make a background check, then the employer must obtain the applicant's written authorization before initiating the inquiry. This is required both by the federal Fair Credit Reporting Act[50] (FCRA) and the New York State Fair Credit Reporting Act.[51] In order to be valid, the authorization must be contained via a stand-alone document that is separate and apart from an employment application or any other documents.[52]

In addition, in order to comply with the FCRA, the job applicant must also be provided with the following documents *at the same time that* the FCRA authorization form is tendered:

- a copy of Article 23-A of the Correction Law; and

---

[50]   15 U.S.C. § 1681c(a).

[51]   Gen. Bus. Law § 380-a.

[52]   Most companies that do employment background checks can supply the required authorization forms.

- a copy of the Summary of Rights under the FCRA.[53]

However, neither the FCRA authorization nor the other two documents should be provided as part of, or with, the employment application.

New York law also requires employers to inform applicants that, upon request, the applicant will be informed whether or not a consumer report was ultimately requested and, if such report was requested, to be informed of the name and address of the consumer reporting agency that furnished the report.[54]

[1.15] May an employer require job applicants to provide references from prior employers as part of a job application?

Yes, but this should be approached with caution. Employers may require applicants to list prior employment and to provide references as part of the application process, but a requirement that is limited to references from prior employers *only* might disadvantage applicants of a disadvantaged race, color, national origin, religion, sex, or other protected class, who may not have prior employers to fulfill such a request. Accordingly, it may be preferable to include an alternative in the job application, such as, "Please provide the names, relationship to you, and contact information for two people who are familiar with your skills and work."

[1.16] May an employer require applicants to submit photographs of themselves in connection with an employment application?

Unless there is a BFOQ that requires an applicant to submit a photograph (for example, an application for an acting or modeling position), employers should not require applicants to submit a photograph of themselves with an application, because a photograph would permit an employer to screen applicants by protected characteristics such as race and ethnicity.

[1.17] May an employer use artificial intelligence programs to screen employment applications?

There is a burgeoning industry in the use of artificial intelligence (AI) to screen prospective employees. While there is no legal prohibition against the use of AI to screen candidates, we urge caution at this time about using AI for the following reasons:

---

53   *See* Consumer Financial Protection Bureau, *A Summary of Your Rights Under the Fair Credit Reporting Act,* https://www.consumer.ftc.gov/articles/pdf-0096-fair-credit-reporting-act.pdf.

54   Gen. Bus. Law § 380-b(b).

First, it will be difficult, if not impossible, for most employers to determine whether the AI program includes built-in biases against certain categories of applicants. For example, if the local labor pool of potentially qualified applicants is 30% minority, but the AI program screens out most or all minority candidates, the employer may be subject to a charge of discrimination.[55]

Second, the use of AI can produce other unintended consequences. Continuing the above example, suppose that an AI program is used to make initial selections from an applicant pool of 100 and generates a list of three candidates for interviews, of whom one is a minority applicant. At that point, if the employer does not select the minority candidate, it risks the argument being made that as soon as the employer got a look at the candidate and saw that he or she was a member of a minority group, the candidate did not get the job.

[1.18] **For how long should employers keep job applications and other submissions from applicants?**

Federal regulations require that résumés and applications submitted by applicants who were not hired should be kept on file for *one year*.[56] In addition, employers must keep application materials submitted by applicants who were offered a conditional offer of employment for *two years*.[57] Further, regulations implementing the federal Equal Pay Act require employers to keep records that "may be pertinent to a determination whether [a wage] differential is based on a factor other than sex"; and, if an employer bases a new hire's wages on information obtained during the hiring process, it should retain those records for *two years*.[58]

As noted in § 1.6 above, the New York State statute of limitations for bringing a discrimination/harassment claim pursuant to the New York State Human Rights Law is three years. Accordingly, we recommend that employers should maintain copies of all résumés and employment applications for at least *three years*.

---

55   See discussion of *State Div. of Human Rights v. Kilian Mfg. Corp.*, 35 N.Y.2d 201, 360 N.Y.S.2d 603 (1974) at § 1.5 above.

56   29 C.F.R. § 1602.14; 29 C.F.R. § 1627.3(b)(1)(i).

57   29 C.F.R. § 1627.3(b)(1)(i).

58   29 C.F.R. § 1620.32.

IV. EMPLOYMENT INTERVIEWS AND DECISIONS

[1.19] What questions may be asked during a job interview?

Employers should limit questions during an interview to those that specifically relate to the position the applicant is seeking. All of the questions set forth in § 1.7 above are permitted during an interview.

Employers may ask questions related to the *bona fide* occupational qualifications for the position that the applicant is seeking. For example, if the position requires the applicant to drive, an employer may ask whether the applicant has a valid driver's license. Similarly, if the position requires the applicant to have the ability to lift a certain amount of weight, or to be able to sit for an extended period of time, employers may inquire whether the individual is able to perform those essential functions of the position.

The nature of the employer also may determine whether there are *bona fide* occupational qualifications. For example, New York law permits qualifying religious organizations to give preference to members of the same religion.[59] Accordingly, qualifying religious organizations may be permitted to inquire about the applicant's religion.[60]

[1.20] What questions may *not* be asked during a job interview?

Employers are prohibited from asking any question that is designed to reveal, or has the predictable effect of revealing, information that an employer is prohibited from considering in making an employment decision. All of the prohibited questions enumerated in § 1.8 above are also prohibited during an interview.

[1.21] Are there special rules for safety-sensitive positions?

Yes, but only to the extent that questions which would otherwise be problematic relate directly to the safety concerns.

Safety-sensitive positions generally include those jobs that require the person in the position to be responsible for his or her own safety or the safety of others. Generally, those holding a safety-sensitive position are subject to mandated drug and alcohol tests to ensure they are of clear mind to perform the position. For example, the Omnibus Transportation

---

59   Exec. Law § 296(11).

60   *See also* Chapter 11 of this book at § 11.6.

Employee Testing Act of 1991[61] requires drug and alcohol testing of all safety-sensitive transportation employees in aviation, trucking, railroads, mass transit, pipelines, and other transportation industries. Because these drug and alcohol tests are mandated by law, it is permissible to explain to applicants who are seeking a safety-sensitive position that they will be required to comply with the drug and alcohol test as set forth by law and ask if they will be able to comply with such requirements.

[1.22] May an employer ask if an applicant has medical conditions which might affect his or her ability to do the job?

Employers should *not* ask an applicant open-ended questions whether he or she has a medical condition that could impact his or her ability to perform the job.

However, employers *may* ask if the applicant is able to perform the essential functions of the job, such as standing for long periods of time or lifting a certain amount of weight, *if* those are truly "essential functions" of the job. Similarly, a statement describing the essential functions of the job followed by a question asking if the applicant is able to perform those functions is generally permissible.

[1.23] What if an applicant has a visible impairment, or volunteers information about a medical condition, or indicates that he or she needs a workplace accommodation?

If an applicant has a visible impairment that the employer believes may require an accommodation, or if an applicant voluntarily discloses the existence of a disability or spontaneously raises the issue of an accommodation for a disability, employers are permitted to ask limited follow-up questions about what type of reasonable accommodation the applicant may need to perform a specific job duty. Under these limited circumstances, the inquiry may be made *before* a conditional offer of employment has been extended to the applicant. The U.S. Equal Employment Opportunities Commission has stated the scope of such authorization as follows:

> Under the law, employers generally cannot ask disability-related questions or require medical examinations until after an applicant has been given a conditional job offer. This is because, in the past, this information was frequently used to exclude applicants with disabilities before their ability to perform a job was evaluated.

---

61   49 U.S.C. § 5331.

Employers are permitted pre-offer to ask limited questions about reasonable accommodation if they reasonably believe that the applicant may need accommodation because of an obvious or voluntarily disclosed disability, or where the applicant has disclosed a need for accommodation.

Also pre-offer, employers may ask if the applicant will need an accommodation to perform a specific job duty, and if the answer is yes, the employer may then ask what the accommodation would be.

The employer may not ask any questions about the nature or severity of the disability pre-offer. However, after making a conditional job offer, an employer may ask any disability-related question or require a medical examination as long as all individuals selected for the same job are asked the same questions or made to take the same examination.[62]

For a more extensive discussion of disabilities, qualifications, the "interactive process," and the obligation to provide "reasonable accommodation," see Chapter 11 of this book at §§ 11.35–11.39.

[1.24] What information can be collected in a background check of an applicant?

For a general discussion of background checks and criminal records, see § 1.4 above.

Federal law, New York State law and New York City law have all placed restrictions on what information a pre-employment "background check" may permissibly disclose, depending on the type of information (such as criminal history or credit history), and by whom the information is collected (i.e., by the prospective employer or by a third party consumer reporting agency).

---

62   U.S. Equal Opportunity Employment Commission, *Pre-Employment Inquiries and Disability*, https://www.eeoc.gov/laws/practices/inquiries_disability.cfm.

[1.24.1] *Federal restrictions*

The federal Fair Credit Reporting Act (FCRA)[63] only imposes restrictions on background checks conducted by external consumer reporting agencies,[64] which may be in the form of a "consumer report" or an "investigative consumer report." A consumer report is any written, oral or other communication by a consumer reporting agency which bears on an individual's credit, character, general reputation, personal characteristics or mode of living.[65] This definition includes credit reports and most criminal background checks. An investigative consumer report is a consumer report based on personal interviews with neighbors, friends or associates, or others with whom the applicant is acquainted or who may have knowledge concerning the applicant.[66]

The FCRA prohibits consumer and investigative consumer reports from containing any of the following information:

- Bankruptcies that are more than 10 years old;

- Civil suits, civil judgments, and records of arrest that are more than seven years old;

- Paid tax liens that are more than seven years old;

- Accounts placed for collection or charged to profit and loss that are more than seven years old;

- Any other adverse items of information (other than records of convictions of crimes) that are more than seven years old;

- The contact information of any medical information furnisher, unless such contact information is reported using codes that do not identify the specific provider or nature of the services provided other than the identity of the consumer; and

- Certain information related to a veteran's medical debt.[67]

---

63   15 U.S.C. §§ 1681–1681x.

64   A consumer reporting agency is an individual or business which, for a fee, regularly assembles or evaluates consumer information. 15 U.S.C. § 1681a(f).

65   15 U.S.C. § 1681a(d).

66   15 U.S.C. § 1681a(e).

67   15 U.S.C. § 1681c(a).

However, the prohibitions as to information other than medical information do not apply to cases in which a consumer credit report is requested in connection with the employment of any individual at an annual salary of $75,000 or more.[68]

[1.24.2] *New York State restrictions*

Like the FRCA, the New York Fair Credit Reporting Act, Gen. Bus. Law § 380-j(f)(1)(i)–(iii) prohibits consumer reports from disclosing: bankruptcies that are more than 14 years old; judgments or paid tax liens that are more than seven years old; and generally any other adverse information that is more than seven years old.[69]

Additionally, the New York law prohibits consumer reporting agencies from reporting:

- Information relative to an arrest or criminal charge unless there has been a criminal conviction for such offense, or unless charges are still pending;

- Information relative to a consumer's race, religion, color, ancestry, or ethnic origin; or

- Information which it has reason to know is inaccurate;[70]

- Accounts placed for collection or charged to profit or loss which are more than seven years old, or accounts placed for collection or charged to profit or loss which have been paid and are more than five years old;

- Records of conviction of crimes which are more than seven years old;

---

68   FCRA, 15 U.S.C. § 1681c(b).The prohibitions also do not apply where the report is requested in connection with a credit transaction involving $150,000 or more or the underwriting of a life insurance policy of $150,000 or more. *Id.*

69   Gen. Bus. Law § 380-j(f)(1).

70   Gen. Bus. Law § 380-j(a).

- Information relating to drug or alcohol addictions where the last reported incident relating to the addiction is more than seven years old; and

- Information relating to past confinement in a mental institution where the date of last confinement is more than seven years old.[71]

However, these restrictions on what information may be included in consumer reports do not apply to situations involving the employment of any individual at an annual salary of $25,000 or more.[72]

[1.24.3] New York City restrictions

For employers in New York City, the New York City "Stop Credit Discrimination in Employment Act," N.Y.C. Admin. Code § 8-107(24)(a), prohibits employers with more than four employees[73] from requesting the consumer credit history of an applicant for employment. This prohibition does not apply to: (a) those applying for positions which require a credit history by either statute or regulation; (b) applicants for the position of police officer or peace officer; and (c) applicants for positions in which they will have signatory authority over funds or assets in excess of $10,000 or the authority to enter into agreements valued at $10,000 or more on the employer's behalf.[74]

---

71 Gen. Bus. Law § 380-j(f)(1).

72 Gen. Bus. Law § 380-j(f)(2). Also exempted are credit transactions involving $50,000 or more and the underwriting of life insurance involving $50,000 or more. *Id.*

73 N.Y.C. Admin. Code § 8-102.

74 Positions as to which a credit report may be required include: (1) police officers, peace officers, or positions with investigatory or law enforcement functions; (2) positions subject to background investigations by the Department of Investigation, if that position is an appointed position with a high degree of public trust; (3) positions for which an employee must be bonded under federal, state or city law; (4) positions for which an employee must have federal or state security clearance; (5) non-clerical positions having regular access to trade secrets, intelligence information, or national security information; (6) positions having signatory authority over third party funds or assets worth $10,000 or more or that involve a fiduciary responsibility to the employer with the authority to make agreements valued at $10,000 or more on behalf of the employer; and (7) positions for which an employee's regular duties allow the employee to modify digital security systems established to prevent the unauthorized use of the employer's or client's networks or databases. N.Y.C. Admin. Code § 8-107(24)(b)(2).

[1.25] May an employer run a criminal history check on a job applicant?

In general, yes, as to actual convictions and pending criminal charges, but not as to prior arrests that did not result in conviction.[75] However, certain localities restrict the time in the hiring process when this may be done, as discussed in § 1.26 below.

For some positions, a criminal history check is legally *required* prior to employment, such as school employees who will come in contact with students,[76] child care providers,[77] nursing home and home care services agency employees,[78] providers of service for alcohol and substance abuse,[79] and providers of services for individuals with special needs.[80]

Even if a criminal history check is not required by law, an employer may wish to conduct criminal history checks of its applicants. We caution, however, that if an employer wishes to conduct a criminal history check of one applicant for a position, the employer should (in addition to complying with any local restrictions, of course) conduct criminal history checks of *all* applicants for that position to avoid allegations of employment discrimination.

If the employer will be utilizing a third party to conduct a criminal history check, it must comply with disclosure and consent requirements discussed in § 1.9 above. Furthermore, applicable "Ban the Box" legislation (*see* § 1.10 above) may affect at what point in the hiring process the employer may make such an inquiry.

As explained in § 1.11 above, an employer must follow the evaluation process required by the New York Correction Law before deciding not to hire an applicant based upon his or her criminal history.

---

75   Criminal history checks, with the exception of applicants for the position of police officer or peace officer, may not include information related to any arrest or criminal accusation which is not currently pending against the individual, was resolved in favor of that individual, resolved by a youthful offender adjudication, or resulted in a sealed conviction. Exec. Law § 296(16).

76   Educ. Law § 3035(1); 8 N.Y.C.R.R. § 87.4.

77   Soc. Serv. Law § 390-b; 18 N.Y.C.R.R. § 413.4.

78   Pub. Health Law § 2899-a; Exec. Law § 845-b(3), 10 N,Y,C,R,R, § 402.6.

79   Mental Hygiene Law § 19.20.

80   Mental Hygiene Law §§ 16.33(a), 31.35(a), Soc. Serv. Law § 378-a(1).

[1.26] **What are the additional local restrictions on criminal history checks?**

In New York City, an employer cannot make any inquiry related to an applicant's criminal background (including by searching publicly available records) before the employer has made a conditional offer of employment.[81] In addition, New York City prohibits employers from asking an applicant about pending arrests until after a conditional offer of employment has been made.[82] Therefore, background checks conducted for New York City employers prior to the extension of a conditional offer of employment should not include information about any pending arrests or criminal cases.

The City of Buffalo and City of Rochester have similar local laws. The City of Buffalo Code, § 154-27, prohibits employers from inquiring about or requiring an applicant to disclose criminal convictions prior to the applicant's first interview. Rochester Mun. Code § 63-14 prohibits employers from inquiring about, or requiring an applicant to disclose, criminal convictions prior to the applicant's first interview, or, if there is no interview, before the employer has made a conditional offer of employment.

Employers in Westchester County may not inquire about an applicant's criminal background until after the applicant has submitted his or her employment application.[83] The Westchester County law also repeats the employer's obligation to perform an analysis of the applicant's criminal record and other factors under Correction Law Article 23-A before taking any adverse employment action based on the applicant's criminal history.

Some other localities have passed similar legislation, which in some localities is applicable only to certain employers. Such legislation has been enacted with respect to the hiring of public employees in Albany County, Dutchess County, Tompkins County, Ulster County, the City of Ithaca, the City of Kingston, the City of Newburgh, the City of Syracuse, the City of Woodstock, and the City of Yonkers.

---

81   N.Y.C. Admin. Code § 8-107(11-a)(3).

82   *Id.*

83   Westchester County Human Rights Law § 700.03(a)(10)(a).

[1.27] How and when is an applicant disqualified by reason of a criminal record?

As explained in § 1.12 above, an employer may not reject an applicant for employment by reason of a prior conviction unless the employer has first considered the eight factors enumerated in Correction Law § 753. As also noted in § 1.12 above, a rejected applicant has the right to request and receive a statement of reasons from the employer.

There must be a *direct* relationship between the crime upon which disqualification is based and the duties of the position applied for, or the underlying crime must have been one that involves an unreasonable risk to safety or property. Further, the employer must consider additional factors such as the seriousness of the underlying offense, the amount of time which has passed since the conviction, the applicant's subsequent record, the age of the applicant at the time of the offense, and any evidence which bears on the applicant's possible rehabilitation.

By way of example, if an applicant for a position as a bookkeeper or bank teller was convicted eight years ago of embezzling funds from a prior employer (or from a church, synagogue or mosque), a prospective employer has legitimate cause to be concerned about hiring that applicant. However, if the underlying conviction was for disorderly conduct at a party when the applicant was 20 years old, and he or she is now 35 and has had no subsequent convictions, it will be very difficult for the employer to explain how an old incident of unrelated conduct bears upon the applicant's fitness for the bookkeeping position.[84]

The analysis is particularly sensitive in localities where a criminal background check may not be considered until *after* the employer has made a conditional offer of employment, because the offer of employment is the employer's acknowledgment that the applicant meets the employer's criteria for hiring—meaning that the criminal record is the *only* reason for the decision not to hire, and must present a legally sufficient reason.

If after following the analysis required under Correction Law § 752, the employer determines that the applicant is disqualified based on his or her criminal history, the employer must, within 30 days of a request from the

---

84   If a *pending* criminal case is for an alleged criminal act that bears no direct relationship to the employment sought, and does not create an unreasonable risk to property or safety, then an employer would likely not be able to disqualify the candidate based on the pending criminal case.

applicant, provide a written statement setting forth the reasons for such denial.[85]

Under the New York City "Fair Chance Act," an employer rejecting an applicant because of his or her criminal record has an *affirmative* obligation to reach out to the applicant before making a final decision about a conviction. The Fair Chance Act requires that, before revoking the conditional job offer that the employer was required to make prior to conducting the criminal background check, the employer must engage in the fair chance process, which means: (1) the employer must explain its reasons for revoking the job offer using the "Fair Chance Notice" or an equivalent form;[86] (2) the employer must provide a copy of the background check or other information it relied upon, including any public records; (3) the employer must give the applicant at least three days to respond to the written information provided and keep the position open during this time; and (4) the employer must affirmatively request information concerning clarification, rehabilitation, or good conduct to rely on in making its determination.[87]

[1.28] May an employer reject an applicant based on a credit check?

Yes, but with two important cautions.

First, an employer should use credit checks on an even-handed basis and as to hiring decisions where there is an actual reason for wanting a credit check as a qualification for the position in question. Otherwise, if credit checks are required only of particular applicants, or if the requirement is likely to disqualify members of a particular group without a relationship to the requirements of the position, then a disparate impact discrimination claim will result.[88]

---

85   Corr. Law § 754.

86   The sample notice is found at https://www1.nyc.gov/assets/cchr/downloads/pdf/FairChance_-Form23-A_distributed.pdf., and begins as follows: "After extending a conditional offer of employment, we checked your criminal record. Based on the enclosed check, we have reservations about hiring you for the position of _____, and may decide to retract our job offer. Below explains why. We invite you to provide us with any information that could help us decide to offer you the job. If you choose to provide us with additional information you have _____ days (must be at least three business days) from the date you receive this to do so."

87   N.Y.C. Administrative Code § 8-107(11-a)(b).

88   For a discussion of "adverse impact" discrimination, *see* Chapter 11 of this book at § 11.24.

Second, the employer must follow the procedure required under the federal FCRA.[89] Specifically, the employer must comply with the following when it has used the services of a consumer reporting agency:

- The employer must provide a copy of the credit report to the applicant and notify the applicant that adverse action is imminent.

- The employer must wait a reasonable period of time before taking final adverse action to give the applicant a fair opportunity to dispute and correct any inaccurate information.

- Upon taking adverse action, the employer must give the applicant written notice of the adverse action.[90] The notice must include the consumer reporting agency's name, address, and telephone number, and a statement that the consumer reporting agency did not make the decision to take the adverse action and is unable to provide the applicant the specific reasons why the adverse action was taken. The notice must also inform the applicant that he or she can obtain a free copy of the consumer report from the agency within 60 days and that he or she has a right to dispute information in the report.

If the employer had a third party that is *not* a consumer reporting agency perform the credit history check, then additional notice and disclosure requirements may apply. In this circumstance, no later than three days after the date on which an investigative consumer report is requested, the employer must:

- Disclose in writing to the applicant that an investigative consumer report, including information as to his or her character, general reputation, personal characteristics, and mode of living (whichever are applicable), may be requested;

- Inform the applicant of his or her right to request a complete and accurate disclosure of the nature and scope of the investigation requested; and

- Provide the applicant with the summary of consumer rights.[91]

---

89   *See* 15 U.S.C. § 1681b(b)(3).

90   15 U.S.C. § 1681m(a).

91   15 U.S.C. § 1681d.

[1.29] May an employer Google information about a job applicant?

Employers are free to use the internet to research job applicants, including reviewing social media sites such as LinkedIn, Facebook, Instagram, and the like. However, the U.S. Equal Employment Opportunity Commission has expressed concern that when doing so, employers may violate federal and state anti-discrimination laws by learning information about an applicant's protected characteristics. As long as the information is not used to discriminate, employers may consider internet and social media information in making hiring decisions.[92]

Employers should be aware that they may not be able to use certain information learned through an internet search to determine whether to hire a candidate. For example, an employer may unintentionally become aware of an applicant's race, sex, religion, or other protected characteristic through an internet search that reveals certain affiliations with groups or images of the applicant. If the applicant is not ultimately chosen for the position and files a complaint alleging employment discrimination, the employer should be prepared to show that it did not take into account the applicant's protected characteristic when making its decision.

With respect to social media sites that may include information which may be viewed only with the data subject's permission (for example, to a Facebook "friend"), New York State has not yet enacted a law prohibiting employers from asking candidates for access to their social media sites; however, many other states have passed laws prohibiting such requests. Additionally, it may not be a best practice to ask for access to a private social media profile due to the possibility that the employer may discover the applicant's protected characteristics or other information that is not allowed to be considered when making a hiring decision.

An employer may not use an internet search to evade the prohibition of inquiring into an applicant's salary history.[93]

Furthermore, employers should bear in mind that Labor Law § 201-d prohibits employment discrimination based on an applicant's participation in

---

92   Of course, information obtained from the internet that has not been put there by the applicant may very well be false or inaccurate, and employers should exercise appropriate caution before relying on it.

93   *See* § 1.13 above.

lawful activities.[94] For example, if a Google search reveals an employee smokes cigarettes or belongs to a motorcycle club—which are lawful activities—that information may not form the basis of the employer's decision not to hire the applicant.

Finally, if an employer conducts Google searches of applicants, all similarly situated applicants should be treated equally and the searches should be conducted uniformly.

[1.30] May an employer verify an applicant's educational credentials?

Yes. Again, however, if this is done, it should be done consistently for all applicants.

Access to educational records—and, accordingly, the information that schools, colleges and universities will be willing to disclose—is governed by the federal Family Educational Rights and Privacy Act (FERPA).[95] FERPA requires consent from the student (or former student) for the release of many types of information, specifically including transcripts of grades. However, student consent is not required for "directory information," which may include information such as a student's name, contact information, date of birth, area of study, dates of attendance, honors and activities, and degree obtained.[96]

Educational institutions will not release an academic transcript without the student's consent. However, if an applicant's receipt of a degree or academic performance is relevant to the employer's hiring decision, the employer may require an applicant to have his or her educational institution send an academic transcript to the employer.

[1.31] May an employer contact a job applicant's past employers as part of a background check?

Yes. However, an employer should not ask a question, or seek information, that is designed to reveal protected characteristics of the applicant.

---

94   See Chapter 8 of this book at §§ 8.22–8.28 for more information about protected lawful activities.

95   20 U.S.C. § 1232g.

96   It is up to each institution to define what it chooses to designate as "directory information," and students have the absolute right to "opt out" of the disclosure of such information. 20 U.S.C. § 1232g. Employers should be wary of asking for dates of attendance because the dates may reveal an applicant's actual or approximate age which could give rise to a claim of age discrimination.

[1.32] What information may a past employer safely provide in response to a reference inquiry?

There is no law that requires any particular information be provided, or withheld, by a past employer in response to a reference inquiry. However, many employers are concerned about being sued by litigious former employees, and, accordingly, make it a practice to limit the response to inquiries with what is colloquially referred to as a "name, rank, and serial number" reference: i.e., the former employee's dates of employment, starting and ending titles, and final salary. Similar references are frequently agreed to between employers and ex-employees as part of the settlement of employment disputes. There is no way for a prospective employer to compel a former employer to provide additional details.

Where a former employer *does* choose to provide additional detail, at least one New York appellate court has found that there is a qualified privilege defense against a defamation claim where a negative reference consists of truthful information: "A qualified privilege exists for the purpose of permitting a prior employer to give a prospective employer honest information as to the character of a former employee even though such information may prove ultimately to be inaccurate."[97] The court explained that in the absence of malice, the employer could not be held liable for providing a negative reference.

There may also be times when a former employer withholds information from its reference, causing the new employer to hire a person who would not have been hired had the new employer known the truth. As a general rule, it is difficult to obtain recourse in these cases, although it is at least theoretically possible for a former employer to be found liable for negligent misrepresentation and/or fraud for giving incomplete or false information as part of a reference.

---

97 *Furci v. A.F.C. Contracting Enters.*, 255 A.D.2d 550, 551, 680 N.Y.S.2d 673 (2d Dep't 1998).

V.   DRUG AND ALCOHOL TESTING/MEDICAL EXAMINATIONS

[1.33]   May an employer require drug or alcohol testing?[98]

[1.33.1] *Drug Testing*

In New York, there is no state law limiting the right of employers to conduct pre-employment drug testing, except that the employer must pay the cost of medical examinations that are required as a condition of employment.[99]

However, effective May 10, 2020, *employers in New York City* are prohibited from requiring prospective employees to submit to testing for the presence of tetrahydrocannabinols (commonly referred to as THC) or marijuana.[100]

Vehicle drivers who perform safety-sensitive functions, as defined in the U.S. Department of Transportation's regulations, *must* undergo testing for controlled substances prior to performing safety-sensitive functions (e.g., driving commercial motor vehicles, repairing or unloading vehicles, etc.). The federal regulations specifically outline the details and requirements of such testing.[101] Under these regulations, and under regulations affecting other classifications of employees such as school bus drivers, employers are not required to, but may, also conduct alcohol screening.

The fact that drug testing may be legal does not mean that an employer can simply use over-the-counter tests. Testing in New York must be conducted by a licensed laboratory, and an employer which wants to conduct *on-site testing* must apply for and be granted a Limited Service Laboratory Registration certificate pursuant to Pub. Health Law § 579 before conducting on-site testing.[102]

---

98   *See also* Chapter 5 of this book at § 5.40.

99   Labor Law § 201-b.

100   N.Y.C. Local Law No. 2019/0Z91.

101   *See* 49 C.F.R. §§ 382.301, 382.107.

102   Pub. Health Law § 579(3)(h).

The penalty for conducting unlicensed testing is significant:

> Any person, partnership, corporation or other entity performing waived tests or provider-performed microscopy procedures without being authorized to do so pursuant to this title shall be subject to a civil penalty of up to five hundred dollars for each test performed, not to exceed two thousand dollars per day for each day tests are performed, in violation of this subdivision.[103]

In addition, drug testing should either be applied even-handedly to all similarly situated applicants (or employees) or based on a particularized, individually fact-based need to testing; otherwise, an employer may be exposed to a discrimination claim.

[1.33.2] *Alcohol Testing*

The EEOC has considered alcohol testing (in contrast to drug testing) to be a medical examination under the Americans With Disabilities Act (ADA), which provides that a job applicant may not be required to take a medical examination until after a conditional job offer has been made.[104] Alcohol testing must be job-related and consistent with business necessity.

If an employer is considering disqualifying a prospective employee based on a failed drug or alcohol test, the employer must be able to demonstrate that the test is accurate and is a valid predictor of job performance.[105]

Employers should also keep in mind that, under the New York State Human Rights Law, medical marijuana users, drug addicts, and alcoholics (including recovered and/or recovering addicts) are considered to be disabled.[106] Accordingly, if a prospective employee fails a drug or alcohol

---

103 Pub. Health Law § 579(3)(h).

104 42 U.S.C. § 12112(d)(2).

105 *Doe v. Roe, Inc.*, 160 A.D.2d 255, 553 N.Y.S.2d 364 (1st Dep't 1990) (holding that where a job applicant was disqualified due to a failed drug test, the employer had to produce evidence establishing that its testing method accurately distinguished between opiate users and consumers of lawful food and/or medications, as well as prove that the test bore a rational relationship to and was a valid predictor of job performance).

106 *See* 9 N.Y.C.R.R. § 466.11(h)(1).

test but is considered disabled and otherwise able to perform his or her job satisfactorily, the employer may be limited in its ability to refuse to hire the individual.

[1.34] When in the hiring process may a drug or alcohol test be administered?

[1.34.1] *Drug Testing*

A drug test may be administered at any time, including *before* a conditional offer of employment has been made.

[1.34.2] *Alcohol Testing*

Because the EEOC considers an alcohol test to be a medical examination under the ADA, an employer may not request or require a job applicant to undergo an alcohol test until *after* a conditional job offer is made. *See* § 1.33 above.

[1.35] What should an employer do if a job applicant is permitted to use medical marijuana?[107]

The New York Compassionate Care Act[108] deems certified medical marijuana patients to be disabled under the New York State Human Rights Law. Therefore, medical marijuana patients are protected from adverse employment actions based on their health conditions and attendant marijuana use.[109] However, employers may enforce a policy prohibiting employees from performing their job duties while impaired by a controlled substance.

Additionally, the Compassionate Care Act does not require an employer to do any act that would violate federal law or cause the employer to lose a federal contract or funding.

[1.36] When may an employer require a job applicant to undergo a medical (physical) examination?

Under federal law, a medical examination is defined as "a [medical] procedure or test that seeks information about an individual's physical or

---

107   *See also* Chapter 11 of this book at § 11.45 and Chapter 12 at § 12.8.

108   Pub. Health Law § 3360–3369-e.

109   *See* Pub. Health Law § 3369(2).

mental impairments or health."[110] Under the ADA, an employer may not require an applicant to undergo a medical examination prior to making a conditional job offer.[111] Further, the New York State Division of Human Rights has ruled that employers may not require a job applicant to submit to a medical examination (including psychological testing) as part of the application process, unless the examination is based on a *bona fide* occupational qualification.

However, under the ADA, an employer may *condition* an offer of employment on the results of a medical examination, provided that the following conditions are met:

- All entering employees in the same job category are required to submit to such an examination;

- Any information obtained about an applicant's medical condition or history is collected and maintained on separate medical forms and in separate medical files as confidential records; and

- The results of the examination are not used to discriminate against otherwise qualified individuals with disabilities.[112]

Similarly, in New York an employer may condition an offer of employment on the results of an applicant's medical exam *if* the medical exam is appropriate based on a *bona fide* occupational qualification, i.e., a qualification that is material to job performance. Employers may require applicants to show that they can perform the physical demands of a job and may conduct tests of physical strength, agility, endurance and stamina, provided the tests are non-discriminatory, can be shown to be job-related, and are given to all applicants for the same job category. Employers must pay the cost of any required medical examinations that are a condition of employment.[113]

Notably, however, under New York State law, "[a] test to determine the illegal use of drugs is not to be considered a medical test."[114]

---

110 EEOC Enforcement Guidance on Disability-Related Inquiries and Medical Examinations of Employees Under the Americans with Disabilities Act, Notice # 915.002 (2000).

111 42 U.S.C. § 12112(d)(2).

112 42 U.S.C. § 12112(d)(3); 29 C.F.R. § 1630.14(b); *see also* EEOC Enforcement Guidance: Pre-employment Disability-Related Questions and Medical Examinations, https://www.eeoc.gov/laws/guidance/enforcement-guidance-preemployment-disability-related-questions-and-medical.

113 Labor Law § 201-b.

114 9 N.Y.C.R.R. § 466.11(h)(6)(i).

[1.37] When may an employer require a job applicant to undergo a psychological examination?

Psychological examinations designed to test personality, intelligence, or aptitude are permissible under the federal ADA, so long as the examination is not likely to provide evidence concerning an applicant's mental disorder or impairment, as categorized in the American Psychiatric Association's Diagnostic and Statistical Manual of Mental Disorders. The ADA prohibits hiring discrimination based on "qualification standards, employment tests or other selection criteria" that tend to screen out disabled individuals and are not job-related or consistent with a business necessity.[115]

In New York, however, Labor Law § 735 prohibits employers from requiring prospective employees to submit to a "psychological stress evaluation," which is defined as questioning or interviewing an individual using a psychological stress evaluator, mechanical device, or instrument to analyze statements for their truth or falsity based on vocal fluctuations or vocal stress.[116] See § 1.39 below for more information on polygraph and psychological "stress testing."

In addition, as noted in § 1.36 above, the New York State Division of Human Rights has ruled that employers may not require a job applicant to submit to a medical examination (including psychological tests) as part of the application process, unless the examination is based on a *bona fide* occupational qualification.

[1.38] May an employer require a job applicant to take a personality, intelligence, or aptitude test as part of the hiring process?

The U.S. Equal Employment Opportunity Commission has opined that employment tests and other selection procedures must be "job-related and consistent with business necessity." The test also should not have the effect of disproportionately excluding persons based on race, color, religion, sex, or national origin if there is a less discriminatory alternative available.[117]

---

115   42 U.S.C. § 12112(b)(6).

116   Labor Law §§ 735–739.

117   EEOC Fact Sheet: Employment Tests and Selection Procedures (Sept. 23, 2010), https://www.eeoc.gov/policy/docs/factemployment_procedures.html.

[1.39] May an employer require a job applicant to take a polygraph (lie detector) test as part of the hiring process?

Federal law generally prohibits employers from using polygraph tests during the hiring process. The Employee Polygraph Protection Act (EPPA)[118] prohibits most private sector employers from requiring, requesting, or suggesting that an employee or job applicant submit to a polygraph or lie detector test, and from using or accepting the results of such tests. The EPPA further prohibits employers from disciplining, discharging, denying employment or discriminating against any employee or applicant: (1) for refusing to take a lie detector test; (2) based on the results of a lie detector test; or (3) for taking any actions to preserve employee rights under the Act.[119]

The EPPA contains limited exemptions to the general ban on polygraph testing. For instance, national defense, security service firms, and employers that manufacture, distribute or dispense controlled substances are permitted to test prospective employees.[120] In order to qualify for the security service firm exemption, the employer's primary business must consist of: (a) providing armored car personnel; (b) persons who design, install, and maintain security alarm systems; or (c) other uniformed or plainclothes security personnel. Thus, a security guard directly employed by an employer which is not in the business of supplying security services would not fall under this exemption.

As noted in § 1.37 above, Labor Law § 735 prohibits employers from requiring prospective employees to submit to a *psychological stress eval-*

---

118   29 U.S.C. §§ 2001–2009.

119   29 U.S.C. § 2002.

120   EPPA, 29 U.S.C. § 2006(e)–(f).

uator examination, although this type of evaluation is slightly different from a polygraph test.[121]

VI. JOB OFFERS AND REJECTIONS

[1.40] What is a conditional offer of employment?

A conditional offer of employment means that the applicant has been offered the job, but that the offer is contingent on the happening of some event, or the obtaining of additional information, and/or can be revoked.

Title 47, Chapter 2-01 of the Rules of the City of New York gives a more detailed definition of a conditional offer of employment (as used in Section 8-107(11-a) of the Administrative Code, i.e., the NYC Fair Chance Act) as a job offer that can only be revoked based on: (1) the results of a criminal background check after the Fair Chance Process has been followed; (2) the results of a medical examination as permitted by the Americans with Disabilities Act of 1990, as amended;[122] or (3) other information the employer could not have reasonably known before making the conditional offer, if based on the information the employer would not have made the offer and the employer can show the information is material.

[1.41] Must an offer of employment be in writing?

There is no requirement under federal or New York State law that a job offer be communicated in writing. However, it is often good practice to put an offer, and the terms of employment, in writing.

---

121 Labor Law § 733(5) defines a "psychological stress evaluator examination" as:

> (a) the questioning or interviewing of an employee or prospective employee for the purpose of subjecting the statements of such employee or prospective employee to analysis by a psychological stress evaluator;
>
> (b) the recording of statements made by an employee or prospective employee for the purpose of subjecting such statements to analysis by a psychological stress evaluator; or
>
> (c) analyzing, with a psychological stress evaluator, statements made by an employee or prospective employee for the purpose of determining the truth or falsity of such statements.

In *Scott v. Transkrit Corp.*, 91 A.D.2d 682, 457 N.Y.S.2d 134 (2d Dep't 1982), the Court held that polygraph tests based on blood pressure, pulse beat, galvanic skin response and breathing pattern are not the psychological stress evaluator exams prohibited by the Labor Law. *See also Nothdurft v. Ross*, 85 A.D.2d 658, 445 N.Y.S.2d 222 (2d Dep't 1981).

122 42 U.S.C. §§ 12101–12213.

Furthermore, pursuant to the New York State Wage Theft Prevention Act, Labor Law § 195(1)(a), all private sector employers are required to provide written notice of wage rates to employees at the time of hiring; *see* Chapter 3 of this book. The notice must be in English and/or the language identified as the employee's primary language, and must set forth the following:

- The rate or rates of pay (including overtime rate, if any), and the basis of pay (i.e., paid by the hour, shift, day, week, salary, piece, commission or other);

- Allowances, if any, claimed as part of the minimum wage, including tip, meal or lodging allowances;

- The regular pay day designated by the employer;

- The name of the employer;

- Any "doing business as" names used by the employer;

- The physical address of the employer's main office or principal place of business, and a mailing address if different; and

- The telephone number of the employer.[123]

The employer should obtain a signed and dated written acknowledgment from the employee when the notice is provided.

[1.42] Should an employer notify rejected candidates in writing?

In general, notices of rejection (for reasons *other* than the results of a background check)[124] are not required to be given, whether orally or in writing. However, it is often good practice to notify candidates who have been rejected, and to do so by a written communication.[125]

---

123 Labor Law § 195(1)(a). *See also* Chapter 8 of this book at § 8.14.

124 *See also* §§ 1.12, 1.14 and 1.27–1.28 above.

125 It is generally preferable for a rejection letter to be "generic" rather than to state specific reasons for rejection.

The federal Fair Credit Reporting Act requires notice to applicants of adverse action taken as a result of a consumer report or investigative report.[126]

Additionally, if an applicant is rejected due to his or her criminal history, the applicant may request a written statement that sets forth the reasons for denying employment and the employer must provide such written statement within 30 days.[127]

In New York City, the NYC Fair Chance Act requires an employer that revokes a conditional offer of employment must: (1) disclose to the applicant a written copy of any inquiry it conducted into the applicant's criminal history; (2) share with the applicant a written copy of its Correction Law Article 23-A analysis; and (3) allow the applicant at least three business days, from receipt of the inquiry and analysis, to respond to the employer's concerns.

---

126   *See* 15 U.S.C. § 1681m. *See also* § 1.28 above.

127   Corr. Law § 754.

CHAPTER TWO

TERMS OF THE EMPLOYMENT RELATIONSHIP

Katherine Ritts Schafer

Edited by Kseniya Premo

CHAPTER OVERVIEW

In this chapter, we consider: (a) the nature of the "employment at-will" doctrine in New York; (b) considerations which relate to employee handbooks; (c) a preliminary discussion of the difference between employees and independent contractors;[1] and (d) what rights employees may be asked to forgo as a condition of employment, The discussion continues in Chapter 8, in which we address additional obligations between employers and employees which are created either by the common law or by legislation and regulatory enactments.

I. "AT-WILL" EMPLOYMENT AND ITS EXCEPTIONS

[2.1] What is "at-will" employment?

[2.2] Is employment "at-will" in New York State?

[2.3] Are there exceptions to the general "employment-at-will rule" in New York?

[2.4] Does an employee's acceptance of an offer letter create an exception to the general "at-will" rule?

[2.5] Does the successful completion of a probationary period mean that an employee is no longer employed "at-will"?

[2.6] If an employee has an employment contract, does that automatically mean the that his or her employment is no longer "at-will"?

[2.7] Are there public policy exception to the "employment-at-will" doctrine in New York?

II. EMPLOYMENT AGREEMENTS

[2.8] Must an employee be given a formal employment agreement?

[2.9] What are the characteristics of written and oral employment agreements?

[2.10] Are oral employment agreements enforceable?

[2.11] What are "promissory estoppel" and "fraudulent inducement"?

III. EMPLOYEE HANDBOOKS

[2.12] What is the purpose of an employee handbook?

[2.13] What are the advantages to of having an employee handbook?

---

1   See Chapter 12 of this book, "Miscellaneous Topics of Interest," at § 12.2 for a more detailed treatment of the differences between employees and independent contractors.

[2.14] What are the disadvantages of having an employee hand-book?

[2.15] What is a progressive discipline policy?

[2.16] What policies should be included in an employee handbook?

[2.17] Should employee handbooks contain a disclaimer of contractual obligations?

[2.18] Should employers include an acknowledgment form with their employee handbook?

[2.19] What considerations apply regarding employee handbooks in a unionized workplace?

IV. EMPLOYEES VS. INDEPENDENT CONTRACTORS

[2.20] What is the difference between an employee and an independent contractor?

V. ARBITRATION AGREEMENTS, WAIVERS AND RELEASES

[2.21] Are agreements to arbitrate employment disputes valid?

[2.22] Are agreements to waive trial by jury valid?

[2.23] Can an employee agree to release claims against his or her employer?

I.   "AT-WILL" EMPLOYMENT AND ITS EXCEPTIONS

[2.1]   What is "at-will" employment?

"At-will" employment means an employment relationship that may be terminated by either party (but, most commonly, by the employer) at any time and for any (or no) reason, so long as the reason is not unlawful.[2] An at-will employee who is discharged by his or her employer has no contractual right to challenge the termination decision regardless of the perceived or actual fairness of the termination decision.

The "at-will" employment doctrine does *not* apply to employees who have been hired for agreed and specific periods of time,[3] or who have been prom-

---

2   An at-will employee may not be terminated for reasons which are discriminatory or in retaliation for the exercise of rights which are protected by law. These restrictions at discussed in Chapter 8 of this book, "Employer and Employee Rights and Obligations," at §§ 8.22–8.28, and Chapter 11, "Discrimination, Harassment and Retaliation," passim.

3   See §§ 2.9–2.10 below.

ised that their employment will not be terminated except for a specific reason or reasons, or who are protected by a collective bargaining agreement that sets rules for how and when an employee may be discharged. Thus, if an employee hired for a definite term is discharged without good cause, the employer can be liable for breach of the employment contract.[4]

[2.2]   Is employment "at-will" in New York State?

Yes. Employment-at-will is the general rule in New York for employees who are not hired for a specific duration.[5]

An at-will employee terminated by his or her employer cannot sue the employer for wrongful or abusive discharge or breach of contract, "absent a constitutionally impermissible purpose, a statutory proscription, or an express limitation in the individual contract of employment."[6] As stated by New York's highest court, the Court of Appeals, "[t]his court has not and does not now recognize a cause of action in tort for abusive or wrongful discharge of an employee; such recognition must await action of the Legislature."[7] *See also* § 2.7 below.

[2.3]   Are there exceptions to the general "employment-at-will" rule in New York?

Yes. While employment-at-will is the general rule in New York, that presumption may be rebutted by a showing that the circumstances surrounding the employer-employee relationship gave rise to a limitation on the right to terminate.

In the landmark case of *Weiner v. McGraw-Hill, Inc.*,[8] the New York Court of Appeals recognized a narrow yet significant exception to the at-will employment doctrine. In that case, an employee hired for an indefi-

---

4   *See Rothenberg v. Lincoln Farm Camp, Inc.*, 755 F.2d 1017 (2d Cir. 1985).

5   *Sabetay v. Sterling Drug, Inc.*, 69 N.Y.2d 329, 514 N.Y.S.2d 209 (1987).

6   *Murphy v. Am. Home Prods. Corp.*, 58 N.Y.2d 293, 461 N.Y.S.2d 232 (1983).

7   *Id. See also Smalley v. The Dreyfus Corp.*, 10 N.Y.3d 55, 58, 853 N.Y.S.2d 270 (2008) (reaffirming the court has "repeatedly refused to recognize exceptions to, or pathways around, [the] principles" set forth in *Murphy*).

8   57 N.Y.2d 458, 457 N.Y.S.2d 193 (1982).

nite term, and subsequently discharged by the employer for "lack of application," brought suit against his employer for breach of contract alleging:

- He was induced to leave his former job based on oral assurances that the company had a firm policy of not terminating employees without "just cause";

- The job application signed by the employee specified that his employment would be subject to the company's handbook on personnel policies and procedures;

- The company handbook expressly provided that the company would resort to dismissal only for just cause, and only after all practical steps toward rehabilitation and salvage of the employee had been taken and failed; and

- He had turned down other offers of employment in reliance on the employer's verbal and written assurances.

The Court held that the employee could maintain a breach of contract action against his employer, even though he had been hired for an indefinite period of time. In so holding, the Court acknowledged that an employer's otherwise unfettered right to terminate an at-will employee can be limited by the inclusion of a "just cause" provision in the employer's employee handbook.

Cases decided in New York since *Weiner* have narrowly interpreted the ruling in that case. Indeed, post-*Weiner* courts have consistently held that restrictions on an employer's right of termination which are contained in an employee handbook or manual will not be enforced as part of the employment contract *unless* the purported restrictions are explicit, specific and unequivocal, and satisfy the high standards set in *Weiner*.[9]

---

9   *See, e.g., Collins v. Hoselton Datsun, Inc.,* 120 A.D.2d 952, 503 N.Y.S.2d 203 (4th Dep't 1986) (general policy statements or supervisory guidelines providing, for example, that "employees should have job security," or that "employees are assured of steady employment as long as you are performing well," are insufficient to alter the at-will relationship); *Wright v. Cayan,* 817 F.2d 999 (2d Cir.), *cert. denied,* 484 U.S. 853 (1987) (completion of probationary period by employee does not limit employer's right to terminate employment at-will); *Coffey v. Tetragenetics, Inc.,* 40 A.D.3d 1247, 836 N.Y.S.2d 718 (3d Dep't 2007) (references in hiring letter to "the end of 2004" fail to establish hiring for a definite period, where references merely set forth timing of salary review and discretionary performance bonus, and letter contained no promises or assurances regarding the length of employment).

Even if an employee can otherwise meet the *Weiner* standard, an employer generally will not be bound by statements contained in an employee handbook unless the employee can show that he or she *knew of the provisions in the handbook at the time of hire and relied upon them in accepting employment.*[10]

As noted above, an employer's right to terminate may also be limited either by statutory prohibition or if the employer acts from an unlawful purpose.[11] Thus, for example, employees-at-will who qualify as "whistleblowers," or who have been discharged for discriminatory reasons, may sue for wrongful discharge; see discussions in Chapter 8 of this book at §§ 8.37–8.38 and Chapter 11, *passim.*

[2.4]   Does an employee's acceptance of an offer letter create an exception to the general "at-will" rule?

Not necessarily. Employers often issue a letter which sets forth the terms of an offer of employment. The mere issuance of such a letter does not create an expectation of continued employment; however, if not drafted carefully, an offer letter may create an exception to the general employment-at-will rule. For example, in *Herman v. Ness Apparel Co., Inc.,*[12] the court denied a motion for summary judgment on breach of contract claim where the prospective employer issued an offer letter containing specific statements regarding the duration of employment contemplated. By contrast, *compare Wright v. Cayan*[13] (an offer letter did not create limitation on employer's right to terminate at-will where the letter stated the employee would serve "at the pleasure of the supervisor for the first two (2) years").

To be safe, employers should consider express contractual disclaimers in their offer letters, such as "this offer is not an assurance of continued employment for any fixed period of time."

---

10   *Brooks v. Key Pharmaceuticals, Inc.,* 183 A.D.2d 1011, 583 N.Y.S.2d 673 (3d Dep't 1992) (at-will employee's breach of contract claim dismissed where the employee never saw the employee handbook prior to accepting offer of employment); *Brown v. General Electric Co.,* 144 A.D.2d 746, 534 N.Y.S.2d 743 (3d Dep't 1988) (plaintiff failed to establish breach of employment contract claim based on statements contained in policy guide, because he did not review the guide until after accepting employment).

11   *Sabetay v. Sterling Drug Co.,* 69 N.Y.2d 329, 337, 514 N.Y.S.2d 209 (1987).

12   305 A.D.2d 217, 760 N.Y.S.2d 142 (1st Dep't 2003).

13   817 F.2d 999, 1000 (2d Cir.), *cert. denied,* 484 U.S. 853 (1987).

[2.5]   Does completion of a probationary period mean that an employee is no longer employed "at-will"?

No. Neither a reference in an offer letter to a probationary period nor the mere fact that an employee has completed a probationary period automatically means that he or she is no longer an at-will employee.[14]

However, we recommend caution when describing (in an employee handbook, an offer letter, or otherwise) what happens after the completion of a probationary period. For example, a handbook might use the term "permanent" to describe the status of employees who survive the probationary period. This term may invite claims that the handbook has established a form of contractual job security not intended by the employer. Instead of "permanent," an employee's status should be described as "regular" or "non-probationary." Employers should also consider including employee handbook language stating that successful completion of any probationary period does not alter the at-will nature of the employment relationship.

[2.6]   If an employee has an employment contract, does that automatically mean that his or her employment is no longer "at-will"?

Probably, but not necessarily. The employment-at-will presumption is rebutted *only* if there is a showing of an "express written policy limiting [the employer's] right of discharge and that the employee detrimentally relied on that policy in accepting the employment."[15] Even where an employee has a written employment agreement, the employment is still presumed to be at-will if the agreement provides that the employer can terminate it on notice, or that employment may be terminated "with or without cause."[16] An express statement in an employment agreement that the employment is at-will precludes a breach of contract claim.[17]

---

14   *Colodney v. Continuum Health Partners, Inc.*, No. 03 Civ. 7276 (DLC), 2004 U.S. Dist. LEXIS 6606 at *17–18 (S.D.N.Y. April 15, 2004); *Wright v. Cayan*, 817 F.2d 999 (2d Cir.), *cert. denied*, 484 U.S. 853 (1987).

15   *De Petris v. Union Settlement Ass'n, Inc.*, 86 N.Y.2d 406, 633 N.Y.S.2d 274 (1995).

16   *Plantier v. Cordiant Plc.*, No. 97 Civ. 8696, 1998 U.S. Dist. LEXIS 15037 (S.D.N.Y. Sept. 24, 1998).

17   *Spivak v. J. Walter Thompson*, 258 A.D.2d 364, 685 N.Y.S.2d 247 (1st Dep't 1999).

[2.7]   Are there "public policy" exceptions to the "employment-at-will" doctrine in New York?

Generally not. While an at-will employee may not be terminated for discriminatory or retaliatory reasons, such an employee cannot challenge termination based on generalized claims of "violations of public policy" or breach of the implied covenant of good faith and fair dealing.[18]

In New York, with one narrow exception, the courts have required *an expression of public policy from the legislature* before an employee can challenge a decision based on "public policy." For example, many states, including New York, have found that terminating an employee in retaliation for filing a workers' compensation claim is prohibited because the public policy of the state encourages the filing of such claims. In New York, such a termination is an exception to the employment-at-will doctrine because N.Y. Workers' Compensation Law § 120 prohibits retaliatory discharge for filing a workers' compensation claim.

The one exception to the more general rule is found in a New York Court of Appeals decision which addressed a claim by a law firm associate that he had been fired because he insisted that the firm report a colleague's unethical conduct. In a narrow holding, the Court found an exception to the employment-at-will doctrine because the attorney code of ethics required reporting, and the core of the relationship between the parties was based on the code.[19] The holding is so narrowly construed that it has not even been applied to other professions.

II.   EMPLOYMENT AGREEMENTS

[2.8]   Must an employee be given a formal employment agreement?

No, with one notable exception for "commission salespersons,"[20] as to whom Labor Law § 191 requires that there be a written and signed

---

18   *See Lobel v. Maimonides Med. Ctr.*, 39 A.D.3d 275, 835 N.Y.S.2d 28 (1st Dep't 2007) (where there is no agreement setting forth a fixed duration for continued employment, employment remains at-will and an employee cannot maintain a claim for wrongful termination or breach of the implied covenant of good faith and fair dealing).

19   *Weider v. Stale*, 80 N.Y. 2d 628, 593 N.Y.S.2d 752 (1992). The *Weider* holding has been so narrowly construed that it has not even been applied to other professions. *E.g., Sabetay v. Sterling Drug Co.*, 69 N.Y. 2d 529, 516 N.Y.S.2d 174 (1981).

20   A commission salesperson is an employee whose principal activity is selling products or services, and who is paid, in whole or in part, on a commission basis; i.e. a.s a percentage of the sales he or she procures.

employment agreement, and which must meet the following requirements:

> A commission salesperson shall be paid the wages, sal-
> ary, drawing account, commissions and all other monies
> earned or payable in accordance with the agreed terms of
> employment, but not less frequently than once in each
> month and not later than the last day of the month follow-
> ing the month in which they are earned; provided, how-
> ever, that if monthly or more frequent payment of wages,
> salary, drawing accounts or commissions are substantial,
> then additional compensation earned, including but not
> limited to extra or incentive earnings, bonuses and special
> payments, may be paid less frequently than once in each
> month, but in no event later than the time provided in the
> employment agreement or compensation plan. The
> employer shall furnish a commission salesperson, upon
> written request, a statement of earnings paid or due and
> unpaid. *The agreed terms of employment shall be reduced
> to writing, signed by both the employer and the commis-
> sion salesperson, kept on file by the employer for a
> period not less than three years and made available to
> the commissioner upon request. Such writing shall
> include a description of how wages, salary, drawing
> account, commissions and all other monies earned and
> payable shall be calculated. Where the writing provides
> for a recoverable draw, the frequency of reconciliation
> shall be included. Such writing shall also provide details
> pertinent to payment of wages, salary, drawing account,
> commissions and all other monies earned and payable in
> the case of termination of employment by either party.*
> The failure of an employer to produce such written terms
> of employment, upon request of the commissioner, shall
> give rise to a presumption that the terms of employment
> that the commissioned salesperson has presented are the
> agreed terms of employment. (Emphasis supplied).

As discussed in § 2.2 above, employment in New York is considered to be
"at-will" *unless* the employer and employee have agreed on a fixed term
during which the employee will remain employed; however, an employer
and an employee may agree, either orally or in writing, on many additional terms of employment such as salary, benefits, expense reimburse-

ment, and many other conditions. The differences between oral and written agreements are discussed in §§ 2.9 and 2.10 below.

It should be noted, however, that even where there is no formal agreement, the common law implies certain rights and obligations as between an employer and an employee, and New York statutory law imposes additional requirements. These include (but are not limited to) the payment of wages, required paid and unpaid leave, protection of employees in the workplace, disability insurance, and unemployment compensation. *See, generally,* the following chapters of this book: Chapter 3, "Wages and Salary," Chapter 4, "Employee Time Off," Chapter 5, "Workers' Compensation and Workplace Safety," Chapter 6, "Disability, Health and Life Insurance," Chapter 7, "Unemployment," Chapter 8, "Employer and Employee Rights and Obligations" and Chapter 9, "Protecting the Employer's Business."

[2.9] What are the characteristics of written and oral employment agreements?

The most significant difference between a written agreement and an oral agreement is the term (duration) of the agreement; *see* § 2.10 below.[21]

An enforceable agreement, whether oral or written, consists of a number of required elements:

- There must have been an "offer and acceptance", and the offer and the acceptance must match up with each other to show that there has been a "meeting of minds." For example, if a potential employer offers a position at a salary of $75,000 per year, and the potential employee says that he or she will be happy to accept the position at $100,000 per year, there has been no meeting of the minds and there is no enforceable agreement.[22]

- There must be "consideration" for the agreement; in other words, a bargained-for exchange of performances. In an employment relationship, this is implicit: the employee agrees to work for the employer, and the employer agrees to compensate the employee.

---

21   There is, of course, another practical difference: it is more difficult to prove the existence of an oral agreement, since a written agreement consists of a physical communication which can be placed in front of a judge or other finder of fact.

22   This situation is sometimes referred to as an "offer-varying acceptance"; and as a matter of law, an acceptance which changes the terms of an offer is a rejection.

- The parties must have agreed on the "material terms" of what each will do for the other, because if there are important terms to which they have not agreed, then there is no enforceable agreement.

In an employment relationship, the basic elements of a valid agreement include: who is the employer and who is the employee; what the employee's position and duties will be; when the relationship will begin (and, if the employment is other than "at-will," when and how it may be ended), and salary and benefits.

An oral agreement is one in which at least some of the material terms were concluded "on a handshake" and without a writing (although other elements of the agreement may appear in written form).

A written agreement is most often a single document, almost always signed by both parties; but courts will also look to other written communications to determine whether an agreement exists. In the absence of one comprehensive document, a court will consider the following factors when deciding whether a contract was formed between two parties:

- Whether there has been an express reservation of the right not to be bound in the absence of a writing;

- Whether there has been partial performance of the contract;

- Whether all of the terms of the alleged contract have been agreed upon; and

- Whether the agreement at issue is the type of contract that is usually committed to writing.[23]

A court has found a binding contract where there was (1) an exchange of emails between the employee and employer with language including "I agree to the following"; (2) the employee started to perform the duties of the position; (3) a material term was agreed to in the emails, such as a severance pay; and (4) and the agreement was not complicated enough that it needed to be in writing.[24]

---

23 *Nusbaum v. E-Lo Sportswear LLC*, No. 17-cv-3646, 2017 U.S. Dist. LEXIS 198032, at *11 (S.D.N.Y. Dec. 1, 2017).

24 *Id.*

[2.10] Are oral employment agreements enforceable?

Generally, yes. So long as the elements of the agreement have been proven to the satisfaction of a court, an oral agreement will be enforced on the same basis as a written agreement, except as to duration. So, for example, if an employer has paid an employee less than the amount agreed to, or has failed to provide an agreed benefit, the employee may sue for arrears whether the employment agreement is written or oral. However, different rules may apply as to claims based on future entitlements.

As noted in §§ 2.1–2.7 above, New York is an "at-will" employment state, meaning that, in the absence of a definite agreement as to duration, both the employer and the employee are free to terminate the relationship at any time for any reason which is not unlawful. However, where an employer has agreed to employ an employee for a fixed period of time, the "at-will" doctrine does not apply and the employer may terminate the employment before the end of the contract period only "for cause."[25] Without "cause," the employer can be liable in damages for discharging the employee prior to the end of the contract.

An employer and employee *can* make an oral agreement that the employment will last for a specified period of time. However, if the oral agreement states a duration that exceeds one year, then the New York "Statute of Frauds" will bar enforcement of the duration provision, because the Statute of Frauds requires certain types contracts to be in writing in order to be valid, specifically including an agreement that "by its terms is not to be performed within one year from the making thereof."[26] Thus, if an employee seeks to enforce a claim that he or she had a right to continued employment for even one day more than a year, he or she will need to produce written proof of the agreement in order to seek enforcement.[27]

[2.11] What are "promissory estoppel" and "fraudulent inducement"?

In the absence of a written agreement for a fixed term of employment, an employer may, generally, withdraw an offer of employment before an

---

25   *See* Chapter 10 of this book, "Discipline," at § 10.6 for a discussion of "cause."

26   Gen. Obligations Law § 5-701.

27   Because the Statute of Frauds can produce harsh results, courts have introduced a limiting factor: if the agreement *could* have been completely performed within one year, then the requirement of a written agreement will not apply.

employee starts work. However, there are some circumstances in which an employer's conduct has been so egregious that the courts will create a remedy.

Promissory estoppel and fraudulent inducement are equitable principles on which a plaintiff may be able to recover damages upon a showing that a promise or fraudulent misrepresentation was made on which the plaintiff relied to his or her detriment.

Fraudulent inducement claims in the employment context arise when an employee is defrauded into making a change in employment status (or not making a change which he or she otherwise would have made) based on false statements made by the employer. Classic examples of fraudulent inducement arise from issues about pay. If an employee accepts a job offer with assurances of a specified pay grade, or is induced not to take a third-party offer by a promise of a matching raise, but in fact is paid less than the promised amount, the employee may sue for fraudulent inducement because he or she would not have taken the job but for the fraudulent statements about compensation.

The requisite elements of any claim for fraud are: (1) a misrepresentation of fact (and it must have been a statement of fact, and not an opinion or general prediction), (2) which was "material" (i.e. critical to the transaction under discussion), (3) which was known by the person making the misrepresentation to be false at the time it was made, (4) which was relied upon by the person to whom it was made in the form either of taking an action which he or she otherwise would not have done or not doing something which he or she otherwise would have done, and (5) which was actually detrimental to the person who relied upon the misrepresentation.

Because an at-will employee has no right to continued employment, at-will employees can only recover for fraudulent statements that induce them into taking a job in the first instance: "[A]n at-will employee, who has been terminated, cannot state a fraudulent inducement claim on the basis of having relied upon the employer's promise not to terminate the contract or upon any representations of future intentions as to the duration or security of his employment."[28]

---

28   *Laduzinski v Alvarez & Marsal Taxand LLC*, 132 A.D.3d 164, 168, 16 N.Y.S.3d 229 (1st Dept. 2015) (citations omitted). The court went on to say that in such a case, the at-will employee could not allege that their employer wrongly fired them, but would rather have to show that they would not have taken the job in the first place if the true facts had been revealed to them.

Courts have upheld claims for fraudulent inducement if plaintiff left other employment, or agreed to remain in a current place of employment, because of a fraudulent statement made by the employer.[29]

A mere promise of non-specific future intent ("If you come to work for me [or if you agree to turn down the other offer and keep working here], you can expect to be vice-president within a year") will not support a successful fraudulent inducement claim. However, intentional misrepresentations made with no intent of performing them ("If you come to work here [or if you agree to turn down the other offer and keep working here] I will double your current salary"), may give rise to an action for fraudulent inducement.[30]

Promissory estoppel is a legal theory that will bind an employer to its promise even if the promise does not satisfy the requirements of an enforceable contract. The elements of a claim for promissory estoppel in New York are: (1) a clear and unambiguous promise, (2) reasonable and foreseeable reliance by the party to whom the promise was made, and (3) an injury to the party to whom the promise was made by reason of his reliance.[31]

The only time an at-will employee can assert a successful promissory estoppel claim for wrongful termination is when "the employer has made a clear, unambiguous promise to terminate only for cause, or only after a certain period of time."[32] An employee's reliance on general assurances of future employment is not enough to maintain a claim.

III. EMPLOYEE HANDBOOKS

[2.12] What is the purpose of an employee handbook?

An employee handbook introduces employees to the organization, provides a summary of the employer's employment policies, and familiarizes employees with the guidelines and benefits that affect the relationship

---

29 *E.g., Jelks v. Citibank, N.A.*, No. 99 Civ. 2955, 2001 U.S. Dist. LEXIS 381 (S.D.N.Y. Jan. 22, 2001).

30 *See Stewart v. Jackson & Nash*, 976 F.2d 86, 89 (2d Cir. 1992).

31 *Apsan v. Gemini Consulting, Inc.*, No. 98 Civ. 1256, 1999 U.S. Dist. LEXIS 1104, at *12–13 (S.D.N.Y. Feb. 4, 1999).

32 *Jaffe v. Aetna Cas. & Sur. Co.*, No. 93 Civ. 0385, 1996 U.S. Dist. LEXIS 8421, at *10 (S.D.N.Y. June 19, 1996).

between them and the employer. Most employee handbooks also summarize at least some legal requirements, such as entitlement to overtime pay, paid family leave, family medical leave, and the like.

An employee handbook should be written in plain, simple language, and should generally try to avoid "legalese"; however, any employee handbook should be reviewed by legal counsel before it is issued or revised, and on a periodic basis as the law changes.

As noted above, an employee handbook should make it clear that the existence of the handbook, and the policies in it, are not intended at convert employees from "at-will" status, or to create contractual rights which the employer cannot change. A sample disclaimer in an employee handbook for XYZ Corporation might read as follows:

> This Handbook addresses the terms and conditions of employment for employees of XYZ Corporation. Employment by XYZ Corporation is at-will unless otherwise stated in a written individual letter of agreement signed by the Chief Operating Officer. This means that either the employee or XYZ Corporation may terminate the employment relationship at any time, for any lawful reason, and with or without notice.

> Nothing in this Handbook is intended to create an employment agreement for any particular term or period of time. All of the policies and procedures set out in the Handbook are subject to change by XYZ Corporation at any time.

> As is the case with all corporate policies, XYZ Corporation has the exclusive right to interpret this policy.

[2.13] What are the advantages of having an employee handbook?

It is helpful to both employers and employees for everyone to understand what is expected in the workplace. By giving managers and employees guidance on what is expected, an employee handbook can reduce or eliminate legal liability, support consistent treatment of similarly situated individuals, and help an employer comply with its obligations under federal, state and local law.

Employee handbooks can also promote desirable workplace conduct by making employer expectations clear; by answering likely employee questions in advance; by creating an atmosphere of fair treatment; and by helping reduce or resolve employee disputes and grievances. Employers (and particularly large employers) which operate on an *ad hoc* basis without written policies often experience confusion, inconsistent treatment, and ensuing dissension.

The advantages of having properly drafted handbooks and policies that are followed consistently and even-handedly easily—especially if the handbook contains appropriate disclaimers—outweigh any legal risks arising from potential contractual implications. That said, however, handbooks are not without risks.

[2.14] What are the disadvantages of having an employee handbook?

One risk of having an employee handbook is the potential for representations made in it to create a contractual obligation and jeopardize the common law rule in New York that employees are hired at-will. For this reason, employers should make sure their employee handbook does not contain any limitations (express or implied) on the employment-at-will rule, that it includes an express contractual disclaimer, and that the employment-at-will status of employees is reiterated where applicable throughout the handbook.

A second risk is that changes in the law may impose requirements different from those set out in a handbook, thus making the handbook obsolete and putting the employer out of compliance.[33] For this reason, it is important to have a handbook reviewed on a regular basis by a lawyer or human resources professional who stays current on the requirements of New York and federal laws affecting the workplace.

A third risk is that a handbook contains policy directives or prohibitions which the employer does not actually follow in practice. When policies are not followed, then the usefulness of the policies, and any employee handbook which contains them, is largely defeated.

We suggest that employers should only make an employee handbook available to employees *after* employment commences. This will avoid

---

33   When this happens, an employer faces a "Catch-22" situation: it can follow the law and put itself out of compliance with its own handbook, or it can follow the handbook and violate the law.

claims by employees that they were induced to accept an offer of employment because of something which appeared in the handbook.[34]

[2.15] What is a progressive discipline policy?

Employee handbooks often contain policies regarding discipline of employees for engaging in misconduct or for poor performance. A "progressive" discipline policy provides that an employer will take several steps, which increase in severity with each violation, in an effort to correct and improve an employee's conduct and/or performance before discharging the employee. These steps may include counseling, oral reprimand, written warning, suspension without pay, and, finally, demotion or termination. Progressive discipline is also discussed in Chapter 10 of this book, "Discipline," at § 10.5.

Contractual liability may result if an employee is discharged in a manner inconsistent with the employer's progressive discipline policy. In *Skelly v. Visiting Nurse Ass'n*,[35] the plaintiff was induced to leave another job and accept employment with the defendant based on oral assurances of job security, together with the employer's personnel manual which was given to her with the offer of employment and which stated that after the probationary period dismissal could occur only after completion of a five-step progressive discipline procedure. The court ruled that the employee was entitled to a trial to consider whether the oral assurances together, with the personnel manual provisions, limited the employer's authority to terminate the plaintiff as an employee at-will.

More frequently (and more problematically), an employer's inconsistent application of (or failure to follow) a progressive discipline policy can serve as a basis for disparate treatment claims under anti-discrimination statutes. In this regard, courts often ask if an employer followed its own handbook's disciplinary procedures in terminating employees. If the steps are not followed, the courts may deny motions to dismiss discrimination

---

34   For the same reason (among others) we suggest that employers *not* post their handbooks (or any other employment policies) to portions of their web sites which are available to the public. Such materials should be posted only to an employer's intranet which is accessible only by current employees, and in a format which cannot be edited by users.

35   210 A.D.2d 683, 619 N.Y.S.2d 879 (3d Dep't 1994).

claims, due to triable issues of fact as to whether the failure to follow the policies was benign or was the result of unlawful discriminatory intent harbored against the terminated employee.[36]

Progressive discipline policies contained in employee handbooks should be described as "guidelines," and not as mandatory procedures for carrying out discipline; and should provide that steps in the process may be skipped by the employer in its discretion, depending on the severity of the offense. To complement this statement, employers should consider providing *an explicitly non-exhaustive* list of examples of behavior that may lead to immediate termination of employment, without progressive discipline (such as theft, physical assault, sexual harassment, etc.).[37]

[2.16] What policies should be included in an employee handbook?

To a large extent, the contents of an employee handbook are optional, although it is the general practice to include a broad range of employer policies and practices so that both management and employees know what is expected of them. That said, certain employment policies are *required* by federal, state, or local law, and an employee handbook is almost always the logical place to include these policies.

For example, in New York, employers are now required to have a sexual harassment prevention policy that complies with the minimum requirements of Labor Law § 201-g.[38]

Employers should also include a reasonable accommodation policy with respect to disabilities, although this is not expressly required. The regulations implementing the New York Human Rights Law Regulations *suggest*, but do not require, that employers provide applicants and new employees notice of their rights with regard to reasonable accommodation of disability, and the procedures to be followed in requesting reasonable accommodation.[39] Again, *see* Chapter 8 of this book for details.

---

36 *See Cosgrove v. Sears, Roebuck & Co.*, 9 F.3d 1033 (2d Cir. 1993) (employer's termination of employee without following progressive discipline policy, coupled with management's knowledge of employee's charges of sexual discrimination and sexual harassment, created inference of retaliatory termination).

37 For example, where an employee seriously assaults a co-worker, or embezzles funds from the employer, no employer will want to be bound by a progressive discipline policy which requires that the only penalty for a first disciplinary offense is an oral warning.

38 *See* Chapter 11 of this book, "Discrimination, Harassment and Retaliation," at § 11.32.

39 9 N.Y.C.R.R. § 466.11(j)(1). *See* Chapter 11 of this book at § 11.35.

Labor Law Section 195(5) requires that covered employers notify their employees, either in writing or by public posting, of the employer's policy on: (1) sick leave; (2) vacation; (3) personal leave; (4) holidays; and (5) work hours.[40] The employee handbook is a good place for this notification.

The New York Labor Law does not require employers to pay employees for accrued but unused paid time off when they terminate their employment *if* the employer has established a policy that such time is forfeited upon termination of employment.[41] For a more detailed discussion of this topic, *see* Chapter 4 of this book, "Employee Time Off," at §§ 4.8–4.13. Again, the employee handbook is the logical place to publish this policy.

Employers should also have policies regarding various leaves of absences, including leave under the federal Family and Medical Leave Act (FMLA), the New York Paid Family Leave Law, and the various leave laws under New York Law, including military spouse leave, blood donation leave, voting leave, and breaks for nursing mothers. Again, *see* Chapter 4 of this book for details.

It is also customary to include most or all of the following policies in an employee handbook: a discipline policy (*see* § 2.15 above), a workplace violence policy, social media and electronic communications policies (establishing an employer's ability to monitor e-mail communication and regulating employees' online activity); a Fair Labor Standards Act "Safe Harbor" policy (to protect employers from losing an employee's exempt status due to improper deductions), and various work rules policies (addressing standards of conduct, like attendance/absenteeism, dress codes/grooming standards, and codes of conduct for employee behavior).

[2.17] Should employee handbooks contain a disclaimer of contractual obligations?

Yes. It is strongly recommended that an employee handbook should include an express disclaimer of contractual obligations, such as:

> This handbook does not create or imply an employment contract, nor does it in any way limit the employer's right to terminate employment at-will.

---

40   Employee time off is discussed in detail in Chapter 4 of this book.

41   *Kolesnikow v. Hudson Valley Hosp. Ctr.*, 622 F. Supp. 2d 98, 120 (S.D.N.Y. 2009) ("An employee's entitlement to receive payment for accrued, unused paid time off upon termination of employment is governed by the terms of the employer's publicized policy.").

Such a disclaimer is an important means by which employers may shield themselves against breach of contract claims, and also preserve the presumption of at-will employment.[42] *See also* § 2.12 above.

Disclaimers should state that:

- The personnel policies, manuals, or handbooks of the employer are intended as general policy statements or guidelines and do not constitute a contract between the parties;

- Management reserves the right to supplement, modify, or abolish any personnel policies, manuals, or handbooks in its discretion and without notice;

- Handbook provisions do not constitute an employment contract for any period of time or a fixed duration;

- Employees hired other than for a mutually-agreed period of time as set forth in a separate writing are employed-at-will, and may terminate their employment, or be terminated, at any time for any reason; and

- The provisions of the handbook supersede all other guidance to employees, whether written or oral.

[2.18] Should employers include an acknowledgment form with the employee handbook?

This is also strongly recommended. It is often extremely helpful to have documentary proof that an employee has received a copy of the handbook, not only to establish that the employee has been informed of and has acknowledged the at-will nature of the employment relationship, but also to establish knowledge of other important policies, such as an anti-harassment policy or a discipline policy.

However, employers should be aware that a signed acknowledgment form has the potential to make it somewhat more likely that the handbook will be considered to be a binding contract of employment rather than just a

---

42 *Lobosco v. N.Y. Telephone Co.*, 96 N.Y.2d 312, 727 N.Y.S.2d 383 (2001) (an employee seeking to rely on a provision in an employee handbook, supposedly creating a promise of employment, must also be held to reliance on any disclaimer language contained in the same handbook); *Baron v. Port Auth. of N.Y. & N.J.*, 271 F.3d 81 (2d Cir. 2001) (New York law makes it clear that conspicuous disclaiming language in an employee handbook preserves the presumption of at-will employment, as far as the provisions in an employee handbook are concerned).

statement of current policy guidelines. For this reason, it is important that contractual disclaimer language be included in both the handbook itself *and* on the acknowledgment form.

Further, if an acknowledgment form is included, employers must be diligent about ensuring that the forms are signed and retained, as the absence of a signed acknowledgment form could support an employee's claim that he or she never received the handbook.

[2.19] What considerations apply regarding employee handbooks in a unionized workplace?

Special issues arise when all or some of an employer's employees are members of a recognized collective bargaining unit. Employers often question whether their handbook should apply to employees represented by a labor union.

Generally, employers should avoid developing a single handbook to cover both unionized and non-unionized workers. For employees represented by a labor union, many (indeed, most) of the terms and conditions of their employment will be set forth in the collective bargaining agreement. Accordingly, large parts of a "one-size-fits-all" employee handbook will either (1) be inapplicable to the unionized segment of the workforce, or (2) conflict with the provisions in the collective bargaining agreement. Further, even if the provisions in the handbook are not covered in the collective bargaining agreement, they may still be problematic if they address issues which are considered "mandatory subjects of bargaining."

An employer violates Sections 8(a)(5) and (1) of the National Labor Relations Act[43] by making material unilateral changes during the term of a collective bargaining agreement as to matters that are mandatory subjects of bargaining.[44] An employer also violates Section 8(a)(5) and (1) of the National Labor Relations Act when it attempts to bypass the union and bargain directly (so-called "direct dealing") with bargaining unit employees.[45]

---

43   29 U.S.C. § 158(a)(5); 29 U.S.C. § 158(a)(1).

44   *NLRB v. Katz*, 369 U.S. 736 (1962).

45   *Heck's, Inc.*, 293 NLRB 1111, 1120 (1989).

In *United Cerebral Palsy of N.Y.C.*,[46] the National Labor Relations Board determined that the employer had violated Sections 8(a)(5) and (1) of the Act by: (1) distributing a handbook which altered terms and conditions of employment without bargaining with the union, and (2) engaging in direct dealing by requiring employees to sign a statement acknowledging that they received the handbook, agreeing to comply with its terms, and acknowledging that the employer could make future changes without notice. The handbook set forth polices concerning such mandatory subjects as vacation, posting of vacancies, and discipline and discharge, and those policies were inconsistent with collective bargaining agreement provisions concerning the same topics. The National Labor Relations Board concluded that only rescission of the entire handbook would fully remedy the unlawful conduct.

Some employers address this issue by adding a disclaimer to the introduction of the employee handbook which states that, in the event of a conflict between the provisions in the handbook and any applicable collective bargaining agreement, the collective bargaining agreement will govern with respect to those employees who are covered by the agreement. The problem with this disclaimer is that it does not clarify which policies actually apply to the unionized segment of the workforce. Unfair labor practice charges can result from the application of policies contained in the handbook.

Employers should consider distributing the employee handbook to non-union employees only, and/or providing a separate handbook for unionized employees which contains only those policies applicable to all employees, such as the employer's anti-harassment policies.

IV. EMPLOYEES VS. INDEPENDENT CONTRACTORS

[2.20] What is the difference between an employee and an independent contractor?

An individual performing work for hire in New York state is typically classified either as an employee or an independent contractor. Throughout this book, the reader will find references to the different application of New York law to employees on the one hand, and independent contractors on the other. Almost none of the legal protections which are afforded to employees are extended to independent contractors; and the latter are

---

46   347 NLRB 603 (2006).

protected only to the extent provided for in the agreements by which their services are engaged. The reader is referred to Chapter 12 of this book at § 12.2 for a more detailed treatment of the differences.

It is crucial for the employers to properly classify individuals working for them, because significant liability can arise when employees are misclassified as independent contractors.

Some of the most substantial risks faced by employers arise when payments to individuals who should have been classified as employees are improperly treated as payments to independent contractors: this results in liability for unpaid federal, state, and local income tax withholdings and liability for Social Security and Medicare contributions, plus associated penalties, fines and interest. Other significant financial risks include unpaid unemployment insurance premiums, unpaid workers' compensation premiums and unpaid overtime compensation and work-related benefits. These liabilities can be potentially devastating for employers. Another substantial risk is a claim of benefit entitlement by or on behalf of common law employees misclassified as independent contractors. Claims have been successfully brought by persons who should properly have been classified as employees for pension and profit-sharing benefits, medical benefits, and even stock options.

There is no single definition of the term "independent contractor" under New York law. To make this determination, the courts and governmental agencies apply a variety of factor-based tests, which are discussed in greater detail in Chapter 12 at § 12.2. As a general rule, however, true independent contractors are generally free from supervision, direction, and control in the performance of their duties.

Courts and administrative agencies often rely on the so-called "*Reid* factors"[47] to determine whether an individual is properly designated as an independent contractor:

- The skill required to perform the work in question: an independent contractor (who might, for example, be an attorney, an electrician, or an accountant) will often have skills that the rest of the employer's work force does not.

- Whether the hired party supplies his or her own tools and equipment: an independent contractor will generally supply his or her

---

47   *Community for Creative Non-Violence v. Reid*, 490 U.S. 730 (1989).

own tools and equipment, and often has an independent location for his or her business.

- The location of the work: an independent contractor will generally have his or her own separate business location.

- The duration of the relationship between the parties: an independent contractor is usually engaged for a specific project and does not perform services for the employer every day.

- Whether the hiring party has the right to assign additional projects to the hired party: an independent contractor is free to turn down additional assignments.

- The extent of the hired party's discretion over when and how long to work: an independent contractor generally decides when, where, and how he or she will get the engagement done.

- The method of payment: an independent contractor generally bills for his or her work and is paid a gross amount without withholding.

- The responsibility for hiring and paying assistants: an independent contractor is usually responsible for hiring and paying his or her own staff.

- Whether the work is part of the regular business of the hiring party: an independent contractor generally has his or her own business and performs functions which the employer does not perform with its own forces.

- Whether the hiring party is in business.

- Whether the hiring party provides benefits to the hired party.

- How the payments to the hired party are treated for tax purposes.

While no one factor is determinative, the degree of control which the hiring party exercises over the hired party can be a decisive: the more control that is exercised over the hired party, the more likely a court or administrative agency is to find that there is an employer-employee relationship.

While independent contractors do not enjoy many of the legal protections afforded to employees, they are afforded protections under the New York City Human Rights Law and are protected from sexual harassment under the N.Y. Executive Law §§ 292(5), 296-d; *see also* Chapter 11 of this book at §§ 11.3.1 and 11.31.

V.   ARBITRATION AGREEMENTS, WAIVERS AND RELEASES

[2.21] Are agreements to arbitrate employment disputes valid?

Yes, with a few specific exceptions. Employers often include arbitration provisions in offer letters and employment agreements, and these requirements will be enforced by the courts.

Thus, for example, the United States Supreme Court has upheld an arbitration agreement requiring workers to waive the right to bring class-action claims on various disputes, primarily over wages and hours.[48]

However, in New York (effective as of October 11, 2019), an employer cannot require an individual to submit future claims of employment discrimination (including but not limited to sexual harassment claims) to mandatory arbitration; and a clause that requires mandatory arbitration of these claims is void except in cases where federal law or applicable collective bargaining agreement are inconsistent.[49]

An employer may refuse to hire, or terminate, an employee if the employee refuses to sign an otherwise-valid arbitration agreement. However, the arbitration agreement must be supported by valid consideration (in other words, a *quid pro quo* for the agreement), such as a payment over and above salary.[50] Often, employers rely on the continuation of employment to serve as consideration in supporting an arbitration agreement, and this can also be valid consideration—but if the employee refuses to sign the agreement and the employer does not terminate the employee, other employees who also signed the agreement may use this as evidence that the agreement lacked consideration when the employer subsequently tries to enforce the arbitration agreement.

---

48   *Epic Sys. Corp. v. Lewis*, 138 S.Ct. 1612, 584 U.S. ___ (2018). However, the requirement will be enforced only where the agreement specifically includes class action proceedings. *See Lamps Plus, Inc. v. Varela*, 139 S. Ct. 1407, 1412 (2019) (citing *Stolt-Nielsen S.A. v. AnimalFeeds Int'l Corp.*, 559 U.S. 662 (2010).

49   CPLR 7515. Note, however, that one federal district court has ruled that the Federal Arbitration Act, 9 U.S.C. §§ 1–307, preempts New York's prohibition of mandatory arbitration clauses.

50   *See Williams v. Parkell Prods., Inc.*, 91 Fed. Appx. 707 (2d Cir. 2003).

[2.22] Are agreements to waive trial by jury valid?

An agreement to have disputes decided only by a judge, and not by a jury, is generally enforceable in New York. In the employment law context, the United States District Court for the Southern District of New York developed a four-factor test to determine the validity of a jury waiver: (1) whether the employer and employee actually negotiated over the waiver provision; (2) the extent to which the waiver provision was conspicuous in the agreement; (3) the relative bargaining power of the parties; and (4) the sophistication of the party who later argues that the waiver should not be enforced.[51] In other words, for an employee's waiver of the right to a jury trial to be effective, he or she must have known about the right and understood what it was, must have intended to waive it, and must have had at least some bargaining power in entering the agreement greater than "take-it-or-leave-it."

[2.23] Can an employee agree to release claims against his or her employer?

Many workplace disputes are settled between employers and employees, whether before or after litigation has been commenced. An employer settling an employee dispute will want the broadest possible protection that the settlement resolves *all* claims which the employee might have asserted (including claims which the employee did not make, but might make in the future).

In New York, an agreement to release claims can contain a general release of "any and all claims" arising from or related to an employee's employment, including future claims. New York courts have consistently upheld the validity of broadly worded releases.

However, certain claims cannot be released, including:

- Claims for unemployment compensation, underpayment for work on public projects, and discrimination based on military service.[52]

---

51   *Schappert v. Bedford, Freeman & Worth Publ'g Group, LLC*, No. 03 Civ. 0058, 2004 U.S. Dist. LEXIS 14153, 2004 WL 1661073 (S.D.N.Y. July 23, 2004).

52   Labor Law § 595(1); Military Law § 318(2).

- In most instances, claims for disability benefits.[53]

- Claims for workers' compensation benefits unless the New York State Workers' Compensation approves a release agreement.[54]

Finally, while an employee can release his or her own claims for employment discrimination, he or she cannot be barred from disclosing certain information, or participating in the adjudication of other discrimination claims; *see* Chapter 11 of this book at § 11.33.

---

53 Employees who are eligible for or receive old age insurance benefits under Title II of the Social Security Act may waive their right to disability benefits by filing a claim for exemption with their employer and the New York Workers' Compensation Board. The statement must be dated, signed by the employee, and notarized. WCL § 218(1).

54 WCL § 32. The release agreement must be on a form approved by the chair of the board or contain the information prescribed by the chair. 12 N.Y.C.R.R. § 300.36(b). Generally, the board will approve a release unless the agreement is unfair, unconscionable, or improper as a matter of law; the agreement is the result of an intentional misrepresentation of material fact; or within 10 days of submitting the agreement, one of the interested parties asks the board to disapprove the agreement and the board determines that it should not be approved. *Id.*

CHAPTER THREE

WAGES AND SALARY

Katherine S. McClung
Andrew D. Bobrek
Dennis A. Lalli

Edited by Jeffrey A. Kehl

CHAPTER OVERVIEW

In this chapter, we address the requirements that New York law imposes on the payment of wages and salary. While New York law in many respects duplicates the requirements of the federal Fair Labor Standards Act (FLSA), 29 U.S.C. §§ 203 *et seq.*, New York imposes significant *additional* requirements that employers must meet.

We discuss the following topics below:

[3.1] **What information about wages are employers required to give to employees?**

[3.1.1] *Time of Hire Notices*

Labor Law § 195(1)(a) requires employers to provide all new hires with specific information about their wages and rate of pay, as well as certain information about the employer and its pay practices. This information must be provided in writing, in the employee's "primary language" as well as in English, on either (1) a form that the New York State Department of Labor (NYS DOL) has promulgated, or (2) a form that the employer may develop for itself—so long as the employer's form provides at least all of the information required to be provided on the DOL's form. The information to be provided is:

> [T]he rate or rates of pay and basis thereof, whether paid by the hour, shift, day, week, salary, piece, commission, or other; allowances, if any, claimed as part of the minimum wage, including tip, meal, or lodging allowances; the benefit portion of the minimum rate of home care aide total compensation as defined in section thirty-six hundred fourteen-c of the public health law ("home care aid benefits"), if applicable; prevailing wage supplements, if any, claimed as part of any prevailing wage or similar requirement pursuant to article eight of this chapter; the regular pay day designated by the employer . . . ; the name of the employer; any "doing business as" names used by the employer; the physical address of the employer's main office or principal place of business, and a mailing address if different; the telephone number of the employer. . . . Each time the employer provides such notice to an employee, the employer shall obtain from the employee a signed and dated written acknowledgement, in English and in the primary language of the employee, of receipt of this notice, which the employer shall preserve and maintain for six years. Such acknowledgement shall include an affirmation by the employee that the employee accurately identified his or her primary language to the employer, and that the notice provided by the employer to such employee pursuant to this subdivision was in the language so identified. . . . For all employees who are not exempt from overtime compensation as established in the commissioner's minimum wage orders

or otherwise provided by New York state law or regulation, the notice must state the regular hourly rate and
overtime rate of pay . . .[1]

At first glance, these requirements seem intimidating, but fortunately, the
NYS DOL has promulgated forms, in multiple languages, that employers
may use to meet these notice obligations.[2]

Labor Law § 195(2) further requires employers to provide written notice
of any changes to the information in the most recent notice that has been
provided to the employee, and this notice must be given at least seven
days before the changes take place. However, the additional notice is not
required if the changes are reflected in the "wage statement" that is provided together with the employee's wages; *see* § 3.1.2 below.

If an employee is not provided with the required "time of hire" notice
within ten days after his or her date of hire, the employee may bring a civil
action, and/or the NYS DOL may commence an administrative proceeding, to recover damages of $50 per work day, subject to a cap of $5,000.
Further, in a civil action brought by an employee, the employee may seek
attorneys' fees. However, the employer has an affirmative defense if
wages due to the employee(s) in question were paid in full and on time.[3]

[3.1.2]   *Wage Statements*

Labor Law § 195(3) also requires employers to provide a "wage statement" (commonly referred to as a "pay stub") with each payment of
wages. The statement must show:

> The dates of work covered by that payment of wages;
> name of employee; name of employer; address and
> phone number of employer; rate or rates of pay and basis
> thereof, whether paid by the hour, shift, day, week, sal-
> ary, piece, commission, or other; gross wages; deduc-
> tions; allowances, if any, claimed as part of the minimum
> wage; the benefit portion of the minimum rate of home
> care aide total compensation as defined in section thirty-
> six hundred fourteen-c of the public health law ("home

---

1   Labor Law § 195(1)(a).

2   *See* Employment Laws/Labor Standards, New York Department of Labor, https://labor.ny.gov/
     formsdocs/wp/ellsformsandpublications.shtm.

3   Labor Law § 198(1-b).

care aide benefits"), if applicable; prevailing wage supplements, if any, claimed as part of any prevailing wage
or similar requirement pursuant to article eight of this
chapter; and net wages. . . . For all [non-exempt]
employees . . . , the statement shall include the regular
hourly rate or rates of pay; the overtime rate or rates of
pay; the number of regular hours worked, and the number of overtime hours worked . . . . Upon request of an
employee, an employer shall furnish an explanation in
writing of how such wages were computed.

If the required wage statements are not provided, an employee may bring
a civil action, and/or the NYS DOL may commence an administrative
proceeding, to recover damages of $250 for each work day that the viola-
tion occurs, subject to a cap of $5,000. Further, in a civil action brought
by an employee, the employee may seek attorneys' fees. Again, however,
the employer has an affirmative defense if wages due to the employee(s)
in question were paid in full and on time.[4]

[3.2]   How frequently must employees be paid in New York?

Labor Law § 191 provides that "manual workers" must be paid weekly,
with payment to be made not later than seven days after the end of the
week in which wages are earned. However, certain larger employers, as
spelled out in Labor Law § 191(a)(ii), may apply to the Commissioner of
Labor for an exemption from this requirement if they demonstrate satisfactory proof of continuing ability to meet payroll responsibilities.

The Appellate Division, First Department of the New York State
Supreme Court has held that manual workers have a private right of
action to sue for a penalty equal to 100% of late-paid wages—which,
when the action involves bi-weekly instead of weekly payment of wages,
applies to the first week of every two-week pay period.[5]

Commission sales employees must be paid in accordance with the agreed
terms of their employment, and, in general, not less frequently than
monthly and not later than the last day of the month following the month
in which their commissions were earned.

Clerical and other workers may be paid not less frequently than semi-
monthly.

---

4   Labor Law § 198(1-d).

5   *Vega v. CM & Assoc. Constr. Mgmt., LLC*, 175 A.D.3d 1144, 107 N.Y.S.3d 286 (1st Dep't 2019).

There is no requirement that applies to the frequency of payment for exempt employees.

At the end of employment, the employer is required to pay all wages owed not later than the regular pay day for the pay period in which the termination occurred.

[3.3] What is the minimum wage in New York?

The statutory minimum wage in New York varies according to geographic region. As of December 31, 2019, the general statutory minimum straight time hourly wage rates are

Location	Minimum Wage
New York City	$15.00/hour
Nassau, Suffolk and Westchester counties	$13.00/hour
The rest of New York State	$11.80/hour

Starting December 31, 2020, the general minimum wage in Nassau, Suffolk and Westchester counties will increase to $14.00/hour, and to $12.50/hour in the rest of the state. In addition, the general minimum wage in Nassau, Suffolk and Westchester counties will increase to $15.00/hour starting December 31, 2021. It is expected that the NYS DOL will promulgate a wage order to provide that starting December 31, 2021 the minimum wage for the rest of the State will increase by an amount yet to be determined.

There are special minimum wage rules for "hospitality industry"[6] employees, as follows:[7]

	New York City	Nassau, Suffolk and Westchester counties	The rest of New York State
Fast food workers	$15.00/hour	$13.75/hour	$13.75/hour
Food service workers	$10.00/hour	$8.65/hour	$7.85/hour
Service employees[a]	$12.50/hour	$10.85/hour	$9.85/hour

a. Primarily workers in job categories where tipping is customary.

---

6 *See* § 3.7.3 below for the regulatory definition of the "hospitality industry."

7 Again, these hourly rates became effective as of December 31, 2019.

"Fast food workers" are those who work in establishments which serve food or drink that patrons pay for before consumption, whether on premises or for take-out or delivery, where there is limited service, and where the establishment is part of a chain that has at least 30 locations nationally. Workers at such establishments whose job duties include customer service, cooking, food or drink preparation, delivery, security, stocking supplies or equipment, cleaning, or routine maintenance, fall within the definition of "fast food workers."

"Food service workers" are those whose principal job duties in any given work week include serving food or beverages to patrons in the hospitality industry (such as waitstaff, bartenders, captains, and bussers) *and* who regularly receive tips above certain threshold amounts.[8] Hospitality industry employers are entitled to take an allowance (commonly called a "tip credit") against the wages of food service employees in amounts that have changed from year to year since 2016 and vary from region to region within the State.[9] However, the tip credit is not available to an employer for any day in which the employee is assigned to work that is not tipped (e.g., setting tables, food service preparation, etc.) for more than two hours or 20% of the shift, whichever is lower. Delivery workers are *not* food service workers.

"Service employees" are workers other than food service workers who customarily receive tips above certain threshold amounts.[10] Hospitality industry employers are entitled to take a tip credit against the wages of service employees in amounts that, like those for food service workers, have changed from year to year since 2016 and vary from region to region within the State.[11] The tip credit available for service employees is smaller than that available for food service workers. Delivery workers are service employees, not food service workers, and the tip credit available to their employers is smaller than the tip credit available for food service workers.

[3.4]   Are employers entitled to take any credits against the minimum wage?

Employers may take limited credits against the minimum wage requirement for tips, and for meals and lodging furnished to employees. These

---

8   12 N.Y.C.R.R. § 146-3.4.

9   *See* 12 N.Y.C.R.R. § 146-1.3(b).

10   12 N.Y.C.R.R. § 146-3.3.

11   *See* 12 N.Y.C.R.R. § 146-1.3(a).

credits are sufficiently complicated that they are discussed only in general terms in this book.

[3.4.1] *The tip credit*

Employers in the hospitality industry may take a credit against the minimum wage owed to "food service workers" and "service employees" if the employee receives tips above certain thresholds.

For "food service workers," *see* definition in § 3.3 above). Again, note that delivery workers are *not* food service workers; rather, they are "service employees."

For "service employees," *see also* definition in § 3.3 above.

Because the tip credit available for service employees is smaller than that available for food service workers, the applicable calculations are different. Using New York City (where the minimum wage has been $15 per hour since December 31, 2018) as an example:

- If a *food service worker* receives tips that average at least $5 per hour in any given week, the employer may take a tip credit of $5 per hour against the employee's wages for that week, and pay a straight-time hours wage of only $10, since the hourly wage of $10 plus the tip credit of $5 per hour equals $15 per hour and thus satisfies the employer's minimum wage obligation.[12]

- However, for a *service employee* (such as a delivery worker), the tips-received threshold is *more* than the tip credit. In New York City, the tip credit has been $2.50 per hour for service employees since December 31, 2018, so that the employer may satisfy its minimum wage obligation by paying $12.50 per hour in wages, since that amount plus the $2.50 per hours tip credit equals $15 per hour. However, the tips-received threshold for service employees is $3.25 per hour.[13] The employer may take the $2.50 per hour tip credit only in weeks in which the service employee receives tips that average at least $3.25 per hour.

For many years, employers in industries *other* than the hospitality were allowed to take a tip credit against the minimum wages of employees who

---

12   12 N.Y.C.R.R. § 146-1.3(b)(1)(i).

13   12 N.Y.C.R.R. § 146-1.3(a)(1)(i).

perform work for which they are tipped.[14] However, to the extent that tip credits were still permitted outside the hospitality industry, in 2020 the tip credit was halved starting June 30, 2020, and is eliminated altogether starting December 31, 2020.

[3.4.2]   *Meals, lodging and utilities.*

With the exception of certain non-profit entitles, and within specific dollar limits (which vary by industry), employers may take credits for the following amenities provided to employees:

- Meals, lodging and facilities in the "Miscellaneous Industries";[15]

- Meals and lodging in the "Hospitality Industry":[16]

- Meals, lodging and utilities on the "Non-Exempt Non-Profitmaking Institutions" sector;[17]

- Apartments and utilities in the "Building Services Industry";[18]

- Meals, lodging and utilities for farm workers.[19]

[3.5]   Can an employer recoup money owed by an employee?

The general rule is that employers may make no deductions from wages except for those specifically authorized by law, as follows:

(a) Wage deductions.

No employer shall make any deductions from wages except those that fall within the following four categories:

(1) any deductions made in accordance with any law, rule or regulation issued by any governmental agency;

---

14   *See* 12 N.Y.C.R.R. § 142-2.5(b).

15   12 N.Y.C.R.R. § 142-2.5(a).

16   12 N.Y.C.R.R. § 146-1.9.

17   12 N.Y.C.R.R. § 142-3.4(a)–(b).

18   12 N.Y.C.R.R. §§ 141-1.5–141-1.6.

19   12 N.Y.C.R.R. § 190-3.1.

(2) deductions specified by, or similar to those specified by, section 193 of the Labor Law, authorized by, and for the benefit of, the employee;

(3) deductions for the recovery of overpayments made in accordance with this Part; and

(4) deductions for the repayment of wage advances made in accordance with this Part.

(b) Separate transactions.

No employer shall make any charge against wages, or require an employee to make any payment by separate transaction unless such charge or payment is permitted as a deduction from wages under this Part or is permitted or required under any provision of a current collective bargaining agreement.[20]

Some deductions (such as income taxes and Social Security contributions) are required by law; others (such as employee welfare benefit and pension plans, charitable contributions, transportation benefits, union dues, and the like) may be made if authorized by a collective bargaining agreement or by the written agreement of an individual employee.

Except as specifically required or permitted by law, payments from an employee to an employer (such as repayment of a loan) must be done other than through payroll. However, there are provisions addressed specifically to the recovery of wage overpayments and repayment of wage advances.[21]

[3.5.1]   *Recouping wage overpayments*

Employers may recover wage overpayments resulting from arithmetic or clerical errors by wage deduction *or* by separate transaction (e.g., by accepting payments from the employee).

However, an employer may recoup an overpayment through wage deduction *only* if the employer provides written notice of intent to recover the overpayment within eight weeks after the overpayment is made. If the over-

---

20   12 N.Y.C.R.R. § 195-2.1.

21   12 N.Y.C.R.R. §§ 195-2.1, 195-5.1, 195-5.2.

payment to be recouped is *less* than the net amount of the employee's next paycheck, the entire amount may be deducted if the employer's written notice is provided at least three days before the deduction is made. If the overpayment to be recouped is *more* than the net amount of the employee's next paycheck, the deductions may not exceed 12.5% of the gross wages in the employee's next paycheck, the remaining pay must equal at least the minimum wage, and notice must be provided at least three weeks before deductions begin. The written notice has to set forth the total amount of the overpayment and the amount to be deducted each pay period.[22]

Further, an employer seeking to recoup a wage overpayment is required to establish a procedure for the employee to dispute the overpayment and the terms of repayment, and to seek a delay in the start of the wage deductions. The Wage Order provides specific steps, timelines, and requirements for these procedures. The employer's notice of its intent to recover the overpayment is required to include a description of this procedure. The employer's failure to make the required procedure available to an employee will create a presumption that the deductions were impermissible.[23]

[3.5.2]   *Recouping loans to employees*

By written agreement with an employee, an employer may take deductions from wages to repay employee wage or salary "advances," which are defined as money provided to employees "based on the anticipation of the earning of future wages." Deductions of interest, fees, or other amounts not specified in an agreement with the employee are *not* permitted. A written agreement between the employer and the employee is required, and must set forth the amount being advanced, the amount of the deductions to me made from each paycheck, and the date when each deduction will be made. It is permissible to require that the unpaid balance will be deducted from the employee's last paycheck upon termination of employment before the last agreed-upon wage deduction is made.[24]

The employer is required to establish a procedure for the employee to dispute the amount and frequency of deductions that are not made in accordance with the written agreement. The procedure is to conform to certain requirements set forth in the Wage Order. A description of this procedure

---

22   12 N.Y.C.R.R. § 195-5.1(a)–(e).

23   *See* 12 N.Y.C.R.R. § 195-5.1(e)–(h).

24   12 N.Y.C.R.R. § 195-5.2.

is to be included in the written loan agreement, and the employer's failure to afford such a procedure to the employee will create a presumption that the contested deductions were impermissible.[25]

[3.6] What requirements apply to overtime pay?

With the exception of employees who are specifically exempted from overtime pay requirements, New York employers must (a) pay employees on an hourly basis, and (b) when they work more than 40 hours in a work week, pay them at an hourly overtime rate equal to 1.5 times the employee's regular straight-time hourly rate for all hours worked in excess of 40. This is the same overtime requirement prescribed by federal law.[26]

When an employer is permitted to take an allowance against the employee's minimum wage (such as food service workers and service employees; see § 3.4 above), the amount of the allowance is *not* increased by 50% for overtime hours.

Example: If a food service worker in New York City receives greater than $5 per hour in a work week that ends after December 31, 2018, the employer is entitled to take a tip credit of $5 against the employee's minimum wage of $15 per hour, and may accordingly pay a straight-time rate of $10 per hour. However, the tip credit of $5 per hour applies to overtime pay the same as to straight-time pay. Since the overtime rate for a $15 per hour food service worker is $22.50 ($15 x 1.5 = $22.50), the employee's overtime wage rate is $17.50 ($22.50 - $5 = $17.50). It is NOT the tipped straight-time rate of $10 times 1.5.

Please note, however, that **an allowance against overtime pay requirements under New York law does not necessarily imply an exemption from overtime pay requirements under the federal Fair Labor Standards Act.**

---

25   *See* 12 N.Y.C.R.R. § 195-5.2(e)–(i).

26   As is also the case under federal law, New York employers are not required to count regular meal breaks as to which employees have no work duties in computing the 40-hour minimum. Thus, an employer that gives employees a one-hour duty-free lunch as part of each 9:00 a.m. to 5:00 p.m. work day has a 35-hour work week; and an hourly employee who works hours above 35 is entitled only to "straight time" (regular hourly) pay until he or she has exceeded 40 hours of actual work.

[3.7]   What employees are exempt from overtime pay requirements?

Some employees and certain types of employers are *exempt* from overtime pay requirements;

[3.7.1]   *The "white collar" overtime exemptions*

So-called "white collar" employees are exempt from overtime pay requirements if they meet both of the "duties" and "salary basis" tests for one or more of the exemptions for executive, administrative, professional, and outside sales employees. Note that salary alone is insufficient to establish an exemption: the employee's position must to meet one of the "duties" tests as well.

While relevant to the duties test analysis, an employee's job title or job description is *not*, by itself, determinative of whether the employee meets the duties test, and a court or administrative agency will consider the employee's actual duties. Accordingly, a title such as "manager" or "executive" does not guarantee that a court or administrative agency will conclude that the employee is exempt.

The employee must also meet the "salary basis" test for the administrative and executive exemptions. This test establishes a minimum salary that the employee must earn in the location where the employee actually performs work in any given week. These minimum salary thresholds are significantly higher than the minimum required under the federal Fair Labor Standards Act.

The salary tests in effect as of December 31, 2019 require that employees earn at least the weekly amounts listed below:[27]

New York City	Nassau, Suffolk and Westchester counties	The rest of New York State
$1,125.00/week ($58,500 per year)	$975.00/week ($50,700 per year)	$885/week ($46,020 per year)

The salary threshold for employees in Nassau, Suffolk and Westchester counties will increase to $1,050 per week ($54,600 per year) starting

---

27   12 N.Y.C.R.R. § 142-2.14(c)(4) (Miscellaneous Industries); *see also* 12 N.Y.C.R.R. § 146-3.2(c)(1) (Hospitality Industry); 12 N.Y.C.R.R. § 141-3.2(c)(1) (Building Services Industry); 12 N.Y.C.R.R. § 143.1(b) (Exempt Nonprofit Making Institutions); 12 N.Y.C.R.R. § 142-3.12(c)(2) (Non-Exempt Nonprofit Making Institutions).

December 31, 2020, and to $1,125 per week ($58,500 per year) starting December 31, 2021. For employees elsewhere in New York State, the threshold increases to $937.50 per week ($48,750 per year) starting December 31, 2020, and will increase further starting December 31, 2021 in an amount that the NYS DOL has not yet determined.

Note also that the white collar exemptions are *not* available with respect to employees covered by the Farm Workers Wage Order; *see* § 3.7.6 below.[28]

The **executive exemption** applies to an employee who, in addition to meeting the salary basis test, meets the following criteria:

(a) The employee's primary duty consists of the management of the enterprise in which he or she is employed or of a customarily recognized department or subdivision of the enterprise;

(b) The employee customarily and regularly directs the work of two or more other employees;

(c) The employee has the authority to hire or fire other employees, or whose suggestions and recommendations as to the hiring or firing and as to the advancement and promotion or any other change of status of other employees will be given particular weight; and

(d) The employee customarily and regularly exercises discretionary authority.[29]

The **administrative exemption** applies to an employee who, in addition to meeting the salary test, meets the following criteria:

(a) The employee's primary duty consists of the performance of office or non-manual field work directly related to management policies or general operations of such individual's employer;

(b) The employee customarily and regularly exercises discretion and independent judgment; and

---

28   *See* 12 N.Y.C.R.R. §§ 190-1.1 *et seq.*

29   12 N.Y.C.R.R. § 142-2.14(c)(4)(i) (Miscellaneous Industries); *see also* 12 N.Y.C.R.R. § 146-3.2(c)(1)(i) (Hospitality Industry); 12 N.Y.C.R.R. § 141-3.2(c)(1)(i) (Building Services Industry); 12 N.Y.C.R.R. § 143.1(b)(1) (Exempt Nonprofit Making Institutions); 12 N.Y.C.R.R. § 142-3.12(c)(2)(i) (Non-Exempt Nonprofit Making Institutions).

(c) The employee regularly and directly assists an employer, or an employee employed in a *bona fide* executive or administrative capacity (such as employment as an administrative assistant); or who performs, under only general supervision, work along specialized or technical lines requiring special training, experience, or knowledge.[30]

The **professional exemption** applies to an employee who meets the following criteria:

(a) The employee's primary duty consists of the performance of work requiring knowledge of an advanced type in a field of science or learning customarily acquired by a prolonged course of specialized intellectual instruction and study, as distinguished from a general academic education and from an apprenticeship, and from training in the performance of routine mental, manual, or physical processes; or original and creative in character in a recognized field of artistic endeavor (as opposed to work that can be produced by a person endowed with general manual or intellectual ability and training), and the result of which depends primarily on the invention, imagination or talent of the employee; and

(b) The employee's work requires the consistent exercise of discretion and judgment in its performance; or

(c) The employee's work is predominantly intellectual and varied in character (as opposed to routine mental, manual, mechanical, or physical work) and is of such a character that the output produced or the result accomplished cannot be standardized in relation to a given period of time.[31]

The professional exemption in New York is not subject to the New York salary test, but *is* subject to a *lower* salary test under the Fair Labor Standards Act.

---

30   12 N.Y.C.R.R. § 142-2.14(c)(4)(ii) (Miscellaneous Industries); *see also* 12 N.Y.C.R.R. § 146-3.2(c)(1)(ii) (Hospitality Industry); 12 N.Y.C.R.R. § 141-3.2(c)(1)(ii) (Building Services Industry); 12 N.Y.C.R.R. § 143.1(b)(2) (Exempt Nonprofit Making Institutions); 12 N.Y.C.R.R. § 142-3.12(c)(2)(ii) (Non-Exempt Nonprofit Making Institutions).

31   12 N.Y.C.R.R. § 142-2.14(c)(4)(iii) (Miscellaneous Industries); *see also* 12 N.Y.C.R.R. § 146-3.2(c)(1)(iii) (Hospitality Industry); 12 N.Y.C.R.R. § 141-3.2(c)(1)(iii) (Building Services Industry); 12 N.Y.C.R.R. § 143.1(b)(3) (Exempt Nonprofit Making Institutions); 12 N.Y.C.R.R. § 142-3.12(c)(2)(iii) (Non-Exempt Nonprofit Making Institutions).

The **outside sales person exemption** applies to an employee who "is customarily and predominantly engaged away from the premises of the employer and not at any fixed site and location for the purpose of:

(a) making sales;

(b) selling and delivering articles or goods; or

(c) obtaining orders or contracts for service or for the use of facilities.[32]

[3.7.2]   *Overtime exemptions for non-profit-making entities*

There are a number of overtime exemptions which apply to non-profit-making institutions:

- **Volunteers.** This exemption applies to "a person who works for a non-profit-making institution under no contract of hire, express or implied, and with no promise of compensation, other than reimbursement for expenses as part of the conditions of work."[33]

- **Learners.** A "learner" is "a person who is participating in a bona fide training program for an occupation in which such person is employed, the required training period for which is recognized to be at least two weeks."[34] The training program must include "either formal instruction or on-the-job training during a period when the learner is entrusted with limited responsibility and is under supervision or guidance."[35] An individual may not be treated as a learner "at an institution in an occupation for which he or she has completed the required training" *or* "after 10 weeks of such training," unless the Commissioner of Labor approves a longer period.[36]

---

32   12 N.Y.C.R.R. § 142-2.14(c)(5) (Miscellaneous Industries); *see also* 12 N.Y.C.R.R. § 146-3.2(c)(2) (Hospitality Industry); 12 N.Y.C.R.R. § 141-3.2(c)(2) (Building Services Industry); 12 N.Y.C.R.R. § 143.1(c) (Exempt Nonprofit Making Institutions); 12 N.Y.C.R.R. § 142-3.12(c)(3) (Non-Exempt Nonprofit Making Institutions).

33   12 N.Y.C.R.R. § 143.1(e) (Exempt Nonprofit Making Institutions); 12 N.Y.C.R.R. § 142-3.12(c)(5) (Non-Exempt Nonprofit Making Institutions).

34   12 N.Y.C.R.R. § 143.1(f) (Exempt Nonprofit Making Institutions); 12 N.Y.C.R.R. § 142-3.12(c)(6) (Non-Exempt Nonprofit Making Institutions).

35   *Id.*

36   12 N.Y.C.R.R. § 143.1(f).

- **Apprentices.** Non-profitmaking institutions can also utilize the apprentice exemption for individuals whose work "[a] is an apprenticeable trade or occupation, and [b] is part of a *bona fide* training program leading to qualification as a journeyman in the trade or occupation."[37]

- **Repayment of Charitable Aid.** This overtime exemption applies to individuals who work in return for charitable aid which they have received. This applies to "any work or duties performed by a person who is not under any express contract of hire, in or for a nonprofitmaking religious or charitable institution, as a means of discharging an obligation to such an institution for charitable aid given to the worker."[38]

- **Members of Religious Orders.** A "religious order" is "a group of persons who are joined together under the authority of a religious leader and are dedicated to the performance of religious works."[39] There is also an exemption for sextons, which applies to "an individual who works as a caretaker at a place where religious services are held, or whose duties at such place are solely of a religious nature, or whose duties are partly religious and partly as a caretaker."[40]

- **Students.** An additional overtime exemption applies to students who also perform services for non-profitmaking institutions. This exemption applies to any "individual who is enrolled in and regularly attends during the daytime a course of instruction leading to a degree, certificate, or diploma offered at an institution of learning, or who is completing residence requirements for a degree."[41] This includes students who are on instructional breaks "during the time

---

37   12 N.Y.C.R.R. § 143.1(g) (Exempt Nonprofit Making Institutions); 12 N.Y.C.R.R. § 142-3.12(c)(7) (Non-Exempt Nonprofit Making Institutions). These sections set out a number of requirements which must be met by the program in order to constitute "a bona fide training program."

38   12 N.Y.C.R.R. § 143.1(j) (Exempt Nonprofit Making Institutions); 12 N.Y.C.R.R. § 142-3.12(c)(10) (Non-Exempt Nonprofit Making Institutions).

39   12 N.Y.C.R.R. § 143.1(h) (Exempt Nonprofit Making Institutions); 12 N.Y.C.R.R. § 142-3.12(c)(8) (Non-Exempt Nonprofit Making Institutions).

40   12 N.Y.C.R.R. § 143.1(i) (Exempt Nonprofit Making Institutions); 12 N.Y.C.R.R. § 142-3.12(c)(9) (Non-Exempt Nonprofit Making Institutions).

41   12 N.Y.C.R.R. § 143.1(k) (Exempt Nonprofit Making Institutions); 12 N.Y.C.R.R. § 142-3.12(c)(11) (Non-Exempt Nonprofit Making Institutions).

that school is not in session if such person was a student during the preceding semester."[42]

- **Impaired workers.** Non-profitmaking institutions may also utilize an overtime exemption covering a disabled person an individual "whose earning capacity for the work to which he or she is assigned to perform is impaired by age, or by physical or mental deficiency or injury."[43] However, a person's earning capacity may not be considered to be impaired by age until that person's 65th birthday.[44]

[3.7.3] *Employees in the hospitality industry*[45]

There are several overtime exemptions for employers and employees in the hospitality industry, which is defined at 12 N.Y.C.R.R. § 146-3.1 as follows:

(a) The term *hospitality industry* includes any restaurant or hotel, as defined herein.

(b) The term *restaurant* includes any eating or drinking place that prepares and offers food or beverage for human consumption either on any of its premises or by such service as catering, banquet, box lunch, curb service or counter service to the public, to employees, or to members or guests of members, and services in connection therewith or incidental thereto. The term *restaurant* includes but is not limited to restaurant operations of other types of establishments, restaurant concessions in any establishment and concessions in restaurants.

(c) The term *hotel* includes:

(1) any establishment which as a whole or part of its business activities offers lodging accommodations for hire to the public, to employees, or to members or guests of members, and services in connection there-

---

42 12 N.Y.C.R.R. § 143.1(k) (Exempt Nonprofit Making Institutions); 12 N.Y.C.R.R. § 142-3.12(c)(11) (Non-Exempt Nonprofit Making Institutions).

43 12 N.Y.C.R.R. § 143.1(*l*) (Exempt Nonprofit Making Institutions); 12 N.Y.C.R.R. § 142-3.12(c)(12) (Non-Exempt Nonprofit Making Institutions).

44 *Id.*

45 *See* the discussion of the hospitality industry in § 3.3 above.

with or incidental thereto. The industry includes but is not limited to commercial hotels, apartment hotels, resort hotels, lodging houses, boarding houses, all-year hotels, furnished room houses, children's camps, adult camps, tourist camps, tourist homes, auto camps, motels, residence clubs, membership clubs, dude ranches, and spas and baths that provide lodging.

(2) An *all-year hotel* is one that does not qualify as a resort hotel under the definition below. Motor courts, motels, cabins, tourist homes, and other establishments serving similar purposes shall be classified as all-year hotels unless they specifically qualify as resort hotels in accordance with the definition below.

(3) A *resort hotel* is one which offers lodging accommodations of a vacational nature to the public or to members or guests of members, and which:

(i) operates for not more than seven months in any calendar year; or

(ii) being located in a rural community or in a city or village of less than 15,000 population, increased its number of employee workdays during any consecutive four-week period by at least 100 percent over the number of employee workdays in any other consecutive four-week period within the preceding calendar year; or

(iii) being located in a rural community or in a city or village of less than 15,000 population, increased its number of guest days during any consecutive four-week period by at least 100 percent over the number of guest days in any other consecutive four-week period within the preceding calendar year.

(d) The *hospitality industry* excludes:

(1) establishments where the service of food or beverage or the provision of lodging is not available to

the public or to members or guests of members, but is incidental to instruction, medical care, religious observance, or the care of persons with disabilities or those who are impoverished or other public charges; and

(2) establishments where the service of food or beverage or the provision of lodging is offered by any corporation, unincorporated association, community chest, fund or foundation organized exclusively for religious, charitable or educational purposes, no part of the net earnings of which inures to the benefit of any private shareholder or individual.

The exclusions set forth in paragraphs (d)(1) and (d)(2) of this section shall not be deemed to exempt such establishments from coverage under another minimum wage order which covers them.[46]

[3.7.4]   *Counselors in children's camps*

This overtime exemption applies to a "person whose duties primarily relate to the guidance, instruction, supervision, and care of campers in a children's camp, whether such work involves direct charge of, or responsibility for, such activities, or merely assistance to persons in charge."[47] It does not apply to any camps that are "open for a period exceeding 17 consecutive weeks during the year."[48] There is also an overtime exemption which applies to "a camper who works no more than four hours a day for a children's camp and at all other times enjoys the same privileges, facilities and accommodations as a regular camper in such camp"; in other words, a "counselor-in-training."[49]

---

46   12 N.Y.C.R.R. § 146-3.1.

47   12 N.Y.C.R.R. § 143.1(m) (Exempt Nonprofit Making Institutions); 12 N.Y.C.R.R. § 142-3.12(c)(13) (Non-Exempt Nonprofit Making Institutions).

48   *Id.*

49   12 N.Y.C.R.R. § 146-3.2(c)(4).

[3.7.5]   *Building industry workers*

Building services employees are exempt from overtime pay requirements if:

- The employee works for an employer that occupies an entire building for its own use *and* the employee works only in that building; or

- The employee works in a "bungalow colony."[50]

[3.7.6]   *Farm workers*

Farm workers are exempt from overtime pay requirements if:

- The employee is "the parent, spouse, child or other member of the employer's immediate family"; or

- The employee is "a minor under 17 years of age employed as a hand-harvest worker on the same farm as the minor's parent or guardian and who is paid on a piece-rate basis at the same piece rate as employees 17 years of age and over."[51]

[3.7.7]   *Government employees*

The Wage Orders specifically exclude "an[y] individual employed by a Federal, State or municipal government or political subdivision thereof."[52] However, as noted above, this does not mean that government employees are exempt from federal overtime requirements under the Fair Labor Standards Act.

[3.8]   What is "call-in pay"?

"Call-in pay" is a minimum amount that an employer is required to pay when an employee who is paid on an hourly basis is required or permitted to come to work, even if there is less (or no) work to be performed after the employee reports to work.

---

50   12 N.Y.C.R.R. § 141-3.2(b)(1)–(2).

51   12 N.Y.C.R.R. § 190-1.3(b).

52   12 N.Y.C.R.R. § 142-2.14(b) (Miscellaneous Industries); *see also* 12 N.Y.C.R.R. § 146-3.2(b) (Hospitality Industry); 12 N.Y.C.R.R. § 141-3.2(b)(3) (Building Services Industry); 12 N.Y.C.R.R. § 143.1(b)(3) (Exempt Nonprofit Making Institutions); 12 N.Y.C.R.R. § 142-3.12(b) (Non-Exempt Nonprofit Making Institutions); 12 N.Y.C.R.R. § 190-1.3(b)(3) (Farm Workers).

Three industries are subject to call-in pay requirements: "miscellaneous industries" employers; non-exempt non-profit-making institutions; and the hospitality industry.

Employers covered by other Wage Orders are not required to provide call-in pay.

[3.9] When are employees entitled to call-in pay?

In the miscellaneous and non-exempt non-profit-making industries, "[a]n employee who by request or permission of the employer reports for work on any day shall be paid for at least four hours, or the number of hours in the regularly scheduled shift, whichever is less, *at the basic minimum hourly wage.*"[53]

Different call-in pay requirements apply to employers in the hospitality industry. In this industry, employers are required to provide call-in pay as follows:

> An employee who by request or permission of the employer reports for duty on any day, whether or not assigned to actual work, shall be paid *at the applicable wage rate*:
>
> > (1) for at least three hours for one shift, or the number of hours in the regularly scheduled shift, whichever is less;
> >
> > (2) for at least six hours for two shifts totaling six hours or less, or the number of hours in the regularly scheduled shift, whichever is less; and
> >
> > (3) for at least eight hours for three shifts totaling eight hours or less, or the number of hours in the regularly scheduled shift, whichever is less.[54]

---

53 12 N.Y.C.R.R. § 142-2.3 (Miscellaneous Industries); 12 N.Y.C.R.R. § 142-3.3 (Non-Exempt Nonprofit Making Institutions) (emphasis supplied).

54 12 N.Y.C.R.R. § 146-1.5 (emphasis supplied). A regularly scheduled shift must be a "fixed, repeating shift that an employee normally works on the same day of each week." If there is variation from week to week in the employee's hours worked or schedule, then there is not a regularly scheduled shift. Employers in the hospitality industry are not entitled to offset the call-in pay obligation based on other wages paid in excess of minimum wage. *See* 12 N.Y.C.R.R. § 146-1.5(e). Call-in pay also cannot "be offset by any credits for meals or lodging provided to the employee." 12 N.Y.C.R.R. § 146-1.5(c).

[3.10] What is "spread of hours pay"?

"Spread of hours" applies with respect to the hospitality and miscellaneous industries, and is one extra hour of pay at the minimum wage rate owed to a non-exempt employee (i.e., an employee who must be paid overtime wages) when the interval between the beginning and end of the employee's workday (the so-called "spread") exceeds 10 hours.[55]

"Spread of hours" refers to the entire period of hours on a given work day during which an employee is expected to be available to his or her employer, and may be greater than the hours actually worked. For example, if, on a given day, an employee is expected to be at work at 8:00 a.m. and not to leave until 7:00 p.m., his or her spread of hours is 11 hours even if two of those hours were not working hours. In this example, the employee would be paid for nine hours actually worked, plus an additional hour of "spread of hours" pay.[56]

The amount of the payment is one hour at the applicable minimum wage rate. *Note*, however, this does not automatically entitle the employee to an additional hour of pay if his or her total compensation for the period of hours is higher than *(the minimum wage rate) x (the number of hours in the spread of hours period plus one hour)*: "[T]he 'spread of hours' regulation does not require all employees to be paid for the additional hour, but merely that the total wages paid be equal to or greater than the total due for all hours at the minimum wage plus one additional hour at the minimum wage."[57]

[3.11] What is "split shift" pay?

A split shift occurs when an employee works two separated shifts on the same day with an unpaid break between shifts which is longer than a meal break: "A split shift is a schedule of daily hours in which the working hours required or permitted are not consecutive. No meal period of one hour or less shall be considered an interruption of consecutive hours."[58]

---

55   12 N.Y.C.R.R. § 142-2.4, 2.18 (Miscellaneous Industries); 12 N.Y.C.R.R. § 142-3.3 (Non-Exempt Nonprofit Making Institutions); 12 N.Y.C.R.R. § 146-1.6 (Hospitality Industry).

56   *See* 12 N.Y.C.R.R. § 146-1.6(d).

57   New York State Department of Labor Opinion Letter RO-06-0037. An example would be the bus driver who drives a morning route from 8:00 to 11:00 a.m. and then has un unpaid break until an afternoon run from 2:00 to 5:00 p.m.

58   12 N.Y.C.R.R. § 142-2.17.

As is the case with spread of hours pay, a split shift entitles the employee to one more hour of pay. Again, however, this may not apply if the employee meets a defined level of compensation for the day: "[S]hould an employee's regular rate of pay exceed the minimum wage rate plus one additional hour's pay at the minimum wage rate, the employee is not required to be paid any additional amount as a result of working a split shift."[59]

[3.12]   Are there additional restrictions on shifts in New York City?

Yes. The New York City Fair Workweek Law imposes additional requirements on shift scheduling, and requires premium pay for some shift changes. The Fair Workweek Law is discussed in Chapter 4 of this book at §§ 4.119–4.130.

---

59   New York State Department of Labor Opinion Letter RO-09-0116.

CHAPTER FOUR

EMPLOYEE TIME OFF

Caroline M. Westover
Kerry W. Langan
Jessica C. Moller
Louis P. DiLorenzo
Mallory A. Campbell

Edited by Kseniya Premo

CHAPTER OVERVIEW

In this chapter, we consider a wide variety of reasons why employers either *may* or *must* give their employees time off. Historically, the decision whether to give paid vacation time, paid personal days, or paid sick leave rested entirely with employers, but in recent years legislative developments have mandated forms of leave which were previously discretionary. Now, some forms of time off may be unpaid, while other types must be paid by the employer as a matter of law.

This chapter addresses New York State statutory requirements. There are additional federal leave requirements—most notably the Family Medical leave Act of 1993[1]—which are simply beyond the scope of this book, but which are of importance to employers.

We should also note that employee leave is a very active area for state legislatures and the United States Congress, and the 2020 COVID-19 pandemic has given rise to multiple state and federal laws in response to the coronavirus crisis, most of which are temporary, but some of which are likely to become permanent.

Finally, it should be noted that in unionized workplaces, additional entitlements and requirements regarding leave may be included in collective bargaining agreements.

The following topics are addressed in this chapter:

I. MEAL BREAKS

[4.1] Must New York employers provide employees with meal breaks?

[4.2] What employees are covered by the meal period requirements?

[4.3] What are New York's meal period requirements?

[4.4] Are there any exceptions to the meal period requirements?

[4.5] What are the penalties for non-compliance?

---

1   29 U.S.C. §§ 2601–2654. A variety of helpful reference materials with respect to FMLA are available at U.S. Department of Labor, *Family and Medical Leave*, https://www.dol.gov/agencies/whd/fmla.

II.   REST PERIODS

[4.6]   Does New York require employers to provide employees with break or rest periods during the workday?

[4.7]   If an employer chooses to provide its employees with breaks or rest periods, must the employees be paid for the break time?

III.   VACATIONS

[4.8]   Must a New York employer provide employees with vacation?

[4.9]   Must a vacation policy be in writing?

[4.10] When an employee resigns or is discharged, must the employer pay out any accrued but unused vacation?

[4.11] Does accrued and unused vacation carry over from one year to the next?

[4.12] Are there other conditions that employers can place on vacation pay?

[4.13] What are the consequences of an employer's failure to pay earned vacation?

IV.   BREAK TIME FOR NURSING MOTHERS (LACTATION BREAKS)

[4.14] Does New York State have a law that permits nursing mothers to express breast milk in the workplace?

[4.15] What employers are covered by lactation requirements?

[4.16] What employees are covered by the lactation requirements?

[4.17] How much break time is a nursing mother entitled to?

[4.18] May an employer tell an employee to postpone her lactation break?

[4.19] Are employers required to pay nursing mothers for lactation breaks?

[4.20] May a nursing mother elect to make up work time that was taken for unpaid lactation breaks?

[4.21] Do employers have to give any notice about lactation breaks?

[4.22] Do employees have to give any notice about the need for lactation breaks?

[4.23] Are employers required to provide a separate space for lactation?

[4.24] When is providing a lactation space "impracticable, inconvenient or expensive" for the employer?

[4.25] When is a lactation space "in close proximity" to an employee's work area?

[4.26] Are there alternatives to a permanent designated lactation space?

[4.27] What must the lactation space contain?

[4.28] What are the penalties for non-compliance?

V. JURY SERVICE

[4.29] Are employees in New York entitled to time off for jury duty?

[4.30] Is jury duty leave paid or unpaid?

[4.31] Is an employer entitled to prior notice of jury service from the employee?

[4.32] What are the penalties for non-compliance?

VI. TIME OFF TO VOTE

[4.33] Are employees entitled to time off to vote?

[4.34] What elections are covered by the law?

[4.35] At what time(s) during the workday may an employee take voting leave?

[4.36] Do employees have to give notice of the desire to take voting leave?

[4.37] May an employer charge paid voting leave time against other accruals of paid time?

[4.38] May an employer require proof of voting eligibility or actual voting?

[4.39] Do employers have to give notice of the right to voting leave?

[4.40] What are the penalties for non-compliance?

VII. CRIME VICTIM AND CRIME WITNESS LEAVE

[4.41] Are victims of, or witnesses to, crimes entitled to time off from work?

[4.42] What employers are covered by the crime victim/witness leave requirement?

[4.43] Who is a "victim" of a crime?

[4.44] What is the purpose of the crime victim/witness time off?

[4.45] Do employees have to give notice of the need to take crime victim leave?

[4.46] Can employers require employees to provide verification or certification of their absence from work?

VIII. BEREAVEMENT LEAVE

[4.47] Are New York employers required to provide employees with bereavement leave?

IX. BLOOD DONATION LEAVE

[4.48] Are employees entitled to time off to donate blood?

[4.49] What notice must an employer give regarding the right to blood donation leave?

[4.50] May an employer require employees to prove that they took leave for an actual blood donation?

[4.51] What are the consequences for non-compliance?

X. BONE MARROW AND ORGAN DONATION LEAVE

[4.52] Are employees entitled to leave for bone marrow or organ donation?

[4.53] Who is eligible to take bone marrow donation leave?

[4.54] What notice must an employer give regarding the right to bone marrow donation leave?

[4.55] What are the penalties for non-compliance?

[4.56] What are the special bone marrow and organ donation rules for New York State employees?

XI. MILITARY SERVICE

[4.57] Are employees entitled to time off for military service?

[4.58] What are the military leave requirements for private sector employers?

[4.59] What military activities qualify for private sector leave and reinstatement?

[4.60] What are the penalties for private sector non-compliance?

[4.61] What are the military leave requirements for public sector employers?

[4.62] Are the spouses of military members entitled to leave?

XII. LEAVE FOR VOLUNTEER EMERGENCY RESPONDERS

[4.63] Are emergency responders entitled to leave for emergency response activities?

XIII. LEAVE FOR VICTIMS OF DOMESTIC VIOLENCE

[4.64] Are victims of domestic violence entitled to leave?

XIV. PAID SICK LEAVE AND PAID FAMILY LEAVE

[4.65] Are employers required to provide sick leave and/or paid family leave?

[4.66] How does the leave required by Labor Law § 196-b coordinate with other required leave?

[4.67] What is Paid Family Leave?

[4.68] What employers are covered by PFL requirements?

[4.69] Are any employers excluded from PFL requirements?

[4.70] What employees are eligible for PFL coverage?

[4.71] May an employee waive PFL coverage?

[4.72] For what purposes can PFL be used?

[4.73] How much PFL may an eligible employee take?

[4.74] Can PFL be taken intermittently, or in less than full-day increments?

[4.75] What notice is an employee required to give the employer of his or her need to use PFL?

[4.76] Can an employer prevent two employees from taking PFL at the same time for the same qualifying event?

[4.77] Can an employee take PFL and be on disability leave at the same time?

[4.78] How are employees paid during PFL leave?

[4.79] Does an employee have to use paid time off concurrently with PFL?

[4.80] How does an employee apply for PFL pay benefits?

[4.81] What happens to an employee's health insurance benefits while an employee is on PFL?

[4.82] What information do employers have to give employees about the availability of PFL?

XV. NEW YORK CITY EARNED SAFE AND SICK TIME ACT

[4.83] What is the NYC Earned Safe and Sick Time Act?

[4.84] What employers and employees are covered by the Act?

[4.85] Are any employees excluded from the Act?

[4.86] For what reasons may an eligible employee take sick leave?

[4.87] Who is considered a "family member" under the Act?

[4.88] For what purposes can safe leave be used?

[4.89] Must employees provide documentation for sick or safe time?

[4.90] How much sick or safe leave are employees entitled to?

[4.91] When does sick or safe leave accrual begin?

[4.92] When may employees begin to use their sick or safe leave?

[4.93] Can an employer require an employee to use a minimum daily increment of leave?

[4.94] When an employee leaves service, is he or she entitled to payment for unused sick or safe time?

[4.95] What happens if an employee returns to service after a break in employment?

[4.96] Can employees donate unused sick or safe leave to other employees?

[4.97] May an employer require an employee who wants to use leave to find a replacement employee for the missed hours?

[4.98] May an employer require an employee to telecommute or work from home instead of taking sick or safe leave?

[4.99] Are employers required to give employees notice of their right to sick or safe leave?

XVI. WESTCHESTER COUNTY EARNED SICK LEAVE LAW

[4.100] Must employers in Westchester County provide employees with sick leave?

[4.101] What employers are covered?

[4.102] What employees are eligible for sick leave?

[4.103] For what purposes can sick leave be used?

[4.104] What is meant by a "family member"?

[4.105] How much leave are employees entitled to?

[4.106] When does an employee begin to earn sick leave?

[4.107] When can employees begin to use sick leave?

[4.108] Can an employee carry over unused sick leave at the end of the year?

[4.109] Can an employer require the employee to provide a doctor's note when he or she uses earned sick leave?

[4.110] Can an employer require an employee to use a minimum daily increment of leave?

XVII. WESTCHESTER COUNTY SAFE TIME LEAVE LAW

[4.111] Must employers in Westchester County provide employees with safe leave?

[4.112] What employers are covered?

[4.113] What employees are eligible for safe leave?

[4.114] For what purposes can safe leave be used?

[4.115] How much leave are employees entitled to?

[4.116] Can an employer require an employee to use a minimum daily increment of leave?

[4.117] Can an employer require an employee to find coverage for safe time leave used?

[4.118] Can an employer require documentation that safe time leave is being used for its intended purpose?

XVIII. NEW YORK CITY'S FAIR WORKWEEK LAW

[4.119] What is New York City's Fair Workweek Law?

[4.120] Who is covered by the Fair Workweek Law?

[4.121] Does the law apply to employers which are not based in New York City?

[4.122] Who is considered to be a "fast food employee"?

[4.123] What are the requirements of the Fair Workweek Law for fast food employers?

[4.124] What are the shift-change "premiums" applicable to fast food workers?

[4.125] Are fast food employers required to pay workers a premium if the schedule changes by just a few minutes?

[4.126] What are the consequences if a fast food employer does not comply with the law?

[4.127] Who is considered to be a "retail employee"?

[4.128] What are the requirements of the Fair Workweek Law for retail employers?

[4.129] What are the consequences if a retail employer does not give employees their schedules 72 hours before the start of work?

[4.130] What is an on-call shift?

XIX. THE DOMESTIC WORKERS' BILL OF RIGHTS

[4.131] What is the Domestic Workers' Bill of Rights?

[4.132] What are the leave provisions applicable to domestic workers?

I.   MEAL BREAKS

[4.1]   Must New York employers provide employees with meal breaks?

Yes. Section 162 of the New York Labor Law mandates that employers provide employees with *unpaid* time off for meal breaks.[2] Employers may, if they wish, pay employees for meal breaks, but are not required to. *See* § 4.3 below for how much meal break time must be provided.

[4.2]   What employees are covered by the meal period requirements?

Section 162 of the Labor Law applies to *all* employees. According to guidance provided by the NYS Department of Labor, Division of Labor Standards, "all categories of workers are covered, including white-collar management staff."[3] In other words, no employees are exempted from the meal break entitlement.

[4.3]   What are New York's meal period requirements?

The meal period requirements vary depending upon (a) the type of establishment in which the employee works, and (b) the hours the employee works.

Individuals employed in a **factory setting** must be allowed at least *sixty minutes* for a meal break between the hours of 11:00 a.m. and 2:00 p.m. (identified in Section 162 as the "noonday meal period").[4]

Individuals employed in a **mercantile or other establishment** who work a shift of more than six hours which extends over the noonday meal period must be allowed at least *thirty minutes* for a meal break between the hours of 11:00 a.m. and 2:00 p.m.[5]

An individual working on a shift that begins prior to 11:00 a.m. and continues past 7:00 p.m. is entitled to *an additional twenty-minute meal break* between 5:00 p.m. and 7:00 p.m.[6]

---

2   *See* Labor Law § 162.

3   N.Y. Department of Labor, *Guidelines for Meal Periods* (LS-443) (Aug. 2019), https://labor.ny.gov/formsdocs/wp/LS443.pdf.

4   Labor Law § 162(1).

5   Labor Law § 162(2).

6   Labor Law § 162(3).

An individual employed in a **factory setting** who works on a shift greater than six hours, between the hours of 1:00 p.m. and 6:00 a.m., is entitled to at least *sixty minutes* for a meal break at the midpoint of the shift.[7]

An individual employed in a **mercantile or other establishment** who works on a shift greater than six hours, between the hours of 1:00 p.m. and 6:00 a.m., is entitled to at least *forty-five minutes* for a meal break at the midpoint of the shift.[8]

[4.4]   Are there any exceptions to the meal period requirements?

Yes. The Department of Labor permits employers to provide a meal period of at least *thirty minutes* to its employees as long as the shortened meal period does not impose a hardship upon the affected employees.[9] For example, a factory employer which is normally required under § 162 to provide its employees with a one-hour meal period may reduce the meal period to no less than thirty minutes, *if* this will not create employee hardship. Under this exception, employers do not need to make any formal permit application to the Department of Labor prior to implementing the shortened meal period.

In special or unusual circumstances, an employer may apply to the Department of Labor for a permit to enable the employer to reduce the meal break to a time period of at least *twenty minutes*.[10] If the Department of Labor grants a permit, the employer is required to display the permit conspicuously in the main entrance to its facility.[11]

Finally, the Department of Labor recognizes an additional exception to the meal period requirements where an employer has only one employee on duty or only one individual in a particular occupation or position. In this situation, the Department of Labor will permit the employee at issue to forgo the meal period and eat while working, so long as the employee voluntarily consents to do so.[12]

---

7   Labor Law § 162(4).

8   *Id.*

9   *Id.*

10   N.Y. Department of Labor, *Guidelines for Meal Periods* (LS-443) (Aug. 2019), https://labor.ny.gov/formsdocs/wp/LS443.pdf.

11   Labor Law § 162(5). It should be noted that the Department of Labor has the authority to revoke the issuance of a special permit at any time.

12   N.Y. Department of Labor, *Guidelines for Meal Periods* (LS-443) (Aug. 2019).

[4.5]   What are the penalties for non-compliance?

Section 218(1) of the New York Labor Law permits the Commissioner of Labor to assess a series of civil penalties against non-compliant employers as follows: (i) up to $1,000 for a first-time offense; (ii) up to $2,000 for a second offense; and (iii) up to $3,000 for third and subsequent offenses. When calculating the penalty amount, the Commissioner will take into account a variety of factors, including the employer's size, the employer's intent to comply with the law, the egregiousness of the violation(s), and the employer's history of any previous wage and hour violations.[13]

II.   REST PERIODS

[4.6]   Does New York require employers to provide employees with break or rest periods during the workday?

No. Other than meal breaks (discussed in §§ 4.1–4.5 above) and lactation breaks (discussed in §§ 4.14–4.28 below), there is no law which obligates employers to provide breaks or rest periods to employees.[14]

[4.7]   If an employer chooses to provide its employees with breaks or rest periods, must the employees be paid for the break time?

If an employer chooses to permit employees to take short breaks of up to twenty minutes, the New York Department of Labor takes the position that such time should be paid as "work time."[15]

III.   VACATIONS

[4.8]   Must a New York employer provide employees with vacation?

No. Under New York law there is no requirement that a New York employer provide vacation or pay for time not worked unless the employer has voluntarily established a policy to grant such pay. If an employer *does* decide to provide a pay-for-time-not-worked benefit such as vacation, personal time, holidays, or other paid time off, the employer

---

13   Labor Law § 218(1).

14   *See* N.Y. Department of Labor, *Wages and Hours: Frequently Asked Questions*, https://labor. ny.gov/workerprotection/laborstandards/faq.shtm#8.

15   *Id.* As to employees who work on public works projects, *see also* 12 N.Y.C.R.R. § 220.4 (stating that "[r]est periods of 20 consecutive minutes or less are considered as time worked upon a public work project and must be compensated as such").

---

can impose almost any reasonable condition on eligibility and receipt of the benefit that it chooses.[16]

[4.9]   Must a vacation policy be in writing?

Technically, yes. Section 195(5) of the New York State Labor Law requires an employer to notify employees in writing (which may be done by a public posting) of "the employer's policy on sick leave, vacation, personal leave, holidays and hours."

The New York State Department of Labor has indicated that in the absence of a written policy, an oral policy (or past practice) may be enforced—but only if the terms of the policy can be confirmed through an investigation. That said, note that the burden in such an investigation (i.e., to prove the existence of a consistent policy, and notice to and acquiescence by the employees) is on the employer.

Labor Law § 198-a contains criminal penalties, and § 197 contains civil penalties, for failing to pay earned wages; and § 198-c defines wage supplements to include vacation pay and makes those penalties available for a failure to pay accrued and unused vacation.

[4.10]   When an employee resigns or is discharged, must the employer pay out any accrued but unused vacation?

The answer depends on the terms of the employer's vacation policy.

If the employer's policy is silent as to vacation pay at the end of employment, then accrued vacation, like earned wages, is to be paid by the next regular payday covering the last pay period worked.

However, a properly written and distributed policy can provide differently, and may include such limitations as the following:

- Accrued vacation is only available as a paid respite from work *while the employee is in service*. Therefore, the policy may provide that any accrued and unused vacation is forfeited upon termination.

---

16   *Glenville Gage Co. v. Indus. Bd. of Appeals*, 70 A.D.2d 283, 421 N.Y.S.2d 408 (3d Dep't 1979), *aff'd*, 52 N.Y.2d 777, 436 N.Y.S.2d 621 (1980).

- Accrued and unused vacation will be paid *except* in certain situations such as:

  - if the employee is discharged for certain specified types of misconduct, then accrued and unused vacation will be forfeited;

  - if the employee fails to give prior notice of resignation in accordance with the employer's policy (such as two weeks or one month), then accrued and unused vacation will be forfeited.[17]

[4.11] Does accrued and unused vacation carry over from one year to the next?

Again, this depends on the terms of the employer's policy.

Many employers prohibit such carry-over, or limit it to some limited amount of time, such as a maximum carry-over of five (or ten) working days. This is done for the following reasons: (a) to avoid the creation of a large, unfunded liability affecting the employer's balance sheet; (b) to prevent employees from "hoarding" vacation for a rainy day as opposed to using it for the intended purpose of a paid respite from work; and (c) to limit employees from creating a quasi-severance or retirement benefit of unused days which will be paid out at a higher rate than the rate at which they were actually earned in prior years.

[4.12] Are there other conditions that employers can place on vacation pay?

Yes. Employer policies often provide for other terms and conditions such as:

- Employees must have been employed for a minimum period of time (such as a year) before they are eligible to receive vacation.

- Vacation entitlements are phased in based on length of service; such as one week after one year of service and two weeks after five years of service. In doing this, some employers use the employee's anniversary date, some use years of service completed at the

---

17   The purpose of the notice period is to give the employer an opportunity to find and train a replacement or find another way to cover the work being performed by the resigning employee. Accordingly, where an employer policy provides for forfeiture where the employee does not give the required notice of resignation, the employer should consider prohibiting the employee from using vacation during any part of the notice period. Otherwise, the employee will, in effect, have received payment for part or all of the accrued or unused vacation without working, and without affording the employer time to cover the work.

beginning of the "vacation period," and others use years of service on the January 1st after the employee reaches the required years of service for eligibility.

- To avoid claims of entitlement to pro-rated vacation, some employers require that employees be employed as of a certain date to be eligible to take the vacation previously earned (such as, the employee must be employed on March 1 following the year in which vacation was "earned"; or must be employed as of December 31st to prevent any claim of a pro rata entitlement to vacation for a partial year of service).

- Employees may earn vacation based on increments of time worked; in other words, a set amount of vacation for each hour, week, month, or partial year of service.

- Employees who earn vacation in increments of time worked may be permitted to "borrow" vacation days not yet earned and may be required to repay the employer for days taken but not subsequently earned.

[4.13] What are the consequences of an employer's failure to pay earned vacation?

Except as set forth in § 4.10 above, if an employee has met an employer's requirements for earning vacation days, the unused days are considered to be a wage supplement under Labor Law § 198-c and there are civil and criminal penalties for an employer (and, in some cases, individuals who work in a managerial capacity) who refuses to pay it.[18]

IV. BREAK TIME FOR NURSING MOTHERS (LACTATION BREAKS)

[4.14] Does New York State have a law that permits nursing mothers to express breast milk in the workplace?

Yes. Section 206-c of the New York Labor Law requires employers to provide nursing mothers with reasonable breaks during the workday for lactation purposes. This break time is *unpaid*; *see* § 4.19 below.

---

18   Labor Law § 195.5.

[4.15]   What employers are covered by lactation requirements?

The lactation requirements of the Labor Law apply to all public and private employers in New York State, regardless of size or industry.[19]

[4.16]   What employees are covered by the lactation requirements?

Section 206-c of the Labor Law does not identify specific eligibility criteria such as length of service with the employer or hours worked in order for a nursing mother to take lactation breaks under this provision. *All* nursing mothers are covered for up to three years after the birth of a child.[20]

[4.17]   How much break time is a nursing mother entitled to?

Section 206-c of the Labor Law does not specify how much time is "reasonable" for lactation breaks. However, the Department of Labor has indicated that lactation breaks shall generally range in length from twenty to thirty minutes every three hours, depending upon the circumstances.[21] In evaluating the appropriate amount of time, employers may need to account for the physical needs of the nursing mother, the amount of time the nursing mother is separated from the infant, the proximity of the lactation room, etc.

[4.18]   May an employer tell an employee to postpone her lactation break?

Yes, but only under limited circumstances. Specifically, an employee's break can be postponed for up to thirty minutes if "she cannot be spared from her duties until appropriate coverage arrives."[22]

---

19   *See* N.Y. Department of Labor, *Guidelines Regarding the Rights of Nursing Mothers to Express Breast Milk in the Work Place* (LS-702) (May 2019), https://labor.ny.gov/formsdocs/wp/LS702.pdf. *See also* N.Y. Department of Labor, *Fact Sheet: Your Right as a Nursing Mother to Pump Breast Milk at Work* (P708) (Sept. 2015), https://labor.ny.gov/formsdocs/factsheets/pdfs/p708.pdf; N.Y. Department of Labor, *Fact Sheet: Rights of Nursing Mothers to Pump Breast Milk at Work – Information for Employers* (P709) (Sept. 2015), https://labor.ny.gov/formsdocs/factsheets/pdfs/p709.pdf.

20   Labor Law § 206-c.

21   N.Y. Department of Labor, *Guidelines Regarding the Rights of Nursing Mothers to Express Breast Milk in the Work Place* (LS-702) (May 2019).

22   *Id.*

[4.19] Are employers required to pay nursing mothers for lactation breaks?

No. The break time that a nursing mother takes to express breast milk is *unpaid*.[23]

However, a nursing mother may elect to take her unpaid lactation break during a regularly scheduled *paid* break or meal period, and in such case this would continue to be paid time.[24] This is the employee's choice, and an employer may not prohibit a nursing mother from taking her regularly scheduled break and/or meal period merely because she has taken additional break time for the purpose of expressing breast milk.[25]

[4.20] May a nursing mother elect to make up work time that was taken for unpaid lactation breaks?

Yes. The Department of Labor states that employers must allow nursing mothers the opportunity to work either before or after their scheduled shifts in order to make up time spent on lactation breaks, if the employee chooses to do so. For purposes of this provision, the make-up time must fall within the employer's normal business hours.[26]

[4.21] Do employers have to give any notice about lactation breaks?

Yes. Employers must provide employees with written notice regarding their rights to take unpaid lactation breaks. This notice must be given either (a) to each affected employee, or (b) communicated to all employ-

---

23   *See* Labor Law § 206-c.

24   *Id.*

25   *See* N.Y. Department of Labor, *Fact Sheet: Your Right As a Nursing Mother to Pump Breast Milk at Work* (P708) (Sept. 2015), https://labor.ny.gov/formsdocs/factsheets/pdfs/p708.pdf; N.Y. Department of Labor, *Fact Sheet: Rights of Nursing Mothers to Pump Breast Milk at Work – Information for Employers* (P709) (Sept. 2015), https://labor.ny.gov/formsdocs/factsheets/pdfs/p709.pdf.

26   *See* N.Y. Department of Labor, *Guidelines Regarding the Rights of Nursing Mothers to Express Breast Milk in the Work Place* (LS-702) (May 2019), https://labor.ny.gov/formsdocs/wp/LS702.pdf; *see also* N.Y. Department of Labor, *Fact Sheet: Your Right As a Nursing Mother to Pump Breast Milk at Work* (P708) (Sept. 2015); N.Y. Department of Labor, *Fact Sheet: Rights of Nursing Mothers to Pump Breast Milk at Work – Information for Employers* (P709) (Sept. 2015).

ees by a written notice posting in a centralized location in the workplace or as a policy published in an employee handbook.[27]

[4.22] Do employees have to give any notice about the need for lactation breaks?

Yes. Employees who wish to take lactation breaks during the workday are required to provide their employers with advance notice. The Department of Labor recommends that the notice be given prior to the employee's return from maternity leave; however, the Department of Labor does not specify whether notice must be given orally or in writing.[28] It should be presumed that oral notice from the employee is sufficient.

[4.23] Are employers required to provide a separate space for lactation?

Yes. Employers are required to make a reasonable effort to identify a private room or designated space in close proximity for employees to express breastmilk in the workplace, unless it would be significantly impracticable, inconvenient or expensive for the employer to do so.[29] "Private" means that the lactation room will be inaccessible by other employees, customers or visitors while a nursing mother is using the space. In addition, the room should have a door with a functional lock, *or* a sign stating that the room is not accessible.[30]

---

27   N.Y. Department of Labor, *Guidelines Regarding The Rights of Nursing Mothers to Express Breast Milk in the Work Place* (LS-702) (May 2019); N.Y. Department of Labor, *Fact Sheet: Your Right As a Nursing Mother to Pump Breast Milk at Work* (P708) (Sept. 2015); N.Y. Department of Labor, *Fact Sheet: Rights of Nursing Mothers to Pump Breast Milk at Work – Information for Employers* (P709) (Sept. 2015).

28   N.Y. Department of Labor, *Guidelines Regarding the Rights of Nursing Mothers to Express Breast Milk in the Work Place* (LS-702) (May 2019); N.Y. Department of Labor, *Fact Sheet: Your Right As a Nursing Mother to Pump Breast Milk at Work* (P708) (Sept. 2015); N.Y. Department of Labor, *Fact Sheet: Rights of Nursing Mothers to Pump Breast Milk at Work – Information for Employers* (P709) (Sept. 2015).

29   *See* Labor Law § 206-c. *See also Guidelines Regarding the Rights of Nursing Mothers to Express Breast Milk In the Work Place* (LS-702), May 2019.

30   N.Y. Department of Labor, *Guidelines Regarding the Rights of Nursing Mothers to Express Breast Milk in the Work Place* (LS-702) (May 2019); *see also* N.Y. Department of Labor, *Fact Sheet: Your Right As a Nursing Mother to Pump Breast Milk at Work* (P708) (Sept. 2015); N.Y. Department of Labor, *Fact Sheet: Rights of Nursing Mothers to Pump Breast Milk at Work – Information for Employers* (P709) (Sept. 2015).

[4.24] When is providing a lactation space "impracticable, inconvenient or expensive" for the employer?

In its published guidelines, the Department of Labor has identified a number of factors that employers should consider to conduct this assessment, including but not limited to: the nature of the work performed by the employer; the size and physical arrangement of the employer's premises; the cost of providing a lactation space; the employer's hours of operation; the employee's work hours, etc.[31] It should be assumed that employers are required to provide lactation space unless true hardship for the employer can be demonstrated.

[4.25] When is a lactation space "in close proximity" to an employee's work area?

The Department of Labor has stated that "close proximity" requires the designated area to be in walking distance from the employee's workspace and should not be so far away as to noticeably extend the employee's break time. Where appropriate and reasonable in terms of distance, an employer may choose to designate a single, centrally located lactation room for use by all nursing employees.[32]

[4.26] Are there alternatives to a permanent designated lactation space?

Not all employers are able to provide a permanent lactation room in the workplace. Where no permanent space is identified, an employer may elect to temporarily use vacant office space and/or another available room(s). If the employer is unable to find a vacant room, it may—as a last resort—have the employee use a cubicle, *provided* that the cubicle is not accessible to the public and is fully enclosed with walls that are at least seven feet tall. However, the Department of Labor has noted that the lactation space cannot be a restroom or a bathroom stall.[33]

In New York City, an employer cannot make an alternative arrangement without first engaging in an "interactive process" with the affected employee about the suitability of the arrangement. The New York City

---

31   *See Guidelines Regarding the Rights of Nursing Mothers to Express Breast Milk in the Work Place* (LS-702) (May 2019).

32   *Id.*

33   *Id.; see also* N.Y. Department of Labor, *Fact Sheet: Your Right As a Nursing Mother to Pump Breast Milk at Work* (P708) (Sept. 2015); N.Y. Department of Labor, *Fact Sheet: Rights of Nursing Mothers to Pump Breast Milk at Work – Information for Employers* (P709) (Sept. 2015).

Commission on Human Rights has set forth a three-requirement standard for lactation accommodations:

> There are three general requirements for employers related to lactation accommodations for employees. Employers must: (1) provide adequate time for employees to express breast milk during the workday; (2) provide a lactation room with all of the components required by law; and (3) have a written policy on lactation accommodations. If providing a lactation room or other accommodations requested by the employee would pose an undue hardship, the employer must engage in a cooperative dialogue with the employee to determine what alternative accommodations may be available that meet the employee's needs. The "undue hardship" standard . . . is a high bar for employers to meet.[34]

[4.27]   What must the lactation space contain?

The space must be well lit, either with natural or artificial light. If a room contains a window, the window must have a curtain or other covering to provide privacy to the employee. The room must also contain a chair, as well as a table or other flat surface.[35]

The Department of Labor also encourages employers to consider providing the following: an electrical outlet; a clean water supply; and access to refrigeration. If an employer elects to provide a refrigerator, the employer is not responsible for safeguarding any breastmilk stored within the refrigerator.[36]

However, in New York City, the employer *must* provide: a lock on the door; an electrical outlet; a chair; a small table or other flat surface; nearby access to running water; and a refrigerator in close proximity

---

34   N.Y.C. Human Rights, *Frequently Asked Questions Lactation Accommodations and Model Policy N.Y.C. Administrative Code § 8-107(22)* Question 3, https://www1.nyc.gov/site/cchr/law/lactation-faqs.page.

35   *See* N.Y. Department of Labor, *Guidelines Regarding the Rights of Nursing Mothers to Express Breast Milk in the Work Place* (LS-702) (May 2019).

36   *Id.*

where breast milk can be stored.[37] The room may be used for other purposes when it is not being used as a lactation space.[38]

[4.28] What are the penalties for non-compliance?

Employers are prohibited from discriminating or retaliating against nursing mothers who exercise their right to express breastmilk in the workplace. Violations may result in civil actions for damages brought by employees, proceedings brought by the Commissioner of Labor for injunctive relief and liquidated damages of up to $20,000, and (in rare cases) criminal penalties.[39]

V.   JURY SERVICE

[4.29] Are employees in New York entitled to time off for jury duty?

Yes. Any employee who receives a summons for jury service is entitled to take time off from work without penalty from the employer.[40]

[4.30] Is jury duty leave paid or unpaid?

Leave for jury service is generally *unpaid*.[41] However, employers who employ more than ten individuals are *required to pay* an employee who must leave work to serve on a jury a minimum of $40.00 per day for *the first three days of jury service*. After three days, these employers are not required to pay for additional jury service.

For an employee who is paid on a salary basis *and* who is "exempt" (in other words, not entitled to statutory overtime pay), an employer may reduce the employee's paycheck by the amount of any daily stipend that the employee receives from the court for his or her jury service. For a discussion of which employees are exempt from overtime under New York State law, *see* Chapter 3 of this book, "Wages and Salary," at § 3.7.[42]

---

37   N.Y.C. Human Rights, *Frequently Asked Questions Lactation Accommodations and Model Policy N.Y.C. Administrative Code § 8-107(22).*

38   *Id.*

39   *See* Labor Law §§ 206-c, 214, 215.

40   Judiciary Law § 519.

41   *Id.*

42   *See also* U.S. Dept. of Labor, Wage & Hour Div., *Fact Sheet #17G: Salary Basis Requirement and the Part 541 Exemptions Under the Fair Labor Standards Act (FLSA)* (rev. Sept. 2019), https://www.dol.gov/agencies/whd/fact-sheets/17g-overtime-salary.

[4.31]   Is an employer entitled to prior notice of jury service from the employee?

Yes. An employee who needs to take time off from work for jury service is required to notify the employer that he or she has been summoned to serve as a juror prior to the commencement of jury duty.[43]

[4.32]   What are the penalties for non-compliance?

Employers are prohibited from discriminating and/or retaliating against employees who lawfully exercise their right to take leave to participate in jury service. An employer who takes an adverse employment action against an employee who needs time off pursuant for jury service will be in criminal contempt and penalized accordingly.[44]

VI.   TIME OFF TO VOTE

[4.33]   Are employees entitled to time off to vote?

Yes. In April 2020, New York State amended its voting leave law to require employers to provide employees with up to two hours of *paid* time off to enable them to vote in "any" election if they do not have "sufficient time" outside of their scheduled working hours to vote.[45] However, despite the reference to "any" election, not all elections are covered; *see* § 4.34 below.

An employee has "sufficient time" outside of his or her working hours to vote if the employee has four consecutive hours between the opening of the polls and the beginning of his or her shift or the end of his or her shift and the closing of the polls.[46] If an employee does not have sufficient time to vote, the employer must permit the employee to take off as much working time as will, when added to the employee's voting time outside of working hours, enable him or her to vote. However, only up to two hours of this time off must be paid.[47]

All employers in New York must comply with the voting leave law.

---

43   Judiciary Law § 519.

44   *See* Judiciary Law §§ 519, 750.

45   N.Y. Elec. Law § 3-110. As originally enacted in 2019, the statute provided for a "blanket" entitlement to *three* paid hours off to vote with no provisions as to "sufficient time" to vote.

46   N.Y. Elec. Law § 3-110(2).

47   N.Y. Elec. Law § 3-110(1).

Any employee who is registered to vote in New York is eligible to take paid time off to vote under this law. The law does not distinguish between full-time and part-time employees, and in the absence of clarifying guidance, employers should assume that part-time employees are covered.

[4.34] What elections are covered by the law?

The statutory language states that the voting leave law applies to "any election." The New York Election Law applies to all public elections for the purpose of nominating or electing an individual and/or deciding a ballot question submitted to the voters, unless a provision of another law applies.[48] In response to the April 2019 amendment, the New York State Board of Elections issued guidance to clarify that "primary and general elections as well as any special elections called by the Governor" are included in this provision.[49]

However, the guidance issued by the New York Board of Elections further states that "school district elections, library district elections, fire district elections or special town elections" are excluded from the voting leave law.[50]

The time off requirements do not apply to early voting periods: the requirement is limited to actual "election days."[51]

[4.35] At what time(s) during the workday may an employee take voting leave?

Employees who wish to take paid time off to vote under this law may only do so at the beginning or end of the work shift, as designated by the employer. However, the law recognizes that the employer and employee may mutually agree to a different time.[52]

---

48   N.Y. Elec. Law § 1-102.

49   N.Y. Board of Elections, *FAQ "Time off to Vote"* at #1 (July 18, 2019), https://www.elections. ny.gov/NYSBOE/elections/TimeOffToVoteFAQ.pdf.

50   *Id.*

51   *Id.*

52   N.Y. Elec. Law § 3-110(2).

[4.36] Do employees have to give notice of the desire to take voting leave?

Yes. Employees must provide employers with notice regarding their intent to take *time off to* vote at least two, but not more than ten, working days prior to the election.[53] For purposes of this provision, the term "working days" means "any day that the employer is operating and/or open for business."[54]

[4.37] May an employer charge paid voting leave time against other accruals of paid time?

The statutory language does not directly address this issue, and there is a lack of case law or other relevant guidance to answer this question.

However, the law states that time off to vote must be provided "without loss of pay."[55] Since earned paid time off is treated as wages in New York (*see* § 4.9 of this chapter), a court may well find that a decrease in other accruals of paid time off constitutes a "loss of pay." Further, the New York Board of Elections has opined that employers cannot require employees to use "personal time" to vote, as it would be "contrary to the intent of the statute."[56]

[4.38] May an employer require proof of voting eligibility or actual voting?

The statute does not provide employers with a mechanism by which to verify either: (a) that an employee is a registered voter; or (b) that an employee has actually voted in a particular election. The guidance issued by the New York State Board of Elections also confirms that the law is silent on the issue of employers requiring voting proof from employees.

However, *as to public sector employees*, the New York State Civil Service Department has specifically stated: "[a]n appointing authority may

---

53   N.Y. Elec. Law § 3-110(3).

54   N.Y. Board of Elections, *FAQ "Time off to Vote"* at #1 (July 18, 2019), https://www.elections.ny.gov/NYSBOE/elections/TimeOffToVoteFAQ.pdf.

55   N.Y. Elec. Law § 3-110(1).

56   N.Y. Board of Elections, *FAQ "Time off to Vote"* at #1 (July 18, 2019).

not require proof of voter registration or proof that an employee actually voted."[57]

[4.39]   Do employers have to give notice of the right to voting leave?

Yes. At least ten working days before an election, the employer is required to post a notice containing information about employees' right to take time off from work to vote.[58] The State Board of Elections published a model notice under the initial 2019 enactment, and it is anticipated that it will publish a revised notice to reflect the 2020 amendments.

[4.40]   What are the penalties for non-compliance?

The voting leave law is silent with respect to the issue of penalties. However, the New York Board of Elections has stated that "civil enforcement remedies (Election Law § 3-104) or misdemeanor criminal charges in instances of 'knowingly and willfully' violating the provision (Election Law § 17-168) are provided for in existing law."[59]

VII.   CRIME VICTIM AND CRIME WITNESS LEAVE

[4.41]   Are victims of, or witnesses to, crimes entitled to time off from work?

Yes. Section 215.14 of the New York Penal Law requires employers to provide *unpaid* time off to employees who are absent from work in connection with the employee's obligations and duties performed as a victim of, or witness to, a crime. This same provision prohibits an employer from taking an adverse employment action—such as discipline, demotion or discharge—against an employee who is absent from work for this purpose.

[4.42]   What employers are covered by the crime victim/witness leave requirement?

Section 215.14 of the New York Penal Code does not restrict the term "employer", nor does it identify any limiting exceptions. Accordingly, the requirements set forth in § 215.14 should be interpreted to apply to all employers.

---

57   N.Y. Civil Service Department, *Attendance and Leave Manual, Policy Bulletin 2019-02-a, Section 21.12* (June 2019), https://www.cs.ny.gov/attend_leave_manual/021AbsenceWithPay/21_12/PolicyBulletin19-02.html.

58   N.Y. Elec. Law § 3-110(4).

59   N.Y. Board of Elections, "FAQ 'Time off to Vote'" at FAQ #8 (July 18, 2019).

[4.43]   Who is a "victim" of a crime?

The law covers an individual who is the victim of a crime *and* an individual who is actually subpoenaed to attend a criminal proceeding as a witness.[60]

In a rather opaque example of legislative drafting, Penal Law § 215.14(2) defines the word "victim" as follows:

> For purposes of this section, the term "victim" shall include the aggrieved party or the aggrieved party's next of kin, if the aggrieved party is deceased as a result of the offense, the representative of a victim as defined in subdivision six of section six hundred twenty-one of the executive law, a good samaritan as defined in subdivision seven of section six hundred twenty-one of such law or a person pursuing an application or enforcement of an order of protection under the criminal procedure law or the family court act.

[4.44]   What is the purpose of the crime victim/witness time off?

A victim or witness is entitled to take time off from work, without penalty, in order to appear as a witness in a criminal proceeding (but only pursuant to a subpoena if the witness is not also a victim); to consult with the prosecutor; or to make a victim impact statement.

[4.45]   Do employees have to give notice of the need to take crime victim leave?

Yes. The law requires that employees notify their employers at least one day in advance before taking time off to exercise their rights as a victim of, or witness to, a crime.[61]

[4.46]   Can employers require employees to provide verification or certification of their absence from work?

Yes. Employers may require employees to submit documentation that confirms their absence from work for a qualifying reason as a victim or witness.[62]

---

60   *See* Penal Law § 215.14(1).

61   Penal Law § 215.14(1).

62   *See* Penal Law § 215.14(1).

VIII. BEREAVEMENT LEAVE

[4.47] Are New York employers required to provide employees with bereavement leave?

No. There are no laws that currently require employers to provide their employees with time off from work for bereavement purposes.

IX. BLOOD DONATION LEAVE

[4.48] Are employees entitled to time off to donate blood?

Yes. Section 202-j of the New York Labor Law requires employers that employ twenty (20) or more individuals in "at least one site" to provide time off from work to employees who seek to donate blood.[63] Eligible employees are those who work for an average of twenty (20) or more hours per week, and who work "at any site owned or operated by an employer."[64]

However, the right to take leave for blood donation does not include a right to take leave for blood *plasma* donation ("apheresis"), although the New York State Department of Labor encourages employers to consider doing so on a voluntary basis.[65]

Employers have two options for providing blood donation leave:

- The first option requires an employer to provide employees with up to three hours of leave during the work day to donate blood once in any calendar year, where the blood donation is made "off-premises."[66] Under this first option, the leave is *unpaid* unless the

---

63   *See* Labor Law §§ 202-j(1)(b) and 202-j(2).

64   *See* Labor Law § 202-j(1)(a).

65   *See* N.Y. Department of Labor, *Guidelines for Implementation of Employee Blood Donation Leave* (LS-703) (Mar. 2016), https://labor.ny.gov/formsdocs/wp/LS703.pdf.

66   *Id.*

employer chooses to pay for it.[67] An employee who wants to take leave for off-premises blood donation(s) must provide notice at least three working days in advance.[68]

- The second option, which applies when the employer chooses the blood donation site (as, for example, in a company "blood drive"), requires an employer to allow employees to donate blood during work hours *at least twice per year* at a convenient time and place. as designated by the employer (referred to herein as "blood donation leave alternatives").[69] This must be granted as *paid* leave, and employers cannot require employees to use accrued, paid time off for their participation.[70] An employee who wishes to take leave under the blood donation leave alternative option must provide the employer with notice at least *two days in advance.*

The New York Department of Labor has established guidelines and requirements that specifically pertain to blood donation leave alternatives.[71] The Department of Labor permits two or more employers to coordinate and/or co-sponsor a blood donation leave alternative at a shared work location.[72]

An employee who wants to take leave for off-premises blood donation(s), must provide notice at least three working days in advance.[73]

---

67   *Id.*

68   The Department of Labor Guidelines contemplate extended notice requirements in certain circumstances. Specifically, where an employee holds a position that is deemed essential to the employer's operation, the employer can require the employee to provide more than three days' advance notice. However, in no event may an employer require an employee in these limited situations to provide more than ten (10) days' advance notice or notice for any period of time longer than is necessary to temporarily fill the employee's position. *See* N.Y. Department of Labor, *Guidelines for Implementation of Employee Blood Donation Leave* (LS-703) (March 2016). The notice may be found at https://www.labor.ny.gov/formsdocs/wp/LS703.pdf. In addition, the Department of Labor recognizes that the employee advance notice provisions may not be applicable in emergency situations where the employee is required to donate blood for his or her own surgery or the surgery of a family member. *Id.*

69   *See* Labor Law § 202-j(2).

70   *See* Labor Law § 202-j(2).

71   *Id.*

72   *Id.*

73   *Id.*

The Department of Labor guidelines for blood donation alternatives include the following (*see* https://www.labor.ny.gov/formsdocs/wp/LS703.pdf):

- Blood donation leave alternatives must be scheduled at a "convenient time and place set by the employer." This means that such leave alternatives must be scheduled during the employee's normal work hours and must be within a reasonable travel distance for the employee.

- If an employee provides the employer with "prompt notice" that he or she is not able to attend the employer's leave alternative because the employee is not in the workplace and if, as a result, the employee will not have the opportunity to participate in at least two blood donation leave alternatives during the applicable calendar year, the employer must either: (i) make another leave alternative available to the employee; or (ii) allow the employee to take off-premises blood donation leave.

- Employees must be allowed sufficient time to donate blood, to recover (e.g., nourishment after donating) and to return to work.

- Notice of a blood donation leave alternative must be posted "prominently" in the workplace at least two weeks in advance of the scheduled alternative. The guidelines further provide that in order for a leave alternative to "count" toward the employer's requirement to provide two leave alternatives in a single calendar year, notice of the leave alternative must be given prior to December 1st of that year.

- Finally, employers are prohibited from scheduling blood donation leave alternatives when a significant number of employees are anticipated to be out of the office (such as major holidays, the last week of December, etc.).

[4.49] What notice must an employer give regarding the right to blood donation leave?

Employers must provide written notice to employees regarding their right to take blood donation leave. The written notice must be given to employees "in a manner that will ensure that employees see it."[74]

---

74   *See* N.Y. Department of Labor, *Guidelines for Implementation of Employee Blood Donation Leave* (LS-703) (Mar. 2016), https://labor.ny.gov/formsdocs/wp/LS703.pdf.

Employers may opt to: (a) post the notice in a "prominent location"; (b) include the notice in an employee handbook; (c) provide notice in employees' paychecks; or (d) use another "comparable method."[75] In an opinion letter, the New York State Department of Labor has stated that electronic postings of such notice on an employer's intranet will also satisfy the acceptable posting requirements and, therefore, be deemed a "comparable method," *provided* that: the posting is placed in a prominent location on the intranet; employees have easy access to the employer's intranet (*for example, that* employees have their own computer stations); and employees may access the intranet during the course of their workday for a reasonable length of time without loss of pay.[76]

Finally, if the employer elects to provide written notice directly to its employees (as opposed to notice via a general workplace posting), it must do so at the time of hire and on an annual basis thereafter (but no later than January 15 of each calendar year).[77]

[4.50] May an employer require employees to prove that they took leave for an actual blood donation?

Yes. Employers may require employees who take leave to make an off-site blood donation to provide "sufficient proof" of their blood donation or good faith effort at blood donation. The Department of Labor Guidelines, do not, however, explain what constitutes "sufficient proof."

[4.51] What are the consequences for non-compliance?

Employers are prohibited from retaliating against employees who request or take blood donation leave under New York law.[78] In addition, Section 215 of the Labor Law makes it unlawful for an employer to "discharge, threaten, penalize, or in any other manner discriminate or retaliate against

---

75   *Id.*

76   N.Y. Department of Labor, *Request for Opinion: Leave for Blood Donation/Breast Milk* Op. RO-08-0095 at 2 (July 31, 2008), https://www.labor.ny.gov/legal/counsel/pdf/Blood%20Donations%20-%20Breast%20Milk/RO-08-0095%20Leave%20for%20Blood%20Donation%20-%20Breast%20Milk.pdf.

77   *See* N.Y. Department of Labor, *Guidelines for Implementation of Employee Blood Donation Leave* (LS-703) (March 2016).

78   *See* Labor Law § 202-j(3).

any employee" who generally exercises any rights protected under the Labor Law.[79] Any employee or the New York Commissioner of Labor may initiate a civil action against an employer for any Section 215 violation.[80]

Section 213 of the Labor Law generally provides that a violation of, or noncompliance with, "any provision of the Labor Law"—not solely limited to Section 202-j—can result in either civil or criminal penalties. Specifically, Section 213 provides a tiered approach to penalties:[81]

First Offense	Monetary fine up to $100
Second Offense	Monetary fine between $100 and $500 *or* up to 30 days' imprisonment *or* both fine and imprisonment
Third Offense and Subsequent Offenses	Monetary fine of at least $300 *or* imprisonment up to 60 days *or* both fine and imprisonment

X. BONE MARROW AND ORGAN DONATION LEAVE

[4.52] Are employees entitled to leave for bone marrow or organ donation?

Yes. Covered employers must provide employees who seek to undergo a medical procedure *to donate bone marrow* with up to twenty-four work hours of leave.[82] This leave is *unpaid* (except for employees of the State of New York), unless the employer chooses to provide paid leave.[83]

The New York Labor Law does not require employers (other than the State of New York as an employer) to provide organ donation leave. However, the United States Department of Labor has opined that organ donation qualifies as a "serious health condition" which entitles an employee who makes an organ donation to take leave under the federal

---

79   *See* Labor Law § 215.

80   *Id.*

81   Labor Law § 213. *See also* N.Y. Department of Labor, *Request for Opinion Leave of Absesnce – Labor Law 202-a Bone Marrow Donation* Op. RO-10-0079 4 (July 1, 2010), https://www.labor.ny.gov/legal/counsel/pdf/Other/RO-10-0079%20Bone%20Marrow%20Donation.pdf.

82   Labor Law § 202-a(2).

83   The law does not specifically state that employers must provide such leave as paid time off. The New York State Department of Labor recognizes that the law does not mandate employers to provide this type of leave on a paid basis; therefore, whether the leave is paid or unpaid is left to the employer's discretion. *See* N.Y. Department of Labor Op. RO-10-0079 (July 1, 2010) at 2.

Family Medical Leave Act;[84] and the New York Paid Family Leave Law was amended in 2018 to provide that Paid Family Leave is available for an employee to care for a family member who needs an organ donation.

See § 4.56 below for the special rules which apply to employees of the State of New York.

This law defines "employer" to include any private entity that employs twenty or more individuals in at least one site, and also includes public entities (such as counties, town, cities, school districts, public authorities or other governmental subdivisions) that employ twenty or more individuals in at least one site.[85]

[4.53]   Who is eligible to take bone marrow donation leave?

An employee who works for an average of twenty or more hours per week and who works "at any site owned or operated by an employer" is eligible to take bone marrow donation leave.[86]

The statute is silent as to a specific number of times that an employee may use or request bone marrow donation leave. As noted above, an employee may take up to twenty-four (24) work hours of leave. In an opinion letter, the New York State Department of Labor has stated that because an employee's workday is not twenty-four (24) hours in length, leave to donate bone marrow can be used in smaller increments.[87]

The New York State Department of Labor suggests that an employer should use a reasonable approach with respect to verification inquiries. For example, the employer may request that the employee provide information from a treating physician regarding the following: confirmation that the employee has, in fact, donated bone marrow; the dates of the bone marrow procedure; the amount of time needed for recovery and follow-up from the procedure, etc.[88]

---

84   U.S. Department of Labor, *Opinion Letter FMLA2018-2-A* (Aug. 28, 2018), https://www.dol.gov/sites/dolgov/files/WHD/legacy/files/2018_08_28_2A_FMLA.pdf.

85   Labor Law § 202-a(1)(b).

86   Labor Law § 202-a(1)(a).

87   N.Y. Department of Labor, *Request for Opinion Leave of Absesnce – Labor Law 202-a Bone Marrow Donation* Op. RO-10-0079 3 (July 1, 2010), https://www.labor.ny.gov/legal/counsel/pdf/Other/RO-10-0079%20Bone%20Marrow%20Donation.pdf.

88   *Id.*

The statute is silent as to how much notice an employee should give to the employer. However, the New York State Department of Labor has stated that when an employee has been scheduled to make a bone marrow donation, the employee should promptly notify the employer that the procedure has been scheduled; and the employee should give the employer at least twenty-four hours' advance notice.

The Department of Labor also takes the position that employees should provide notice to their employers as soon as they receive the request to donate bone marrow—even if a procedure has not yet been scheduled.[89]

[4.54] What notice must an employer give regarding the right to bone marrow donation leave?

While the New York State Department of Labor encourages employers to notify employees of their right to take time off to donate bone marrow through policies and handbooks, the statute does not formally require employers to provide such notice.[90]

[4.55] What are the penalties for non-compliance?

See § 4.51 above: the same penalties apply.

[4.56] What are the special bone marrow and organ donation rules for New York State employees?

Any employee of the State of New York is entitled to take leave for purposes of organ *and bone marrow donation*. In contrast to other employers, this leave for State employees is *paid* leave.[91]

The amount of leave available to a State employee depends upon the type of leave. A State employee is entitled to up to seven days of leave to donate bone marrow, and up to thirty days of leave to serve as an organ donor.[92]

State employees must provide the State with at least fourteen days of advance written notice regarding their need to take leave under Section

---

89   *Id.* at 4.

90   N.Y. Department of Labor, *Request for Opinion Leave of Absence – Labor Law 202-a Bone Marrow Donation*, Op. RO-10-0079 (July 1, 2010) at 4.

91   Labor Law § 202-b(1).

92   *See* Labor Law § 202-b(1).

202-b, but this requirement can be waived in the event of a medical emergency, which must be documented by a physician.[93]

The State may require an employee to submit documentation from the employee's physician that verifies the purpose for, and length of, the leave requested.[94]

XI.   MILITARY SERVICE

[4.57]   Are employees entitled to time off for military service?

Yes. Both private and public employers are required to provide *unpaid* leave time (and reinstatement rights) for military service. *These requirements are in addition to requirements under federal law,* as provided in the Uniformed Services Employment and Reemployment Rights Act of 1994 and its corresponding regulations.[95]

New York State's provisions governing *private employers* are codified in Article XIII of the New York Military Law, referred to as the "New York Soldiers' and Sailors' Civil Relief Act of 1951" (referred to here as the "Civil Relief Act").[96] Sections 317 and 318 address reinstatement rights and discrimination protections following an individual's return to private sector employment following military leave.

The provisions governing *public employers* are codified in Article XI of the New York Military Law. Sections 242 and 243 address leave rights, reinstatement rights, and pay during leave following an individual's return to public sector employment following military leave.

---

93   Labor Law § 202-b(1).

94   *See* Labor Law § 202-b(1).

95   *See* 38 U.S.C. §§ 4301–4335. Also note that, for employers whose employees need to hold professional licenses, N.Y. Military Law § 308-b (extension of license, certificate or registration) provides that the professional licenses of persons who are on military leave are extended if they would otherwise expire during the period of military service. There is a similar extension of license provided for by N.Y.C. Admin. Code § 22-503.

96   *See* Mil. Law § 328.

[4.58] What are the military leave requirements for private sector employers?

The Civil Relief Act does not identify a minimum number of employees for an employer to be covered by the law. Therefore, "any private employer" is deemed to be covered under the Civil Relief Act.[97]

The Civil Relief Act does not set a limit regarding how much time an employee may take for military service purposes. Reinstatement rights are afforded to any employee—other than a temporary employee—so long as all of the following criteria are satisfied:

- The employee has taken time off from work to perform military service;

- The employee has obtained a duly-executed military completion certificate;

- The employee remains qualified to perform the duties of his or her position with the employer; and

- The employee has applied for re-employment within a certain period of time (i.e., within 10 days, within 60 days, or within 90 days, depending on the type of service) after being relieved from military service.[98]

Section 317 does not specify how much advance notice an employer must give his or her employer *prior* to taking military leave.[99] However, as noted above, the law does require an employee to provide notice to the employer regarding a request for reinstatement *following* the individual's release from military service.

[4.59] What military activities qualify for private sector leave and reinstatement?

Individuals in the United States armed forces, reserves, and/or New York State National Guard (referred to in the statute as "the Organized Militia")

---

97   *See* Mil. Law § 317(5).

98   *See* Mil. Law § 317(1)–(3). Because the statute is complicated, employers should refer directly to the statute, which can be found at http://public.leginfo.state.ny.us/lawssrch.cgi?NVLWO under the drop-down menu "LAWS" and then at the link "MIL."

99   It is, of course, the case that employees with military service obligations may be called to active duty essentially without notice from the government.

may take leave to participate in a variety of military functions in addition to active duty deployment, such as: assemblies for drill or other similar training; reserve duty training, instruction or duties; annual full-time training duty; active duty for training or other annual trainings as required by United States law; initial full-time training; and/or initial active-duty training.[100] However, Section 317 does *not* cover individuals who participate in routine Reserve Officer Training Corps (ROTC) training, unless the training is "advanced."[101]

The law provides that an employee who has taken leave for a qualifying military activity must be restored or returned to his or her position or to a position of "like seniority, status and pay." However, an employer is not obligated to provide reinstatement when a change in the employer's circumstance would render it impossible or unreasonable to do so.[102]

Section 317 also prohibits employers from discharging a returning employee without cause within one year of the employee's reinstatement following a return from military leave.[103]

An employee who takes military leave is entitled to continue any applicable employer-provided insurance coverage(s) and/or other employee benefits on the same terms and conditions as other employees who have taken a non-military furlough or leave of absence.[104]

[4.60]   What are the penalties for private sector non-compliance?

Section 318 of the Civil Relief Act prohibits employers from discriminating against, or refusing to hire and otherwise employ, any individual because of military service obligations.[105]

Employees cannot be asked, required, or forced to waive their rights under the Civil Relief Act.[106]

---

100   *See* Mil. Law § 317(2), (2)(a) and (3).

101   *See* Mil. Law § 317(3).

102   *See* Mil. Law § 317(1)(c).

103   *See* Mil. Law § 317(4).

104   *See* Mil. Law § 317(4).

105   *See* Mil. Law § 318(1).

106   Mil. Law § 318(2)(a).

Any employer who knowingly disregards this anti-waiver provision is guilty of a misdemeanor and shall be subject to penalties including: imprisonment (not to exceed one year); a fine (not to exceed $1,000); or a combination of imprisonment and a monetary fine.[107] In addition, an employer that knowingly violates the anti-waiver provisions may also be subjected to a civil penalty of up to $5,000 per occurrence.

[4.61] What are the military leave requirements for public sector employers?

Public sector employers are governed by N.Y. Military Law §§ 242 and 243. Officers and employees of public bodies in New York are entitled to leave: (a) "while engaged in performance of ordered military duty"; (b) while voluntarily or involuntarily attending "any service school or schools conducted by the armed forces of the United States"; or (c) "while performing full-time training duty or active duty for training with or in an armed force of the United States," including reserve or National Guard training. This leave is not considered to be a break in service.[108]

In addition, public sector employees are entitled to be paid by their employers for their military service, as follows:

- For the greater of thirty calendar days or twenty-two working days in any calendar year "while engaged in the performance of ordered military duty, and while going to and returning from such duty"; *and*

- For an additional five working days for an employee who has served "in a combat theater or combat zone of operations" as certified by the United States Department of Defense for health-related services arising from such duty.[109]

N.Y. Military Law § 243 provides that public sector employees (with the exception of police officers, unless such police officers have obtained prior permission from their public sector employers) are entitled to reinstatement to their positions after the end of military duty, so long as they have not received a dishonorable or bad conduct discharge.[110] In the case of "volun-

---

107   Mil. Law § 318(2)(b).

108   Mil. Law § 242.

109   In cities of one million or more, Mil. Law § 242 imposes additional requirements.

110   The section contains an exception to the dishonorable or bad conduct discharge exception for "LGBT veterans."

tary" (enlisted) service, the reinstatement right expires after four years of military service, *unless* "the service in excess of four years is at the request and for the convenience of the federal government" *or* "is performed during a period of war, or national emergency declared by the president."

[4.62] Are the spouses of military members entitled to leave?

Yes. Section 202-i of the New York Labor Law provides that employees who are married to persons in military service must be granted up to ten days of *unpaid* leave if: (a) the spouse in military service is on leave from the United States Armed Forces, National Guard or reserves; *and* (b) the spouse in military service has been deployed during a "period of military conflict" to a combat theater or a combat zone of operations.[111] However, this provision only applies to employees employed by an employer that employs twenty (20) or more individuals in at least one site.[112]

These provisions are designed to enable to enable an employee to join his or her spouse who is on leave from a conflict deployment.

XII. LEAVE FOR VOLUNTEER EMERGENCY RESPONDERS

[4.63] Are emergency responders entitled to leave for emergency response activities?

Yes. All employers, other than New York State itself, are required to provide *unpaid* leave for employees who serve as voluntary emergency responders (as defined in the next paragraph of this section) during state or local emergencies as declared by the Governor or an appropriate local executive.[113] Emergency responder leave is *unpaid*, unless an employee elects to use accrued paid time off for some or all of the emergency responder leave period.[114]

---

111   *See* Labor Law § 202-i(2). A "period of military conflict is defined as: (i) a period of war declared by Congress; or (ii) circumstances where reserve members of the United States Armed Forces are called to active duty pursuant to certain provisions under the United States Code. Labor Law § 202-i(1)(c).

112   Labor Law § 202-i(1)(b).

113   *See* Labor Law § 202-l(1); *see also* Exec. Law §§ 24, 28.

114   *See* Labor Law § 202-l.

In order to qualify for voluntary emergency responder leave, an employee must meet the following criteria:

- First, the employee must be either a volunteer firefighter or a member of a volunteer ambulance service (duly recognized under Article 30 of New York's Public Health Law);

- Second, the employee must have previously provided the employer with written notice of his or her status as a volunteer firefighter or a member of the volunteer ambulance service. Such notice must have been confirmed by the head of the applicable fire department or ambulance service; and

- Finally, the employee's volunteer duties must be related to a "declared emergency" as defined by Executive Law § 24 or § 28.[115]

Section 202-l does not identify a maximum amount of time that must be afforded to an employee for this type of leave. Presumably, an employee is entitled to take leave to provide voluntary emergency response services any time a qualifying emergency has been declared and the employee's services are needed.

The law recognizes an exception to the leave requirement where an employer determines that the leave would cause an undue hardship to the employer's business.[116] An undue hardship is defined as a significant expense and/or difficulty to the employer as a result of providing the requested leave. The factors that are considered in the undue hardship analysis are the same factors that employers must consider when determining whether a request for a workplace accommodation constitutes an undue hardship (for example: the cost of lost productivity, or the number of individuals needing leave or accommodation).[117]

Employers may request that employees provide a notarized statement from the head of the applicable fire department or ambulance service that

---

115 Executive Law § 24 covers emergencies declared by the local chief executive of a "county, city, town or village"; and Executive Law § 28 covers emergencies declared by the Governor.

116 *See* Labor Law § 202-l(1).

117 *See* Exec. Law § 296(10)(d).

certifies the period of time that the employee responded to an emergency under this provision.[118]

XIII. LEAVE FOR VICTIMS OF DOMESTIC VIOLENCE

[4.64] Are victims of domestic violence entitled to leave?[119]

Yes. In 2019, New York State enacted legislation that requires covered employers to accommodate employees who are victims of domestic violence by providing them with *unpaid* time off from work for qualifying reasons.[120] It is unlawful for an employer to discriminate against a person who is a domestic violence victim; *see* Chapter 11 of this book, "Discrimination, Harassment and Retaliation," at § 11.59.

As originally enacted, a covered employer was an employer with four or more employees, but effective February 8, 2020 the definition of a covered employer was expanded to include *all* employers within the New York State, regardless of size.[121]

Domestic violence leave is unpaid, but an employer has the option to require that an employee who takes time off for domestic violence leave purposes must use available accrued paid time off and/or sick time; any additional domestic violence leave extending past available paid leave is unpaid unless the employer has provided otherwise in its policies or an applicable collective bargaining agreement.[122]

The law does not require that an employee have been employed for a minimum period of time, or that an employee have worked some minimum number of hours in order to be eligible for domestic violence leave. Rather, the law simply requires that leave be made available to an employee who is a "victim of domestic violence" as defined under Section 459-a of the New York Social Services Law.[123]

---

118   Labor Law § 202-l(4).

119   See also §§ 4.83–4.99 and §§ 4.111–4.118 below, which discusses similar rights afforded by New York City and Westchester County.

120   Exec. Law §§ 292, 296.

121   Exec. Law § 292(5).

122   Exec. Law § 296(22)(c)(1).

123   *See* Exec. Law §§ 292(34) and 296(22)(c)(1) and (2).

The law permits an employee who is a victim of domestic violence to take leave for the following reasons:

- To seek medical attention for injuries caused by domestic violence, including injuries to a child who is a victim of domestic violence, provided that the employee seeking leave did not cause the child's injuries;

- To obtain "services from a domestic violence shelter, program, or rape crisis center as a result of domestic violence";

- To obtain psychological counseling associated with an incident(s) of domestic violence, which also includes counseling for a child who is a victim of domestic violence, so long as the employee is not the "perpetrator of the domestic violence against the child";

- To participate in safety planning and other actions designed to increase the employee's safety against future incidents of domestic violence, including temporary or permanent relocation; or

- To obtain legal services, to aid and assist in the prosecution of criminal offense(s), or to appear in legal proceedings that relate to the incident(s) of domestic violence.[124]

Employers are not required to provide domestic violence leave where the employee's absence from work would constitute an "undue hardship."[125] For discussion of what constitutes "undue hardship," *see* §§ 4.24, 4.26 and 4.63 of this chapter, and Chapter 11 of this book, "Discrimination, Harassment and Retaliation," at §§ 11.39 and 11.59.

Employees who need time off from work for qualifying reasons related to domestic violence must provide the employer with "reasonable" advance notice, unless advance notice is not feasible. However, the statute does not provide any standard for what notice will be considered "reasonable." If it is *not* feasible for an employee to provide an employer with reasonable advance notice, the employee must, upon request from the employer, provide documentation to certify the employee's absence. Documentation may include one of the following:

---

124   Exec. Law § 296(22)(c)(2).

125   Exec. Law § 296(22)(c)(3).

- A police report indicating that the employee or his or her child was a victim of domestic violence;

- A court order protecting or separating the employee or his or her child from the perpetrator of an act of domestic violence;

- Other evidence from a court or prosecuting attorney that the employee appeared in court; or

- Documentation from a medical professional, domestic violence advocate, health care provider, or counselor that the employee or his or her child was undergoing counseling or treatment for physical or mental injuries or abuse resulting in victimization from an act of domestic violence."[126]

An employee who is entitled to domestic violence leave is entitled to the continuation of any health insurance coverage during his or her absence from work, without any change of benefits.[127]

Employers are required to "maintain the confidentiality of and information regarding an employee's status as a victim of domestic violence."[128]

An employee with a physical or mental disability resulting from domestic violence can request reasonable accommodations, and is to be treated in the same manner as any other employee with a disability; *see generally* Chapter 11 of this book, "Discrimination, Harassment and Retaliation," at §§ 11.35–11.46.

XIV. PAID SICK LEAVE AND PAID FAMILY LEAVE

[4.65] Are employers required to provide sick leave and/or paid family leave?

Yes. Since 2018, private sector employers have been required to provide "paid family leave," which is paid for through New York State via payroll deductions from employees' wages (*see* §§ 4.67–4.82 below).

---

126   Exec. Law § 296(22)(c)(4) and (5).

127   Exec. Law § 296(22)(c)(1).

128   Exec. Law § 296(22)(d).

In addition, however, during the coronavirus crisis of 2020, the Legislature added additional requirements in the form of a new Labor Law § 196-b which, depending on the size of the employer's workforce, may impose an obligation to provide sick leave paid for by the employer.

Labor Law § 196-b requires employers to provide sick leave beginning on January 1, 2021 as follows:

Employers with four or fewer employees and net income of $1 million or less[a]	Up to 40 hours of *unpaid* leave per calendar year
Employers with four or fewer employees and net income of more than $1 million	Up to 40 hours of *paid* leave per calendar year
Employers with between five and 99 employees	Up to 40 hours of *paid* leave per calendar year
Employers with 100 or more employees	Up to 56 hours of *paid* leave per calendar year

a.   Income as reported in the employer's previous tax year.

The employer's number of employees is counted as the number of employees employed in the previous January 1–December 31 year, but for purposes of counting the period in which the required leave is available, the employer may pick any regular and consecutive twelve-month period.

Employees earn the sick leave entitlement at the rate of one hour per every thirty hours worked. Staring on January 1, 2021, there will be a wide variety of purposes for which employees may use this leave, many of which are unrelated to illness. Included are:

- The mental or physical illness, injury or health condition of the employee or the employee's family member,[129] "regardless of whether such illness, injury, or health condition has been diagnosed or requires medical care";

- Diagnosis of, care for, treatment of and/or preventive care for a mental or physical illness, injury or health condition of the employee or the employee's family member;

---

129   "Family member" is broadly defined as "an employee's child, spouse, domestic partner, parent, sibling, grandchild or grandparent, and the child or parent of an employee's spouse or domestic partner. "Child" is broadly defined as a child to whom the employee stands in loco parentis, whether biological, adopted, foster, or otherwise.

- Absence attributable to the fact that the employee or the employee's family member has been a victim of domestic violence (*see* § 4.88 of this chapter, below), for the purpose of:

    (a) Obtaining services from a domestic violence shelter, rape crisis center, or "other services program";

    (b) Participating in safety planning, temporarily or permanently relocating, or taking other action to increase the safety of the employee or the employee's family members;

    (c) Meeting with an attorney or social service provider to get information or advice, or prepare to participate in a criminal or civil proceeding;

    (d) Filing a domestic incident report with law enforcement;

    (e) Meeting with a district attorney's office; or

    (f) "To take any other actions necessary to ensure the health or safety of the employee or the employee's family member or to protect those who associate or work with the employee."[130]

The statute provides that an employer may not require the disclosure of confidential information as a condition of leave, which by inference suggests that an employer may ask for the reason for the leave to the extent that confidential information is not involved. This will, presumably, be clarified by regulation.

Paid leave must be paid at the employee's regular rate, but the employer may require that it be taken in minimum four-hour increments.

Unused leave must carry over from year to year, except that an employer with fewer than 100 employees may limit the *use* of sick leave to 40 hours per year, and an employer with 100 or more employees may limit the *use* of sick leave to 56 hours per year. The statute specifically provides that unused leave has no cash value at separation from employment.[131]

---

130   2020 N.Y. Laws ch. 56, to be codified at Labor Law § 196-b.

131   *Id.*

Employers are prohibited from retaliating or taking any other adverse employment action against an employee who uses or requests statutory sick leave.

When an employee returns from statutory sick leave, he or she must be restored to his or her previous position and rate of pay.

Effective September 30, 2020, Labor Law § 195(4) was amended to require that an employer's weekly "payroll records" must include the "amount of sick leave provided to each employee." The amendment does not, however, require employee pay stubs to include this same sick leave information.

Upon request (either written or oral) from an employee, the employer must, within three business days, furnish the employee with a summary of how much sick leave the employee has accrued and used in the current calendar year and (if requested) in any previous calendar year.

In unionized workplaces, an employer may negotiate with the employee union for different leave provisions, but the agreement must recite that the agreement varies from the requirements of Labor Law § 196-b.

[4.66] How does the leave required by Labor Law § 196-b coordinate with other required leave?

The leave requirements of § 196-b overlap to a significant extent with crime victim and crime witness leave (*see* §§ 4.41–4.46 above), domestic violence leave (*see* § 4.64 above), other paid family leave requirements (*see* §§ 4.67–4.82 below), and local safe and sick time laws (*see* §§ 4.83–4.118 below). They may also impact on required blood donation leave (*see* §§ 4.48–4.51 above) and bone marrow and organ donation leave (*see* §§ 4.52–4.56 above).

It is simply not clear at the time this book is first being written how these various provisions will be coordinated in the period before § 196-b becomes effective

[4.67] What is Paid Family Leave?

Starting in 2018, through amendments to the Workers' Compensation Law and its enabling regulations, employees of private-sector employers in New York State have been entitled to take Paid Family Leave (PFL) for certain qualifying events. PFL was enacted as a paid mechanism to enable eligible employees to take time off from work to care for family members under various circumstances.

PFL is funded through New York State via payroll deductions to pay PFL premiums. The premiums are paid entirely by deductions from employee wages, and not from other employer funds. Employees who qualify for Paid Family Leave receive partial wage replacement from an insurance policy that is funded by weekly, post-tax employee payroll deductions (established annually in accordance with state law). Payroll deductions begin on the employee's first day of employment even though the employee is not yet eligible for PFL.[132]

[4.68]   What employers are covered by PFL requirements?

A private sector employer that employees one or more employees for at least thirty (30) days in any calendar year is a covered employer for purposes of PFL. Once covered, an employer will continue to be a covered employer for PFL purposes until it no longer employs at least one or more employees for thirty (30) days, in which case the employer will lose its covered status at the end of the calendar year during which its employee count dropped below the one or more threshold.[133]

[4.69]   Are any employers excluded from PFL requirements?

Yes. The State of New York, municipal corporations, local governmental agencies and other political subdivisions and/or authorities are not subject to PFL requirements. A public sector employer *may* opt-in to PFL but is not required to do so.[134]

[4.70]   What employees are eligible for PFL coverage?

Employee eligibility for PFL depends on the number of hours an employee is regularly scheduled to work for the employer. For purposes of PFL, "full-time employees" are those employees who are regularly scheduled to work 20 or more hours per week for the employer, and "part-time employees" are those employees who are regularly scheduled to work less than 20 hours per week for the employer.

A part-time employee is eligible to take PFL after he or she has worked 175 days for the employer.[135]

---

132   *See* 12 N.Y.C.R.R. § 380-7.2(b)(1) ("A covered employer may deduct employee contributions prior to the effective date of the policy and prior to an employee's eligibility for paid family leave.").

133   WCL § 202; 12 N.Y.C.R.R. § 355.4(a).

134   WCL § 201(4).

135   12 N.Y.C.R.R. § 380-2.5(b).

A full-time employee will be eligible to take PFL after he or she has been employed by the employer for 26 consecutive weeks. A full-time employee does not have to actually come to work in each of the 26 weeks necessary to meet the eligibility threshold, but needs to be employed for that length of time. Periods of paid time off (e.g., vacation, sick time, personal leave, bereavement leave, etc.) count towards the 26-week employment threshold for full-time employees; however, periods of paid short-term disability leaves of absence will not count towards the 26-week employment threshold. Periods of absence that are due to the nature of the employment, such as semester breaks or periods of time when the employer is closed, also will not count towards this 26-week employment threshold.[136]

[4.71] May an employee waive PFL coverage?

Only some employees may opt out of PFL coverage. Because PFL is funded through employee payroll deductions, certain employees are permitted to opt out of coverage, but otherwise all employees are required to participate in PFL. Only the following employees are permitted to waive PFL coverage:

- if the employee's regular work schedule is 20 or more hours per week, but the employee will not work for the covered employer for 26 consecutive weeks; or

- if the employee's regular work schedule is less than 20 hours per week *and* the employee will not work for the covered employer for 175 days during a consecutive 52-week period.[137]

If an employee elects to waive PFL coverage, the covered employer may not take PFL payroll deductions from that employee.

An employee who wishes to waive PFL coverage must do so in writing, and the Workers' Compensation Board has published a specific form entitled "Employee Opt-Out Of Paid Family Leave Benefits," which is available on the State's Paid Family Leave website.[138] The employee must

---

136   12 N.Y.C.R.R. § 380-2.5(a).

137   12 N.Y.C.R.R. § 380-2.6(a).

138   http://www.wcb.ny.gov/content/main/forms/PFLWaiver.pdf.

submit the PFL waiver form to the employer, and the employer must retain a copy of the employee's written waiver for the duration of the employee's employment.[139]

A PFL waiver may be revoked by the employee at any time. In addition, if an employee who had previously waived PFL coverage has a change in circumstance such that he or she no longer meets the criteria for waiver set forth above, the waiver that the employee previously signed will be automatically revoked by operation of law.[140] For example, if a temporary full-time employee who was originally hired for a limited period of time (less than 6 months) and therefore not expected to be employed for 26 consecutive weeks, now has his or her term of employment extended such that the employee will be employed for more than the 26-week threshold, the waiver that the employee previously signed would automatically be revoked under the law.

Once the PFL waiver is revoked, the employer must notify the employee of the change and begin taking PFL payroll deductions. Although the law permits an employer to recoup PFL payroll deductions retroactively from the employee's date of hire, the employer is not required to do so and may instead take payroll deductions in the amount necessary to prevent the covered employer from having to pay the PFL insurance premium applicable to that employee now that his or her PFL coverage waiver is no longer valid.[141]

[4.72]   For what purposes can PFL be used?

PFL may not be used for an individual's own disability or serious health condition. PFL is intended to be used only for leave necessitated for the following family-related events:

- *Caring*: To provide care for the employee's child (regardless of age), parent (including parent-in-law), grandparent, grandchild, spouse and/or domestic partner with a "serious health condition."[142] For this purpose, the phrase *"providing care"* includes: necessary physical care, emotional support, visitation, assistance in treatment, transportation, arranging for a change in care, assistance with essential daily living matters, and personal attendant

---

139   12 N.Y.C.R.R. § 380-2.6(c).

140   12 N.Y.C.R.R. § 380-2.6(b).

141   *Id.*

142   WCL § 201(15)(a) and (20); *see also* 12 N.Y.C.R.R. § 380-2.1(a).

services.[143] In addition, the phrase "serious health condition" means: an illness, injury, impairment, or physical or mental condition (including the need for an organ transplant) that involves either in-patient care or continuing treatment (or supervision) by a health care provider.[144]

- *Bonding*: To bond with the employee's child following the child's birth, adoption, or placement in foster care.[145] For PFL taken in connection with the *birth* of a child, PFL must be used within one year of the child's birth.[146] For the *adoption of a child or placement of a child in foster care*, PFL may be taken *prior to* the adoption or placement if the employee's absence is necessary for the placement or adoption to proceed, and the leave must be used within one year of either the first day of PFL leave or the date of the adoption/placement, whichever is earlier.[147]

- *Preparing*: To prepare for, or attend to, a qualifying exigency (as that phrase is defined and interpreted under the federal Family and Medical Leave Act). A qualifying exigency must arise out of the fact that the employee's spouse, domestic partner, child, or parent is on active duty or has been notified of an impending call to active duty in the Armed Forces of the United States.[148]

[4.73] How much PFL may an eligible employee take?

When PFL was first implemented in 2018, the maximum amount of leave available in a 52-week period[149] was 8 weeks; but as PFL has been phased

---

143   12 N.Y.C.R.R. § 380-2.1(b).

144   *See* WCL § 201(18).

145   WCL § 201(15)(b); *see also* 12 N.Y.C.R.R. § 380-2.2.

146   WCL § 201(15)(b); *see also* 12 N.Y.C.R.R. § 380-2.2(b).

147   12 N.Y.C.R.R. § 380-2.2(a).

148   *See* WCL § 201(15)(c); *see also* 12 N.Y.C.R.R. § 380-2.3(a).

149   Unlike FMLA, where the employer can determine the "leave year" to be used for purposes of calculating whether the maximum amount of leave that has been used by an employee, under PFL the "leave year" is always going to be defined on a rolling backwards basis as the 52 calendar weeks immediately preceding each day of PFL leave that is used.

in, the maximum amount of leave available has increased and will continue to increase until 2021 as follows:[150]

Effective Date	Maximum Amount of PFL
January 1, 2020	10 weeks
January 1, 2021 and continuing thereafter	12 weeks

If a continuous PFL leave spans across calendar years, the maximum amount of PFL available for that leave is set at the start of the leave and does not increase during the leave. In the event an employee also collects short-term disability benefits for his or her own disability, the maximum combined amount of time that the employee can take for short-term disability and PFL is 26 weeks in a 52 week period.[151] Although the maximum benefit available to eligible employees is discussed in terms of weeks, it is important to note that employees are not required to use PFL in week blocks and instead may use PFL in daily increments. When an employee uses PFL in daily increments instead of as a weekly benefit, the maximum amount of PFL leave available to the employee per "week" of leave will be determined not by calendar weeks but rather by the number of days the employee is regularly scheduled to work each week. For example, an employee that is regularly scheduled to work 3 days per week will be able to use 3 days of PFL per week up to a maximum 10 weeks for a total of 30 PFL days in 2020, or up to a maximum of 12 weeks for a total of 36 PFL days in 2021.[152]

[4.74] Can PFL be taken intermittently, or in less than full-day increments?

PFL can be taken intermittently for any of the qualifying reasons for which leave is available, including bonding.[153]

However, PFL must be used in full-day increments *unless* (a) the employer agrees otherwise, *and* (b) any FMLA leave which is available for the same absence is also taken intermittently in less than full-day increments, and the employee is paid for working the remaining part of the day. In that situation, the employer can track the amount of FMLA

---

150   WCL § 204(2)(a); 12 N.Y.C.R.R. § 380-2.5(c).

151   12 N.Y.C.R.R. § 380-2.5(f).

152   12 N.Y.C.R.R. § 380-2.5(c)(2).

153   This is in contrast to the federal Family Medical Leave Act, which permits intermittent use of leave for bonding purposes only with the employer's consent.

leave used by the employee and deduct one day from the employee's PFL allotment when the employee's cumulative partial-day intermittent FMLA leave use totals the length of his or her regular workday.[154]

[4.75] What notice is an employee required to give the employer of his or her need to use PFL?

The amount of notice required depends on whether an employee's need for PFL is foreseeable.

When the employee's need for PFL is foreseeable, an employee generally must provide at least 30 days' notice of his or her need for PFL in advance of the first date of the leave. Foreseeable events include an expected birth, placement for adoption or foster care; planned medical treatment for a serious health condition of a family member; the planned medical treatment for a serious injury or illness of a covered service member; or another known military exigency. If an employee fails to provide 30 days' advance notice of foreseeable PFL, the employee's request for PFL may be denied for up period of up to 30 days from the date notice is provided.[155]

However, if the need is foreseeable but 30 days' advance notice is not practicable—for example, where the employee only learns of the need for leave less than 30 days in advance—notice must be given as soon as practicable (generally the same day or the next business day).[156]

When the need for leave is not foreseeable, an employee must notify the employer as soon as practicable under the circumstances of his or her need for leave. In this situation, as soon as practicable means as soon as both possible and practical, taking into account all of the facts and circumstances in the individual case.[157]

As to intermittent family leave the employer may require the employee to provide notice as soon as is practicable before each day of intermittent leave.[158]

---

154 12 N.Y.C.R.R. § 380-2.5(g)(5).

155 12 N.Y.C.R.R. § 380-3.5.

156 WCL § 205(5); 12 N.Y.C.R.R. § 380-3.1(a)–(b).

157 *Id.*

158 12 N.Y.C.R.R. § 380-3.1(c).

[4.76] Can an employer prevent two employees from taking PFL at the same time for the same qualifying event?

Yes. If more than one eligible employee seeks to take PFL for the same qualifying event, those employees will not be permitted to take PFL at the same time. For example, if both parents of a newborn child work for the same employer, their employer may prevent both parents from taking PFL during the same period of time even though ultimately both parents must be permitted to take time off with their newborn child.

[4.77] Can an employee take PFL and be on disability leave at the same time?

No. PFL may not be used at the same time that an employee is receiving disability benefits.[159] An employee's own illness or health condition is not one of the qualifying reasons for which PFL may be taken.

[4.78] How are employees paid during PFL leave?

Except where an employer is self-insured for PFL, employees do not receive pay from their employer during periods of PFL. Instead, an employee on PFL will generally receive a partial wage replacement benefit directly from the employer's PFL insurance carrier after the employee files a claim with that insurance carrier (see below).

The amount of the partial wage replacement benefit is set by state law as a percentage of the employee's weekly wage up to a maximum amount. The benefit amount available has increased since PFL was first imple-

---

159   WCL § 205(4); *see* 12 N.Y.C.R.R. § 380-2.2(c).

mented in 2018 and will continue to increase as follows until 2021 when PFL is fully phased in, as set forth below:

Effective Date	Maximum Amount of Benefit
January 1, 2018	50% of the employee's average weekly wage, capped at a maximum benefit of $652.96 per week
January 1, 2019	55% of the employee's average weekly wage, capped at a maximum benefit of $746.41 per week
January 1, 2020	67% of the employee's average weekly wage, capped at a maximum benefit of $840.70 per week
January 1, 2021 and continuing thereafter	67% of the employee's average weekly wage, capped at a maximum benefit equal to 60% of the New York State average weekly wage[a]

a.   The maximum benefit amount for 2021 and thereafter will be determined by New York State on March 31st when the NYS Commissioner of Labor reports the New York State Average Weekly Wage to the NYS Superintendent of Financial Services.

If a continuous PFL leave spans across calendar years, the employee's benefit amount is set at the start of the leave and does not increase during the leave.

[4.79]   Does an employee have to use paid time off concurrently with PFL?

No. Unlike the federal Family Medical Leave Act, where employees can be required to use their accrued paid time off concurrently during periods of unpaid FMLA leave, under PFL, employees cannot be required to do so. An employer may *permit* an employee on PFL to concurrently utilize accrued paid time off so that the employee can continue to receive 100% of his or her wages during PFL, but if an employee does not wish to do that, and instead prefers to save his or her accrued paid time off to use at a future date, the employer cannot require the employee to run his or her PFL and paid time off concurrently.[160]

[4.80]   How does an employee apply for PFL pay benefits?

In order to receive pay benefits while on PFL, an employee must submit a claim using the *Request for Paid Family Leave* form (PFL-1) to the employer's PFL insurance carrier (or the employer where the employer is self-insured for PFL), as well as the appropriate certification form (PFL-2 for bonding; PFL-3/PFL-4 for providing care; or PFL-5 for military-

---

160   12 N.Y.C.R.R. § 380-6.2.

related leave) and supporting documentation. These claim forms are available on New York State's PFL website[161] and provide details regarding the specific documentation that is required to support an employee's request to be paid PFL.

If an employee is seeking payment for time off that he or she previously took (for example, for time off taken because of an unforeseeable emergency), the employee's PFL claim must be filed with the PFL insurance carrier within 30 days of the date(s) for which payment is sought. However, employees are generally encouraged to file PFL claims as quickly as possible to ensure prompt payment of benefits for qualifying leaves.

Prior to submitting the *Request for Paid Family Leave* form to the employer's PFL insurance carrier, an employee must provide the form to their employer (generally to the Human Resources Department) so that the employer can complete the employer section (Part B) of that form. The employer has three business days to complete that section and return the form to the employee.

Employees are generally responsible for timely filing their own PFL claim forms, certification forms, and supporting documentation with the employer's PFL insurance carrier (or the employer where the employer is self-insured for PFL). Employers are not obligated to file a PFL claim form on an employee's behalf

Once a claim for PFL has been filed, the employer's PFL insurance carrier (or employer where the employer is self-insured for PFL) must either pay or deny an employee's PFL claim within 18 days of when the completed PFL claim form, certification form, and supporting documents are submitted by the employee. No PFL benefit will be paid to an employee until the employee's PFL claim is fully submitted and approved (by the carrier or by the self-insured employer, as the case may be).

[4.81] What happens to an employee's health insurance benefits while an employee is on PFL?

An employee who receives health insurance from his or her employer is entitled to have health insurance continued during periods of PFL on the same terms as would have applied if the employee had continued to work. If an employee is required to pay a portion of the health insurance premium while actively working, that employee is required to continue pay-

---

161   N.Y. State, *Paid Family Leave Forms*, https://paidfamilyleave.ny.gov/forms?q=/forms%3Ff%5B0%5D%3Dfilter_term%3A1061&_wrapper_for mat=drupal_ajax&.

ing his or her portion of the premium while on PFL. If the employee fails to pay his or her portion of the premium for 30 days, the employer may stop providing health insurance to the employee if it notifies the employee that payment has not been received and provides 15 days advanced notice to the employee that coverage will be dropped as of a specified date.[162] However, if health insurance coverage lapses because an employee has not made the required premium payments, the employer must restore the employee's health coverage upon the employee's return to work at the same level of coverage as the employee would have had if PFL had not been taken and the premium payment(s) had not been missed.[163]

[4.82] What information do employers have to give employees about the availability of PFL?

If an employer maintains an employee handbook, policy manual, or similar guidance document concerning employee benefits or leave rights, the employer must include within that same document a written PFL policy concerning the leave available and employee's obligations with regard to PFL (e.g., notice requirements, what an employee has to do to apply for PFL, etc.). If an employer does not have a written employee handbook, policy manual, or similar guidance document, the employer is required to provide all employees with written guidance concerning their rights and obligations under PFL, including information on how to file a claim for PFL.[164]

Employers must also post, in plain view in a location where all employees can readily see it, a typewritten or printed notice concerning PFL in a form prescribed by the NYS Workers Compensation Board.[165] The PFL posting that has been approved by the NYS Workers Compensation Board for 2020 is available online.[166]

---

162   12 N.Y.C.R.R. §§ 380-7.3(a)–(d), 380-7.4.

163   12 N.Y.C.R.R. § 380-7.3(e).

164   12 N.Y.C.R.R. § 380-7.2(a).

165   12 N.Y.C.R.R. § 380-7.2(e).

166   http://docs.paidfamilyleave.ny.gov/content/main/forms/PFLDocs/PFL271S_2020.pdf.

XV. NEW YORK CITY EARNED SAFE AND SICK TIME ACT

[4.83]   What is the NYC Earned Safe and Sick Time Act?

Section 20 of the N.Y.C. Administrative Code, which went into effect on April 1, 2014, mandates that N.Y.C. employers provide employees with sick leave and "safe leave." For some employers, the leave must be *paid* leave; for others, it can be *unpaid*.[167]

On September 28, 2020, the New York City Mayor signed a bill amending the original mandate. The New York City Department of Consumer Protection and Worker Protection posted guidance regarding the amendment at https://www1.nyc.gov/site/dca/about/paid-sick-leave-what-employers-need-to-know.page.

Employers must treat medical information received from employees about themselves or their family members in connection with sick time use as *confidential*.[168]

[4.84]   What employers and employees are covered by the Act?

The Act applies to all private employers in New York City, including not-for-profit employers, that have one or more employees.[169]

- Employers with fewer than five employees and a net annual income of less than $1 million in the previous tax year must provide up to 40 hours of *unpaid* sick leave.

- Employers with fewer than five employees and a net annual income of $1 million or more in the previous tax year must provide up to 40 hours of *paid* sick leave.

- Employers with five to 99 employees must provide up to 40 hours of *paid* sick leave.

---

167   N.Y.C. Admin Code §§ 20-911–20-925.; *see* § 4.73 *supra*.

168   N.Y.C. Admin Code § 20-921.

169   N.Y.C. Admin Code § 20-913(a). So long as the employee actually works in New York City, it does not matter where the employee actually lives. *See* N.Y.C. Consumer Affairs, *Paid Safe and Sick Leave: Frequently Asked Questions* (Sept. 20, 2018), https://www1.nyc.gov/assets/dca/downloads/pdf/about/PaidSickLeave-FAQs.pdf.

- Employers with 100 or more employees must provide up to 56 hours of *paid* sick leave. However, in 2020, these employers may limit the use of paid leave to 40 hours.

- Employers one or more domestic workers must provide two days of *paid* sick leave to any domestic worker who has worked for the employer for more than one year.[170]

The leave requirements apply only to employees who work more than 80 hours in a calendar year.

Family members who work in a business, *per diem* workers, "on-call" workers, and undocumented employees ("illegal aliens") are all covered, as are "industrial home workers" who do work in their homes in New York City (no matter where their employer is located), and employees who telecommute to work, so long as they work.[171] An employee who works for more than one employer is entitled to coverage from *both* (or all) of the employers.

Employers are prohibited from retaliating against anyone who exercises the rights conferred by the Act, including but not limited to a person "who mistakenly but in good faith alleges a violation of the Act.[172]

[4.85] Are any employees excluded from the Act?

The law does not apply to the following categories of persons:[173]

- Employees who work 80 hours or fewer in a twelve-month period;

- Employees of government agencies;

- Students in federal work study programs;

---

170   This safe and sick leave is in addition to the three days of paid rest to which domestic workers are entitled under Section 161(1) of New York State Labor Law. *See* https://www1.nyc.gov/assets/dca/downloads/pdf/about/PaidSickLeave-FAQs.pdf.

171   N.Y.C. Consumer Affairs, *Paid Safe and Sick Leave: Frequently Asked Questions* (Sept. 20, 2018), https://www1.nyc.gov/assets/dca/downloads/pdf/about/PaidSickLeave-FAQs.pdf.

172   N.Y.C. Admin. Code § 20-918. No person may take an adverse action against any employee that "penalizes an employee for, or is reasonably likely to deter an employee from, exercising or attempting to exercise rights" under the N.Y.C. law.

173   *Id.*

- Licensed physical therapists, occupational therapists, speech language pathologists, and audiologists who (a) set their own hours of work and (b) make at least four times the federal minimum wage;

- Independent contractors who do not meet the definition of an employee under the New York Labor Law;[174]

- Participants in Work Experience programs; and

- *Some* employees covered by a collective bargaining agreement:

> The law does not apply to employees covered by a valid collective bargaining agreement that was in effect on April 1, 2014 . . . until that collective bargaining agreement expires. For employees covered by a collective bargaining agreement that came into effect or [was] renewed after April 1, 2014 or May 5, 2018, the law does not apply if the collective bargaining agreement expressly waives the law's provisions and the agreement provides a comparable benefit to employees, such as paid time off. Otherwise, the law applies to these employees.[175]

[4.86]   For what reasons may an eligible employee take sick leave?

An eligible employee is entitled to use sick leave for:

- The employee's own mental or physical illness, injury or health condition or need for medical diagnosis, care or treatment of a mental or physical illness, injury or health condition, or need for preventive care;

- Care of a family member who needs medical diagnosis, care or treatment of a mental or physical illness, injury, or health condition, or who needs preventive medical care; or

- The closure of the employee's place of business by order of a public official due to a public health emergency or such employee's need to care for a child whose school or child care provider has

---

174   For a discussion of independent contractor status, *see* Chapter 12 of this book, "Miscellaneous Topics of Interest."

175   N.Y.C. Consumer Affairs, *Paid Safe and Sick Leave: Frequently Asked Questions* (Sept. 20, 2018), https://www1.nyc.gov/assets/dca/downloads/pdf/about/PaidSickLeave-FAQs.pdf.

been closed by order of a public official due to a public health emergency.[176]

Elective organ donation surgery, both for the employee and for the employee's family members, is covered by the sick leave entitlement.[177]

[4.87] Who is considered a "family member" under the Act?

"Family member" means "an employee's child, spouse, domestic partner, sibling, grandchild or grandparent; the child or parent of an employee's spouse or domestic partner; any other individual related by blood to the employee; and any other individual whose close association with the employee is the equivalent of a family relationship."[178]

[4.88] For what purposes can safe leave be used?

In addition to leave for illness, an employee covered by the New York City law is entitled to take "safe leave" if the employee or a family member of the employee has been a victim of a family offense matter, human trafficking, sexual offense, or stalking.

An employee can use safe leave:

- To obtain services from a domestic violence shelter, rape crisis center, or other shelter or services program for relief from a family offense matter, sexual offenses, stalking, or human trafficking;

- To participate in safety planning, to be temporarily or permanently relocated, or to take other actions to increase the safety of the employee or employee's family members from future family offense matters, sexual offenses, stalking, or human trafficking;

- To meet with a civil attorney or other social service provider to obtain information and advice on, and prepare for or participate in, any criminal or civil proceeding, including but not limited to, matters related to a family offense matter, sexual offense, stalking,

---

176 N.Y.C. Admin Code § 20-914(a).

177 https://www1.nyc.gov/site/dca/about/paid-sick-leave-FAQs.page.

178 N.Y.C. Admin Code § 20-912. *See also* N.Y.C. Consumer Affairs, *Paid Safe and Sick Leave: Frequently Asked Questions* (Sept. 20, 2018), https://www1.nyc.gov/assets/dca/downloads/pdf/about/PaidSickLeave-FAQs.pdf.

human trafficking, custody, visitation, matrimonial issues, orders of protection, immigration, housing, discrimination in employment, housing, or consumer credit;

- To file a complaint or domestic incident report with law enforcement;

- To meet with a district attorney's office;

- To enroll children in a new school; or

- To take other actions necessary to maintain, improve, or restore the physical, psychological, or economic health or safety of the employee or the employee's family member or to protect those who associate or work with the employee.[179]

[4.89] Must employees provide documentation for sick or safe time?

An employer may require reasonable documentation from a medical provider to support a sick or safe leave of more than three consecutive work days *if* the requirement is set out on an employer's written policy.[180] However, an employer requiring such documentation must reimburse the employee for any fee charged by the employee's health care provider to furnish the documentation.[181]

An employer may take disciplinary action, up to and including termination, against an employee who abuses safe or sick time for unauthorized purposes.[182] Under the rules promulgated by the New York City Department of Consumer Affairs Office of Labor Policy and Standards, examples of "abuse"

> may include, but are not limited to a pattern of: (1) use of unscheduled safe time and sick time on or adjacent to weekends, regularly scheduled days off, holidays, vacation or pay day, (2) taking scheduled safe time and sick time on days when other leave has been denied, and (3)

---

179   N.Y.C. Admin Code § 20-914(b).

180   N.Y.C. Admin Code § 20-914(e)(2).

181   *Id.*

182   N.Y.C. Admin Code § 20-914(f).

taking safe time and sick time on days when the employee is scheduled to work a shift or perform duties perceived as undesirable.[183]

[4.90] How much sick or safe leave are employees entitled to?

Employees earn one hour of leave for every 30 hours worked, up to the maximum set out in § 4.84 above. An employer may, but is not required to, pay employees for unused sick and safe time at the end of a calendar year.

Up to 40 hours of unused leave (or up to 56 hours where the employer employees 100 or more employees) can be carried over to the following calendar year *unless*: (a) the employer has paid the employee for the unused leave, *or* (b) the employer "front-loads" sick or safe time at the beginning of each year (in other words, makes the leave available to employees *before* they have worked the required number of hours).[184]

However, employers are only required to allow employees to use up to 40 hours (or 56 hours where the employer employs 100 or more employees) of sick leave per year, even if they have carried over hours from a prior year.[185]

[4.91] When does sick or safe leave accrual begin?

Employees begin to accrue sick and safe leave on the first day of their employment.[186] Non-exempt employees (employees who are entitled to statutory overtime) accrue leave for *all* hours worked, including overtime. Exempt employees accrue based on a 40-hour workweek.[187]

[4.92] When may employees begin to use their sick or safe leave?

Employees may start using their accrued leave as soon as it has accrued.[188]

---

183 6 R.C.N.Y. § 7-215.

184 N.Y.C. Admin Code § 20-913(h).

185 *Id.* Of course, this 40-hour upper limit applies only to the maximum number of hours of leave required by the New York City law. To the extent that a collective bargaining agreement, individual agreement or employer policy allows for a greater amount of (paid or unpaid) sick leave, then the 40-hour limit does not set an upper limit to leave.

186 N.Y.C. Admin Code § 20-913(d)(1).

187 N.Y.C. Admin Code § 20-913(e).

188 N.Y.C. Admin Code § 20-913(d)(1).

[4.93] Can an employer require an employee to use a minimum daily increment of leave?

Yes. The law permits an employer to set a "reasonable" minimum increment for the use of leave, but this minimum cannot be more than four hours per day.[189]

[4.94] When an employee leaves service, is he or she entitled to payment for unused sick or safe time?

No.[190]

[4.95] What happens if an employee returns to service after a break in employment?

If the employee is rehired *within six months*, the employer must reinstate previously accrued sick or safe leave, *unless* the employer had already paid the employee for unused leave when the employee left service, and the employee agreed to be paid out.[191]

The rehired employee may use accrued sick or safe leave immediately after resuming employment.

If, however, the employee's break in service is *more than six months*, then the law does not require the employer to reinstate unused leave. The employee would have a zero balance of accrued leave on the first day of reemployment and would not be eligible to use leave until a new leave entitlement has accrued.[192]

[4.96] Can employees donate unused sick or safe leave to other employees?

Yes, but only if the employer chooses to permit it. An employer may have a policy that allows employees to donate unused sick leave to other employees, as long as participation is voluntary.

---

189 N.Y.C. Admin Code § 20-913(g).

190 N.Y.C. Admin Code § 20-913(i).

191 N.Y.C. Admin Code § 20-913(j).

192 *Id.*

[4.97] May an employer require an employee who wants to use leave to find a replacement employee for the missed hours?

No.[193]

[4.98] May an employer require an employee to telecommute or work from home instead of taking sick or safe leave?

No. However, an employer may offer the employee the option of working from home or telecommuting. If the employee voluntarily agrees to work from home or telecommute the employee would retain the leave that he or she accrued.[194]

[4.99] Are employers required to give employees notice of their right to sick or safe leave?

Yes. Employers must give a Notice of Employee Rights to covered new employees when they begin employment.[195] Employers must also post this notice "in an area accessible to employees."[196]

Employers must also provide, either on pay stubs or in another form of written documentation given to the employee each pay period, the amount of sick and safe leave accrued and used during the pay period, and the employee's total balance of accrued leave.[197]

XVI. WESTCHESTER COUNTY EARNED SICK LEAVE LAW

[4.100] Must employers in Westchester County provide employees with sick leave?

Yes. Westchester County's Earned Sick Leave Law went into effect on April 10, 2019, and provides for mandatory sick leave as follows:

- For employers of five or more employees, the leave must be *paid*.

---

193 N.Y.C. Admin Code § 20-914(e).

194 *Id.*

195 N.Y.C. Admin Code § 20-919(a)(1). The Notice of Employee Rights is available in 26 languages at https://www1.nyc.gov/site/dca/about/Paid-Safe-Sick-Leave-Notice-of-Employee-Rights.page.

196 N.Y.C. Admin Code § 20-919(a)(1).

197 N.Y.C. Admin Code § 20-919(c).

- For domestic workers, regardless of the number of employees, the leave must be *paid*.

- For employers of one to five employees, the leave can be *unpaid*.[198]

[4.101] What employers are covered?

All employers in Westchester County are covered *except* government agencies.[199] However, employees of Westchester County who are not covered by a collective bargaining agreement are entitled to sick leave under the Westchester County law.[200]

[4.102] What employees are eligible for sick leave?

Any employee who has worked for more than 80 hours in a calendar year.[201] In contrast to the New York City Law, the Westchester law provides that "calendar year" means from January 1 to December 31.[202]

[4.103] For what purposes can sick leave be used?

Earned sick time may be used for:

- An employee's mental or physical illness, injury or health condition; an employee's need for medical diagnosis, care, or treatment of a mental or physical illness, injury or health condition; an employee's need for preventive medical care;

- The care of a family member with a mental or physical illness, injury or health condition; care of a family member who needs a medical diagnosis, care, or treatment of a mental or physical illness, injury or health condition; and care of a family member who needs preventive medical care;

---

198   Westchester County Code § 585.03(2). An information page is available at https://human-rights.westchestergov.com/resources/earned-sick-leave-law and an FAQ sheet is available at https://humanrights.westchestergov.com/images/stories/pdfs/2019slemployerfaqr2.pdf.

199   Westchester County Code § 585.02(7).

200   Westchester Human Rights Commission, *Westchester's Earned Sick Leave Law: What Employers Need to Know* (July 2, 2019), https://humanrights.westchestergov.com/images/stories/pdfs/2019slemployerfaqr2.pdf.

201   Westchester County Code § 585.02(6).

202   Westchester County Code § 585.02(1).

- The closure of the employee's place of business by order of a public official due to a public health emergency; or

- The closure of a day care or elementary or secondary school attended by an employee's child where such closure was due to a public health emergency.[203]

[4.104] What is meant by a "family member"?

A "family member" means the "employee's child, spouse, domestic partner, parent, sibling, grandchild or grandparent; and the child or parent of an employee's spouse, domestic, partner or household member."[204] "Parent" includes "biological, foster, step- or adoptive parent."[205] "Child" means "regardless of age, a biological, adopted, foster child, legal ward or a person to whom the employee stands *in loco parentis* or to whom the employee stood *in loco parentis* when that person was a minor."[206]

[4.105] How much leave are employees entitled to?

Covered employees are entitled to take up to 40 hours of paid leave in any calendar year or "year" as determined by the employer.[207] Employees earn one hour of sick leave for every 30 hours worked up to 40 hours of leave per year, except that *domestic workers* earn one hour per seven days worked, up to 40 hours.[208] Employers have the option of "front-loading" the leave so that it is available at the start of the year and does not have to be earned *pro rata*.[209]

[4.106] When does an employee begin to earn sick leave?

On the first day of employment.[210]

---

203   Westchester County Code § 585.06(1).

204   Westchester County Code § 585.02(8).

205   Westchester County Code § 585.02(10).

206   Westchester County Code § 585.02(2).

207   Here, "year" means a regular and consecutive 12-month period as determined by the employer. Westchester County Code § 585.02(14).

208   Westchester County Code § 585.04. *See also* Westchester Human Rights Commission, *Westchester's Earned Sick Leave Law: What Employers Need to Know* (July 2, 2019), https://humanrights.westchestergov.com/images/stories/pdfs/2019slemployerfaqr2.pdf.

209   Westchester Human Rights Commission, *Westchester's Earned Sick Leave Law: What Employers Need to Know* (July 2, 2019).

210   Westchester County Code § 585.03(1).

[4.107] When can employees begin to use sick leave?

After 90 days of employment.[211]

[4.108] Can an employee carry over unused sick leave at the end of the year?

Yes. An employee can carry over up to 40 hours of unused accrued sick leave into the following year.[212] However, employers can limit the employee's use of sick time to 40 hours per year.

[4.109] Can an employer require the employee to provide a doctor's note when he or she uses earned sick leave?

Yes. An employer can require documentation from a health care provider if the employee uses more than three consecutive workdays as sick leave. However, the employer cannot require the health care provider to specify the medical reason for sick leave.[213]

[4.110] Can an employer require an employee to use a minimum daily increment of leave?

Yes. An employee may use a minimum of four hours and, if more time is needed, then the smallest increment that the employer's payroll system uses to account for absence or use of other time.[214]

XVII. WESTCHESTER COUNTY SAFE TIME LEAVE LAW

[4.111] Must employers in Westchester County provide employees with safe leave?

Yes. Westchester County's Safe Time Leave for Victims of Domestic Violence and Human Trafficking Law went into effect on October 30, 2019. This leave is *paid* regardless of the number of employees.[215]

---

211   Westchester County Code § 585.06(2).

212   *See* Westchester Human Rights Commission, *Westchester's Earned Sick Leave Law: What Employers Need to Know* (July 2, 2019).

213   Westchester County Code § 585.07(5).

214   Westchester County Code § 585.06(3).

215   Westchester County Code § 586.01–586.13. *See* Westchester Human Rights Commission, *Westchester's Earned Sick Leave Law: What Employers Need to Know* (July 2, 2019), https://humanrights.westchestergov.com/images/stories/pdfs/2019slemployerfaqr2.pdf.

[4.112] What employers are covered?

All employers in Westchester County are covered except government agencies. However, Westchester County employees who are *not covered by a collective bargaining agreement* are entitled to safe time leave under the Westchester Safe Time Leave Law.[216]

[4.113] What employees are eligible for safe leave?

Any employee who has worked for more than 90 days in a calendar year and is the victim of domestic violence or human trafficking is eligible for the leave.[217]

[4.114] For what purposes can safe leave be used?

Covered employees can use safe time leave:

- To attend or testify in criminal and or civil court proceedings relating to domestic violence;

- To attend or testify in criminal and or civil court proceedings relating to human trafficking; or

- To move to a safe location.[218]

[4.115] How much leave are employees entitled to?

Covered employees are entitled to take up to 40 hours of paid leave in any calendar year or "year" as determined by the employer.[219] This leave does not "accrue" on a *pro rata* basis: after the first 90 days of employment, employees are entitled to take up to the full 40 hours of safe live in any year at any time.[220]

---

216   Westchester County Code § 586.03(4).

217   Westchester County Code § 586.03(3).

218   Westchester County Code § 586.04.

219   Westchester County Code § 586.04.

220   Westchester County Code § 586.05.

[4.116] Can an employer require an employee to use a minimum daily increment of leave?

Yes, although it is not clear what increments are permitted. Absent clarification, we would suggest that employers adopt minimum increments of four hours; *see* § 4.110 above.

[4.117] Can an employer require an employee to find coverage for safe time leave used?

No. An employer may not require, as a condition of an employee's use of safe time leave, that the employee find another employee to work during the time of the employee's absence.[221]

[4.118] Can an employer require documentation that safe time leave is being used for its intended purpose?

Yes. An employer may require the employee to provide reasonable documentation that the safe time leave has been used for a purpose covered by the Safe Time Leave Law.[222]

XVIII. NEW YORK CITY'S FAIR WORKWEEK LAW

[4.119] What is New York City's Fair Workweek Law?

New York City's Fair Workweek Law went into effect on November 26, 2017, and requires retail and fast food employers in New York City to give workers predictable work schedules, and requires fast food employers to give existing workers the opportunity to work open shifts before hiring new workers.[223]

[4.120] Who is covered by the Fair Workweek Law?

The law applies to (a) employees of fast food establishments which are part of a chain of 30 or more such establishments nationally, and (b) retail businesses which primarily sell consumer goods and employ 20 or more workers in New York City.[224]

---

221   Westchester County Code § 586.05(3).

222   Westchester County Code § 586.05(4).

223   N.Y.C. Admin Code §§ 20-1201–20-1263. N.Y.C. Consumer Affairs, *Fair Workweek and Fast Food Deductions Laws: Frequently Asked Questions* (Nov. 11, 2017), https://www1.nyc.gov/assets/dca/downloads/pdf/workers/FAQs-FairWorkweek-Deductions.pdf.

224   N.Y.C. Admin Code § 20-1201.

[4.121] Does the law apply to employers which are not based in New York City?

Yes. The law applies to all employers that employ workers in New York City and meet the above definitions of coverage.

[4.122] Who is considered to be a "fast food employee"?

Workers at a fast food establishment in New York City who perform at least one of the following functions are covered: customer service; cooking; food or drink preparation; delivery; security; stocking supplies or equipment; cleaning; or routine maintenance. It does not include employees who are salaried (i.e. paid on an annual rather than an hourly basis).[225]

[4.123] What are the requirements of the Fair Workweek Law for fast food employers?

For fast food workers, the Fair Workweek Law requires the following:

- Covered employees must, not later than their first day of work, be given a written "Good Faith Estimate," of the days, times, locations, and total number of hours that they can expect to work (including "on-call" shifts) each week.[226] The Good Faith Estimate must be updated when a worker's actual hours are changed from the estimate after three (3) consecutive weeks or three (3) weeks in a six-week period.[227]

- Covered employees must be given fourteen days' (two weeks') advance notice of work schedules, and schedule change premiums when schedules are changed on less than fourteen days' notice. *See* § 4.124 below for a discussion of premiums.

- When new shifts become available, before advertising for, or hiring, a new worker, employers must notify current workers who have worked at least eight hours within the previous 30 days about available shifts at any of their locations by: (a) posting the information in the workplace; and (b) providing each worker with information electronically, by text or e-mail.[228]

---

225 *Id.*

226 *See* § 4.130 below for a definition of "on-call" shifts.

227 N.Y.C. Admin Code § 20-1221(a).

228 The notification must include detailed information about shifts, shift structure and procedures for assignment. *Id.*

- A fast food worker must consent in writing before being scheduled to work two shifts over two calendar days when the first shift ends a day and there are fewer than 11 hours between shifts.[229] In addition, the employer must pay the fast food worker a $100 premium for working this assignment.[230]

[4.124] What are the shift change "premiums" applicable to fast food workers?

If a fast food employer changes workers' schedules less than 14 days before the start of the schedule, the employer must pay each worker a schedule change premium. Workers can accept or decline additional shifts.

Amount of Notice	Additional work time or shift	Changes to shifts but no change to total work time	Reduced work time or shifts
Less than 14 days but at least 7 days	$10 per change	$10 per change	$20 per change
Less than 7 days but at least 24 hours	$15 per change	$15 per change	$45 per change
Less than 24 hours	$15 per change	$15 per change	$75 per change

The premiums are excused where: (a) the employer's operations cannot begin or continue due to (i) threats to the employees or the employer's property; (ii) the failure of a public utility or the shutdown of public transportation; (iii) fire, flood or other natural disaster; (iv) a state of emergency declared by the president of the United States, governor of the state of New York, or the mayor of the City of New York; or (v) severe weather conditions that pose a threat to employee safety; (b) the employee requested in writing a change in schedule; (c) two employees voluntarily trade shifts with one another; or (d) the employer is required to pay the employee overtime pay for a changed shift.[231]

---

229   Referred to as "clopenings," these shifts usually involve both closing and opening the establishment.

230   N.Y.C. Admin. Code § 20-1221(a).

231   N.Y.C. Admin Code § 20-1222.

[4.125] Are fast food employers required to pay workers a premium if the schedule changes by just a few minutes?

No. Employers only need to pay a premium if changes to a shift add up to more than 15 minutes per shift. However, the worker must still consent in writing to any additional time worked.[232]

[4.126] What are the consequences if a fast food employer does not comply with the law?

When a fast food employer fails to comply with the good faith estimate, or to provide a written notice of a work schedule before the first day of work and at least 14 days before subsequent schedule changes, the employer must pay the employee $200 for each violation.[233]

When a fast food employer does not pay a premium for a schedule change, an employer owes the employee the premiums withheld plus $300 for each violation.[234]

When a fast food employer requires employees to work two shifts with fewer than 11 hours between shifts without the employee's consent, the employer must pay the employee $500 for each violation.[235]

An employer may be penalized for multiple violations of the Fair Work-week Law as follows:

> a. For each violation of this chapter, an employer is liable for a penalty of $500 for the first violation and, for subsequent violations that occur within two years of any previous violation of this chapter, up to $750 for the second violation and up to $1,000 for each succeeding violation.
> b. The penalties imposed pursuant to this section shall be imposed on a per employee and per instance basis for each violation.[236]

---

232 *Id.*

233 N.Y.C. Admin Code § 20-1208(3)(b).

234 N.Y.C. Admin Code § 20-1208(3)(c).

235 N.Y.C. Admin Code § 20-1208(3)(d).

236 N.Y.C. Admin Code § 20-1209(a).

[4.127] Who is considered to be a "retail employee"?

A retail employee is *any* employee of a retail employer. There is no exception for supervisors or managers: in other words, it applies to all employees, whether salaried or hourly.

[4.128] What are the requirements of the Fair Workweek Law for retail employers?

For retail workers, the Fair Workweek Law requires the following:

- The employer must provide the employee with a written work schedule at least 72 hours before the first shift on the work schedule. The schedule must be conspicuously posted in a location that is accessible and visible to all retail employees at least 72 hours before the beginning of the scheduled hours of work. Retail employers must also electronically send the schedule to employees if that is how the employer usually communicates with workers.[237]

- "On-call" shifts are prohibited.

- "Call-in" shifts within 72 hours of the start of the shift are prohibited.

- Shift cancellations with less than 72 hours' notice are prohibited.

- Shift additions with less than 72 hours' notice are prohibited unless the employee consents in writing.

- The employer must provide an updated written schedule if changes are made with less than 72 hours' notice.[238]

[4.129] What are the consequences if a retail employer does not give employees their schedules 72 hours before the start of work?

A retail employer violates the law and may be required to pay $300 to each affected worker, as well as any other damage or relief required to remedy the harm to the affected workers. The employer may also have to pay a penalty of at least $500 for each violation depending on whether this is the first time the employer violated the law.[239]

---

237   N.Y.C. Admin Code § 20-1252.

238   *Id.*

239   N.Y.C. Admin Code §§ 20-1208(a)(3)(g) and 20-1209.

[4.130] What is an on-call shift?

An on-call shift occurs when an employer requires the employee to be available to work, regardless of whether the employee actually works and regardless of whether the employer actually requires the employee to report to a work location.[240]

For fast food workers, any on-call shifts must be included in the Good Faith Estimate (*see* § 4.123 above).

A retail employer cannot require an employee to be ready and available to work at any time the employer demands.[241]

XIX. THE DOMESTIC WORKERS' BILL OF RIGHTS

[4.131] What is the Domestic Workers' Bill of Rights?

The Domestic Workers' Bill of Rights is a New York State law designed, through amendments to a number of statutes, to provide the following basic protections to domestic workers:

- The right to overtime pay at time-and-a-half after 40 hours of work in a week, or after 44 hours of work for workers who live in their employer's home;[242]

- A day of rest (24 hours) every seven days, or overtime pay if the employee agrees to work on that day;[243]

- Three paid days of rest each year after one year of work for the same employer;[244] and

- Protection under New York State Human Rights Law from sexual or racial harassment.[245]

---

240 N.Y.C. Admin Code § 20-1201.

241 *Id.*

242 Labor Law § 170.

243 Labor Law § 161.

244 *Id.*

245 N.Y. Executive Law § 296-b. *See* New York State Department of Labor, *Domestic Workers' Bill of Rights*, https://labor.ny.gov/legal/domestic-workers-bill-of-rights.shtm. *See also* Chapter 11 of this book, "Discrimination, Harassment and Retaliation," at §§ 11.3.3 and 11.26–11.34 for discussion of the harassment provisions of this law.

[4.132] What are the leave provisions applicable to domestic workers?

In addition to the requirement that a domestic worker is entitled to one day of rest in every seven days (or overtime pay if the employee *agrees* to work a seven-day week), employers of domestic workers must provide three days of *paid* leave in each calendar year (i.e. beginning each January 1). If any of the three paid leave days are not provided, the employee must be paid for those days at his or her regular rate of pay.[246]

However, this mandatory paid leave for domestic workers is *not* in addition to other paid vacation or sick leave; in other words, if an employer already provides three paid sick or vacation days, the employer's obligation has been met.[247]

---

246   N.Y. Department of Labor, *Domestic Workers Legislation: Frequently Asked Questions,* https://labor.ny.gov/legal/laws/pdf/domestic-workers/domestic-workers-faqs.pdf.

247   *Id.*

CHAPTER FIVE

WORKERS' COMPENSATION AND WORKPLACE SAFETY

Patrick V. Melfi

CHAPTER OVERVIEW

In this chapter, we consider the two principal statutory schemes for protecting employees in the workplace: the worker's compensation framework, and the regulatory schemes for maintaining a safe workplace. Disability issues are discussed in Chapter 6 of this book, and unemployment insurance is discussed in Chapter 7.

The following questions are addressed:

I. WORKERS' COMPENSATION

[5.1] What is workers' compensation?

[5.2] What employers are covered by the WCL?

[5.3] Who is an "employee" covered by the WCL?

[5.4] What is an "independent contractor"?

[5.5] Are part-time employees covered by the WCL?

[5.6] Are "leased" employees covered by the WCL?

[5.7] Are volunteers covered by the WCL?

[5.8] Are employees of not-for-profit entities covered by the WCL?

[5.9] Are racetrack jockeys covered by the WCL?

[5.10] Are sole proprietors and partners in partnerships covered by the WCL?

[5.11] Are individuals who work in construction covered by the WCL?

[5.12] Are out-of-state employers covered by the WCL if they have employees working in New York?

[5.13] What are the obligations of employers who are subject to the WCL?

[5.14] What does workers' compensation insurance cover?

[5.15] Are there any exceptions to WCL exclusivity?

[5.16] What are an employer's options with respect to workers' compensation insurance?

[5.17] What happens if an employer fails to maintain required workers' compensation coverage?

[5.18] What benefits does the WCL provide to employees?
    [5.18.1] Medical treatment
    [5.18.2] Wage replacement
    [5.18.3] Disability benefits
    [5.18.4] "Scheduled Loss of Use"
    [5.18.5] Death benefits

[5.19] Is every workplace accident or injury covered by the WCL?

[5.20] Are recreational activities covered by the WCL?

[5.21] Is "horseplay" covered by the WCL?

[5.22] Is an employee who gets hurt while conducting personal business covered by the WCL?

[5.23] Is an employee who is assaulted by a co-worker covered by the WCL?

[5.24] Are injuries sustained while commuting covered by the WCL?

[5.25] Are non-occupational injuries or illnesses covered by the WCL?

[5.26] Are injuries sustained in a "home office" covered by the WCL?

[5.27] Is an employee who is injured while violating a work rule covered by the WCL?

[5.28] Is an employee who is injured while on a business trip covered by the WCL?

[5.29] What if an accident or injury does not cause a new injury, but merely aggravates a pre-existing non-occupational injury?

[5.30] Are occupational diseases covered by the WCL?

[5.31] Are psychological and psychiatric conditions covered by the WCL?

[5.32] How are workers' compensation claims presented and decided?

[5.33] What are some of the important forms and deadlines for WCB cases?

[5.34] What is a "return to work" program?

[5.35] Is an employer required to offer injured employees light or modified duty?

[5.36] Is an employer required to hold an injured employee's job open until he or she can return to work?

[5.37] When can an employer discharge an employee who has claimed or is receiving WCL benefits?

[5.38] When can an employer do about fraudulent WCL claims?

II.   WORKPLACE SAFETY

[5.39] What is DOSH?
    [5.39.1] The Industry Inspection Bureau (IIB)
    [5.39.2] The License and Certification Unit
    [5.39.3] The Asbestos Control Unit
    [5.39.4] The Boiler Safety Bureau
    [5.39.5] The Mine Safety Training Program

I.   WORKERS' COMPENSATION

[5.1]   What is workers' compensation?

In 1913, the New York State Constitution was amended to give the Legislature the power to enact workers' compensation legislation. The Legislature enacted the New York Workers' Compensation Law (WCL) the following year. The legislation provided that employees were to be compensated on a "no-fault" basis, regardless of any negligence on their own part, for all injuries "arising out of and in the course of" their employment[1]. As Chief Judge Cardozo opined in 1928, the statute was enacted for humanitarian purposes to insure that injured employees might "be saved from becoming one of the derelicts of society, a fragment of human wreckage."[2]

[5.2]   What employers are covered by the WCL?

The Workers' Compensation Board (WCB), which administers the WCL, has noted that "virtually all employers in New York State must provide workers' compensation coverage for their employees."[3] Indeed, the definition of "employer" in the WCL supports this generalization by defining an employer to be a person or entity that has "one or more persons in employment."[4] Toward this goal of broad coverage, the WCL also specifically identifies and lists hundreds of different "employments" that fall within more than 20 groupings that are covered by the law.[5]

---

1   WCL § 10.

2   *Surace v. Danna*, 248 N.Y. 18, 20–21 (1928).

3   *See* Workers' Compensation Board, *Employer's Handbook to Workers' Compensation in NYS,* at 16 (Dec. 2011), www.wcb.ny.gov/content/main/Employers/EmployerHandbook.pdf.

4   WCL § 2(3).

5   As examples of the level of detail in these groupings, the manufacture of butter is covered and falls under Group 3; operation of a horse-drawn carriage is covered and falls under Group 7; grave digging is covered and falls under Group 13, and so on. WCL § 3.

[5.3]   Who is an "employee" covered by the WCL?

Generally speaking, all "employees" of a covered employer fall within the protections of the WCL.[6] The New York courts have used two tests to determine whether an employer/employee relationship exists.[7]

The older test—called the common-law "control" test—turns on an analysis of four factors: (1) whether there is direct evidence of the owner's right to control (or exercise of actual control over) the claimant; (2) the method of payment to the claimant; (3) the extent to which the owner furnishes equipment; and (4) whether the owner retains the right to discharge the claimant.[8]

The newer test—called the "relative nature of the work" test—focuses on the following factors: (1) the character of the claimant's work; (2) how much of a separate calling that work is from the owner's occupation; (3) whether that work is continuous or intermittent; (4) whether that work is expected to be permanent; (5) the importance of that work in relation to the owner's business; and (6) whether the claimant should be expected to carry his or her own accident insurance.[9]

The two tests have been applied separately, but the recent trend has been for the courts to employ a combination of the factors in both tests when confronted with workers' compensation questions.[10]

[5.4]   What is an "independent contractor"?[11]

Independent contractors are not employees, and are not covered by the WCL.[12] However, an employer cannot avoid WCL responsibility simply

---

6   *See In re Clumber Transp. Corp.,* 160 A.D.2d 1186, 555 N.Y.S.2d 196 (3d Dep't 1990) ("Workers' compensation legislation must be construed remedially and beneficially, with a view to carrying out fairly and fully the legislative purpose, and with a view to bringing all workers within its purview and the operation of such social legislation").

7   *See Commissioners of State Ins. Fund v. Lindenhurst Green & White Corp.,* 101 A.D.2d 730, 475 N.Y.S.2d 42 (1st Dep't 1984).

8   *Id.* (citing *Mace v. Morrison & Fleming,* 267 A.D. 29, 44 N.Y.S.2d 672 (3d Dep't 1943), *aff'd,* 293 N.Y. 844 (1944)).

9   *Gordon v. New York Life Ins. Co.,* 300 N.Y. 652 (1950).

10   *Commissioners of State Ins. Fund,* 101 A.D.2d at 731.

11   *See also* Chapter 2 of this book at § 2.20 and Chapter 12 at § 12.1.

12   *Commissioners of the State Ins. Fund v. Fox Run Farms,* 195 A.D.2d 372, 600 N.Y.S2d 239 (1st Dep't 1993); *Renouf v. N.Y. Cent. R.R. Co.,* 254 N.Y. 349 (1930).

by calling someone an independent contractor, so it is important to understand the difference between and independent contractor and an employee.

The factors that a workers' compensation law judge will consider in determining whether an individual is an independent contractor, and not an employee, include the following:

1. Does the individual control the time and manner in which the work is to be done?

2. Has the contractor obtained a Federal Employer Identification Number from the Federal Internal Revenue Service, or has it filed business or self-employment income tax returns with the IRS based on work or service performed the previous calendar year?

3. Does the individual maintain a separate business establishment from the business to which he or she is rendering service?

4. Does the individual perform work that is different than the primary work of the business to which he or she is rendering service, and does he or she perform work for other businesses?

5. Does the individual operate under a specific contract, with responsibility for the satisfactory performance of the work, and subject to profit or loss in performing the specific work under the contract (so as to be in a position to succeed or fail if the business's expenses exceed income)?

6. Has the individual obtained a liability insurance policy (and if appropriate, workers' compensation and disability benefits insurance policies) under his or her own legal business name and federal employer identification number?

7. Does the individual have recurring business liabilities and obligations?

8. If the individual has business cards or advertises, do those materials identify the contractor or another entity?

9. Does the individual provide all equipment and materials necessary to fulfill the contract?

10. Does the individual work under his or her own operating permit, contract or authority?[13]

Whether an employer-employee relationship exists is a factual issue for the WCB to decide, and its determination will be upheld by the courts so long as it is supported by (the comparatively low standard of) "substantial evidence."[14] If the evidence is equivocal or inconclusive, WCL § 21(1) contains a statutory presumption that "it shall be presumed in the absence of substantial evidence to the contrary [t]hat the claim comes within the provisions of this chapter"). The WCB routinely relies on the Section 21 presumption in holding a WCL-covered employment relationship exists.[15]

[5.5]   Are part-time employees covered by the WCL?

Yes.[16]

[5.6]   Are "leased" employees covered by the WCL?

Generally, a business may not "borrow" or "lease" employees from another business without each business having workers' compensation

---

13 *See* Workers' Compensation Board, *Workers' Compensation Coverage: Identifying Independent Contractors in Non Construction Industries*, http://www.wcb.ny.gov/content/main/Employers/Coverage_wc/emp_empDefinition.jsp#indContractor.

14 *See Bugaj v. Great Am. Transp., Inc.*, 20 A.D.3d 612, 798 N.Y.S.2d 529 (3d Dep't 2005) (citing *Topper v. Cohen's Bakery*, 295 A.D.2d 872, 744 N.Y.S.2d 260 (3d Dep't 2002)); *see also Taylor v. Kranichfeld*, 2 A.D.3d 1099, 769 N.Y.S.2d 335 (3d Dep't 2003); *Jhoda v. Mauser Serv.*, 279 A.D.2d 853, 719 N.Y.S.2d 388 (3d Dep't 2001); *Kissena Beverages*, 2019 N.Y. Wrk. Comp. LEXIS 11490 (N.Y. WCB, October 4, 2019). In New York law, the term "substantial evidence" has a specific meaning. The New York State Court of Appeals has defined "substantial evidence" as "proof within the whole record of such quality and quantity as to generate conviction in and persuade a fair and detached fact finder that, form that proof as a premise, a conclusion or ultimate fact may be extracted reasonably—probatively and logically." *300 Gramatan Ave. Assoc. v. State Div. of Human Rights*, 45 N.Y.2d 176, 181, 408 N.Y.S.2d 54 (1978). The standard is "such relevant proof as a reasonable mind may accept as adequate to support a conclusion or ultimate fact," but it is "less than a preponderance of the evidence." *Id.* at 180 (emphasis supplied).

15 *See State Ins. Fund*, 2005 N.Y. Wrk. Comp. LEXIS 849 (N.Y. WCB, Jan. 26, 2005) ("The information provided by the parties is insufficient to tilt this balancing test in favor of an employment relationship or independent contractor status. *Workers' Compensation Law 21 provides that, in the absence of sufficient evidence to the contrary, a claim is deemed to come within the provisions of the Workers' Compensation Law.*") (emphasis supplied).

16 "[T]here is no precedent to support an argument that part time versus full time status has any bearing on the determination of employer-employee relationship." *Vaad Hakashruth*, 2015 N.Y. Wrk. Comp. LEXIS 3497 (N.Y. WCB, April 29, 2015).

coverage in its own legal name. The only exception is when a business obtains all of its employees from a Temporary Service Agency (TSA). Temporary employees "are generally considered to be the employees of the [TSA] since that agency hires, fires, and has direction and control over these individuals."[17]

[5.7]   Are volunteers covered by the WCL?

The WCL provides that employers are *not* required to provide workers' compensation insurance for "persons engaged in voluntary service not under contract of hire." WCL § 3(1) (Group 18). "However, simply because an employer considers a worker to be a volunteer within the general meaning of the word does not mean that the worker is a volunteer for the purposes of the [WCL]."[18]

A volunteer can be found to be an employee within the meaning of the statute depending on various factors, with no single factor being dispositive.[19] If an individual receives a financial benefit from the arrangement, he/she may not be a volunteer.[20] By way of example, an unpaid ski patrol member who was reimbursed for buying a ski patrol parka and received free skiing privileges was found to be an employee for workers' compensation purposes.[21] By contrast, however, an individual was found to be a pure volunteer on the following findings of fact by the WCB:

> There was no financial consideration given to the claimant. There was no expectation that the claimant would return on any kind of regular basis to render the volunteer service. The claimant did not have to render any services if he chose not to. . . . The Board Panel finds that the volunteer services of the claimant were not 'employment' within the meaning of the provisions of WCL.[22]

---

17   *Capital Cleaning Servs.*, 2017 N.Y. Wrk. Comp. LEXIS 4781 (N.Y. WCB, Jan. 25, 2017).

18   *You Gotta Believe*, 2008 N.Y. Wrk. Comp. LEXIS 3996 (N.Y. WCB, May 2, 2008).

19   See *Fitzpatrick v. Holimont Inc.*, 247 A.D.2d 715, 669 N.Y.S.2d 88 (3d Dep't 1998).

20   *LeCelle v. N.Y. Conf. of Seventh-Day Adventists*, 235 A.D.2d 694 (3d Dep't 1997) (WCL-covered claimant received tuition credits).

21   *Fitzpatrick*, 247 A.D.2d at 716.

22   *Gaelic Park Sports Centre*, 2016 N.Y. Wrk. Comp. LEXIS 52 (N.Y. WCB, Jan. 4, 2016).

[5.8]   Are employees of not-for-profit entities covered by the WCL?

Generally, yes. Employees who work for not-for-profit organizations, and are compensated for their services, are covered, but some employees of not-for-profit entities may, in the employer's discretion, be excluded, as follows:[23]

- *Clergy and Religious Orders.* Paid clergy and members of religious orders are exempt from mandatory coverage (but can be covered voluntarily). This exemption for clergy and members of religious orders only applies to the performance of religious duties. For example, in *Geddes v. Salvation Army*,[24] the court found that a minister who was injured while operating a baling machine was entitled to workers' compensation benefits because at the time he was not engaging in ministerial (or non-manual) duties, but engaged in hazardous employment. Thus, while an individual may fall with the Group 18 exemption as a minister or pastor, he/she will be covered by the WCL if injured while performing non-exempt work.[25]

- *Amateur Athletes.* Individuals engaged in supervised amateur athletic activities operated on a nonprofit basis (*provided* that they are not otherwise engaged or employed by any person, firm, or corporation participating in such athletic activity) are exempt.[26]

- *Teachers in "religious, charitable or educational institutions."* Paid individuals engaged in a teaching capacity in or for a religious, charitable, or educational institution (if qualified under Section 501(c)(3) of the Internal Revenue Code) are also exempt from mandatory coverage (but can also be covered voluntarily). WCL § 3(1). The exemption, however, only applies to the performance of teaching duties.

---

23   WCL §§ 2(4) and 3 (Group 18).

24   37 A.D.2d 640, 37 A.D.640 (3d Dep't 1971).

25   *See also Tioga Co. Open Door Mission Inc.,* 2000 N.Y. Wrk. Comp. LEXIS 113248 (N.Y. WCB, May 25, 2000) (holding exclusion not applicable where "claimant was not performing his work as a pastor, but engaged in his job as the superintendent").

26   *See Yonkers Bd. of Educ.,* 2017 N.Y. Wrk. Comp. LEXIS 8255 (N.Y. WCB, June 7, 2017) (claim disallowed because claimant was participating as a volunteer assistant football coach in a supervised amateur athletic activity operated on a non-profit basis) (citing *Community College*, 2010 N.Y. Wrk. Comp. G0154911 (N.Y. WCB, 2010) (claim disallowed because claimant was injured while acting as a volunteer assistant coach of a collegiate baseball team funded by student activity fees)).

- *Persons Working in Exchange for Charitable Aid.* Persons receiving charitable aid from a religious or charitable institution (as qualified under Section 501(c)(3) of the Internal Revenue Code) who perform work in return for that aid and certain persons receiving rehabilitation services in a sheltered workshop may be excluded.[27]

[5.9]   Are racetrack jockeys covered by the WCL?

There is a "jockey fund" that provides jockeys connected with New York's horse racing industry with coverage under the WCL.[28] The provision covers "a jockey, apprentice jockey or exercise person . . . performing services for an owner or trainer in connection with the training or racing of a horse at a facility of a racing association or corporation subject to article two or four of the racing, pari-mutuel wagering and breeding law and subject to the jurisdiction of the New York state gaming commission."[29]

[5.10]   Are sole proprietors and partners in partnerships covered by the WCL?

A sole proprietor is not an employee and is ordinarily not covered by the WCL.[30] Similarly, working partners in a partnership are not covered by the WCL.[31] However, sole proprietors and partners may elect to be covered and obtain insurance.[32]

[5.11]   Are individuals who work in construction covered by the WCL?

Generally, yes. The 2010 New York State Construction Industry Fair Play Act[33] creates a presumption of employment in the construction industry.

---

27 WCL § 3(1) (Group 18). "Recipients of charitable aid from a religious or charitable institution who perform work in or for the institution which is incidental to or in return for the aid conferred, and not under any express contract of hire, shall not be deemed to be employed or engaged in employment under the terms of this section." *Id. See, e.g., Salvation Army Adult Rehab.,* 2010 N.Y. Wrk. Comp. LEXIS 6521 (N.Y. WCB, June 22, 2010) (employer-employee relationship did not exist, because "[w]hile [the claimant] performed work, the record indicates that such work was a component of the claimant's overall recovery program and it was provided for the purpose of returning the claimant to the work force.").

28 *See* WCL § 2(5).

29 *Id.*

30 WCL § 54(8).

31 *Id.*

32 *Id.*

33 Labor Law art. 15-B.

Specifically, the Fair Play Act presumes that any person performing services for a construction contractor is an employee of that contractor.[34] The law defines construction as "constructing, reconstructing, altering, maintaining, moving, rehabilitating, repairing, renovating or demolition of any building, structure, or improvement, or relating to the excavation of or other development or improvement to land."[35]

The Fair Play Act creates a three-part test to determine whether a construction industry worker is legitimately exempt from coverage as an "independent contractor":

(a) Is the individual free from control and direction in performing the job, both under his or her contract and in fact?

(b) Are the services performed outside the usual course of business for which the service is performed?

(c) Is the individual customarily engaged in an independently established trade, occupation, profession, or business that is similar to the service at issue?[36]

All three parts of the test must be satisfied.

With respect to the third prong of the three-part test described above, the Fair Play Act requires application of a mandatory 12-part test to determine when "a sole proprietor, partnership, corporation or entity that may be a contractor under this section shall be considered a separate business entity from the" business to which services are provided. To satisfy that prong of the test, a separate business entity must:

1. be performing the service free from the direction or control over the means and manner of providing the service subject only to the right of the contractor to specify the desired result;

2. not be subject to cancellation when its work with the contractor ends;

3. have a substantial investment of capital in the entity beyond ordinary tools and equipment and a personal vehicle;

---

34   Labor Law § 861-c.

35   Labor Law § 861-b(1).

36   Labor Law § 861-c(1).

4. own the capital goods and gain the profits and bear the losses of the entity;

5. make its services available to the general public or business community on a regular basis;

6. include the services provided on a federal income tax schedule as an independent business;

7. perform the services under the entity's name;

8. obtain and pay for any required license or permit in the entity's name;

9. furnish the tools and equipment necessary to provide the service;

10. hire its own employees without contractor approval, pay the employees without reimbursement from the contractor and report the employees' income to the Internal Revenue Service;

11. *not* hold out the entity or the employees of the entity to be its own employees to its customers; and

12. have the right to perform similar services for others on whatever basis and whenever it chooses.[37]

The entity must meet all 12 criteria to be considered a separate business entity.

[5.12] Are out-of-state employers covered by the WCL if they have employees working in New York?

In 2007, the Chair of the WCB issued an opinion letter advising that "all out-of-state employers with employees working in New York State will be required to carry a full, statutory New York State workers' compensation insurance policy." Thereafter, the WCB posted the "Out-of-State Employers Policy" on its website which details when out-of-state employers are required to obtain coverage.[38] Specifically, the policy pro-

---

37   Labor Law § 861-c(2).

38   Workers' Compensation Board, *Change in Workers' Compensation Coverage Requirements for Out-of-State Employers with Employees Working in New York State*, http://www.wcb.ny.gov/content/main/onthejob/CoverageSituations/outOfStateEmployers.jsp.

vides that "an out-of-state employer with an individual or individuals working in New York is required to have a full NYS workers' compensation insurance policy if that employer (as defined in the WCL) meets any of the following criteria":

- the employer is required to register with the NYS Department of Labor and pay Unemployment Insurance for any period in question;

- the employer has a permanent physical location in New York or has one or more employees whose primary work location is in New York;.

- the employer is operating in New York under a permit, contract, or license granted by the State of New York, its counties or any municipality as defined under § 57 of the WCL;

- the employer is working as a contractor/general contractor/ sub-contractor on a construction project in New York; or

- in the previous year, the employer had one or more employees physically in New York for: (a) at least 40 hours of every week for a period of longer than 2 consecutive weeks; or (b) had employees present in New York for 25 or more individual days (e.g., 5 employees working for 5 days in New York equals 25 individual employee days).[39]

Out-of-state employers may also be required to have coverage when they employ residents of New York who are injured on the job outside of New York, provided there are sufficient contacts between the employment at issue and New York State. "When a claimant seeks compensation for an injury sustained outside of New York, the Board possesses subject matter jurisdiction over that claim if sufficient significant contacts between the claimant's employment and the state are found to exist."[40] The inquiry

---

39   *Id.*

40   *Sanchez v. Clestra Cleanroom*, 11 A.D.3d 781, 783 N.Y.S.2d 676 (3d Dep't 2004).

does not focus on the location of the employer, but upon the location of the employment.[41]

Subsequent cases have identified many different factors that may be considered in finding New York employment, including the location of the employer's office, as well as the location of the employee's performance, the locations where the employee was recruited and hired, and whether the employee resided in New York, was regularly contacted there by the out-of-state employer and was expected to return to New York after out-of-state assignments.[42]

The case law that has developed in this area has not established a "bright line" test of when the WCB possesses jurisdiction over an out-of-state employer.[43]

[5.13]   What are the obligations of employers who are subject to the WCL?

An employer's threshold obligation is to obtain and keep in effect workers' compensation insurance coverage for covered employees, and there must be no lapse in coverage even when switching insurance carriers. Employers must also post a notice of workers' compensation coverage.[44] This notice is known as "Form C-105" and is most often obtained from the insurance carrier (e.g., after securing of workers' compensation insur-

---

41   *Nashko v. Standard Water Proofing Co.*, 4 N.Y.2d 199, 173 N.Y.S.2d 565 (1958). The Court of Appeals discussion of the issue in *Standard Water Proofing* is particularly instructive:

> The Workmen's Compensation Law contains no explicit definition of its territorial scope and this court has not attempted to fix a single inflexible and conclusive standard for all cases. [citations omitted]. What has developed is an approach whereby certain factors tending to show substantial connection with this State are looked for in the factual patterns of each individual case. If sufficient significant contacts with this State appear so that it can reasonably be said that the employment is located here, then the Workmen's Compensation Board has jurisdiction. [citations omitted]. If on the other hand the circumstances and elements of the employment are such as to indicate that the employment is in fact located in another State then the claimant is not protected by our statute. But at all times the determination as to the employment's location is governed by the facts of the particular case. *Id.* at 200–01.

42   *See Coley v. Endicott Johnson Corp.*, 60 A.D.3d 1213, 875 N.Y.S.2d 337 (3d Dep't 2009); *Edick v. Transcontinental Refrigerated Lines*, 300 A.D.2d 848, 752 N.Y.S.2d 153 (3d Dep't 2002); *Williams v. Roadkill, Inc.*, 277 A.D.2d 764, 716 N.Y.S.2d 478 (3d Dep't 2000).

43   *Cf. Transcontinental Refrigerated Lines*, 300 A.D.2d at 849 (finding jurisdiction); *Williams*, 277 A.D.2d at 765 (finding jurisdiction); *US Xpress Inc.*, 2018 N.Y. Wrk. Comp. LEXIS 12046 (N.Y. WCB, Dec. 24, 2018) (finding no jurisdiction).

44   WCL § 51.

ance, the employer's insurance carrier or licensed agent can email the WCB at certificates@wcb.ny.gov to obtain controlled forms not available on the agency's website).

An employer is also obligated to keep accurate payroll and workplace accident records. Specifically, an employer must keep accurate records of the number of WCL-covered employees, classifications, wages, and accidents for their business for four years.[45] An employer that fails to keep accurate payroll records may, in addition to all other penalties, fines or assessments, be penalized $1,000 for each ten-day period of noncompliance, or a sum not in excess of two times the cost of compensation for its payroll for the period of such failure.[46] If the employer is a corporation, its president, secretary, and treasurer shall be liable for the penalty.

There can also be criminal liability in the form of fines for the failure to secure required workers' compensation insurance.[47] For example, an employer with five or fewer employees that fails to secure coverage faces a fine of between $1,000 to $5,000.[48] For employers with more than five employees, the failure to secure coverage can constitute a Class E Felony, subject to a fine of between $5,000 to $50,000.[49] Any subsequent violations will result in a Class D Felony, and fines of no less than $10,000 but no higher than $50,000.[50]

[5.14] What does workers' compensation insurance cover?

When employers buy workers' compensation insurance, the carrier is assuming the employer's statutory obligation to pay medical, indemnity, and death benefits under the law, including the following: (i) medical services; (ii) temporary disability payments to the employee to help replace lost wages; (iii) permanent disability payments to the employee to compensate for permanent effects of a workplace accident or illness; (iv) a death benefit for the employee's survivors in the event of a fatal injury; and (v) legal representation for the employer by the insurance carrier.

---

45   WCL § 131(1).

46   WCL § 131(2).

47   WCL § 52.

48   WCL § 52(1)(a).

49   *Id.*

50   WCL § 52(1)(b).

When an employee's on-the-job injury or disease is eligible for workers' compensation coverage, that coverage is the injured or sick employee's sole remedy, and the employee cannot sue the employer for other damages.

With the rare exceptions noted in § 5.15 below, the employer cannot be sued for civil damages arising from the injury or disease suffered by the employee. This is an important protection for both employees and employers: the employee is assured of compensation for his or her lost income and medical expense; and the employer is assured that it will not be sued in court for huge damages. WCL § 11 provides as follows:

> The liability of an employer . . . shall be exclusive and in place of any other liability whatsoever, to such employee, his or her personal representatives, spouse, parents, dependents, distributees, or any person otherwise entitled to recover damages, contribution or indemnity, at common law or otherwise, on account of such injury or death.

This "exclusivity rule" has been stated by the Court of Appeals as follows:

> It is well recognized that the compensation statute was designed to provide a swift and sure source of benefits to the injured employee or to the dependents of the deceased employee. The price for these secure benefits is the loss of the common-law tort action in which greater benefits might be obtained. Thus, unless the employee can establish the existence of a limited number of exceptional circumstances, the sole remedy is workmen's compensation.[51]

WCL § 11 also restricts an employer's exposure to actions by third party non-employers for contributory negligence and/or indemnification to cases involving "grave injury":

> An employer shall not be liable for contribution or indemnity to any third person based upon liability for injuries sustained by an employee acting within the scope of his or her employment for such employer unless such third person proves through competent medical evidence

---

51   *O'Rourke v. Long*, 41 N.Y.2d 219, 222, 391 N.Y.S.2d 553 (1976).

that such employee has sustained a "grave injury" which shall mean only one or more of the following: death, permanent and total loss of use or amputation of an arm, leg, hand or foot, loss of multiple fingers, loss of multiple toes, paraplegia or quadriplegia, total and permanent blindness, total and permanent deafness, loss of nose, loss of ear, permanent and severe facial disfigurement, loss of an index finger or an acquired injury to the brain caused by an external physical force resulting in permanent total disability.

[5.15] Are there any exceptions to WCL exclusivity?

Yes. There are two commonly-invoked exceptions to the finality and exclusivity provisions of WCL § 11.

The first exception is where the employer fails to procure insurance for the purpose of securing the payment of compensation.[52]

The second exception is where the injury complained of is the product of an intentional and deliberate act **by the employer**; in other words, an act by the employer itself, and not an act by somebody else.[53] The intentional act exception applies "[w]here injury is sustained to an employee due to an intentional tort perpetrated by the employer or at the employer's direction."[54] This, in turn, requires "an intentional or deliberate act by the employer directed at causing harm to the particular employee."[55]

[5.16] What are an employer's options with respect to workers' compensation insurance?

There are four basic ways for an employer to secure coverage:

---

52   *See* § 5.13 above.

53   *See Blanchard v. Integrated Food Sys.*, 220 A.D.2d 895, 632 N.Y.S.2d 329 (3d Dep't 1995) (claim by fast food employee who was shot during robbery was not exception to WCL's exclusive liability rule where there was no evidence of employer's willful intent to harm employee in requiring her to work past lawful hours); *Acevedo v. Consolidated Edison Co.,* 189 A.D.2d 497, 596 N.Y.S.2d 68 (1st Dep't 1993) (employees exposed to asbestos at work had exclusive remedy under the WCL even though they were not warned by their employer of the potential danger).

54   *Finch v. Swingly,* 42 A.D.2d 1035, 348 N.Y.S.2d 266 (4th Dep't 1973) (exception did not apply where the employee was working underneath an automobile hoist in the employer's garage when the lift collapsed and injured him).

55   *Mylroie v. GAF Corp.*, 81 A.D.2d 994, 440 N.Y.S.2d 67 (3d Dep't 1983).

1. *Private Insurance.* Employers can purchase a workers' compensation insurance policy from any private insurance carrier authorized by the New York State Department of Financial Services to provide workers' compensation insurance to employers.

2. *The New York State Insurance Fund ("NYSIF").* Employers can purchase workers' compensation insurance policy from the NYSIF, which is a public insurance carrier in New York State. The NYSIF was created by statute and acts as a state agency.[56]

3. *Self-Insurance.* An individual employer has the option of meeting its obligation to ensure coverage by applying for and receiving permission to self-insure.[57] This option is generally reserved for large employers that can demonstrate the financial strength to self-insure.

4. *Group Self-Insurance.* The WCL allows employers performing related activities in a given industry to join together and assume the workers' compensation liabilities of each associated member.[58] Groups must maintain a trust fund dedicated to the payment of the workers' compensation obligations of the employer members.[59] Members of a group self-insured trust must also file an application for participation in the group as well as an indemnity agreement acknowledging their joint and several liability to the trust and the other trust members.[60] All members of the group are subject to assessments when the group fund has defaulted and is unable to make payments.[61]

It is worth noting that both private and NYSIF insurance coverage include so-called "EL" ("Employer's Liability") coverage. Let us assume that employee John Doe is gravely injured at work when his desk chair collapses and he is thrown to the floor. Mr. Doe's remedy against the employer is a workers' compensation claim—but he may also decide to sue the manufacturer of his desk chair in court, claiming that the chair

---

56   WCL § 76.

57   WCL § 50(3).

58   WCL § 50(3-a).

59   *Id.*

60   WCL § 50(3).

61   WCL § 50(5).

was a defective product. Mr. Doe's claim against the chair manufacturer is not subject to workers' compensation limits, and the possibility exists that the chair manufacturer will implead (claim over against) the employer, claiming that the chair was improperly maintained or located in the workplace, and that the employer is thus responsible for any damages which may have to be paid by the manufacturer. EL coverage will provide a defense for the employer against that lawsuit.

However, *self-insurance arrangements do not include EL coverage.* Accordingly, any employer deciding to self-insure should make sure that there is separate liability coverage in place to defend against these claims.

It should also be noted that WCL § 29 provides employers and their insurance carriers a right to reimbursement, subject to certain limitations, where the employee recovers at law against a third-party tortfeasor. When the employee has won such a recovery, the employer/carrier can sue the third party within one year after the accident or six months following the WCB's compensability award, *provided* that the employer must have given injured employee 30-days advance notice in writing.[62]

In addition, the WCL's subrogation provision provides that, where the employee has recovered against a third party, the employer may have a lien on the proceeds of a third-party settlement "after the deduction of the reasonable and necessary expenditures, including attorney's fees, incurred in effecting such recovery."[63]

[5.17] What happens if an employer fails to maintain required workers' compensation coverage?

There are several consequences:

A threshold consequence for failure to secure coverage is that an injured employee can either claim workers' compensation benefits under the WCL *or proceed against the employer in court under a theory of general tort liability.*[64] Jury awards are likely to be far higher than statutory WCB awards; and further, if the employee chooses to go to court and sue on a

---

62   WCL § 29(1).

63   *Id.*

64   WCL § 11.

tort theory, the employer loses several common-law defenses (assumption of risk, contributory negligence by the injured employee, and active negligence by a co-employee).[65]

There are also *civil penalties* for failing to secure coverage. For example, WCL § 52(5) authorizes the Chair of the WCB, upon finding that an employer has failed for a period of ten or more consecutive days to make provision for the payment of compensation, to "impose upon such employer, in addition to all other penalties, fines or assessments, a penalty of $2,000 dollars for each ten day period of non-compliance or a sum not in excess of two times the cost of compensation for its payroll for the period of such failure, which sum shall be paid into the uninsured employers' fund."

Finally, there are *criminal penalties* for failing to secure coverage. WCL § 52(1)(a) provides that a failure to secure the payment of compensation for five or fewer employees within a 12-month period is a misdemeanor punishable by a fine of not less than $1,000 nor more than $5,000. Failure to secure the payment of compensation for more than five employees within a 12-month period is a class E felony punishable by a fine of not less than $5,000 nor more than $50,000. WCL § 52(1)(b) provides that conviction for a subsequent violation within five years is a class D felony, subject to a fine of not less than $10,000 nor more than $50,000.

[5.18]   What benefits does the WCL provide to employees?

There are five categories of benefits:

[5.18.1]   *Medical Treatment*

A claimant may receive necessary medical care directly related to the original injury or illness and the recovery from his or her disability.[66] The treating health care provider must be authorized by the Workers' Compensation Board, except in an emergency situation.[67]

[5.18.2]   *Wage Replacement*

A claimant who is totally or partially disabled and unable to work for more than seven days receives a cash benefit to replace lost wages.[68]

---

65   *Id.*

66   WCL § 13(a).

67   *Id.*

68   WCL § 12.

The amount that a worker receives is based on his or her average weekly wage for the previous year. The following formula is used to calculate benefits: 2/3 x average weekly wage x % of disability = weekly benefit. Therefore, a claimant who was earning $400 per week and is totally (100%) disabled would receive $266.67 per week. A partially disabled claimant (50%) would receive $133.34 per week. In addition, there are maximum weekly amounts, which are re-set from year to year; by way of example, in the year beginning July 1, 2019, the maximum weekly wage replacement benefit was $934.11.

[5.18.3] *Disability Benefits*

WCL § 15(1)–(5) provides for disability payments to be paid to workers whose occupational illness or injury results in permanent total disability, permanent partial disability, temporary total disability, or temporary partial disability. These amounts are set as a percentage of the employee's average weekly wage, with maximum amounts.

[5.18.4] *"Scheduled Loss of Use"*

A Scheduled Loss of Use award is a generally a lump sum cash benefit intended to compensate the individual for lost earning power resulting from a permanent functional impairment to a specific body part as a result of an on-the-job injury, in accordance with loss schedules set by the WCB.[69]

[5.18.5] *Death Benefits*

If a worker dies from a compensable injury, his or her surviving spouse and/or minor children (or if none, other dependents as recognized by law), are entitled to weekly cash benefits. The amount is equal to 2/3 of the deceased worker's average weekly wage for the year before the accident. The weekly compensation may not exceed the weekly maximum, despite the number of dependents. The death benefit rates and percentages provided for in WCL § 16 have been summarized by the WCB on "Board Form C-500, Disability Benefits, Rates and Awards."[70] If there are no

---

69   See Workers' Compensation Board, *Understanding Your Schedule Loss of Use Award*, www.wcb.ny.gov/content/main/Workers/ScheduledLossUse.jsp.

70   See Workers' Compensation Board, *Death Benefits, Rates and Awards* (June 2016) www.wcb.ny.gov/content/main/forms/C500_1.pdf.

surviving dependents eligible to receive compensation, the surviving parents or the estate of the deceased worker may be entitled to payment of a sum of $50,000.[71]

Funeral expenses may also be paid. For deaths on and after June 8, 2016, the maximum amount for funeral expenses is $12,500 in Metropolitan New York counties, and $10,500 in all other counties.[72]

[5.19]   Is every workplace accident or injury covered by the WCL?

No. Although WCL § 21 creates a *presumption* that workplace injuries are compensable, not every accident or injury is in fact covered.

To be compensable, an injury must "arise out of and in the course of employment."[73] Activities that are "purely personal pursuits" are not within the scope of employment and compensation is not recoverable for injuries sustained while engaging in them.[74] In addition, WCL § 10 bars compensation when the injury: (i) has been caused solely by intoxication of the injured employee while on duty; or (ii) is the result of the deliberate intent of the injured employee to bring about injury or death; or (iii) the injury is sustained in off-duty athletic events under specific circumstances.[75]

The test for determining whether a particular activity is within the scope of employment or is purely personal is whether the activity is both reasonable and sufficiently work related under the circumstances. An employee "may indulge in any reasonable activity [while on a business trip], and if he does so the risk inherent in such activity is an incident of his employment."[76] The determination of whether activity is unreasonable is factual, and the WCB is afforded "great latitude" in deciding whether the employee's conduct is disqualifying.[77]

---

71   *Id.*

72   *Id.*

73   *See* WCL § 10.

74   *See, e.g., Pasquel v. Coverly,* 4 N.Y.2d 28, 31, 171 N.Y.S.2d 848 (1958).

75   For athletic events, see § 5.18 above.

76   *Capizzi v. Southern Dist. Reporters,* 61 N.Y.2d 50, 55, 471 N.Y.S.2d 554 (1984), quoting *Davis v. Newsweek,* 305 N.Y. 20, 28 (1953).

77   *Anadio v. Ideal Leather Finishers,* 32 A.D.2d 40, 299 N.Y.S.2d 489 (3d Dep't 1969).

As with other WCB determinations, the line between what is reasonable and unreasonable is not always bright, and with some exceptions, courts and the WCB have frequently found that injuries arising from personal activities are compensable when they happen on business trips or during breaks in the workday.[78]

[5.20] Are recreational activities covered by the WCL?

Sometimes, depending on the facts. For cases arising other than from injuries sustained on business trips, WCL § 10(1) provides that there is no coverage "where the injury was sustained in or caused by voluntary participation in an off-duty athletic activity not constituting part of the employee's work related duties . . . unless the employer (a) requires the employee to participate in such activity, (b) compensates the employee for participating in such activity or (c) otherwise "sponsors the activity."[79]

[5.21] Is "horseplay" covered by the WCL?

Again, sometimes. The Court of Appeals has held that injuries resulting from horseplay (defined by the Court as instances where "employees momentarily abandon work to play, tease, test one another or satisfy their curiosity") are compensable if they result from conduct which "may reasonably be regarded as an incident of the employment."[80]

However, the Appellate Division, Third Department, has observed that:

---

78   *Compare Pasquel v. Coverly*, 4 N.Y.2d 28, 171 N.Y.S.2d 848 (1958), *with Leonard v. Peoples Camp Corp.*, 9 A.D.2d 420, 194 N.Y.S.2d 863 (3d Dep't 1959), *aff'd*, 9 N.Y.2d 652, 212 N.Y.S.2d 69 (1961); *Rizzo v. Syracuse University*, 2 A.D.2d 641, 151 N.Y.S.2d 724 (3d Dep't 1956); *Simmons v. The Hedges*, 286 A.D. 1044, 144 N.Y.S.2d 828 (3d Dep't 1955); *Gabunas v. Pan American Airways*, 279 A.D. 697, 108 N.Y.S.2d 372 (3d Dep't 1951).

79   This mirrors the New York Court of Appeals decision in *Congdon v. Klett,* 307 N.Y. 218 (1956), which ruled that injuries sustained by an employee engaged in recreational activities will be compensable if:

> (a) they occur on the premises during a lunch or recreation period as a regular incident of the employment; or (b) the employer, by expressly or impliedly requiring participation, or by making the activity part of the services of an employee, brings the activity within the orbit of the employment; or (c) the employer derives substantial direct benefit from the activity beyond the intangible value of improvement in employee health and morale that is common to all kinds of recreation and social life.

80   *Lubrano v. Malinet,* 65 N.Y.2d 616, 617-18, 491 N.Y.S.2d 148 (1985) (a compensable injury was found where employee tried to recreate a "trick" performed by a co-worker that involved tossing a lighted match into a bucket containing a residue of oil, gasoline and grease without causing an explosion).

[a]lthough recoveries for injuries resulting from horse-play have been permitted, they have been limited to instances where the horseplay arises "out of a regular and foreseeable feature of the employment . . . or where the claimants were the passive victims of a co-employee's prank . . . or were injured by a 'tempting instrumentality' kept on the work premises by the employer."[81]

Unfortunately, a clear delineation between compensable "playing, teasing, or testing" and non-compensable "isolated acts of foolery" is difficult to discern at the WCB level.[82]

[5.22] Is an employee who gets hurt while conducting personal business covered by the WCL?

Once again, sometimes.

The general rule is that "[a]ctivities which are purely personal pursuits are not within the scope of employment and are not compensable under the [WCL], with the test being whether the activities are both reasonable and sufficiently work related under the circumstances."[83] The determination of whether an activity constitutes a purely personal pursuit is one of fact for the WCB to resolve.[84]

---

81   *Gladwell v. C & S Communications,* 224 A.D.2d 775, 637 N.Y.S.2d 502 (3d Dep't, 1996) (injury not compensable where it resulted from an "obviously unauthorized and 'isolated incident of foolery'"; employee was injured because he "performed a stunt which involved his leaning backward outside a van door while the vehicle was moving.").

82   *Compare Roosevelt Union Free Sch. Dist.,* 2019 N.Y. Wrk. Comp. LEXIS 79 (N.Y. WCB, Jan. 3, 2019) (a compensable injury was found where security guard who "was playfully interacting with one of the students when she was injured" was engaged in "the type of activity [which] is a reasonably foreseeable extension of [her] duties"), *with Button v. Button,* 166 A.D.3d 1258, 86 N.Y.S3d 805 (3d Dep't 2017) (affirming WCB determination that an injury was not compensable where claimant rode the employer's all-terrrain vehicle to his employer-provided residence (which was located across the street from the workplace), "grabbed a beer," and was struck by an oncoming vehicle because he failed to yield to oncoming traffic up on his return to work).

83   *Vogel v. Anheuser-Busch,* 265 A.D.2d 705, 696 N.Y.S.2d 571 (3d Dep't 1999) (reversing WCB and holding injury was compensable where employee was injured in the employer's parking lot while assisting a co-worker whose motorcycle would not start).

84   *Pagano v. Anheuser Busch,* 301 A.D.2d 977, 754 N.Y.S2d 700 (3d Dep't 2003) (affirming WCB determination that fatal injury was not compensable where employee suffered heart attack because his "death was caused by his health problems and his own activity of running, rather than by any external condition or event in the parking lot. It is also clear that he decided to run, rather than walk, solely because he was behind schedule").

It is important to note that "[m]omentary deviation[s] from the work routine for a customary and accepted purpose will not bar a claim for benefits."[85] This can lead to apparently bizarre results, such as a finding that a WCL death benefit was properly awarded where an employee fell off the roof he was supposed to be working on even though at the time he fell, he was trying to steal copper for his personal use).[86]

Furthermore, "[a]ccidents that occur during an employee's short breaks, such as coffee breaks, are considered to be so closely related to the performance of the job that they do not constitute an interruption of employment."[87]

[5.23] Is an employee who is assaulted by a co-worker covered by the WCL?

The test for whether the victim of an assault is entitled to workers' compensation is whether the assault originated from work-related differences, or if it arose from pure personal animosity between the combatants. An award of compensation is appropriate as long as there is a connection between the motivation for the assault and the employment.[88]

The connection between the assault and the workplace does not need to be particularly strong or clear and convincing for the resulting injury to be compensable. "An award of compensation may be sustained even though the result of an assault . . . so long as there is any nexus, however slender, between the motivation for the assault and the employment."[89]

---

85   *Richardson v. Fiedler Roofing,* 67 N.Y.2d 246, 502 N.Y.S.2d 125 (1986).

86   *Id.*

87   *Pabon v. N.Y.C. Transit Authority,* 24 A.D.3d 833, 805 N.Y.S.2d 183 (3d Dep't 2005); *Giovanni's Italian Restaurant,* 2017 N.Y. Wrk. Comp. LEXIS 13888 (N.Y. WCB, December 6, 2017).

88   *Baker v. Hudson Valley Nursing Home,* 233 A.D.2d 608, 649 N.Y.S.2d 105 (3d Dep't 1996) (employee suffered compensable injury when assaulted by co-worker who accused employee of "spreading gossip about [her]"); *Privatera v. Yellow Cab Co.,* 158 A.D.2d 835, 551 N.Y.S.2d 419 (3d Dep't 1990) (compensable injury found where 75-year old claimant was pushed by co-worker after dispute concerning "work-related topic").

89   *Seymour v. Rivera Appliances Corp.,* 28 N.Y.2d 406, 409, 271 N.Y.S.2d 243 (1971) (internal citation omitted). ("Arguments among employees and their escalation into violence, especially during regular breaks, must be anticipated by employers") *Id.*

[5.24] Are injuries sustained while commuting covered by the WCL?

Sometimes. The New York Court of Appeals has explained the governing principle as follows:

> While the general rule is that accidents occurring on the public highway, away from the place of employment and outside regular working hours, do not arise out of and in the course of employment, it is equally true that, as the employee comes in closer proximity with his employment situs, there develops "a gray area" where the risks of street travel merge with the risks attendant with employment and where the mere fact that the accident took place on a public road or sidewalk may not ipso facto negate the right to compensation.[90]

The Court of Appeals further stated,

> When the employee advances to the point where he is engaging in an act or series of acts which are part and parcel of the entrance into the employment premises, the test of compensability is whether there is such a relationship existing between the accident and the employment as to bring the former within the range of the latter.[91]

There must be (1) "a special hazard at the particular off-premises point" and (2) a "close association of the access route with the premises, so far as going and coming are concerned."[92]

---

90   *Husted v. Seneca Steel Serv., Inc.,* 41 N.Y.2d 140, 144, 391 N.Y.S.2d 78 (1976) (affirming WCB determination that injury occurred in the compensable "gray area" when car accident occurred "not 'more than a foot, maybe even closer' to" the employer's parking lot).

91   *Id.* at 141–42.

92   *Id.*

At the WCB level, the cases focus on whether the employee was on a special errand for the employer or was subjected to some special hazard that employees had to navigate to gain entry to the workplace.[93]

[5.25] Are non-occupational injuries or illnesses covered by the WCL?

No. Non-occupational accidents, injuries or illnesses are not covered: a compensable injury must "arise out of and in the course of employment."[94]

See Chapter 6 of this book for a discussion of statutory disability benefits, which *do* cover non-occupational illnesses and injuries.

[5.26] Are injuries sustained in a "home office" covered by the WCL?

Generally not, but the WCB and the courts recognize an exception from the general rule on non-compensability for home offices "where it is shown that an employee's home has become part of the employer's premises"[95]:

> As it is commonplace for many professional and managerial level employees to take work home, the exception is applied cautiously and generally only after consideration of the following indicia: the quantity and regularity of the work performed at home, the continuing presence of work equipment at home and the special circumstances of the particular employment that made it necessary and not merely personally convenient to work at home.[96]

---

93   *NYS Dep't of Educ.*, 2018 N.Y. Wrk. Comp. LEXIS 5955 (N.Y. WCB, June 28, 2018) (claimant did not fall within the compensable gray area where she "parked her car on the public street and was around the corner from the entrance she wished to utilize for her entrance at the time she sustained her injury"); *Niagara Falls Memorial*, 2018 N.Y. Wrk. Comp. LEXIS 3898 (N.Y. WCB, April 27, 2018) (claimant did not fall within the compensable gray area when the "motor vehicle accident occurred near the hospital but it was in an intersection on a public street [and] [t]he record does not contain any evidence that the location of the accident was a special hazard that employees of the hospital had to navigate"); *Dep't of Educ.*, 2018 N.Y. Wrk. Comp. LEXIS 352 (N.Y. WCB, January 10, 2018) (claimant fell within the gray area when she fell on ice-covered sidewalk that employer had a duty to remove; these factors support the claimant's contention that her slip and fall injury occurred in the "gray area" pursuant to *Husted* and that a special hazard existed from the ice and there was a close association of the access route with the premises).

94   *See* WCL § 10. *See also Dorosz v. Green & Seifter,* 92 N.Y.2d 672, 685 N.Y.S.2d 406 (1999) ("in applying WCL § 10 the threshold test is whether, in the words of the statute, the activity constitutes "part of the employee's work related duties").

95   *Bobinis v. State Ins. Fund*, 235 A.D.2d 955, 653 N.Y.S.2d 408 (3d Dep't 1997).

96   *Id*. at 956.

Thus, an employee's home can achieve "the status as a place of employment where the record showed that he regularly took work home, had work equipment at his house and it was necessary and beneficial to his employer for him to perform duties at home."[97]

[5.27] Is an employee who is injured while violating a work rule covered by the WCL?

This issue was addressed by the New York Court of Appeals in *Merchant v. Pinkerton's Inc.*[98] In that case, a security guard was killed on the job by his personal firearm which the he brought to work despite signing an application acknowledging that he was forbidden to carry a firearm, and in violation of the employer's regulation that violation of the rule would result in immediate discharge. Ruling that this did *not* disqualify the decedent's estate from claiming workers' compensation, the Court set forth the framework for evaluation of "work rule" cases as follows:

> As a general rule, the misconduct of an employee, whether framed in terms of simple negligent dereliction of duty or even willful disobedience of the rules of the workplace, has no bearing upon whether an injury is compensable. Under the Workers' Compensation Law, fault of the respective parties simply has no bearing to the basic test of coverage . . . there has never developed a rule of general applicability to the effect that an employee forfeits his compensation coverage by performing his duties in a needlessly dangerous way or in conscious disregard of the employer's instructions.[99]

The Court went on to say that work rule cases are to be decided according to the general premise that compensation will not be denied where the

---

97   *Hille v. Gerald Records*, 23 N.Y.2d 135, 139, 295 N.Y.S.2d 645 (1968). The WCB has applied the exception sparingly. *E.g.*, IBM Corp., 2015 N.Y. Wrk. Comp. LEXIS 6682 (N.Y. WCB, June 23, 2015) (refusing to apply exception; "[t]here is nothing in the record that concludes it was necessary for the claimant to perform his work duties at home and the claimant derived the benefit from working at home"); *Alliance Capital Mgmt., LLP,* 2005 N.Y. Wrk. Comp. LEXIS 7953 (N.Y. WCB, September 12, 2005) (refusing to apply exception; "Being able to work from home allowed the claimant to perform her job duties and still take care of her children, a clear benefit to her. Furthermore, a review of the record shows that it was not the norm for the claimant to work at home. Rather it was a rare occurrence for the benefit of the claimant. Finally, it was not a necessity, as it was not required by the employer that the claimant work from home, she did so for her convenience.").

98   50 N.Y.2d 492, 429 N.Y.S.2d 598 (1980).

99   *Id.* at 495.

---

rule relates to the "method of accomplishing the ultimate work," as opposed to "overstepping the boundaries defining the ultimate work to be done."[100]

The WCB and Third Department have consistently applied *Merchant*, and thus, disqualification from benefits for violation of work rules is rare.

[5.28] Is an employee who is injured while on a business trip covered by the WCL?

Almost always. Traditionally, injuries sustained by an employee while traveling in the business of his employer have been found to be compensable if they occurred while the employee was actually acting in furtherance of his employer's business. In fact, this theory of compensability has been expanded in recognition of the fact that a change in environment creates a greater risk of injury to the employee so that injuries to a traveling employee may be compensable even if the employee at the time of the accident was not engaged in the duties of his employment.[101]

Thus, the cases generally hold that risks inherent in travel arise out of the employment where travel is required for the job. In fact, the WCB and courts have been somewhat reluctant to disqualify traveling employees from benefits even if they are arguably engaged in personal pursuits at the time of the injury.[102]

---

100   *Id.*

101   *See Lepow v. Lepow Knitting Mills,* 288 N.Y. 377 (1942) (compensable injury where employee was bitten by a disease-bearing insect indigenous to a tropical country; "[w]e hold in the present case that the decedent was sent to South Africa upon a mission arranged by his employer solely to promote its business interests, and that the risks incidental to his itinerary through regions infested by a death-bearing insect were special in character").

102   *See, e.g., Lewis v. Knappen Tippetts Abbett Eng. Co.,* 304 N.Y. 461 (1952) (compensable injury where employee was shot while on sightseeing trip in a war-torn country; "[claimant] was sent by his employer to a country where there had been warfare for a long time and where an uneasy truce was in effect. The employer knew all about that, but for its own profit sent him there, nevertheless"); *Markoholz v. General Electric Co.,* 13 N.Y.2d 163, 243 N.Y.S.2d 853 (1963) (compensable injury where decedent attended international conference at employer's request and was killed in airplane accident at the end of a week's vacation following the conference; "where the employment is far from home, the employee has no fixed hours, excursions to nearby places of interest are available and expected"); *Mount Vernon Cent. Sch. Dist.,* 2015 N.Y. Wrk. Comp. LEXIS 6239 (N.Y. WCB, June 17, 2015) (compensable injury where employee on business trip injured at shopping mall; "[t]he employer put the claimant in the Albany/Troy, NY area and therefore, since the claimant was in travel status, the employer assumes the risk of any injuries sustained by the claimant while engaging in reasonable activities").

There is a point, however, where an employee's actions may be so unreasonable as to defeat coverage; as, for example, in the case of the manager on out-of-town trip for training purposes who became intoxicated, broke into hotel's closed outdoor pool and "dove into the shallow end of the pool without taking note that the pool had been partially drained that day to be closed for the season."[103]

[5.29] What if an accident or injury does not cause a new injury, but merely aggravates a pre-existing non-occupational injury?

The fact that an injury relates to a preexisting condition will not preclude the claimant from workers' compensation coverage where it is demonstrated that the claimant's employment exacerbated the condition "in such a manner as to cause a disability which did not previously exist."[104] The courts have found a number of injuries compensable notwithstanding a wide variety of preexisting medical conditions.[105]

[5.30] Are occupational diseases covered by the WCL?

Yes. WCL § 2 defines an occupational disease as "a disease resulting from the nature of employment and contracted therein."

However, to establish an occupational disease, a claimant must demonstrate a "recognizable link" between the alleged condition and a "distinctive feature" of his or her work.[106]

[5.31] Are psychological and psychiatric conditions covered by the WCL?

Sometimes. For a mental injury premised on work-related stress to be compensable, "a claimant must demonstrate that the stress that caused the

---

103   *Grady v. Dun & Bradstreet,* 265 A.D.2d 643, 696 N.Y.S.2d 258 (3d Dep't 1999).

104   *Ochsner v. New Venture Gear,* 273 A.D.2d 715, 710 N.Y.S.2d 443 (3d Dep't 2000).

105   *See Johannesen v. New York City Dep't of Hous. Preservation & Dev.,* 84 N.Y.2d 129, 615 N.Y.S.2d 336 (1994) (claimant's bronchial asthma was an accidental injury under workers' compensation laws, even though it was gradual, because the record substantiated that her working environment was highly dangerous and aggravated the condition); *Masse v. Robinson Co.,* 301 N.Y. 34, 37 (1950)("[a] heart injury such as coronary occlusion or thrombosis when brought on by overexertion or strain in the course of daily work is compensable, though a pre-existing pathology may have been a contributing factor"); *Lynch v. Rockland County Dept. of Social Services,* 124 A.D.2d 430, 507 N.Y.S.2d 529 (3d Dep't 1986) (aggravation of preexisting arthritic condition).

106   *See Ball v. New Era Cap Co.,* 21 A.D.3d 618, 799 N.Y.S.2d 334 (3d Dep't 2005) (citing *Aldrich v. St. Joseph's Hosp.,* 305 A.D.2d 908, 759 N.Y.S.2d 603 (3d Dep't 2003)).

claimed mental injury was greater than that which other similarly situated workers experienced in the normal work environment."[107] There are two lines of cases in this area, which reflect two different types of stress-inducing factors in the normal work environment.

The first line of cases involves emotional injury claimed to have been caused by the nature of the work itself. If the work inherently involves stress to which all employees are exposed, exposure to that stress does *not* result in a compensable injury.[108]

The second line of cases involves claims that a supervisor or co-worker has created a stressful work environment, causing emotional injury. The inquiry in these cases is whether the offensive conduct may be considered a "normal" feature of employee interaction in the particular workplace, or in a similar work environment. For example, in *Clark v. Oswego County*,[109] the claimant was subjected to the office manager's yelling and use of profanity. In rejecting the claim that the resulting stress constituted an accident, the court noted that the record established that arguments in which voices were raised and profanities were used were not unusual, and claimant had been involved in such arguments in the past.

Thus, compensable stress cases turn on a factual determination by the WCB that the "claimant experienced far greater than typical work-related stress."[110] However, two additional considerations have been articulated by the courts. First, the injury "need not be caused by a discrete, identifi-

---

107   *Guess v. Finger Lakes Ambulance,* 28 A.D.3d 996, 812 N.Y.S.2d 393 (3d Dep't 2006).

108   *See Charlotten v. N.Y. State Police,* 286 A.D.2d 849, 730 N.Y.S.2d 377 (3d Dep't 2001) (police officer exposed to gruesome traffic accidents did not experience compensable injury); *Guess v. Finger Lakes Ambulance,* 28 A.D.3d 996, 812 N.Y.S.2d 393 (3d Dep't 2006) (no compensable injury where paramedic in attending to a dying man experienced trauma).

109   17 A.D.3d 882, 793 N.Y.S.2d 258 (3d Dep't 2005). Similarly, in *Pecora v. City of Westchester,* 13 A.D.3d 916, 786 N.Y.S.2d 653 (3d Dep't 2004) the court found that one incident of name-calling and sarcastic references to the claimant were "of the nature normally encountered" in work in a waste water treatment plant. *See also Curley v. Allstate Ins. Co.,* 2 A.D.3d 995, 768 N.Y.S.2d 400 (3d Dep't 2003).

110   *Cook-Schoonover v. Corning Hosp.,* 291 A.D.2d 715, 738 N.Y.S.2d 118 (3d Dep't 2002) (affirming WCB determination employee experienced far greater than typical work-related stress; claimant "experienced a verbally harassing work environment that led to hospitalizations for hyperventilation, chest pain, rapid heart-beat and dizziness").

able psychic trauma, but can result from emotional stress extending over a period of months."[111] Second, "the fact that claimant may have a particular vulnerability will not preclude an award of benefits."[112]

[5.32] How are workers' compensation claims presented and decided?

Employees can initiate a workers' compensation claim on-line or in-person at any WCB office. Insurers will often accept a claim and promptly begin paying benefits. Alternatively, an insurer can dispute or contest a claim for various reasons. Contested claims are initially heard by a WCL Administrative Law Judge ("ALJ") who conducts hearings and renders the initial decision on compensability.[113] While ALJ decisions are binding, parties may seek review of an ALJ decision with the Administrative Review Division of the WCB.

On an appeal, a three-member panel of the WCB constitutes the first-level appeal. If there is *not* a unanimous decision by the panel, a mandatory full Board review by all thirteen Commissioners may be requested within 30 days of the filing date of the Board panel's decision. If the decision of the panel *is* unanimous, a party may request discretionary full Board review, which the Board may or may not decide to entertain.

WCB panel decisions (if full Board review is not available) and Board review decisions, may then be appealed to the Appellate Division, Third Department, of the Supreme Court of the State of New York.[114]

The WCB has broad authority to resolve factual issues based on credibility of witnesses and draw any reasonable inference from the evidence in the record.[115] Questions of credibility, reasonableness, and weight of medical evidence are for the WCB to decide, and it is within the province of the WCB to resolve conflicts in the medical testimony as well as to determine the reasonableness of, weight, and credibility to be given to, that testimony.[116] Where there is conflicting testimony, it is the WCB that

---

111   *Velazquez v. Triborough Bridge & Tunnel Authority*, 156 A.D.2d 922, 550 N.Y.S.2d 139 (3d Dep't 1989).

112   *McDonald v. Danforth*, 286 A.D.2d 845, 730 N.Y.S.2d 571 (3d Dep't 2001).

113   WCL § 25.

114   WCL § 23.

115   *See Korczyk v. City of Albany*, 264 A.D.2d 908, 695 N.Y.S.2d 429 (3d Dep't 1999).

116   *See Forrest v. Grossman's Lumber*, 175 A.D. 2d 498, 572 N.Y.S.2d 774 (3d Dep't 1991).

determines which witnesses are credible, and which testimony to accept or reject.[117] As long as credibility determinations are supported by sufficient evidence, the fact that some contradictory evidence was also introduced will not change the result.[118]

[5.33] What are some of the important forms and deadlines for WCB cases?

Within 48 hours of the first medical treatment rendered to a workers' compensation claimant, the doctor must complete a preliminary medical report (Form C-4) and mail it to the appropriate WCB District Office, with copies to the employer or its insurance carrier, the injured worker, and his or her representative (if any).[119]

Within 10 days after an on-the-job injury or illness, the employer must submit a notification of work-related injury/illness report (Form C-2).[120]

Within 14 days after an employer's submission of the work-related injury/ illness report, the employer's insurer must provide the injured worker with a written statement of his or her rights under the law (Form C-430S).[121]

Within 15 days after the first medical treatment, the doctor must complete a 15-day report of the injury and treatment and mail it to the WCB District Office.[122]

Within 18 days after the first day of disability (*or* within 10 days after the employer first has knowledge of the alleged accident, *or* within 10 days after the carrier receives the Form C-2, whichever of these three periods is longer), the insurer must begin the payment of benefits or dispute the claim if lost time exceeds seven days. If the claim is being disputed, the insurer must so inform the WCB, the claimant, and the claimant's representative (if any). If the claim is not disputed, but payment is not being

---

117   *Wright v. Golden Arrow Line, Inc.*, 206 A.D.2d 759, 615 N.Y.S.2d 473 (3d Dep't 1994).

118   *Scollo v. Joseph J. Pietrafesa Co.*, 105 A.D.2d 515, 481 N.Y.S.2d 464 (3d Dep't 1984).

119   WCL § 13.

120   WCL § 110.

121   *Id.*

122   WCL § 13-a(4)(a).

made for specific reasons stated on the notice, (such as, that there is no lost time or that the duration of the disability is less than the 7-day waiting period), the insurer must also notify all the parties.[123]

When the WCB notifies an employer or its insurance carrier that a workers' compensation case has been indexed against the employer, and the employer or insurance carrier decides to contest the claim, a "notice of controversy must" be filed with the WCB within 25 days from the date of mailing of the notice of indexing.[124]

[5.34]   What is a "return to work" program?[125]

A "return to work" (RTW) program is an employer-sponsored program allowing workers who are unable to perform their usual and customary job duties because of a compensable injury or illness to return to work in a temporary, limited, or light duty capacity while they recover. **Employers are not required to sponsor RTW programs**, but there can be a financial incentive to do so: the indemnity benefit that an injured employee receives is offset by the amount he or she is receiving in wages while working in a RTW program.[126] The WCB has suggested that, "according to the NYSIF, companies that have return to work programs have seen savings up to 20–40 percent or more in workers' compensation costs." RTW programs are common and the WCB has published a "best practices" handbook for employers on implementation of a RTW program.[127]

[5.35]   Is an employer required to offer injured employees light or modified duty?

The WCL does not have any provision that obligates an employer to provide light or modified duty. However, there may be circumstances in which it is appropriate to offer a "light duty" position as an accommodation to a temporary disability; *see* discussion in Chapter 11 of this book at §§ 11.40–11.41.

If an employer opts to offer of light or modified duty, and that offer is unreasonably rejected, that *may* allow the employer to stop paying indem-

---

123   WCL § 25.

124   *Id.* at n. 2.

125   *See* Chapter 11 of this book.

126   WCL § 15(5-a).

127   *See* Workers' Compensation Board, *Return to Work Program*, http://www.wcb.ny.gov/content/main/ReturnToWork/RTW_Handbook.pdf.

nity benefits under the WCL. However, it is for the WCB, and not for the employer or its carrier, to make the determination of whether or not the employee's rejection of the offer was reasonable.[128]

[5.36]   Is an employer required to hold an injured employee's job open until he or she can return to work?

The WCL does not require that a position be held open indefinitely.[129] However, despite the absence of an affirmative obligation to that effect, employers should consider whether any other federal and state disability discrimination or leave laws apply, such as the federal Americans With Disabilities Act and Family Medical Leave Act, or the New York Human Rights Law. *See* Chapter 4 and Chapter 11 at § 11.42.

[5.37]   When can an employer discharge an employee who has claimed or is receiving WCL benefits?

An employer *may not discharge* an employee in retaliation for filing a workers' compensation claim, for receiving WCL benefits, or because it is believed that the employee may file for or receive benefits in the future.[130]

However, an employer *may discharge* an employee who has filed workers' compensation claims and/or is receiving benefits if the termination is for a "valid business reason" such as insubordination, lack of work/economic reasons, misconduct, lengthy absence from work, inability to perform the job, or poor job performance, so long as the employer's motivation is not retaliatory.[131]

---

128   *See Okonski v. Pollio Dairy Products Corp.*, 184 A.D.2d 871, 585 N.Y.S.2d 121 (3d Dep't 1992) ("The issue of whether a partially disabled claimant's failure to accept light duty work constitutes a voluntary withdrawal from the labor market is a factual one, and if supported by substantial evidence the Workers' Compensation Board's decision on that issue cannot be disturbed.").

129   *See Conklin v. City of Newburgh*, 205 A.D.2d 841, 613 N.Y.S.2d 287 (3d Dep't 1994) (citing *Duncan v. N.Y. State Dev. Ctr.*, 63 N.Y.2d 128, 481 N.Y.S.2d 22 (1984) ("An employer should be permitted to take reasonable steps to secure a steady, reliable, and adequate work force.")).

130   WCL § 120 n. 7.

131   *E.g., Gallo v. Jam Towing, Inc.*, 30 A.D.3d 656, 816 N.Y.S.2d 229 (3d Dep't 2006) (employer had valid business reason for termination; claimant "was absent approximately 14 days, with no advance warning on at least six of those days, and was late on numerous other occasions"); *Monroe v. Cortland County*, 275 A.D.2d 510, 711 N.Y.S.2d 636 (3d Dep't 2008) (same; claimant discharged from his position, and offered a reassignment, based upon his inability to operate the skid steer for more than 40 minutes per day); *Lawrik v. Superior Confections, Inc.*, 300 A.D.2d 777, 752 N.Y.S.2d 121 (3d Dep't 2002) (same; "claimant was discharged due to ongoing insubordination and a persistent inability to get along with her coworkers").

The WCL's no-retaliation provision does not confer a right to sue the employer in court; rather, retaliation claims must be submitted to and decided by the WCB.[132] The remedies available in a § 120 proceeding include reinstatement, back pay, attorneys' fees, and a penalty of not less than one hundred dollars or more than five hundred dollars. As with WCB benefit determinations, WCB retaliation determinations are given considerable deference when judicially reviewed.[133]

An employee claiming retaliation has the burden of proving "both a causal nexus between the employee's activities in obtaining compensation and the employer's conduct against the employee [*i.e.*, the adverse employment action], so that it clearly appears that the employee attempting to exercise his rights under the compensation or disability status is treated detrimentally when compared to other groups of employees."[134]

[5.38] What can an employer do about fraudulent WCL claims?

WCL § 114-a provides that a compensation claimant who "knowingly makes a false statement or representation as to a material fact . . . shall be disqualified from receiving any compensation directly attributable to such false statement or representation."[135] The WCB also instructs employers to report suspected fraud to the Office of the Fraud Inspector General for investigation and potential prosecution by the New York State Attorney General's Office. Reports can be made anonymously to a telephone complaint line.[136]

Employers should remember that they cannot discipline or terminate employees based on their own unilateral decision that an employee has committed worker's compensation fraud.[137] Instead, the suspected fraud should be reported to the WCB.

---

132   WCL § 120.

133   *Id.*

134   *Johnson v. Moog, Inc.*, 114 A.D.2d 538, 494 N.Y.S.2d 152 (3d Dep't 1985) (citing *Duncan v. N.Y. State Dev. Ctr.*, 63 N.Y.2d 128, 134 (1984)).

135   *Kodra v. Mondelez Intl., Inc.*, 145 A.D.3d 1131, 1132, 42 N.Y.S.3d 467 (3d Dep't 2016).

136   (800) 367-4448 or https://ig.ny.gov/workers-comp-complaint.

137   *E.g., Gillen v. U.S. Air, Inc.*, 260 A.D.2d 853, 688 N.Y.S.2d 761 (3d Dep't 1999).

II.   WORKPLACE SAFETY

Most private sector employers in New York are subject to the federal Occupational Safety and Health Act of 1970,[138] and the health and safety standards promulgated by the Occupational Safety and Health Administration (OSHA).[139] While those OSHA standards will govern the vast majority of safety issues in the private sector, there are several licensing requirements and agencies in New York that cover workplace safety issues.

[5.39] What is DOSH?

OSHA oversees and monitors approved state plans that are operated by individual states or U.S. territories. While a number of states have adopted plans covering some or all private sector employees, New York State has not done so; accordingly, *private sector employers* operating in New York are subject to OSHA's jurisdiction and all applicable health and safety rules, regulations, and standards.[140]

By contrast New York State *has* adopted an OSHA-approved state plan which covers *public sector employers*, which is embodied in the New York Public Employee Safety and Health ("PESH") plan. PESH is overseen by the New York Division of Safety and Health (DOSH), which enforces OSHA standards at state and local government workplaces (including state, county, town, and village governments; state and local government authorities, including school districts, and paid and volunteer fire departments; etc.). PESH does not have jurisdiction over private sector employers.

DOSH is part of the New York State Department of Labor Worker Protection Bureau, and oversees PESH and eight other specific safety programs which do include private sector employers; as follows:

---

138   29 U.S.C. §§ 651–678.

139   29 C.F.R. Pts. 1902–2400.

140   In the absence of an OSHA-approved state plan, any New York State law that attempted to regulate any area covered by an OSHA regulation or standard would likely be preempted by federal law. *See Gade v. National Solid Wastes Mgmt. Ass'n,* 505 U.S. 88, 98 (1992) *(OSHA* "pre-empts all state 'occupational safety and health standards relating to any occupational safety or health issue with respect to which a federal standard has been promulgated'" *Id.* (citing 29 U.S.C. § 667(b)).

[5.39.1] *The Industry Inspection Bureau (IIB)*

The IIB enforces regulations for the protection of the public in specific subject matter areas, including amusement rides, certain grandstands, tents and bleachers, places of public assembly, passenger tramways/ski lifts, storage of explosives, certain types of coin-operated machines, the installation/maintenance of elevators in factories and stores, and window cleaning. By way of example, a few of the more common areas of IIB safety regulation and enforcement include the following:

- Inspections to ensure compliance with inspection requirements for elevators and escalators in factory and mercantile establishments.

- Inspections to ensure window cleaning equipment meets the design and safety standards and also investigates accidents involving window cleaning equipment.

- Regulation and inspection of coin-operated machines that perform a manufacturing process (e.g., clothes washing and drying).

- Regulation and inspection of ski areas and investigation of accidents involving skiers and snowboarders.[141]

[5.39.2] *The License and Certification Unit*

The DOSH License and Certification (L&C) Unit issues licenses and certificates in the following safety-sensitive jobs and industries: Asbestos Certificate of Competence; Asbestos Handling License; Crane Operator's Certificate of Competence; Blaster's Certificate of Competence; Explosives Dealer/Manufacturer License; Explosives Purchase/Own/Possess/Transport License; and Pyro-technician Certificate of Competence. The L&C Unit also certifies safety consultants and specialists who provide consultation and evaluation services to employers who are participating in safety and loss prevention programs pursuant to WCL § 134. One of these prevention programs, known as Industrial Code Rule 59, requires a comprehensive safety and loss prevention consultation and evaluation for any employer with either: (1) an annual payroll of over $800,000; or (2) a workers' compensation experience modification rating of more than 1.20.[142] Another prevention program is a voluntary program known as

---

141   A complete list can be found at https://labor.ny.gov/workerprotection/safetyhealth/DOSH_INDEX.shtm.

142   *See* § 5.39.6 below.

Industrial Code Rule 60, which can result in reduced workers compensation costs for self-insured employers or insured employers with an experience rating of less than 1.30 and an annual workers' compensation premium of at least $5,000.

[5.39.3] *The Asbestos Control Unit*

The Asbestos Control Bureau is charged with protecting the public against toxic hazards from asbestos fiber exposure associated with the demolition, rehabilitation, and renovation of buildings and other structures containing asbestos. The Bureau enforces Industrial Code Rule 56 which regulates the demolition, rehabilitation and renovation of buildings and other structures containing asbestos.

[5.39.4] *The Boiler Safety Bureau*

The Boiler Safety Bureau is responsible for the inspection of all high-pressure boilers and all low-pressure boilers (except those located in dwellings of less than six families). In accordance with Industrial Code Rules 4 and 14, inspections for high-pressure boilers are required each year and for low-pressure boilers every other year.

[5.39.5] *The Mine Safety Training Program*

The Mine Safety Training Program provides safety instruction to mining employees in New York State. The program is funded by a grant through the federal Mine Safety and Health Administration (MHSA). The training is specific to guidelines and regulations issued by MSHA which cover mining operations.[143]

[5.39.6] *The Workplace Safety and Loss Prevention Program (WSLPP)*

The WSLPP oversees and enforces Industrial Code Rule 59 which requires a comprehensive safety and loss prevention consultation and evaluation for any employer with: (i) an annual payroll of over $800,000; or (ii) a workers' compensation experience modification rating of more than 1.20.[144] Employers which receive notice of their required participation are subject to the following deadlines and requirements:

- Within 30 days from receipt of the notice, the employer must make an appointment for a consultation and evaluation;

---

143   30 C.F.R. Pt. 46.

144   *See* § 5.39.2 above.

- Within 10 days after making the appointment, the employer must tell its insurer and the Labor Department (by letter, email, or fax) the date of the evaluation and the name, address, and Certification Number of the Consultant who will do it;

- The consultation and evaluation must be completed within 75 days.

- A Safety and Loss Prevention Consultant certified by the L&C Unit must complete the consultation.

The WSLPP also oversees the workers' compensation incentive program created by *Industrial Code Rule 60*. Under this voluntary program, employers may apply to the Department of Labor for a discount in their workers' compensation costs if they establish one or more of the following programs: (i) a safety program; (ii) a drug and alcohol prevention program; or (iii) a return to work program. The program is for employers insured through the State Insurance Fund (except those in a recognized safety group) or any other insurer that issues policies for workers' compensation. Employers may apply if they:

(i)   pay an annual premium of at least $5,000;

(ii) maintain an experience rating of under 1.30;

(iii) do not have a mandatory safety and loss program due to a high experience rating; and

(iv) implement any of the three voluntary programs.

Approved employers can receive a credit to their workers' compensation insurance premium or security deposit for an initial credit period of three years.

[5.39.7] *The Hazard Abatement Board*

The Hazard Abatement Board is a five-member board appointed by the Governor. It awards grants for programs that provide safety and health training for public and private employers, labor unions, educational institutions, non-profit organizations, and trade associations.

[5.39.8] *The On-Site Consultation Program*

The On-Site Consultation Program is a resource for safety and health issues that is free to businesses. The services available to employers include: on-site consultation surveys to identify safety hazards; industrial hygiene surveys to determine air contaminant or noise exposure levels and other health hazards; and suggestions for mitigation, controlling or eliminating these safety and health hazards.

[5.40]   Drugs, Alcohol, Tobacco and Weapons in the Workplace

See generally Chapters 8, 11 and 12 of this book.

[5.40.1] *Drug testing*[145]

New York does not restrict a private employer's decision to conduct pre-hire, post-accident and/or random drug testing. However, an employer cannot simply use over-the-counter tests. Testing must be conducted by a licensed laboratory.[146] Employers who want to conduct *on-site testing* must apply for and be granted a Limited Service Laboratory Registration certificate pursuant to Public Health Law § 579 before conducting on-site testing.

The penalty for conducting unauthorized testing is significant:

> Any person, partnership, corporation or other entity performing waived tests or provider-performed microscopy procedures without being authorized to do so pursuant to this title shall be subject to a civil penalty of up to five hundred dollars for each test performed, not to exceed two thousand dollars per day for each day tests are performed, in violation of this subdivision.[147]

[5.40.2] *Smoking in the workplace*

Article 13-E of New York's Public Health Law, also known as the Clean Indoor Air Act, prohibits smoking and vaping in almost all private sector workplaces, including restaurants and bars. The purpose of the Act is to

---

145   *See* Chapter 1 at §§ 1.33–1.34, Chapter 7 at § 7.26, and Chapter 11 at § 11.45.

146   Public Health Law § 579(3)(h).

147   *Id.*

protect workers and the public from exposure to harmful secondhand tobacco smoke and vaping aerosols.[148]

[5.40.3] *Weapons in the workplace*

New York does not have any specific laws that restrict an employer's ability to prohibit employees from storing firearms in cars parked in a company parking lot or to prohibit employees from carrying firearms into the workplace.

[5.41] What is the New York "Scaffold Law"?

Labor Law § 240 (known as "the Scaffold Law") is one of the most frequent sources of litigation in the New York courts and provides, in relevant part, as follows:

> All contractors and owners and their agents . . . in the erection, demolition, repairing, altering, painting, cleaning or pointing of a building or structure shall furnish or erect, or cause to be furnished or erected for the performance of such labor, scaffolding, hoists, stays, ladders, slings, hangers, blocks, pulleys, braces, irons, ropes, and other devices which shall be so constructed, placed and operated as to give proper protection to a person so employed.[149]

The Scaffold Law "imposes liability even on contractors and owners who had nothing to do with the plaintiff's accident, and where a violation of the statute has caused injury, any fault by the plaintiff contributing to that injury is irrelevant."[150] The Legislature, however, afforded this extraordinary protection only to workers "employed" in the "erection, demolition, repairing, altering, painting, cleaning or pointing of a building or structure."[151]

---

148   *See* Chapter 12 at § 12.8.

149   Labor Law § 240(1).

150   *Dahar v. Holland Ladder & Mfg. Co.*, 18 N.Y.3d 521, 941 N.Y.S.2d 31 (2012).

151   *Joblon v. Solow*, 91 N.Y.2d 457, 672 N.Y.S.2d 286 (1998) (emphasis in original) (citing Labor Law § 240(1)).

CHAPTER SIX

DISABILITY, HEALTH, AND LIFE INSURANCE BENEFITS

Daniel J. Nugent
Stephen C. Daley
Thaddeus J. Lewkowicz

Edited by Thomas G. Eron

CHAPTER OVERVIEW

In this chapter, we consider short-term disability benefits (which must be provided by "covered employers"); long-term disability benefits (which are not required); health coverage (which is not required under state law, but is nonetheless subject to significant requirements); and provide a brief overview of requirements under federal law that may apply to employers providing these benefits.

Specific questions considered are as follows:

I.   SHORT-TERM DISABILITY BENEFITS

[6.1]   Are employers required to provide short-term disability benefits for their employees?

[6.2]   What employees are eligible to receive short-term disability?

[6.3]   What employment relationships are exempt from the short-term disability requirements?

[6.4]   What types of disabilities are covered by short-term disability?

[6.5]   How long must an employee be disabled to qualify for short-term disability benefits?

[6.6]   Are short-term disability benefits available to ex-employees?

[6.7]   What are the benefits payable for short-term disability?

[6.8]   For how long is an employee entitled to short-term disability benefits?

[6.9]   What will disqualify a claimant from receiving disability benefits?

[6.10] Can an employee receive short-term disability benefits and unemployment insurance benefits at the same time?

[6.11] May an employee waive short-term disability benefits?

[6.12] Are there any notices which must be given to an employee who becomes disabled?

[6.13] How does an employee file a claim for New York's short-term disability benefits?

[6.14] What are the employer's obligations when a disability benefits claim is filed?

[6.15] May an employee be required to undergo a physical examination to support a claim for short-term disability benefits?

[6.16] How soon must New York's short-term disability benefits be paid?

[6.17] Who must pay for the cost of disability insurance?

[6.18] How can an employer meet its obligation to provide short-term disability coverage?

I.   SHORT-TERM DISABILITY BENEFITS

[6.1]   Are employers required to provide short-term disability benefits for their employees?

The New York Workers' Compensation Law provides that all *private-sector* employers (with some specific exceptions discussed in § 6.3 below) must, if they have employed one or more employees in New York State on each of at least 30 days in any calendar year, provide short-term disability benefits for its employees after the expiration of four weeks following the 30th day of such employment.[1]

---

1   WCL §§ 2, 202(1).

It is worth noting at the outset that *public-sector* employers in New York State are *not* required to provide short-term disability benefits.

An employer of personal or domestic employees in a private home is required to provide short-term disability benefits for its employees *if* the employer employs at least one employee who works 40 or more hours per week for that employer.[2]

Any employer that, by operation of law, becomes a successor to a covered employer or that acquires by purchase or otherwise the trade or business of a covered employer automatically becomes a covered employer, and is required to provide short-term disability benefits for its employees.[3]

Short-term disability coverage does not cover work-related injuries or illnesses. Coverage for work-related injuries or illnesses is covered in Chapter 5 of this book.

[6.2] What employees are eligible to receive short-term disability benefits?

Full-time employees who are employed by a covered employer for four or more consecutive weeks are eligible to receive short-term disability benefits.[4]

Part-time employees are eligible to receive short-term disability benefits on the 25th day of regular employment with a covered employer.[5]

An employee who has previously completed four or more consecutive weeks in employment with a covered employer and who returns to work with that same covered employer after an agreed and specified unpaid leave of absence or vacation without pay becomes eligible for benefits immediately upon return to that employment.[6]

---

2   WCL § 202(2).

3   WCL § 202(4).

4   WCL § 203.

5   *Id.*

6   *Id.*

[6.3]   **What employment relationships are exempt from the short-term disability requirements?**

As noted in § 6.1 above, employers of personal or domestic employees in a private home are exempt from New York's short-term disability requirements if those employees do not work at least 40 hours per week.[7]

In addition, short-term disability benefits do not need to be provided to employees in any of the following employment relationships:

- the minor children of an employer;

- a priest, a rabbi, a sexton, a Christian Science reader, a member of a religious order, or a duly ordained, commissioned, or licensed minister;

- an executive officer or an officer of a corporation who at all times during the period involved owns *all* of the issued and outstanding stock of such corporation;

- an executive officer of an incorporated religious, charitable or educational institution;

- persons engaged in a professional or teaching capacity, volunteers, persons participating in and receiving rehabilitative services in a sheltered workshop under a certificate issued by the United States Department of Labor, or recipients of charitable aid who perform work in, or for, an institution that is incidental to or in return for the aid conferred and not under an express contract of hire, in, or for, or operated by, a religious, charitable, or educational institution;

- persons performing services for New York State, a municipal corporation, a local government agency, or other political subdivision or public authority;

- persons employed under the federal Railroad Unemployment Insurance Act;[8]

- persons performing services as officers or crew members of vessels on navigable waters inside or outside the United States;

---

7   WCL § 202(2).

8   45 U.S.C. §§ 351 *et seq.*

- persons performing services as farm laborers;

- persons engaged in casual employment, and the first 45 days of extra employment of employees not regularly in employment;

- persons performing services as golf caddies;

- students performing service during all or any part of a school year or regular vacation periods as a part-time worker, if they are in regular attendance during the daytime as students in an elementary or secondary school; or

- if certain requirements are met, the services of a licensed real estate broker or sales associate, licensed insurance agent or broker, or media sales representative.[9]

Independent contractors are *not* employees and, therefore, are not eligible for short-term disability benefits.[10]

[6.4] What types of disabilities are covered by short-term disability?

New York's short-term disability benefits cover injuries or sickness occurring while the employee is employed that do *not* arise out of and in the course of employment, but that render the employee unable to perform either (a) the regular duties of his or her employment, or (b) the duties of any other employment that the employer may offer the employee at the employee's regular wages.[11]

Pregnancy is considered a disability covered by New York's short-term disability requirements.[12]

The disabilities that arise during periods of unemployment are discussed in § 6.6 below.

---

9   WCL §§ 201(5), 201(6)(a), 201(6)(d).

10   The Workers' Compensation Board has published a guide entitled *Who Is An Employee Under the Disability Benefits Law?* which is available at http://www.wcb.ny.gov/content/main/ DisabilityBenefits/Employer/employeeDef.jsp. *See also* Chapter 12 of this book at § 12.1 for a general discussion of independent contractor status.

11   WCL § 201(9)(a).

12   WCL § 201(9)(b).

[6.5]   How long must an employee be disabled to qualify for short-term disability benefits?

Employees become eligible to receive New York's short-term disability benefits on the eighth consecutive day of disability.[13]

[6.6]   Are short-term disability benefits available to former employees?

A former employee will continue to be eligible for short-term disability benefits for a period of four weeks after his or her employment with a covered employer ends, regardless of whether he or she performs any work for remuneration or profit in non-covered employment.[14] If, during that four-week period, the employee performs any work for a *different* covered employer, then he or she immediately becomes eligible for disability benefits with respect to that employment.[15]

If a terminated employee's disability first begins *during* the first four weeks after he or she leaves employment, then the employee's last covered employer (or that employer's insurance carrier) is responsible for paying the employee's short-term disability benefits just as if the employee became disabled while employed.[16]

If a terminated employee's disability begins *more* than four weeks after he or she leaves employment, and the terminated employee is entitled to unemployment insurance benefits, then the employee is entitled to receive short-term disability benefits directly from the State Fund.[17]

A terminated employee who becomes ineligible for benefits being claimed under the unemployment insurance law solely because of disability during a period of unemployment within 26 weeks immediately following such termination of employment is eligible for short-term disability benefits for each week of disability during which he or she would have received unemployment insurance benefits had there been no disability if:

---

13   WCL § 204(1).

14   WCL § 203.

15   *Id.*

16   *See* WCL § 203.

17   *See* WCL §§ 207(1), 207(3).

- the employee's employment was terminated by a covered employer;

- the only reason the employee could not receive unemployment benefits for 26 weeks after the termination was that he or she was disabled; and

- on the day his or her disability commences, the employee is not employed or working for remuneration or profit and is not otherwise eligible for job-related Workers' Compensation Benefits.[18]

A terminated employee is eligible for short-term disability benefits during a period of unemployment within 26 weeks immediately following such termination of employment even if he or she would *not* have been eligible for unemployment insurance benefits if all of the following conditions are met:

- the employee's employment with a covered employer is terminated;

- the employee was employed by one or more covered employers in each of 20 calendar weeks during the 30 calendar weeks immediately preceding the date he or she last worked for such covered employer and was paid wages of at least 13 dollars in such employment in each of those weeks;

- the employee is not eligible for unemployment insurance benefits because of a lack of qualifying wages;

- the employee has evidenced his or her continued attachment to the labor market during unemployment; and

- the employee is not employed or working for remuneration or profit and is not otherwise eligible for job-related Workers' Compensation Benefits.[19]

A terminated employee who becomes disabled and continues to be disabled for at least eight consecutive days, and who meets the eligibility criteria set forth above, will be entitled to receive short-term disability benefits beginning with the eighth consecutive day of that disability for each week of continuing disability thereafter.[20]

---

18   WCL § 207(1).

19   WCL § 207(2).

20   *Id.*

[6.7]   What are the benefits payable for short-term disability?

Under New York's short-term disability law, covered employers are required only to provide cash payment disability benefits.[21] The weekly cash disability benefit for a disabled employee is 50% of the employee's weekly wage, up to $170.00 per week.[22]

[6.8]   For how long is an employee entitled to short-term disability benefits?

Short-term disability benefits are paid for a maximum of 26 weeks of disability in any 52-consecutive-week period.[23]

[6.9]   What will disqualify a claimant from receiving disability benefits?

Any one or more of the following facts can make short-term disability benefits unavailable:

- The disabled employee is not under the care of a doctor;

- The disability is caused by the willful intention of the employee to bring about the injury or sickness, or the injury or sickness was sustained during the perpetration of an illegal act by the employee;

- The employee is being paid to perform work;

- The employee is entitled to receive payments from his or her employer, or from a fund to which the employer has contributed, in an amount equal to or greater than the amount of the short-term disability benefits;

- The employee is subject to suspension or disqualification of the accumulation of unemployment insurance benefit rights, or would be subject if he or she were eligible for such benefit rights, except for ineligibility resulting from the employee's disability;

---

21   WCL § 204(2).

22   *Id.*

23   WCL § 205(1)(a).

- The employee's disability has been caused by an act of war, declared or undeclared; or

- The disability commenced before the employee first became eligible for short-term disability benefits.[24]

[6.10] Can an employee receive short-term disability benefits and unemployment insurance benefits at the same time?

No. Disability benefits are not payable with respect to any week for which payments are received under any of the following:

- The Unemployment Insurance Law;

- The Volunteer Firefighters' Benefit law;

- Any other workers' compensation act, occupational disease act, or similar law;

- Any employers' liability act or similar law;

- Any other temporary disability or cash sickness benefits act or similar law;

- The federal Employers' Liability Act; or

- The maritime doctrine of maintenance, wages, and cure.[25]

[6.11] May an employee waive short-term disability benefits?

Generally not. With the one specific exception discussed in the paragraph below, an agreement by an employee to waive his or her rights to short-term disability benefits is invalid and unenforceable.[26]

However, an employee who is receiving or is entitled to receive old-age insurance benefits under the Social Security Act *may* waive short-term disability benefits by filing a waiver with the Chair of the Workers' Compensation Board and with his or her employer. An employee filing such a

---

24   WCL §§ 205(1)(b), 205(3).

25   WCL § 206(1).

26   WCL § 218(1).

waiver does not have to contribute to the cost of any short-term disability benefits, and his or her employer is relieved from any responsibility to provide short-term disability payments for that employee.[27]

[6.12] Are there any notices that must be given to an employee who becomes disabled?

Yes. When an employee is eligible for short-term disability benefits and has been absent from work due to a disability for more than seven consecutive days, the employer must provide the employee with a written statement of the employee's rights to short-term disability benefits.[28] This statement must be provided within five business days after the employee's seventh consecutive day of absence due to disability, or within five business days after the employer has received notice that the employee's absence is due to disability, whichever is later.[29]

The written statement of the employee's rights is provided by the NYS Workers' Compensation Board in form DB-271S.[30]

[6.13] How does an employee file a claim for short-term disability benefits?

Written notice, proof of disability, and a claim for short-term disability benefits must be given to the employer by, or on behalf of, the employee (or, in the case of a claimant who has been unemployed for more than four weeks, notice must be given to the Chair of the Workers' Compensation Board) within 30 days after the start of the disability.[31] The employer or its insurance carrier (or the Chair of the Workers' Compensation Board) may require additional proof of disability from the employee, but not more often than once per week.[32]

---

27   WCL § 235.

28   WCL § 229(2).

29   *Id.*

30   *See* Workers' Compensation Board, Statement of Rights (May 2019), http://www.wcb.ny.gov/content/main/forms/db271s.pdf.

31   WCL § 217(1).

32   *Id.*

The claim form is Form DB-450.[33] The written notice, proof of disability, and claim must also include a statement of disability from the claimant's attending physician.[34]

[6.14] What are the employer's obligations when a disability benefits claim is filed?

The employer must provide the statement of employee rights discussed in § 6.12 above. The employer is entitled to investigate the claim, require additional information, and potentially reject the claim. However, if either the employer or the employer's disability carrier rejects the claim, then the employer (or carrier, as the case may be) is required to send a written notice of rejection to the employee by first class mail within 45 days of receipt of the employee's original claim.[35] Failure to mail the notice of rejection within the required time period precludes the employer (or carrier) from contesting the employee's eligibility for short-term disability benefits, unless it is shown that it was not reasonably possible to have done so and that the notice was mailed as soon as possible.[36]

[6.15] May an employee be required to undergo a physical examination to support a claim for short-term disability benefits?

Yes. An employee claiming short-term disability benefits must, if requested by the employer or insurance carrier, periodically submit (but not more often than once a week) to an examination by a physician, podiatrist, chiropractor, dentist, psychologist, or certified nurse midwife designated by the employer or carrier.[37]

In addition, in cases where (a) the claim for short-term disability is being contested, (b) the claimant becomes disabled after more than four weeks of unemployment, or (c) in other cases as the Chair of the Workers' Compensation Board may require, the Chair may direct the claimant to submit to an examination by a health care provider designated by the Chair.[38]

---

33   *See* http://www.wcb.ny.gov/content/main/forms/db450.pdf.

34   WCL § 217(1).

35   WCL § 217(6).

36   *Id.*

37   WCL § 217(2).

38   WCL § 217(3).

Any required medical examination shall be without cost to the employee and shall be held at reasonable times and places.[39]

If a claimant refuses to submit to any required physical examination without good cause, then he or she shall be disqualified from receiving any short-term disability benefits, except as to benefits already paid.[40]

[6.16] How soon must New York's short-term disability benefits be paid?

The first payment of short-term disability benefits is due on the 14th day of disability, and benefits for that period are to be paid directly to the employee within four business days thereafter, or within four business days after the filing of required proof of claim, whichever is later. After that, benefits are due and payable biweekly.[41]

[6.17] Who must pay for the cost of disability insurance?

Both employers and employees must contribute, although the employee contribution is essentially *de minimis.*

Every covered employee is supposed to contribute to the cost of providing short-term disability benefits, with the contribution computed as 0.5% of the employee's wages, up to a limit of $0.60 per week (which comes out to $31.20 per year).[42] The employer may collect employee contributions through payroll deductions.[43]

If the employer fails to make the deduction for an applicable payroll period, the employer may, within one month thereafter, deduct from payroll for the missed contribution.[44]

---

39   WCL § 217(2).

40   WCL § 217(4).

41   WCL § 208(1). The Chair of the Workers' Compensation Board may determine that short-term disability benefits are to be paid monthly or semi-monthly if wages were paid on a monthly basis. *Id.*

42   WCL §§ 209(1), 209(3).

43   WCL § 209(4).

44   *Id.*

Every covered employer shall contribute the additional cost of providing short-term disability benefits if the cost of the coverage is in excess of the contributions collected from its employees.[45]

[6.18] How can an employer meet its obligation to provide short-term disability coverage?

A covered employer has the following options:

- Purchasing coverage directly from the State Insurance Fund;

- Purchasing short-term disability insurance from a stock or mutual corporation or reciprocal insurer authorized to transact the business of accident and health insurance in New York State; or

- Through self-insurance, after furnishing satisfactory proof to the Chair of the Workers' Compensation Board of the employer's financial ability to pay such short-term disability benefits.[46]

If a covered employer chooses the third option above (i.e., self-insurance), it will be required to make a security deposit with Workers' Compensation Board in an amount deemed necessary by the Chair to comply with the Workers' Compensation Laws.[47]

[6.19] What happens if an employer fails to meet its obligations with respect to short-term disability coverage?

A failure to make provision to cover short-term disability benefits within 10 days of the time that an employer becomes a covered employer (*see* § 6.1, *supra*) is a misdemeanor punishable by a fine of between $100 and $500 or imprisonment for not more than one year, or both a fine and imprisonment.[48] Where the employer is a corporation, the president, secretary, and treasurer (or officers exercising corresponding functions) are individually liable for these penalties.[49]

In addition, upon making a finding that an employer has failed to make provision for the payment of short-term disability benefits, the Workers'

---

45   WCL § 210.

46   WCL § 211(1)–(3).

47   WCL § 211(3).

48   WCL § 220(1).

49   *Id.*

Compensation Board *shall* impose a penalty on the employer in an amount up to 0.5% of the employer's weekly payroll for the period of such failure, and *may* impose an additional penalty of up to $500.[50]

Additionally, when a covered employer fails to provide for the payment of short-term disability benefits, any employee entitled to benefits will be paid directly from the State Fund, and the employer will be required to reimburse the State Fund in an amount computed as the *greater* of (a) the amount paid to the employee, or (b) 1% of the employer's payroll for its employees in employment during the period of non-compliance, which-ever is greater.[51]

[6.20] How do New York's short-term disability benefits coordinate with other disability benefits?

New York's short-term disability benefits will generally be offset by dis-ability benefits *other than* disability benefits under a veteran's disability program or a permanent disability policy or program of an employer for whom the employee has performed services.[52] Additionally, there is no such offset against short-term disability benefits if the claim for short-term disability benefits is based on a disability other than the permanent disabil-ity for which the permanent disability benefit or annuity was granted.[53]

II.   LONG-TERM DISABILITY BENEFITS

[6.21] Are employers in New York required to provide long-term disability benefits for their employees?

No. Although New York State requires employers to provide short-term disability benefits for a period of up to 26 weeks, employers are *not* required to provide long-term disability benefits (i.e., disability benefits for a period exceeding 26 weeks).

If a New York employer provides insured long-term disability benefits, those benefits must comply with applicable New York Insurance Law requirements.[54]

---

50   WCL § 220(2).

51   WCL § 213(1). However, if the Chair of the Workers' Compensation Board is satisfied that the employer's non-compliance of the employer was inadvertent, the penalties may be reduced. *Id.*

52   WCL § 206(1)(a).

53   *Id.*

54   Ins. Law § 1113(a)(3).

Further, the New York Labor Law requires employers to give written notice to any employee who is terminated from employment of the date of cancellation of long-term disability benefits (as well as any other benefits). The notice must be provided within five working days after the date the employee is terminated.[55]

III. HEALTH INSURANCE REQUIREMENTS

[6.22] Are employers in New York required to provide health benefits for employees?

No. New York State does not require private employers to maintain health coverage for their employees, but most larger New York employers do provide such coverage. In addition, the federal Patient Protection and Affordable Care Act of 2010 ("Affordable Care Act") imposes penalties on employers that do not provide "affordable coverage" for employees; however, the requirements of the Affordable Care Act are beyond the scope of this book.

While New York State does not require health coverage, it does impose requirements when coverage is provided.

[6.23] What are the significant New York requirements that apply to group health insurance benefits that an employer provides to its employees?

The New York Insurance Law imposes numerous requirements on health insurance policies issued in New York. Among these requirements are several mandated types of medical coverage, and these mandates have increased the costs of health insurance policies for New York employers. Some employers in New York have elected to self-fund or self-insure their health plans in order to avoid the mandates applicable to insurance plans.

Among the types of mandates that apply to health insurance policies in New York are:

- **Extension of Health Continuation Coverage Requirements.** An extension of health continuation coverage is provided for eligible employees and dependents losing employer-provided medical

---

55   Labor Law § 195(6).

insurance coverage, from 18 months for employees to 36 months for employees' dependents, regardless of the size of the employer.[56]

- **Coverage for Unmarried Children Through Age 29.** New York health insurers are required to allow an employee's unmarried child to elect coverage through age 29, even if that child is not financially dependent upon a parent, as long as that child lives, works, or resides in New York or the service area of the insurer and is not eligible for another medical plan or Medicare.[57]

- **Coverage Requirements for Dependent Children and Grand-children.** There are special requirements applicable to dependent children and grandchildren for New York health insurance policies regarding which dependent children and grandchildren must be covered; for example, a prohibition on denying enrollment of a child under the health coverage of the child's parent on the ground that the child was born out of wedlock, was not claimed as a dependent on the parent's tax return, or does not reside with the parent or in the insurer's service area.[58]

- **Requirements Regarding Coverages for Women and Children.** There are requirements for New York health insurance policies regarding the types of health coverage that must be provided for women and children, including maternity care, mastectomy care, post-mastectomy reconstruction, mammography screening, donor human breast milk, and autism spectrum disorder treatment.[59]

- **Other Requirements Regarding the Types of Health Insurance Coverage That Must Be Offered.** There are requirements regarding several other types of health coverages that must be offered, including, but not limited to, preventive care and screenings, enumerated cancer screenings and treatments, diabetes care, enumerated alcohol and drug abuse treatments, enumerated mental health coverages, infertility, home health care, preadmission testing, sec-

---

56   Ins. Law §§ 3221(m), 4305(e). This is the New York version of federal "COBRA" continuation coverage, which entitles employees to continue their own health and hospitalization benefits, and coverage for their dependents, provided that the employee can be required to pay the actual premium cost of the continuation coverage plus a 2% administrative fee.

57   Ins. Law §§ 4235(f)(1)(B), 4304(d)(1)(B), 4305(c)(1)(B).

58   Ins. Law §§ 2608-a, 4305(c)(1), 4235(f)(1).

59   Ins. Law §§ 3221, 4303.

ond surgical opinions, emergency services, enteral formulas, chiropractic care, certain experimental or investigational services, bone mineral density tests and treatments, out-of-network dialysis, contraceptive drugs and devices, nursing home care, ambulatory care, hospice care, and out-of-network benefits.[60]

New York also requires small health insurance plans covering from one to 100 employees to use "community rating" when setting premiums, which can make these plans more expensive than "experience-rated" plans which look to a more limited pool of covered persons.[61]

When an employee is "separated from employment," New York employers must provide written notice of the cancellation of group health insurance benefits (as well as other benefits) connected with the employee's termination, and the notice must be provided within five working days after the date the employee's employment is terminated.[62]

IV. LIFE INSURANCE

[6.24] Are employers in New York required to provide life insurance benefits for their employees?

No. New York State does not require private employers to provide employees with life insurance benefits.

[6.25] If an employer provides group term life insurance benefits to its employees, what are the important New York requirements that apply to those benefits?

If an employer in New York provides group life insurance benefits to its employees, the insurance must comply with the requirements of N.Y. Insurance Law §§ 3220 and 4216 with respect to matters such as employer contributions, coverage, incontestability, and conversion right requirements.

When an employee is separated from employment, a New York employer is required to provide written notice of the cancellation of group life insurance benefits (as well as any other benefits, including accident and

---

60 Ins. Law §§ 3221, 3241(b), 4303.

61 Ins. Law §§ 3231(a), 4317(a).

62 Labor Law § 195(6). This requirement is in addition to any notices which may be required under federal law, such as notice of the right under COBRA to continue health insurance for the employee and his or her dependents.

health insurance) connected with the employee's termination, and such notice must be provided within five working days after the date the employee's employment is terminated.[63]

V.   FEDERAL BENEFIT REQUIREMENTS

[6.26] Overview of the interplay between New York and federal law

While the subject of this book is New York law, employers need to be aware that the employee benefits either must or may be provided under New York law may also be subject to federal laws creating additional obligations. This section presents a general overview and is by no means intended to be a comprehensive enumeration or treatment. Compliance with federal requirements should be informed by legal counsel and/or financial advisors familiar with applicable tax and Employee Retirement Income Security Act (ERISA).[64]

Federal benefit requirements derive from a variety of sources, such as the Affordable Care Act,[65] ERISA (which includes the Consolidated Omnibus Budget Reconciliation Act of 1985, or COBRA), the Internal Revenue Code, the Health Insurance Portability and Accountability Act of 1996 (HIPAA),[66] and various other federal laws.

In some instances, New York law may be preempted by federal law, which is the case with ERISA. In other instances, New York requirements exceed federal requirements. Accordingly, an analysis is required to determine whether federal law, New York law, or a combination of the two apply to the benefits being offered. For example, ERISA will preempt the New York short-term disability law unless an exemption applies (such as a regulatory exemption for payroll practices or a statutory exemption for a plan that is maintained solely for the purpose of complying with applicable workers' compensation or disability insurance laws). If ERISA preempts New York law, then various ERISA requirements must be met.

Employers offering disability, group health, and group life insurance benefits in New York also need to consider the various tax consequences under the Internal Revenue Code. Taxation of these benefits will depend on,

---

63   Labor Law § 195(6).

64   29 U.S.C. §§ 1001–1461.

65   42 U.S.C. §§ 18001 *et seq.*

66   42 U.S.C. §§ 1302d *et seq.*

among other factors, who pays the premiums for the benefits offered and whether the benefits satisfy "nondiscrimination coverage" requirements.[67]

There are other federal requirements to consider when providing disability, group health, and group life insurance benefits in New York. Among the more important of these other federal benefit requirements are the following:

- **Employment Law Discrimination Prohibitions**. Benefits should be provided in a manner consistent with federal statutes that preclude employment law discrimination including, but not limited to, the Age Discrimination in Employment Act,[68] the Older Workers Benefit Protection Act,[69] the Americans with Disabilities Act,[70] Title VII of the Civil Rights Act of 1964[71] (including the 1978 Pregnancy Discrimination Act), and the Genetic Information Nondiscrimination Act of 2008.[72] *See generally* Chapter 11 of this book.

- **Requirements for Collectively Bargained Plans**. Several statutes impose requirements that could affect collectively bargained benefit plans, including the National Labor Relations Act of 1935,[73] the Labor Management Relations Act of 1947,[74] and the Labor-Management Reporting and Disclosure Act of 1959.[75]

---

67   In this context, "discrimination" does not refer to discrimination on the basis of race, color, creed, etc.; rather, it refers to benefits which discriminate in favor of higher-paid employees over lower-paid employees.

68   29 U.S.C. § 621–634.

69   29 U.S.C. § 626(f).

70   42 U.S.C. §§ 12101–12213.

71   42 U.S.C. §§ 2000e–2000e-17.

72   122 Stat. 881 (2008).

73   29 U.S.C. §§ 151–169.

74   29 U.S.C. §§ 141–197.

75   29 U.S.C.§§ 401–531.

CHAPTER SEVEN

UNEMPLOYMENT INSURANCE

Mark A. Moldenhauer

Edited by John Gaal

CHAPTER OVERVIEW

In this chapter, we address the scope and application of New York State's requirement that employers participate in a statewide program of unemployment insurance. Specific questions addressed are as follows:

I. WHAT THE UNEMPLOYMENT INSURANCE LAW COVERS

[7.1] What is the New York State unemployment insurance program?

[7.2] What is the relationship between the New York State unemployment insurance program and the federal unemployment insurance program?

[7.3] What do the terms "employment" and "employee" mean for purposes of unemployment insurance?

[7.4] Is "interstate" work covered by the New York Unemployment Insurance Law?

[7.5] Is work performed entirely outside New York covered by the Unemployment Insurance Law?

[7.6] What employers are covered by the Unemployment Insurance Law?

[7.7] Are non-profit organizations covered by the Unemployment Insurance Law?

[7.8] Are corporate officers and directors covered by the Unemployment Insurance Law?

[7.9] Are business partners covered by the Unemployment Insurance Law?

II. HOW EMPLOYERS FUND THE UNEMPLOYMENT INSURANCE PROGRAM

[7.10] How is the New York unemployment insurance program funded?

[7.11] What are employer "contributions" and when are employers liable for them?

[7.12] When and how must employers make contributions?

[7.13] What is a "payment in lieu of contribution"?

[7.14] What happens if an employer fails to make required contributions?

[7.15] How, and when, are employer contribution rates determined?

[7.16] How is an employer's experience rating calculated?

[7.17] What happens when a business changes hands?

III. ELIGIBILITY FOR UNEMPLOYMENT BENEFITS

[7.18] Who is eligible for unemployment insurance benefits?
    [7.18.1] What is the "statutory waiting period?"
    [7.18.2] What is a "valid original claim"?
    [7.18.3] What does it mean to be "able to work and available for work"?
    [7.18.4] When is a claimant subject to disqualification from benefits?
    [7.18.5] What is a claimant's "benefit year"?
    [7.18.6] What is the "base period" and how is it relevant to a claimant's eligibility for benefits?
    [7.18.7] What does it mean to be "totally unemployed"?
    [7.18.8] What about employees of educational institutions during "break" periods?

[7.19] Is a claimant entitled to partial unemployment insurance benefits for part-time work?

[7.20] What impact does the receipt of accrued vacation pay or similar paid time off benefits have on a claimant's eligibility for unemployment insurance benefits?

[7.21] Can a claimant attend school and collect unemployment benefits?

[7.22] Is a claimant eligible for unemployment benefits after retirement?

[7.23] Will dismissal or severance pay affect a claimant's eligibility for unemployment benefits?

[7.24] What is the "Shared-Work Program" and how do employers participate in it?

IV. DISQUALIFICATION FROM RECEIVING UNEMPLOYMENT BENEFITS

[7.25] Under what circumstances will an otherwise eligible claimant be disqualified from receiving, unemployment benefits?
    [7.25.1] What constitutes good cause for leaving employment and still being eligible for unemployment benefits?
    [7.25.2] When is a voluntary separation deemed to be without good cause?

[7.26] What constitutes "misconduct" for purposes of disqualifying a claimant from receiving benefits?

[7.27] Can a claimant's criminal conduct lead to a disqualification from benefits?

I. WHAT THE UNEMPLOYMENT INSURANCE LAW COVERS

[7.1] What is the New York State unemployment insurance program?

The New York State Unemployment Insurance program provides temporary financial benefits to workers who (generally) lose their jobs through no fault of their own. It is intended to provide a level of economic protection to someone who is out of work but seeks to remain in the labor market. Eligible claimants are paid from a state-maintained fund financed by employer contributions made in the form of an unemployment insurance tax on payrolls.

The New York Commissioner of Labor is authorized to make rules and regulations to administer the program and, subject to civil service law requirements, appoint officers and employees in furtherance of that purpose.[1]

Initial determinations as to whether claimants are eligible for unemployment insurance benefits are made by the New York State Department of Labor, Unemployment Division. If a dispute exists as to a claimant's eligibility, a hearing will be held before an administrative law judge appointed by the Commissioner of Labor. Ultimate responsibility for deciding issues of eligibility and employer contribution liability resides with a five-member Unemployment Insurance Appeal Board appointed by the governor. Determination, hearing, and appeal processes are discussed at §§ 7.36–7.40 below.

[7.2]   **What is the relationship between the New York State unemployment insurance program and the federal unemployment insurance program?**

Under the Federal Unemployment Tax Act (FUTA), the federal government imposes an annual unemployment insurance tax on all employers liable to offer unemployment benefits. This amount is in addition to the employer payments required by New York State. Monies from that federal tax are used to administer state unemployment insurance programs, including the New York State Unemployment Insurance program.

The FUTA tax rate is currently 6% of wages up to the first $7,000 in annual wages paid to an employee. However, an employer paying a state unemployment insurance tax receives a credit of up to 5.4% against its FUTA obligation, thus reducing the effective FUTA tax rate to .6%. To receive the full credit for a calendar year, an employer must pay its state contribution in full by January 31 of that calendar year.[2]

[7.3]   **What do the terms "employment" and "employee" mean for purposes of unemployment insurance?**

The term "employment" is defined to mean "any service under any contract of employment for hire, express or implied, written or oral," unless

---

1   Labor Law § 530(1).

2   *Topic No. 759 From 940 – Employer's Annual Federal Unemployment,* Internal Revenue Service (Apr. 13, 2020), https://www.irs.gov/taxtopics/tc759.

specifically excluded by law.[3] It includes services performed on a full-time, part-time, or casual basis.

Independent contractors are not employees covered by unemployment insurance. However, an employer cannot avoid an unemployment insurance obligation by simply classifying a worker as an independent contractor. The important distinction between employees and independent contractors is discussed in Chapter 12 of this book, "Miscellaneous Topics of Interest," at § 12.1.

Several other statutory exclusions exist with respect to the definition of "employment." These include services rendered by: the employer's spouse or child under the age of 21;[4] golf caddies;[5] day students;[6] individuals subject to the Federal Railroad Unemployment Insurance Act;[7] minor babysitters at the home of the employer;[8] persons under the age of 21 engaged in yard work or household chores in a residential setting or on the premises of a non-profit, noncommercial operation, and not involving the use of power-driven machinery;[9] and children under the age of 14.[10] Other exceptions arise with respect to certain work performed by maritime workers, students and students' spouses at educational institutions, college students, students employed by seasonal camps, freelance shorthand reporters, qualified real estate agents, qualified insurance agents or brokers, and newspaper delivery persons.[11] Effective January 1, 2020, the term "employment" expressly includes agricultural labor, including all services performed on a farm or incidental to farming operations.[12]

---

3   Labor Law § 511(1)(a).

4   Labor Law § 511(7).

5   Labor Law § 511(8).

6   Labor Law § 511(9).

7   Labor Law § 511(10).

8   Labor Law § 511(12).

9   Labor Law § 511(13).

10   Labor Law § 511(14).

11   Labor Law §§ 511(11) and 511(15)–511(23).

12   Labor Law § 511(6). Prior to January 1, 2020, agricultural labor was generally excluded from the definition of "employment," unless specifically covered pursuant to Section 564 of the Labor Law.

The enumeration above is not intended to be an exhaustive list of the statutory exceptions to the definition of "employment," or the various circumstances under which those exceptions apply.[13]

[7.4]   Is "interstate" work covered by the New York Unemployment Insurance Law?

If an employee's services are "localized" within New York State, that employee must be covered by the Unemployment Insurance Law even if the work is performed both in and out of New York State.[14] Service is deemed "localized" in New York State if it is performed either entirely within the state, or both inside and outside the state if the portion performed outside the state is incidental to the service inside the state.[15] Work performed outside the state that is temporary or transitory, or that involves isolated transactions, will generally be deemed "incidental" for unemployment insurance coverage purposes.[16]

If an employee's services are not localized in any state, they may still be considered covered "employment" under the Unemployment Insurance Law so long as any services are performed within New York and any of the following apply: (1) the employee's base of operations is in New York; (2) the employee's work is directed or controlled from New York and he or she has no base of operations in any other state where the service is performed; or (3) the employee resides in New York and he or she has no base of operations in, and is not directed or controlled out of, any state where the service is performed.[17]

[7.5]   Is work performed entirely outside New York covered by the Unemployment Insurance Law?

In general, the term "employment" does not include services performed solely outside New York during a calendar year *if* contributions are required under the unemployment insurance law of some other state or by the federal government.[18] However, services performed within the United

---

13   *See generally* Labor Law § 511.

14   Labor Law § 511(2).

15   *Id.*

16   *Id.*

17   Labor Law § 511(3).

18   Labor Law § 511(3).

States, the Virgin Islands or Canada will be considered covered "employment" within New York if: (1) contributions are *not* required with respect to such service by another jurisdiction; and (2) the services are directed or controlled from within New York State.[19]

An employer may elect to provide New York unemployment insurance coverage for work which would not otherwise be covered if: (1) contributions are not required with respect to those services under the laws of a different jurisdiction; (2) the employer makes an application to provide such coverage; and (3) the Commissioner of Labor approves the application in writing.[20]

[7.6]   What employers are covered by the Unemployment Insurance Law?

The Unemployment Insurance Law broadly defines "employer" to include the State of New York, other governmental entities, Indian tribes as defined by Labor Law § 566, "and any person, partnership, firm, association, public or private, domestic or foreign corporation, the legal representatives of a deceased person, or the receiver, trustee, or successor of a person, partnership, firm, association, public or private, domestic or foreign corporation."[21]

Thus, employees of New York State and of public entities in New York (such as counties, cities, towns, villages, school districts, etc.) are covered by the Unemployment Insurance Law.[22] However, specifically *excluded* are: (1) elected officials, members of a legislative body or the judiciary; (2) members of the State National Guard or Air National Guard (except for someone who renders such services as a regular State employee); (3) persons serving on a temporary basis in case of fire, storm, snow, earthquake, flood or similar emergency; (4) persons in a major non-tenured policymaking or advisory position; (5) persons in policymaking or advisory positions when the duties of the position do not ordinarily require more than eight hours per week to perform; or (6) inmates of a custodial or penal institution.[23]

---

19   Labor Law § 511(4)(a).

20   Labor Law § 561(2)(a).

21   Labor Law § 512(1).

22   Labor Law § 565(1).

23   Labor Law § 565(2).

In general, federal public employees are covered by the unemployment laws of the states where they work.[24]

[7.7]   Are non-profit organizations covered by the Unemployment Insurance Law?

Generally, yes. A "non-profit organization" is defined for purposes of the Unemployment Insurance Law as "any corporation, unincorporated association, community chest, fund, or foundations organized and operated exclusively for religious, charitable, scientific, literary or education purposes, no part of the net earnings of which inures to the benefit of any private shareholder or individual."[25]

While non-profit organizations are covered employers, some services rendered for non-profit organizations are excluded from the definition of "employment," including services by:

- A duly ordained, commissioned or licensed minister of a church acting "in the exercise of his [or] her ministry," or by a member of a religious order "in the exercise of duties required by such order";

- A lay member who is elected or appointed to an office within the discipline of a *bona fide* church and engaged in religious functions;

- A person employed at a place of religious worship as a caretaker and/or for the performance of religious duties, unless the employer voluntarily applies to have such services included as employment eligible for benefits and the Commissioner of Labor approves such application;

- A person who receives rehabilitation services in a facility which offers a rehabilitation program for individuals whose earning capacity is impaired by age or a physical or mental condition, or a person who is given "remunerative work" in a facility which exists for purposes of providing such work to individuals with an impaired physical or mental condition who cannot be readily absorbed in the competitive labor market;

- An inmate of a custodial or penal institution; and

---

24   *See* 26 U.S.C. § 3305(b).

25   Labor Law § 563(1).

- A person who participates in a youth service program designed to foster a commitment to community service and occupational and educational development and who, while participating in such a program, performs services in the community or attends school and receives a stipend designed to cover expenses incurred in performing such services or attending school, and who is eligible for an award or scholarship upon leaving the program.[26]

[7.8] Are corporate officers and directors covered by the Unemployment Insurance Law?

In general, officers and directors of a corporation who provide employment-like services are considered to be employees who are eligible for unemployment insurance benefits and as to whom an employer is liable for contributions based on remuneration paid.[27] This is true even if an officer is a shareholder who receives no salary for services he or she performs.[28]

On the other hand, members of a governing board who meet infrequently and act solely in a policy-making capacity are *not* employees entitled to unemployment insurance benefits.[29]

[7.9] Are business partners covered by the Unemployment Insurance Law?

The general partners of a partnership are not employees for unemployment insurance purposes and, thus, are not entitled to benefits.[30] However, a signatory to a partnership agreement who had made no investments in the partnership, had no right to participate in the manage-

---

26   The foregoing list is not exhaustive; *see* Labor Law § 563.2 for a full enumeration.

27   *See In re Regan & Regan, P.C.*, 256 A.D.2d 829, 681 N.Y.S.2d 675 (3d Dep't 1998); *R.S. Smero, Inc. v. Levine*, 51 A.D.2d 273, 381 N.Y.S.2d 337 (3d Dep't 1976); *J.H.H. Voss Co. v. Lubin*, 2 A.D.2d 626 (3d Dep't 1956).

28   *See In re JD Sta. Plaza Realty, Inc.*, 127 A.D.3d 1451, 1452, 7 N.Y.S.3d 673 (3d Dep't 2015) (affirming Unemployment Insurance Appeal Board determination that an S-corporation owed unemployment insurance contributions based on the remuneration paid to its president and sole shareholder who, despite earning no salary, received net income from the corporation); *see also In re Salamanca Nursing Home, Inc.*, 117 A.D.2d 903, 904, 499 N.Y.S.2d 229 (3d Dep't 1986) (affirming determination that payments to stockholders should be treated as wages, since they provided administrative services as corporate officers), *aff'd*, 68 N.Y. 2d 901, 508 N.Y.S.2d 939 (1986).

29   *See In re Manhattan Manor Nursing Home*, 117 A.D.2d 885, 887, 498 N.Y.S.2d 895 (3d Dep't 1986); *In re Baldwinsville Sav. & Loan Ass'n*, 263 App. Div. 895 (3d Dep't 1942).

30   *See In re Heymann*, 192 A.D.2d 861, 596 N.Y.S.2d 532 (3d Dep't 1993).

ment of the partnership, and was paid only for hours worked has been found to qualify for unemployment insurance benefits.[31]

The earnings of sole-proprietors and of members of a limited liability company are not subject to contributions, and such individuals are not eligible to collect unemployment insurance benefits.[32]

II.   HOW EMPLOYERS FUND THE UNEMPLOYMENT INSURANCE PROGRAM

[7.10] How is the New York unemployment insurance program funded?

The Unemployment Insurance Law calls for the establishment of three funds: the Unemployment Insurance Fund, the Unemployment Administration Fund and the Special Fund.[33]

The Unemployment Insurance Fund consists of all contributions, interest and penalties paid into it by operation of the Unemployment Insurance Law, moneys credited to the state pursuant to the Federal Social Security Act, and property and securities acquired through the use of such funds.[34] The primary purpose of the Unemployment Insurance Fund is to finance the payment of benefits to eligible claimants.

The Unemployment Administration Fund covers the expenses associated with administering the Unemployment Insurance Law.[35] It consists of monies received by the State of New York or the Commissioner of Labor for the administration of the Unemployment Insurance Law, as well as monies that may be transferred from the Unemployment Insurance Fund pursuant to the Federal Social Security Act.

The Special Fund consists of, among other things, interest and penalties collected from employers with delinquent contributions.[36] It is used to

---

31   *See In re O'Shea (Cayuga Emergency Physicians, LLP)*, 140 A.D.3d 1358, 33 N.Y.S.3d 551 (3d Dep't 2016).

32   *See* N.Y. Department of Labor, *Covered or Excluded Employment*, https://labor.ny.gov/ui/dande/covered1.shtm.

33   Labor Law §§ 550–552.

34   Labor Law § 550(1)(a).

35   Labor Law § 551(1).

36   Labor Law § 552(1).

fund operations deemed necessary by the Commissioner of Labor for the administration of the Unemployment Insurance Law. It may also be used to finance administrative operations while awaiting federal funds and defray the costs associated with vocational and other training courses.[37]

Other funds have been established in furtherance of the unemployment insurance program. The Re-employment Service Fund is funded by employer contributions equaling .075% of quarterly wage payments and is used to finance the Department of Labor's re-employment service initiatives.[38] The Unemployment Insurance Control Fund consists of penalties collected from employers who file late quarterly withholding reports and unemployment insurance returns.[39] It is used, in part, to identify and prevent fraud and abuse and support collection and enforcement activities.[40]

[7.11] What are employer "contributions" and when are employers liable for them?

"Contributions" is the term used to describe the payments made by covered employers into the Unemployment Employment Insurance Fund, and which will ultimately be used to pay benefits to eligible claimants. An employer must notify the Department of Labor when it first hires employees to allow for its liability status and contribution rate to be determined.

Contributions are based on "wages" paid, which includes "all remuneration" up to a statutorily prescribed amount.[41] "Remuneration" is defined broadly to mean "every form of compensation paid by an employer to his employee," including "salaries, commissions, bonuses, and the reasonable value of board, rent, housing, lodging, or similar advantage received."[42] It also includes gratuities, whether or not received directly

---

37   Labor Law §§ 552(2), 552(3).

38   Labor Law § 552-a(2).

39   Labor Law § 552-b(2).

40   *Id.*

41   Labor Law § 518.1(a). The maximum amount of wages on which contributions are paid is $11,600 as of January 1, 2020, with incremental increases scheduled to occur annually thereafter through January 2026. After 2026, the wage base will adjust on January 1 of each year to 16% of the state's average annual wage, rounded up to the nearest $100.

42   Labor Law § 517(1).

from the employer.[43] However, "remuneration" does *not* include: (1) payments to employees or dependents under a plan or system providing for retirement, sickness or accident disability, or medical or hospitalization expenses for the employee or dependents; (2) payments made by an employer, without payroll deductions, for FICA taxes required from employees; (3) insurance or annuity payments to an employee for retirement; (4) payments on account of sickness or accident disability made by an employer to, or on behalf of, an employee after six months from when the employee last worked; (5) payments from, or to, a trust described in Section 401(a) of the Internal Revenue Code; (6) payments made to employees over the age of 65 for periods in which the employee did not work, other than vacation or sick pay; and (7) dismissal payments. [44]

The triggering date when contributions must begin varies depending on the type of employer:

- In general, a for-profit employer becomes liable for contributions under the Unemployment Insurance Law as of the first day of the calendar quarter in which it pays remuneration totaling $300 or more.[45]

- An employer of domestic or household workers becomes liable for contributions as of the first day of the calendar quarter in which it pays cash remuneration of $500 or more.[46]

- A governmental entity or Indian tribe becomes liable for contributions as of the first day of the calendar quarter in which it pays remuneration to any person in covered employment.[47]

- A non-profit organization becomes liable for contributions as of the first day of either: (1) the calendar quarter in which it pays cash remuneration totaling $1,000 or more; or (2) the calendar year in

---

43   *Id.* If gratuities are received from someone other than the employer, the value of the gratuities will be determined by the Commissioner of Labor and deemed part of the remuneration paid by the employer.

44   Labor Law § 517(2). Notwithstanding any of the exclusions under § 517 of the Labor Law, compensation paid by an employer to an employee is considered "wages" if the employer is liable for a tax on such compensation under FUTA. Labor Law § 518(1)(b).

45   Labor Law § 560(1).

46   *Id.*

47   Labor Law §§ 565(3), 566(3).

which it employs four or more persons on at least one day in each of 20 different weeks during that year or the preceding year.[48]

[7.12] When and how must employers make contributions?

An employer must report its payroll and pay its required unemployment contributions for each calendar quarter on or before to the last day of the month following the close of the quarter during which the wages were paid.[49] If the amount of wages is not determined before the close of the quarter, contributions must be paid on or before the first day of the month following the close of the quarter in which the wages are determined.[50]

Contributions may be paid by cash or check, money order, or draft made payable to the "New York State Unemployment Insurance Fund," and mailed to the New York State Department of Labor, Unemployment Insurance Division, W. Averell Harriman Campus, Unemployment Insurance Division, Employer-Account Adjustment Section, Albany, NY 12240-0425.

[7.13] What is a "payment in lieu of contribution"?

Governmental entities, tax-exempt non-profit organizations and Indian tribes may opt out of the contribution system and instead make a "payment in lieu of contribution" equal to the amount of the benefits actually paid to claimants.[51] In effect, this is "self-insurance." An employer exercising this option must cover all unemployment payments made to its employees, regardless of the amount.

[7.14] What happens if an employer fails to make required contributions?

An employer will be assessed interest at the rate of 1% for each month a contribution payment is late.[52] If the late payment is the result of fraud with intent to avoid payment, a penalty equal to 50% of the deficiency will also be assessed.[53]

---

48 Labor Law § 563(3)(a).

49 12 N.Y.C.R.R. § 472.3.

50 *Id.*

51 Labor Law §§ 563(4), 566(4).

52 Labor Law § 570(3).

53 Labor Law § 570(4).

The following acts or omissions constitute misdemeanors punishable by a fine of not more than $500, up to one-year imprisonment, or both (Labor Law § 630):

- Making a willful false statement or representation which results in the receipt, for oneself or another, of a benefit or payment under the Unemployment Insurance Law, or to reduce the amount of contributions owed;[54]

- Willfully refusing or failing to pay contributions owed;[55]

- Refusing to allow the Department of Labor to inspect payroll or other records or documents relative to the enforcement of the Unemployment Insurance Law;[56] and

- Making deductions from the remuneration owed to an employee in order to cover any portion of the employer's contribution owed.[57]

If a corporation is found guilty of any violation under the Unemployment Insurance Law, its president, secretary, treasurer, or functionally equivalent officer will be found guilty of a misdemeanor.[58]

[7.15] How, and when, are employer contribution rates determined?

In general, the Unemployment Insurance Law sets a "normal" contribution rate which is calculated annually based on an employer's individual experience in the unemployment insurance system. It takes into account various factors, including the amount of wages subject to contributions and the amount of unemployment benefits paid to former employees.[59] In addition, employers are assessed a "subsidiary rate" which varies depending on both the financial status of the State Unemployment Insurance Fund and the employer's experience rating history.[60] Whereas nor-

---

54   Labor Law § 632(1).

55   Labor Law § 633.

56   Labor Law § 634.

57   Labor Law § 635.

58   Labor Law § 631.

59   Labor Law § 570(1).

60   Labor Law § 577(2).

mal contributions are credited against an individual employer account, *see* § 7.16 below, subsidiary contributions are paid into a general account maintained by the State.

Employers are also liable for contributions to the Re-Employment Service Fund, which is discussed at § 7.10 above.[61] Non-profit, governmental, and Indian tribe employers electing to make payments in lieu of contributions are excluded from this additional contribution requirement.[62]

A covered employer must report its wages paid, and remit unemployment insurance contributions to, the New York State Department of Labor each calendar quarter; *see* § 7.12 above. Failure to report wages accurately, and failure to submit contributions on a timely basis, may subject the employer to liability for interest and penalties. It may also cause the employer's contribution rate to be adjusted upward and, ultimately, result in an enforcement action to collect delinquent contributions and penalties.

To qualify for a normal contribution rate based on experience, the employer (or its predecessor) must have: (1) been in the unemployment insurance system for five calendar quarters ending as of the most recent computation date (December 31); and (2) paid some remuneration to employees in the payroll year (October 1 through September 30) preceding that computation date. Newly liable employers which are not qualified for an experience rate are assigned a normal contribution rate, which is fixed each year according to the size of the Unemployment Insurance Fund in an amount not to exceed the statutory maximum of 3.4%.[63] The employer normal contribution rate for 2020 is 2.5%.

[7.16] How is an employer's experience rating calculated?

The Department of Labor's Unemployment Insurance Division establishes an individual account as a bookkeeping device for each employer required to make contributions. An employer's account is used to calculate its "account balance," which, in turn, is used to determine the employer's contribution rate as of December 31 of each year.

Normal contributions paid in a timely manner are credited to the employer's account. Benefits paid to former employees are debited against the account. Contributions not paid in a timely manner (defined as

---

61   Labor Law § 581-b.

62   *Id.*

63   Labor Law § 581(2)(c).

within 60 days after the due date) will not be credited to the employer's account, but rather to a general account established under the Unemployment Insurance Law, and will therefore adversely affect the employer's future contribution rate.[64]

The employer's account balance is divided by its five-year average payroll subject to contribution. If the employer has been liable for less than five years, the average will be computed from the initial date of liability to the end of the last payroll year. The result is referred to as the employer's "account percentage," which, depending on the condition of the Unemployment Insurance Fund, will correspond to a normal rate listed on the Unemployment Insurance rate table.

In general, an employer with a "positive account balance"—meaning that its contribution paid into the unemployment insurance system exceeds the benefits debited against its account—will be assigned a lower contribution rate. An employer with a "negative account balance" will receive a higher contribution rate.

An employer typically has the option of reducing its contribution rate by making non-refundable voluntary payments in addition to its required contributions. However, this option is not available if the employer has not paid all contributions regularly due, has failed to file all required returns, did not make its voluntary payment prior to March 31, or otherwise failed to provide requested information.

[7.17]   What happens when a business changes hands?

When a business operation is transferred, the transferee takes over the original employer's account and experience rating, in proportion to the payroll or number of employees assigned to the transferee organization. This account remains chargeable for benefits paid that are based on employment with the business prior to the transfer.[65]

A transfer will be *not* be deemed to have occurred if the Commissioner of Labor finds that all of the four following conditions have been met: (1) the transferee has *not* assumed any of the transferring employer's obligations; (2) the transferee has *not* acquired any of the transferring employer's goodwill; (3) the transferee has *not* continued or resumed the business of the transferring employer either in the same establishment or

---

64   Labor Law § 581(1)(d).

65   Labor Law § 581(4)(a).

elsewhere; and (4) the transferee has *not* employed substantially the same employees as the transferring employer in connection with the organization, trade, business, or part thereof transferred.[66]

Additionally, no transfer is deemed to have occurred until and unless the transferring employer or the transferee employer has given notice to the Commissioner of Labor before the end of the calendar year following the calendar year when the transfer occurred.[67]

A notice of transfer may be entered on the employer's quarterly contributions report or sent separately to the Liability and Determination Section of the Unemployment Insurance Division. If an employer wants a transfer to be recognized for experience rating purposes, it must give notice of the transfer *prior* to the end of the year following the calendar year in which the transfer occurred. The contribution rates for the transferring employer and transferee will then be determined or re-determined as of December 31 of the preceding year. The new rates will apply to wages paid from the date of the transfer to the end of the calendar year in which the transfer occurred.

III.   ELIGIBILITY FOR UNEMPLOYMENT BENEFITS

[7.18]   Who is eligible for unemployment insurance benefits?

The Unemployment Insurance Law provides cash benefits to claimants who become involuntarily unemployed.[68] To be eligible for benefits, a claimant must satisfy a "statutory waiting period" and submit a "valid original claim" showing that he or she is "totally unemployed." [69] Additionally, a claimant must register with a local unemployment insurance office and satisfy all reporting obligations.[70]

[7.18.1]   *What is the "statutory waiting period"?*

An otherwise eligible claimant must accumulate four "effective days," or the equivalent of one full week of unemployment, before he or she will

---

66   Labor Law § 581.4(c). This finding may be made on the Commissioner's own motion or upon the application of any interested party. *Id.*

67   Labor Law § 581(4)(d).

68   Labor Law § 501.

69   Labor Law § 590. See § 7.18.7 below for the meaning of "total unemployment."

70   Labor Law § 596.

become entitled to benefits.[71] This four-day statutory waiting period can be satisfied by counting effective days accumulated over a single week or multiple weeks.[72]

An "effective day" is accumulated in any Monday-Sunday week during which a claimant had four or more days of "total unemployment," excluding the first three days of total unemployment in that week.[73] Thus, a claimant who has no days of employment in a Monday-Sunday week will accumulate four effective days and satisfy the statutory waiting period based on his or her total unemployment in that week alone. However, a claimant who has two days of employment in a Monday-Sunday week will only accumulate two effective days, and this claimant must accumulate an additional two effective days in subsequent weeks before he or she is entitled to benefits.

[7.18.2] *What is a "valid original claim"?*

In general, a "valid original claim" is a claim filed by a claimant who meets the following four criteria:

- The claimant must be *able* to work and *available* for work;

- The claimant must not be subject to any *disqualification* from benefits;

- The claimant's previously established "benefit year" (if any) must have expired; and

- The claimant must have received the requisite amount of remuneration from employers liable for contributions (or payments in lieu of contributions) during the "base period."[74]

[7.18.3] *What does it mean to be "able to work and available for work"?*

An essential requirement to receive unemployment insurance benefits is that the claimant must be available for work and ready, willing, and able to work in his or her usual employment, or in other employment for which

---

71   Labor Law § 590(7).

72   *Id.*

73   Labor Law § 523.

74   Labor Law § 527.

he or she is reasonably suited by training and experience.[75] The Unemployment Insurance Law expressly requires a claimant to be "actively seeking work," which is defined to mean "engaged in systematic and sustained efforts to find work," in order to be eligible for benefits.[76]

A claimant who is unable to work due to medical restrictions is not eligible for unemployment insurance benefits.[77] However, a different determination may be warranted if the employer failed to provide an accommodation which would have enabled the claimant to continue performing the functions of his or her job.[78]

[7.18.4] *When is a claimant subject to disqualification from benefits?*

A claimant who becomes unemployed as a result of his or her own conduct, such as because of a voluntary separation of employment, discharge for misconduct or other good cause, or a loss of employment due to criminal conduct, will be disqualified from receiving benefits. Likewise, a claimant will become disqualified by refusing a suitable offer of employment. A claimant who makes a false statement or representation to the Department of Labor in an attempt to obtain unemployment insurance benefits will forfeit his or her right to future benefits for up to a 20-week period.[79]

[7.18.5] *What is a claimant's "benefit year"?*

A claimant's "benefit year" is the 52-consecutive week period beginning on the first Monday after he or she files a claim for unemployment insur-

---

75   Labor Law § 591(2).

76   *Id.*

77   *In re Ormanian*, 167 A.D.3d 1183, 1184, 89 N.Y.S.3d 760 (3d Dep't 2018).

78   *Id.* at 1184 (finding that the medical documentation in the record, together with claimant's receipt of workers' compensation benefits, showed that she was unable to perform required job duties, and noting that "inasmuch as the essential job functions required of [claimant] included the performance of various physical tasks, including the manual operation of a school bus door three times in a certain amount of time, we are unpersuaded by claimant's contention that, at the time she applied for benefits and during the time period in question, no accommodation was made for her injury"); *see also In re Allen*, 2 A.D.3d 951, 952, 767 N.Y.S.2d 682 (3d Dep't 2003) (holding that substantial evidence demonstrated that anxiety and depression prevented claimant from returning to work as a correction officer, and claimant's contention that no accommodation was made for his disability was unpersuasive").

79   *See* §§ 7.25–7.30 below for a more detailed discussion of disqualification.

ance benefits.[80] In general, benefits may not be paid for more than 104 effective days (26 weeks) of total unemployment in a benefit year.[81]

[7.18.6] *What is the "base period" and how is it relevant to a claimant's eligibility for benefits?*

Eligibility for benefits is determined by the claimant's employment record during the base period. The "basic base period" is the first four of the last five completed calendar quarters ending on the Sunday immediately prior to a claimant filing a claim for unemployment insurance benefits.[82] An "alternate base period" is the last four completed calendar quarters prior to the claim being filed.[83]

A claimant must have worked and been paid wages in at least two quarters of the base period. The total wages paid to the claimant throughout the base period must be at least one and one-half times the "high" quarter wages. In 2020, the maximum amount used as "high" quarter wages is $11,088. Therefore, an employee who was paid at least this amount must have earned at least $5,544 in the other base period quarters to be eligible for unemployment insurance benefits.[84]

The Department of Labor will first look to the basic base period to determine if a claim is established. If a claimant is not qualified based on the basic base period, the alternative base period will be used to calculate benefit eligibility.

If eligible, a claimant's weekly benefit rate will equal 1/26 of his or her highest quarter earnings during the base period used to establish the claim.[85] If a claimant's highest quarter earnings are $3,575 or less, the weekly benefit rate will be 1/25 of the earnings, with a minimum benefit rate of $104 per week beginning January 1, 2020.[86] The maximum weekly benefit rate was increased from $450 to $504 effective October 7,

---

80   Labor Law § 521.

81   Labor Law § 590(4).

82   Labor Law § 520(1).

83   Labor Law § 520(2).

84   N.Y. Department of Labor, *How Your Weekly Unemployment Insurance Benefit is Calculated*, (Sept. 2019), https://www.labor.ny.gov/formsdocs/factsheets/pdfs/p832.pdf.

85   Labor Law § 590(5)(a).

86   *Id.*

2019. Thereafter, the maximum rate is expected to increase as of the first Monday of October in each year through 2026, when it will be set at 50% of the state's average weekly wage.[87]

[7.18.7] *What does it mean to be "totally unemployed"?*

"Total unemployment" means the "total lack of any employment on any day."[88] Whether an individual receives compensation for services is not determinative as to whether he or she was engaged in employment for purposes of benefit eligibility. For example, a claimant who volunteers services for a family-owned business will not be deemed to have had a "total lack of employment."[89] The same is true for a self-employed individual.[90]

[7.18.8] *What about employees of educational institutions during "break" periods?*

Educational employees who do not work during regular school break (vacation) periods are *not* considered to be unemployed during those periods, so long as they have received a "reasonable assurance" that their employment will continue at the end of the break period.[91]

[7.19] Is a claimant entitled to partial unemployment insurance benefits for part-time work?

Yes. A claimant who works fewer than four days in a week and does not earn over the maximum benefit rate will remain eligible for partial benefits as follows: (1) a claimant who performs one day of work will receive 3/4 of his or her full weekly benefit rate; (2) a claimant who performs two

---

87   *Id.*

88   Labor Law § 522.

89   *In re Claim of Wilson*, 102 A.D.2d 556, 480 N.Y.S.2d 53 (3d Dep't 1984) (claimant was ineligible for benefits when he performed work on his brother's farm, despite not being paid for the work).

90   *In re Swan*, 40 A.D.3d 1295, 1295, 835 N.Y.S.2d 774 (3d Dep't 2007) ("It is well settled that a claimant who performs activities on behalf of an ongoing business will not be considered totally unemployed even if such activities are minimal, provided that the claimant stands to benefit financially from the continued existence of the business").

91   *See* https://labor.ny.gov/ui/claimantinfo/school-personnel-faq.shtm#6.

days of work will receive 1/2 of his or her full weekly benefit rate; and (3) a claimant who performs three days of work will receive 1/4 of his or her full weekly benefit rate.[92]

[7.20] What impact does the receipt of accrued vacation pay or similar paid time off benefits have on a claimant's eligibility for unemployment insurance benefits?

No unemployment benefits are payable to a claimant during a paid vacation period or paid holiday.[93] The term "vacation period" is defined to include "the time designated for vacation purposes in accordance with the collective bargaining agreement or the employment contract or by the employer, his union, or his representative."[94] If no collective bargaining agreement or employment contract exists, or if it does not make such a designation, then a period designated or announced by the employer in advance is deemed to be a vacation period.[95]

In addition, courts have declined to disturb determinations by the Unemployment Insurance Appeals Board (UIAB) that a claimant is ineligible to receive benefits while receiving a payout of accrued sick, personal and vacation days post-termination.[96]

---

92   Labor Law § 523. *See In re Robinson*, 125 A.D.3d 1038, 1040, 3 N.Y.S.3d 117 (3d Dep't 2015) ("claimants performing part-time work who have worked four or more days per week or who have earned more than [the maximum benefit rate] regardless of the number of days worked have been deemed not to be totally unemployed and, therefore, ineligible to receive benefits for those weeks").

93   Labor Law § 591(3)(a).

94   Labor Law § 591(3)(b).

95   *Id.* Although § 591.3(b) of the Labor Law provides that the designation of vacation pay shall be "in writing," the Department of Labor has long taken the position that a verbal designation of vacation suffices to render an individual not "totally unemployed" and, thus, ineligible for unemployment insurance benefits. *See, e.g.*, N.Y. Department of Labor Unemployment Insurance Division Adjudication Services Office, Appeal Board Case No. 68, 256-59 (Aug. 20, 1959) (reversing referee determination to grant benefits because the vacation period was not designated in writing and holding "that such a construction and interpretation of the statute does violence to its intent and purpose. The statute is designed specifically to prevent the payment of unemployment insurance benefits during the period for which the employee receives vacation monies for the very purpose of refraining from work and obtaining a temporary respite therefrom").

96   *Berger v. Ross*, 41 N.Y.2d 1065, 396 N.Y.S.2d 184 (1977) (holding that "[t]he board's determination that the employer-employee relationship continued until the claimant exhausted all of his leave credits was rational and should not be disturbed"). *See also In re Claim of Jowers*, 239 A.D. 2d 638, 657 N.Y.S.2d 122 (3d Dep't 1997) (citing *Berger v. Ross* and holding that the claimant's continued receipt of a paycheck post-termination and until his accrued leave credits were exhausted constituted substantial evidence to support the UIAB holding that he was not totally unemployed).

[7.21] Can a claimant attend school and collect unemployment benefits?

Generally, the decision to attend school instead of working disqualifies a claimant from receiving unemployment insurance benefits.[97] However, a claimant remains eligible for benefits if he or she regularly attends a vocational training course or course in basic education skills that has been approved by the Commissioner of Labor as satisfying statutory requirements.[98]

[7.22] Is a claimant eligible for unemployment benefits after retirement?

Someone who voluntarily retires when the option of continuing to work remains available is generally not eligible for unemployment benefits.[99] This is true even as to someone who was enticed to retire by a severance package[100] or by an early retirement incentive,[101] notwithstanding the claimant's assertion that he or she felt pressure to resign.[102] An employee who chooses to accept an early retirement incentive in lieu of exercising a contractual right to "bump" a less senior employee has also been deemed ineligible for benefits.[103]

However, an individual who retires when it is clear that continuing work would not be available will not be not disqualified from receiving benefits.[104]

Upon retirement, the claimant's weekly benefit rate will be reduced by pension or 401(k) payments *if* the base period employer contributed to the underlying plan.[105] If the claimant was the sole contributor to the pension, 401(k) or other retirement plan, then no benefit reduction will apply.[106]

---

97 *In re Dowling*, 21 A.D.3d 1210, 800 N.Y.S.2d 870 (3d Dep't 2005).

98 Labor Law § 599(1).

99 *In re Polisseni*, 73 A.D.3d 1266, 902 N.Y.S.2d 672 (3d Dep't 2010).

100 *In re Lucht*, 49 A.D.3d 1048, 854 N.Y.S.2d 568 (3d Dep't 2008).

101 *In re Standford*, 54 A.D.3d 1095, 864 N.Y.S.2d 184 (3d Dep't 2008).

102 *Id.*

103 *In re Slezak*, 252 A.D.2d 644, 675 N.Y.S.2d 202 (3d Dep't 1998).

104 *In re Mineo*, 307 A.D.2d 611, 762 N.Y.S.2d 186 (3d Dep't 2003).

105 Labor Law § 600(1)(a).

106 Labor Law § 600(1)(b).

[7.23] Will dismissal or severance pay affect a claimant's eligibility for unemployment benefits?

The receipt of dismissal pay or severance pay upon separation may impact a claimant's eligibility for unemployment benefits; and as explained in §§ 7.25 and 7.26 below, a termination for misconduct will result in complete ineligibility.

A claimant is not eligible for benefits if he or she is receiving weekly dismissal or severance payments in an amount greater than the maximum weekly benefit rate.[107] If the amount is paid in a lump sum, the Department of Labor will consider the time period covered by the termination agreement or plan to determine if the pro-rated weekly benefit is greater than the maximum weekly benefit rate. If no agreement or plan exists, or if the agreement or plan is silent as to the period covered by the lump sum dismissal or severance payment, the Department of Labor will determine the *pro rata* amount based upon the claimant's average weekly pay.[108]

However, payments which are made to a claimant more than 30 days after the last date of employment are not treated as dismissal or severance pay, and thus do not affect unemployment insurance eligibility.[109]

The term "dismissal pay" does not include payments for pension, retirement, accrued leave and health insurance, or payments for supplemental unemployment benefits.[110] However, as discussed in §§ 7.20 and 7.22 above, a claimant's receipt of pension, retirement, or accrued leave payouts following separation may otherwise impact his or her eligibility for unemployment benefits.

[7.24] What is the "Shared-Work Program" and how do employers participate in it?

The Department of Labor has adopted the "Shared-Work Program" to give employers an alternative to laying off workers during temporary downturns in business. Under this program, employees may collect partial unemployment insurance benefits while working a reduced schedule for a period up to 26 weeks. In effect, it creates an exception to the general rule that a claimant must be "totally unemployed" to be eligible to receive

---

107   Labor Law § 591(6).

108   Labor Law § 591(6)(c).

109   Labor Law § 591(6)(d).

110   Labor Law § 591(6)(c).

benefits. It allows an employer to spread the impact of downturn more evenly across its workforce, lessening or eliminating the need for layoffs, and making it possible for the employer to retain staff and more quickly ramp-up operations once the business climate improves.

To take advantage of the Shared-Work Program, an employer must design a shared work plan and submit a plan application to the Department of Labor.[111] The plan can cover the total workforce, or just one or more shifts or work units. The application must be submitted at least three weeks, but no more than four weeks, before the proposed effective date.

An employer must have employed at least two employees working in New York State and must have paid contributions (or, as applicable, made payments in lieu of contributions) for four consecutive calendar quarters in order to participate in the Shared-Work Program. Additionally, the employer's plan must: (1) reduce work hours and corresponding wages by 20–60%; (2) apply to employees who normally work no more than 40 hours per week; (3) not reduce or eliminate fringe benefits unless such benefits are also being reduced or eliminated for the entire workforce; (4) not extend beyond 53 weeks (unless a new plan is approved); and (5) allow an employer to avoid a layoff of a number of employees equivalent to the reduced hours. Moreover, the employer cannot hire additional employees for the work group covered by the plan. If the affected employees are subject to a collective bargaining agreement, the union must agree to participation in the Shared-Work Program.[112]

IV. DISQUALIFICATION FROM RECEIVING UNEMPLOYMENT BENEFITS

[7.25] Under what circumstances will an otherwise eligible claimant be disqualified from receiving unemployment benefits?

As a general rule, a claimant who becomes unemployed through no fault of his or her own will receive unemployment insurance so long as he or she satisfies the "statutory waiting period" and submits a "valid original claim" demonstrating "total unemployment."[113] However, a claimant who

---

111   Labor Law § 605.

112   *Id.* Information about the Shared-Work Program is available in a series of "Frequently Asked Questions" on the Department of Labor website: https://labor.ny.gov/ui/claimantinfo/sharedworkclmtfaq.shtm.

113   Labor Law § 590. *See* § 7.18 above.

quits his or her job without "good cause," or who is terminated for misconduct or due to a criminal act, or who refuses a suitable offer of employment is disqualified from receiving benefits.

A claimant's right to receive unemployment benefits may also be delayed or suspended under other circumstances, including if he or she participates in a strike or makes a willful misrepresentation in support of a claim for benefits.

> **[7.25.1]** *What constitutes good cause for leaving employment and still being eligible for unemployment benefits?*

The Unemployment Insurance Appeals Board has discretion to determine whether the circumstances underlying a voluntary separation of employment amount to "good cause" for purposes of awarding benefits. Good cause to support a voluntary separation has been found to exist in circumstances: (a) where a claimant resigned in the face of disciplinary charges for actions which did not constitute misconduct;[114] (b) where the claimant feared for her personal safety due to threatening behavior by her supervisor;[115] and (c) where the claimant was unable to arrange appropriate child care despite demonstrable efforts.[116] Good cause has also been found to exist when a claimant experienced a substantial change in the terms and conditions of employment, including changes to: days of work and earning capacity,[117] scheduled hours and employer-provided benefits,[118] or the type of job responsibilities to be performed.[119]

Additionally, the Unemployment Insurance Law has identified several scenarios under which "good cause" exists for an individual voluntarily to separate from employment. These include "compelling family reasons" such

---

114   *In re Cohen*, 91 A.D.3d 998, 936 N.Y.S.2d 717 (3d Dep't 2012).

115   *In re Claim of Perkins*, 256 A.D.2d 800, 681 N.Y.S.2d 383 (3d Dep't 1998).

116   *See In re Cottone*, 109 A.D.3d 1044, 972 N.Y.S.2d 342 (3d Dep't 2013). *But see In re Denson*, 34 A.D.3d 893, 823 N.Y.S.2d 585 (3d Dept. 2006) (voluntary separation was without good cause when the claimant failed to contact a referral service identified by the employer to help secure appropriate child-care at the conclusion of the claimant's maternity leave).

117   *In re Alemic*, 140 A.D.3d 1565, 34 N.Y.S.3d 711 (3d Dep't 2016).

118   *In re Claim of Knoblach*, 239 A.D.2d 761, 762, 657 N.Y.S.2d 250 (3d Dep't 1997). *But see In re Claim of Rowe*, 258 A.D.2d 803, 803–04, 685 N.Y.S.2d 871 (3d Dep't 1999) (a reduction in hours due to the hiring of a new staff member which was intended to reduce the claimant's workload and stress and was largely offset by an increase to the claimant's pay did not amount to such a substantial change as to constitute good cause for leaving employment).

119   *In re Claim of Lavecchia*, 265 A.D.2d 724, 695 N.Y.S.2d 780 (3d Dep't 1999).

as: (1) domestic violence, if it is shown that claimant reasonably believes that continued employment will jeopardize his or her safety or the safety of an immediate family member; (2) illness or disability of an immediate family member which necessitates care for a longer period of time than the employer is willing to grant leave; and (3) relocation to accompany one's spouse to a place from which it is not practical to commute and due to a change in the spouse's employment.[120] Good cause also exists if the claimant waives his or her right to retain employment during a temporary layoff due to lack of work, as contemplated by a collective bargaining agreement or written employer plan.[121] Moreover, voluntary separation will not disqualify a claimant from benefits if circumstances have developed which would have justified a refusal of employment in the first place.[122]

[7.25.2] *When is a voluntary separation deemed to be without good cause?*

A voluntary separation has been deemed to be without good cause when the claimant left employment due to a dissatisfaction with wages,[123] a dispute over the payment of commissions,[124] the decision to pursue other work opportunities,[125] a desire to change careers,[126] dissatisfaction with legitimate job responsibilities,[127] a refusal to relocate to the downtown office where the claimant was expected to work at the time of hire,[128] a preference for particular work hours,[129] a desire not to work additional hours as requested by the employer,[130] a belief by the claimant that he would not pass a required test,[131] a refusal to comply with the employer's

---

120 Labor Law § 593(1)(b).

121 Labor Law § 593(1)(a).

122 *Id.*

123 *In re Claim of Fluman*, 254 A.D.2d 649, 679 N.Y.S.2d 440 (3d Dep't 1998).

124 *In re Claim of Huntington*, 295 A.D.2d 736, 743 N.Y.S.2d 209 (3d Dep't 2002).

125 *In re Claim of Gadamowitz*, 213 A.D.2d 912, 624 N.Y.S.2d 72 (3d Dep't 1998).

126 *In re Kremsky*, 32 A.D.3d 602, 819 N.Y.S.2d 350 (3d Dep't 2006).

127 *In re Tineo*, 117 A.D.3d 1307, 985 N.Y.S.2d 773 (3d Dep't 2014).

128 *In re Claim of Hidy*, 169 A.D.2d 914, 564 N.Y.S.2d 828 (3d Dep't 1991).

129 *In re Claim of De Angelis*, 199 A.D.2d 739, 605 N.Y.S.2d 471 (3d Dep't 1993).

130 *In re Claim of Marcheschi*, 306 A.D.2d 613, 759 N.Y.S.2d 716 (3d Dep't 2003).

131 *Gordon v. Levine*, 51 A.D.2d 613, 378 N.Y.S.2d 122 (3d Dep't 1976).

no-smoking policy,[132] and the claimant's anticipation of discharge for performance reasons.[133] In all of these situations, unemployment compensation was denied.

Similarly, an inability to get along with co-workers or the claimant's dissatisfaction with the work environment likewise does not constitute good cause to voluntarily separate from employment.[134] Nor does the claimant's perception that a supervisor was unfairly critical of his work constitute good cause.[135] Alleged workplace discrimination or harassment was found not to constitute good cause when the facts showed that the claimant never brought the purported conduct to management's attention, thereby preventing the employer from addressing it prior to the claimant's resignation.[136]

Finally, a claimant who provokes his or her own discharge will, at least in some cases, be treated as a voluntary separation without good cause, thus resulting in a disqualification from benefits.[137]

Affirmative employee misconduct as creating ineligibility to receive unemployment benefits is discussed in §§ 7.26 and 7.27 below.

[7.26]   What constitutes "misconduct" for purposes of disqualifying a claimant from receiving benefits?

An employee who has been discharged for misconduct "in connection with his or her employment" is disqualified from receiving unemployment benefits until he or she has subsequently worked in employment and earned at least ten times his or her weekly benefit rate.[138] While the term

---

132   *In re Wacher*, 175 A.D.2d 975, 573 N.Y.S.2d 781 (3d Dep't 1991).

133   *In re Kanter*, 138 A.D.3d 1283, 28 N.Y.S.3d 353 (3d Dep't 2016).

134   *In re Ayad*, 41 A.D.3d 1126, 840 N.Y.S.2d 439 (3d Dep't 2007).

135   *In re Claim of Fradys*, 308 A.D.2d 672, 764 N.Y.S.2d 661 (3d Dep't 2003).

136   *In re Gilyard*, 170 A.D.3d 1419, 96 N.Y.S.3d 696 (3d Dep't 2019) (alleged sexual harassment); *In re Logghe*, 39 A.D.3d 1003, 834 N.Y.S.2d 350 (3d Dep't 2007) (alleged discrimination in regards to administration of benefits); *In re Roman*, 32 A.D.3d 1067, 820 N.Y.S.2d 860 (3d Dep't 2006) (alleged sexual harassment and discrimination in regards to the assignment of projects).

137   *Miller v. Levine*, 37 A.D.2d 873, 325 N.Y.S.2d 6 (3d Dep't 1971) (refusal by attorney to be fingerprinted as a condition of employment and under threat of discharge); *Moran v. Catherwood*, 34 A.D.2d 694, 309 N.Y.S.2d 642 (3d Dep't), *aff'd*, 27 N.Y.2d 946, 318 N.Y.S.2d 318 (1970) (refusal by newspaper editor to follow rules governing editorial process); *In re Oxios*, 33 A.D.2d 858, 305 N.Y.S.2d 869 (3d Dep't 1969) (refusal by messenger to make deliveries as directed by the employer).

138   Labor Law § 593(3).

"misconduct" is not defined by statute, courts interpret it to mean a voluntary act or omission which is "detrimental to the employer's interest or a violation of a reasonable work condition."[139] An employee's off-the-clock behavior *may* constitute disqualifying misconduct, but only if it "raises serious questions as to a worker's integrity."[140] It must be borne in mind that "not every discharge for cause rises to the level of misconduct for unemployment insurance purposes."[141]

Examples of acts or omissions which rise to the requisite level of "misconduct" include: insubordination (such as refusing to accept a reasonable work assignment or other reasonable request of management);[142] willful or deliberate failure to follow an established policy (particularly if the claimant received prior warnings about the consequences of such failure);[143] chronic absenteeism;[144] dishonesty;[145] theft;[146] drug abuse or

---

139 *In re Cedrone*, 69 A.D.3d 1251, 1252, 896 N.Y.S.2d 481 (3d Dep't 2010).

140 *In re Claim of Bruggeman*, 101 A.D.2d 973, 973, 477 N.Y.S.2d 449 (3d Dep't 1984).

141 *In re Salcedo*, 171 A.D.3d 1437, 1438, 99 N.Y.S.3d 118 (3d Dep't 2019).

142 *In re Elbaz*, 30 A.D.3d 954, 954, 817 N.Y.S.2d 450 (3d Dep't 2006) (dishwasher's refusal to clean up garbage under threat of termination constituted disqualifying misconduct); *In re Lambert*, 34 A.D.3d 948, 948, 823 N.Y.S.2d 616 (3d Dep't 2006) (custodian's refusal to sign weekly inspection report despite knowing that his signature was simply to acknowledge receipt and not to indicate agreement with the contents thereof rose to the level of disqualifying misconduct).

143 *In re Trunzo*, 145 A.D.3d 1308, 1309, 42 N.Y.S.3d 693 (3d Dep't 2016) (registered nurse engaged in disqualifying conduct when she included over-the-counter medication in a patient's mediset without a physician's order over the course of six months, despite being aware of the employer's policy to the contrary); *In re Strang*, 112 A.D.3d 1254, 978 N.Y.S.2d 395 (3d Dep't 2013) (employee engaged in disqualifying misconduct where she shared confidential information pertaining to her employer's business affairs with a former employee despite being aware of the employer's written policy against such conduct); *In re Ghoulian*, 6 A.D.3d 908, 774 N.Y.S.2d 460 (3d Dep't 2004) (teaching assistant engaged in disqualifying misconduct where she took students off school premises in her car despite previously warnings that doing so would result in termination).

144 *In re Claim of Iglesias*, 297 A.D.2d 849, 850, 746 N.Y.S.2d 853 (3d Dep't 2002) (security guard terminated for misconduct in the form of excessive absenteeism following repeated oral and written warnings).

145 *In re Congdon*, 41 A.D.3d 1013, 1013–14, 839 N.Y.S.2d 263 (3d Dep't 2007) (claimant terminated for not accurately reporting the amount of money in his cash drawer).

146 *In re Claim of Alexander*, 3 A.D.3d 827, 827, 771 N.Y.S.2d 259 (3d Dep't 2004) (claimant terminated for theft of cell phone, when evidence showed recent calls were linked to him).

refusing to take a required drug test;[147] using alcohol at work;[148] or engaging in workplace violence[149] and harassment.[150]

On the other hand, it is well-established that an act of "[m]ere negligence"—even if it was enough to justify firing the employee—does not by itself rise to the level of misconduct for purposes of denying a claimant unemployment benefits (although "persistent" acts of negligence may support denial).[151] Poor performance or inefficiency and bad judgment,[152] or merely technical violation of an employer's rules or procedures will generally not constitute disqualifying misconduct.[153] Moreover, isolated poor behavior occurring in the absence of prior warnings may not result in a claimant's disqualification from benefits even if it otherwise would be considered misconduct if the incidents were repeated, or the claimant had been on notice that disciplinary action would result.[154]

---

147   *In re Jenkins*, 27 A.D.3d 863, 864, 810 N.Y.S.2d 561 (3d Dep't 2006) (claimant engaged in disqualifying misconduct when he refused to comply with a reasonable request for a drug test after a manager smelled marijuana and rolling papers in the vicinity of him and other employees).

148   *In re Holder*, 49 A.D.3d 1131, 1131, 853 N.Y.S.2d 717 (3d Dep't 2008) (despite his belated assertion that his speech was slurred due to the use of medication, the credible evidence established that the claimant engaged in disqualifying misconduct by reporting to work under the influence of alcohol). *But see In re McCarthy*, 150 A.D.3d 1587, 1588, 54 N.Y.S.3d 763 (3d Dep't 2017) ("[a]lcoholism is a recognized disease that may excuse what is otherwise disqualifying misconduct if substantial evidence establishes that (1) claimant is an alcoholic, (2) the disease caused the misbehavior for which he or she was terminated, and (3) claimant was available for and capable of employment") (internal citations and alterations omitted).

149   *In re Smith*, 177 A.D.3d 1064, 1065, 109 N.Y.S.3d 922 (3d Dep't 2019) (claimant engaged in disqualifying misconduct when he became agitated and then grabbed, shoved and struck a supervisor who told him to turn off music).

150   *In re Campon*, 122 A.D.3d 1228, 1229, 995 N.Y.S.2d 865 (3d Dep't 2014) (claimant was disqualified from receiving benefits based on his "prolonged campaign of harassment against a coworker").

151   *In re Claim of Weinfeld*, 135 A.D.2d 880, 881, 522 N.Y.S.2d 278 (3d Dep't 1987). *But see In re Claim of Mitch*, 247 A.D.2d 738, 739, 669 N.Y.S.2d 73 (3d Dep't 1998) ("persistent negligence in spite of prior warnings can constitute misconduct").

152   *In re Stewart*, 175 A.D.3d 780, 105 N.Y.S.3d 624 (3d Dep't 2019) (poor performance); *In re Claim of Lackey*, 81 A.D.2d 955, 439 N.Y.S.2d 712 (3d Dep't 1981) (inefficiency, negligence and bad judgement).

153   *In re Claim of Watson*, 189 A.D.2d 1088, 592 N.Y.S.2d 893 (3d Dep't 1993).

154   *In re Salcedo*, 171 A.D.3d 1437, 1438–39, 99 N.Y.S.3d 118 (a claimant who "sent a harassing message and spoke loudly and rudely to [a] supervisor" did not engage in disqualifying misconduct when the conduct occurred in isolation).

[7.27] Can a claimant's criminal conduct lead to a disqualification from benefits?

Yes, if it is employment-related criminal conduct. A claimant is disqualified from receiving benefits when he or she "loses employment as a result of an act constituting a felony in connection with such employment, provided the claimant is duly convicted thereof or has signed a statement admitting that he or she has committed such an act."[155] The disqualification from benefits will continue for a period of 12 months after the loss of employment.[156]

A felony is deemed to be "in connection with employment" if it causes a "breach of a duty, express or implied, [that] the claimant owes to the employer."[157] "[C]onduct is disqualifying 'when it evinces a willful disregard of standards of behavior which employers have the right to expect of their employees.'"[158] Such conduct may occur either while the claimant was actively engaged in job responsibilities,[159] or during nonworking hours.[160]

[7.28] Can a claimant's refusal of an employment offer result in a disqualification from benefits?

Yes. As a general rule, a claimant who has rejected a suitable offer of employment is disqualified from receiving unemployment benefits. A "suitable offer" is one which the claimant is "reasonably suited by training and experience."[161]

A desire for higher wages will not justify a claimant's refusal of an otherwise suitable offer if the rate of pay is consistent with the prevailing wage

---

155 Labor Law § 593(4).

156 *Id.*

157 *In re Gunn*, 172 A.D.3d 1865, 1868, 102 N.Y.S.3d 304 (3d Dep't 2019) (quoting *In re Sinker*, 89 N.Y.2d 485, 488, 655 N.Y.S.2d 842 (1997)).

158 *Id.* (quoting *In re Sinker*, 89 N.Y.2d at 488).

159 *In re Cardillo*, 129 A.D.3d 1423, 1424, 12 N.Y.S.3d 634 (3d Dep't 2015) (claimant disqualified from benefits after pleading guilty to securities fraud-related felonies, which "clearly violated a duty that he owed to [his] hedge fund [employer] . . . to conduct business in a fair and honest manner").

160 *In re Gunn*, 172 A.D.3d at 1868 (claimant disqualified from benefits due to felony driving while intoxicated conviction, which "cast a negative light on the Police Department and exhibited a deliberate disregard for the standards of behavior that the Police Department had a right to expect from its employees").

161 *In re Neuman*, 105 A.D.3d 1216, 1217, 962 N.Y.S.2d 813 (3d Dep't 2013) (quoting *In re Schirra*, 45 A.D.3d 1067, 1068, 846 N.Y.S.2d 419 (3d Dep't 2007)).

in the locality for comparable positions.[162] Nor will a preference for a shorter commute warrant the rejection of a suitable offer.[163]

However, a refusal of employment will not disqualify a claimant from receiving benefits if:

- Accepting the offer would interfere with the claimant's right to join or retain union membership or otherwise violate the terms of a collective bargaining agreement; or

- There is a strike, lockout, or other industrial controversy taking place at the place where employment was offered; or

- The employment is at an unreasonable distance from the claimant's residence or involves substantially greater travel expense than the claimant's former job; or

- The wages or benefits offered to the claimant are substandard; or

- The offer is for a full-time position but the claimant has customarily worked only part-time and is unable or unwilling to work a full-time schedule.[164]

[7.29]   Are striking employees entitled to unemployment benefits?

Yes, but generally a strike must have lasted for 14 consecutive days before a striking employee is eligible for unemployment insurance benefits.[165] However, a striking employee will become eligible sooner if the employer locks out employees, or if the striker remains unemployed after the labor dispute ends.[166] Additionally, a striking employee becomes immediately eligible for benefits if the employer hires a permanent replacement worker for the striking employee's position.[167]

---

162   *Id.* at 1217.

163   *Id.* ("dissatisfaction with the length of one's commute does not constitute good cause for rejecting an otherwise suitable offer of employment") (quoting *In re Pelle*, 12 A.D.3d 750, 751, 783 N.Y.S.2d 729 (3d Dep't 2004)).

164   Labor Law § 593(2).

165   Labor Law § 592(1)(a). Until February 2020, a longer period applied.

166   *Id.*

167   Labor Law § 592(1)(b)(i).

For purposes of the Unemployment Insurance Law, a replacement worker is automatically presumed to be "permanent" *unless* the employer certifies in writing that the employee can return to his or her prior position once the strike ends.[168] If the employer makes such a certification and then does not allow the employee to return to his or her position at the conclusion of the strike, the employee is entitled to recover any benefits lost as a result of the 14-day suspension of benefits, and the Department of Labor may impose a penalty on the employer of up to $750 per employee per week of lost benefits.[169]

V. FILING FOR BENEFITS

[7.30] How does someone file for unemployment benefits?

A person seeking unemployment insurance benefits must file a claim at the local state employment office serving the area in which he or she was (a) last employed or (b) currently resides.[170] Claims may also be filed online at the Department of Labor website or by telephone.[171]

A claimant must have been unemployed for a full week before he or she will begin receiving unemployment insurance benefits.[172] It generally takes three to six weeks for the Unemployment Insurance Division to process and review a claim.

[7.31] What is an "initial determination"?

The determination issued by the Commissioner of Labor as to the validity of a claim for unemployment insurance benefits and the amount of benefits payable to the claimant is known as the "initial determination."[173]

[7.32] What happens if a claimant disagrees with the initial determination?

A claimant who disagrees with the initial determination, either as to the validity of the claim or as to the amount of benefits payable, has the right to a hearing before an administrative law judge. A request for a hearing

---

168 *Id.*

169 *Id.*

170 Labor Law § 596(1).

171 https://dol.ny.gov/unemployment/file-your-first-claim-benefits.

172 Labor Law § 590(7).

173 Labor Law § 597(1).

must be made within 30 days of the mailing or personal delivery of the notice of determination.[174]

[7.33] What happens if the employer disagrees with the initial determination?

An employer also has the right to contest the initial determination by requesting a hearing before an administrative law judge within 30 days of the mailing or personal delivery of the notice of determination.[175]

[7.34] What happens if a claimant submits false information in support of a claim for unemployment insurance benefits?

A claimant who is found willfully to have made a false statement or misrepresentation in furtherance of an unemployment insurance claim is subject to a forfeiture of benefits for up to 20 weeks.[176] If benefits were previously awarded based on such false statements or representations, the claimant will be required to refund all moneys and to pay a civil penalty of $100 or 15% of the total overpayment, whichever is greater.[177]

VI.   HEARINGS AND APPEALS

[7.35] What are the procedures for an unemployment hearing?

The administrative law judge is authorized to conduct an unemployment hearing "in such order and manner and with such methods of proof and interrogation as the judge deems best suited to ascertain the substantial rights of the parties," which may include having the administrative law judge examining the witnesses himself or herself.[178] The parties (i.e., the former employee and the employer) are to be afforded a full opportunity to present testimony and documents or other evidence. The administrative law judge is not, however, bound by common law of statutory rules of evidence or by technical or formal rules of procedure.[179]

---

174   Labor Law § 620(1)(a).

175   Labor Law § 620(2).

176   Labor Law § 594(1).

177   Labor Law § 594(4).

178   12 N.Y.C.R.R. § 461.4(a).

179   *Id.*

The testimony taken during a hearing is to be under oath or by affirmation and a verbatim record of the proceeding shall be made.[180] The parties (or their attorneys or agents) have the right to call, examine, and cross-examine parties and witnesses.[181]

In reaching a decision, the administrative law judge may consider only evidence presented at the hearing and those facts and law of which "official notice" may be taken.[182]

Adjournments will be permitted for good cause shown, with adjourned hearings to be rescheduled on an expedited basis.[183]

[7.36] Can the parties compel the appearance of witnesses or other evidence for a hearing?

Yes. The parties (or their attorneys or agents) may request that the administrative law judge issue subpoenas to compel the appearance of relevant witnesses or the production of relevant documents, records, or other evidence.[184]

[7.37] Is an administrative law judge's decision subject to appeal?

Yes, but with somewhat differing requirements based upon the procedural "posture" of the claim.

A claimant may appeal an administrative law judge's decision by filing a notice of appeal within 20 days of its mailing or personal delivery.[185]

If the hearing was requested by the claimant, the employer may likewise appeal the administrative law judge decision within 20 days.[186]

---

180 12 N.Y.C.R.R. § 461.4(b).

181 *Id.*

182 12 N.Y.C.R.R. § 461.4(j). In addition, attorneys have the independent power under the New York Civil Practice Law and Rules to issue subpoenas in administrative hearings. CPLR 2302(a).

183 12 N.Y.C.R.R. § 461.6(a).

184 12 N.Y.C.R.R. § 461.4(c). In addition, attorneys have the independent power under the New York Civil Practice Law and Rules to issue subpoenas in administrative hearings. CPLR 2302(a).

185 12 N.Y.C.R.R. § 463.1(b).

186 12 N.Y.C.R.R. § 463.1(c).

However, if the hearing was requested by the employer, the employer has the right to an appeal *only* if it appeared at the hearing, in which case the same 20-day timeframe applies.[187]

Appeals from an administrative law judge's decision are heard by the Unemployment Insurance Appeals Board.

The Unemployment Insurance Appeals Board typically renders its decision without a new hearing, based on the testimony and other evidence accepted into the record by the administrative law judge and the written arguments of the parties on appeal.[188] However, it may hold a hearing on appeal, either in its own discretion or upon the application of a party.[189]

Evidence that was not introduced at the original administrative hearing many only be considered by the Unemployment Insurance Appeals Board if all parties consent or if there is a further hearing.[190] If further a hearing is granted or directed, the Unemployment Insurance Appeals Board may limit the parties to oral argument or, if it chooses, permit the calling of witnesses or the introduction of further evidence.[191]

[7.38] Is an Unemployment Insurance Appeals Board decision subject to review?

Yes. Any party which appeared at the Unemployment Insurance Appeals Board, or the New York State Commissioner of Labor, may appeal to the Appellate Division, Third Department within 30 days following the mailing or personal delivery of the notice of the Unemployment Insurance Appeals Board decision.

The Appellate Division will decide questions of law based upon its own reading of the law. For mixed questions of fact and law, the Appellate Division's review is limited to whether the decision being challenged is supported by a rational basis.[192] For pure questions of fact, the Appellate

---

187   12 N.Y.C.R.R. § 463.1(d).

188   12 N.Y.C.R.R. § 463.1(f).

189   12 N.Y.C.R.R. §§ 463.1(f), 463.3.

190   12 N.Y.C.R.R. § 463.1(f).

191   12 N.Y.C.R.R. § 463.3(b).

192   *Fisher v. Levine*, 36 N.Y.2d 146, 150, 365 N.Y.S.2d 828 (1975).

Division will uphold an Unemployment Insurance Appeals Board decision if it is supported by "substantial evidence," even if the evidence on the record might support a contrary conclusion.[193]

[7.39] Do decisions or evidence from an unemployment proceeding have any impact on other disputes between the employer and the employee?

If there is a dispute between an employer and an ex-employee as to the ex-employee's entitlement to unemployment insurance, there is a good chance that there are other disputes between the parties, such as wrongful termination, breach of contract, constructive discharge, and/or employment discrimination. It is, accordingly, of interest to employers whether what happens in an unemployment dispute will have an impact on other disputed matters.

The Unemployment Insurance Law explicitly provides that except for proceedings before other tribunals (i.e. a court or another administrative agency) *which relate to a claim for unemployment insurance benefits*, no finding of fact or law contained in the decision of an administrative law judge, the Unemployment Insurance Appeals Board, or a court rendered under the Unemployment Insurance Law shall preclude the litigation of an issue of fact or law in a subsequent action or proceeding.[194] In other words, a finding made in an unemployment case, while it may be final as to the issue of unemployment benefits, is not determinative of any other dispute between the parties, and those disputes may be re-litigated.

In addition, Labor Law § 537(2)(b) provides that "unemployment insurance information" is for the exclusive use of the Commissioner of Labor in relation to the administration of the Unemployment Insurance Law; and this broadly includes "information obtained by the [Department of Labor] from employers and employees" in connection with a claim for benefits.[195] Unemployment insurance information may not be used "in any court action or proceeding pending therein" unless (a) the Commissioner of Labor is a party, or (b) the information was disclosed to a federal, state, or local agency under limited circumstances and with assurances that the information will remain confidential and be used only

---

193   *Id.*

194   Labor Law § 623(2).

195   Labor Law § 537(1)(a)(i).

for prescribed "legitimate governmental purposes."[196] Any person who discloses unemployment insurance information in violation of § 537 of the Labor Law shall be guilty of a misdemeanor.[197]

Courts have interpreted the foregoing to mean that Labor Law § 537 prohibits the use of testimony and written statements introduced during an unemployment insurance hearing in subsequent proceedings.[198]

VII. RECORD-KEEPING AND POSTING REQUIREMENTS

[7.40] What record-keeping and posting requirements apply?

Employers are required to keep a record of each person employed, including the employee's name and Social Security number, the amount of remuneration paid, and any other records which may be required by regulations promulgated by the Commissioner of Labor.[199] These records are subject to inspection by the New York State Department of Labor, and the Commissioner of Labor may require that information from such records be reported.[200] Employers that fail to maintain required records, or willfully falsify records or file false reports, may be prosecuted for criminal misdemeanors.[201]

Every employer subject to the Unemployment Insurance Law, (*except* for employers of employees in personal or domestic service), must conspicuously post and maintain notices to inform employees that the employer is registered with the New York state Department of Labor.[202]

Employers must also notify each person who is separated from employment for *any* reason of his or her right to apply for unemployment insurance benefits. This notice is required even in the event of a temporary

---

196   Labor Law §§ 537(2)(b), 537(3)(g).

197   Labor Law §§ 537(2).

198   *Wilson v. Bratton*, 266 A.D.2d 140, 141 (1st Dep't 1999); *Seymour v. New York State Elec & Gas*, 215 A.D.2d 971, 972–73 (3d Dep't 1995).

199   Labor Law § 575(1).

200   *Id.*

201   *Id.*

202   12 N.Y.C.R.R. § 472.7. The posting of Form IA 133, *Unemployment Insurance Notice to Employees*, satisfies this requirement; *see Notice to Employees* Poster, N.Y. Department of Labor (Sept. 2019), https://www.labor.ny.gov/formsdocs/ui/IA132.pdf.

separation which is expected to result in more than three days of covered unemployment. The notice must include the employer's name, the employer's registration number with New York State, the mailing address where payroll records are kept, and a statement advising the employee that he or she should bring the notice with him or her so that the information can be presented to the Department of Labor when an application for unemployment insurance is filed.[203]

---

203   12 N.Y.C.R.R. § 472.8. An employer's use of Form IA 12.3, Record of Employment, will satisfy these requirements; *see* https://www.labor.ny.gov/formsdocs/ui/IA12_3.pdf.

CHAPTER EIGHT

EMPLOYER AND EMPLOYEE RIGHTS AND OBLIGATIONS

James Holahan
Subhash Viswanathan

Edited by R. Daniel Bordoni

CHAPTER OVERVIEW

In this chapter, we consider the general obligations which exist between employers and employees. These obligations arise from legislation in some cases, and from the "common law" in others. Congress, the New York State Legislature, and local county and municipal legislatures enact many laws regulating the employer-employee relationship, and these requirements exist side-by-side with an extensive set of duties that employers and employees owe to each other under what is called "the common law," which is a body of accumulated judicial precedent.

Specific questions addressed in this chapter are as follows:

[8.1] What is the "common law"?

[8.2] What common law duties does the employee owe to the employer?

[8.3] What common law duties does the employer owe to the employee?

[8.4] What can an employer do about an employee who violates the duties owed by the employee to the employer?

[8.5] What is the employee's common law duty of loyalty?

[8.6] What is the employee's common law duty of competence?

[8.7] What is the employee's common law duty to protect confidential information?

[8.8] If an employee has not signed a confidentiality agreement, is the employer still protected against the disclosure of confidential information?

[8.9] Do all employees owe the same duties?

[8.10] Can an employer require an employee to sign an employment agreement?

[8.11] Can an employee be required to arbitrate any employment disputes?

[8.12] What is the "faithless servant" doctrine?

[8.13] Does an employee have an obligation to respond to an employer's work-related questions?

[8.14] What information must an employer provide to employees in writing *at the time of* employment?

[8.15] What information must an employer provide to employees *during* employment?

[8.15.1] Wage Statements

[8.15.2] Benefits Disclosures

[8.15.3] Workplace Posting Requirements

[8.16] What information must an employer provide to employees *at the end* of employment?

[8.17] What workplace records must an employer retain, and for how long?

[8.18] Are employers required to protect employee information from third parties?

[8.19] What ongoing documents and information must an employer provide to employees?

[8.20] Do employees have access to the contents of their personnel files?

[8.21] What information must an employee provide to the employer?

[8.22] Can an employer regulate an employee's off-premises political activities?

[8.23] What types of political activities are protected under New York Labor Law § 201-d?

[8.24] Can an employer regulate an employee's off-premises recreational activities?

[8.25] Can an employer regulate an employee's off-premises romantic activities with another employee?

[8.26] Can an employer take action against an applicant or employee because the individual smokes cigarettes or drinks alcoholic beverages outside of work hours?

[8.27] Can an employer take action against an applicant or employee for pro-union activity?

[8.28] What remedies are available for violations of New York Labor Law § 201-d?

[8.29] Can an employer maintain a policy restricting an employee's personal use of social media outside of work hours?

[8.30] Can an employer discharge or discipline an employee for inappropriate social media activity?

[8.31] Can an employer restrict employee use of workplace computers and electronic systems?

[8.32] Can an employer discharge or discipline an employee for inappropriate use of workplace computers and electronic systems?

[8.33] Can an employer maintain a policy prohibiting employees from taking photographs or secretly recording conversations in the workplace?

[8.34] Can an employer discharge or discipline an employee for taking photographs or secretly recording conversations in the workplace?

[8.1]   What is the "common law"?

The common law consists of rules for human behavior in general, and includes workplace behavior, which has been derived from centuries of English judicial decisions, imported to the American colonies prior to 1776, and then elaborated upon by American courts. It is a body of judicial decisions resolving personal disputes between litigants based on the particular facts of each case. These decisions become "precedent" for future decisions involving similar facts.

From judicial decisions rendered over centuries of time, the common law established certain duties that a "servant" owed to a "master" as well as certain duties that a "master" owed to a "servant." The common law of "master and servant" has evolved into the common law of "employer and employee."

Though the phrase "master–servant" has an uncomfortable sound in modern usage, the fundamental principles developed by the English courts for defining the duties owed between master and servant continue to shape the employment relationship in New York and in other states, and the common law continues to evolve and remain relevant to this day. It impacts many determinations, including, among other issues, who is an "employee" and whether that employee may be terminated "at will."[1]

[8.2]   What common law duties does the employee owe to the employer?

Decisions by New York courts recognize a number of common law duties that an employee owes to an employer.[2] These common law duties prohibit employees from acting in ways that, although not forbidden by any

---

1   "At will" employment is discussed in Chapter 2 of this book at §§ 2.1–2.7. The differences between employees and independent contractors are discussed in Chapter 2 at § 2.16, Chapter 5 at § 5.4, and Chapter 12 at § 12.1.

2   *See Western Elec. Co. v. Brenner*, 41 N.Y.2d 291, 295, 392 N.Y.S. 2d 409 (1977).

express understanding, would deprive the employer of the right to receive the intended benefits of the employment relationship.[3] Simply put, an employee may not act against his or her employer's interest.

Related common law duties include: the duty to follow the employer's reasonable rules and directions; the duty to protect and preserve the employer's property (including its confidential information) and to return it when the employment ends; and the duty to devote sufficient time and attention to the employer's work and avoid any competing responsibilities.[4]

The employee's common law duties of loyalty, competence, and to protect the employer's confidential information are discussed in Sections 8.5 through 8.7 below.

Not every bad act by an employee necessarily violates a common law duty. It is only where the employee acts directly against the employer's interests—as in embezzlement, improperly competing with the current employer, or usurping business opportunities—that a breach of the duty of loyalty will be found.[5] For example, an executive who allegedly violated the employer's policy prohibiting sexual harassment, but did not act directly to harm the employer's interests, was found not to have breached his duty of loyalty.[6] (Of course, the employee's conduct may have violated various state laws dealing with workplace harassment; see discussion in Chapter 11 of this book at §§ 11.26–11.34).

[8.3]   What common law duties does the employer owe to the employee?

The common law also recognizes a number of duties that a "master" owes a "servant," including the duty to provide a safe working environment.[7] (This common law duty to provide a safe working environment continues

---

3   *Gettinger Assoc., L.P. v. Abraham Kamber Co.*, 83 A.D.3d 412, 414, 920 N.Y.S.2d 75 (1st Dep't 2011), *quoting Jaffe v. Paramount Commc'ns, Inc.*, 222 A.D.2d 17, 22–23, 644 N.Y.S.2d 43 (1st Dep't 1996); *see Aventine Inv. Mgmt., Inc. v. Canadian Imperial Bank of Commerce*, 265 A.D.2d 513, 514, 697 N.Y.S.2d 128 (2d Dep't 1999).

4   *Onsite Cos, Inc. v. Comfort*, 21 A.D.3d 1306, 1308, 802 N.Y.S.2d 578 (4th Dep't 2005).

5   *Veritas Capital Mgmt., L.L.C. v. Campbell*, 82 A.D.3d 529, 530, 918 N.Y.S.2d 448 (1st Dep't 2011); *Linder v. Innovative Commercial Sys. LLC*, 41 Misc. 3d 1214(A), 981 N.Y.S.2d 636 (Sup. Ct., N.Y. Co. 2013), *aff'd,* 127 A.D.3d 670, 8 N.Y.S.3d 191 (1st Dep't 2015); *Sullivan & Cromwell LLP v. Charney*, 15 Misc. 3d 1128(A), 841 N.Y.S.2d 222, (Sup. Ct., N.Y. Co. 2007).

6   *Pozner v. Fox Broadcasting Co.*, 59 Misc. 3d 897, 900–02 (Sup. Ct., N.Y. Co. 2018).

7   *Hammond v. Int'l Paper Co.*, 161 A.D. 914, 914, 557 N.Y.S. 2d 477 (3d Dep't 1990).

today, but has been reinforced and expanded by statute and regulation.)[8] Chapter 5 of this book, "Workers' Compensation and Workplace Safety," addresses workplace safety in greater detail.

Employers also have a common law duty to adopt reasonable rules, and to take reasonable measures, to protect their employees from harm that is reasonably foreseeable.[9] This duty includes the responsibility to hire competent personnel in sufficient numbers to minimize any reasonably preventable risk of harm to employees that might arise from failing to do so.[10]

[8.4]   What can an employer do about an employee who violates the duties owed by the employee to the employer?

Remedies for breach of employee and employer common law duties are largely the same remedies as are available for correcting a breach of contract.[11] An action may be brought in the appropriate New York court (and, in certain circumstances, may also be brought in federal court if federal jurisdictional requirements are met).[12] However, for breach of the duty of loyalty, an employer may, as an alternative to more traditional contract damages, instead elect to recover all of the salary, commissions, and expenses paid to the disloyal employee during the period of disloyalty.[13]

The remedies available from the courts depend in part on the nature of the injury and also on what needs to be done to rectify the harm. For example, an employee may not take a benefit from someone else as a reward for what the employee should be doing for his or her employer.[14] Accordingly, an employee who, "on the side," makes a profit or receives a benefit for ser-

---

8   *Id.*

9   *Id.*

10   *See Melendez v. Figler*, No. 161439/2015, 2018 N.Y. Slip Op. 30417(U), 2018 N.Y. Misc. Lexis 830 at *12 (Sup. Ct., N.Y. Co. Mar. 5, 2018).

11   *NYWC, Inc. v. Pro Beauty Concepts, Inc.*, 44 Misc. 3d 1209(A), 997 N.Y.S.2d 99 (Sup. Ct., Queens Co. 2014).

12   *Pure Power Boot Camp, Inc. v. Warrior Fitness Boot Camp, LLC*, 813 F. Supp. 2d 489, 524 (S.D.N.Y. 2011).

13   *Corporate Interiors, Inc. v. Pappas*, 2 Misc. 3d 1009(A), 784 N.Y.S.2d 919 (Sup. Ct., Queens Co. 2004).

14   *Sokoloff v. Harriman Estates Dev.*, 96 N.Y.2d 409, 416, 729 N.Y.S.2d 425 (2001).

vices performed for his or her employer is under a duty to give that profit or benefit to his or her employer.[15] If the employee does not turn over the profit or benefit, the employer may sue the employee for restitution.[16]

If a material breach of the common law duties is proven, then the remedies available to the injured party are designed to make that person or entity whole and to recover any profit or gain that the employee realized by the wrongful behavior.[17] This can include monetary relief (e.g., cash compensation for economic loss caused by the breach) and injunctive relief (e.g., judicial orders that direct that the offending conduct cease and place the injured party in the position it would have enjoyed but for the breach of duty).[18] In addition, an employee who breaches his or her common law duties may be fired.[19]

It should be noted that the remedies for breach of contract or the breach of an employee's common-law duties in New York do *not* include damages for pain and suffering or recovery of attorneys' fees. Depending on the nature and severity of an employee's conduct, punitive damages can be awarded to serve as a deterrent,[20] but punitive damages are awarded only in rare cases involving extremely serious misconduct.

Chapter 9 of this book, "Protecting the Employer's Business," contains a further discussion of what employers may do about employees whose disloyalty damages the employer's business.

[8.5]   What is the employee's common law duty of loyalty?

An employee owes a duty of good faith and loyalty to the employer in the performance of the employee's duties. An employee breaches that duty

---

15   *Epstein Eng'g, P.C. v. Cataldo*, 41 Misc. 3d 1218(A), 981 N.Y.S.2d 634 (Sup. Ct., N.Y. Co. 2013), *aff'd*, 124 A.D.3d 420, 1 N.Y.S.3d 38 (1st Dep't 2015).

16   *Id. See also W. Elec. Co. v. Brenner*, 41 N.Y.2d 291, 295, 392 N.Y.S.2d 409 (1977) (any compensation secretly or improperly received from others beyond the compensation to which the employee is entitled is deemed to be held by him in trust for his or her employer).

17   *Gomez v. Bicknell*, 302 A.D.2d 107, 114, 756 N.Y.S.2d 209 (2d Dep't 2002).

18   *Gassman & Gassman v. Salzman*, 112 A.D.2d 82, 82, 491 N.Y.S.2d 641 (1st Dep't 1985).

19   *Anderson v. Anderson*, 120 A.D.3d 1559, 1560–61, 993 N.Y.S.2d 220 (4th Dep't 2014).

20   *Pure Power Boot Camp, Inc.*, 813 F. Supp. 2d 489, 526 (S.D.N.Y. 2011).

by using the employer's time, facilities, or confidential information for personal gain, or by acting in a way that is harmful to the employer.[21]

For example, an employee violates the duty of loyalty by making his or her own personal expenses appear to be employer expenses.[22]

Similarly, an employee who used his or her employer's proprietary secrets to build and conduct a competing business while still in the employ of his or her employer has breached his or her duty of loyalty.[23]

Likewise, an employee who created a company which then overcharged his or her employer for shipping goods overseas violated his or her duty to the employer.[24]

A breach of the duty of loyalty arises when an employee, while still employed, accepts employment with a competitor or uses his or her employer's property, including confidential information, to benefit himself or another.[25] The duty may be breached where an employee uses his or her employment for personal gain, even though his or her employer suffered no direct harm. Diverting a corporate advantage that an employee acquires because of his or her employment for the benefit of the employee or another is also a breach of the duty of loyalty. Similarly, an employee may not use the employer's facilities or equipment or time that should have been devoted to the employer's business to advance the employee's personal or business interests or the interests of another.[26]

[8.6]   What is the employee's common law duty of competence?

Employees have a general duty of competence, diligence, and good faith.[27] They must act, in all circumstances, in the interest of the

---

21   *Wallack Freight Lines, Inc. v. Next Day Express, Inc.*, 273 A.D.2d 462, 463, 711 N.Y.S.2d 462 (2d Dep't 2000); *Mahuson v. Ventraq, Inc.*, 118 A.D.3d 1267, 1269, 988 N.Y.S.2d 309 (4th Dep't 2014).

22   *In re the Jud. Dissolution of Stony Cr. Indus. Inc.*, 6 Misc. 3d 1019(A), 800 N.Y.S.2d 349 (Sup. Ct., Nassau Co. 2005).

23   *Laro Maint. Corp. v. Culkin*, 267 A.D.2d 431, 433, 700 N.Y.S.2d 490 (2d Dep't 1999).

24   *Hartford v. DM Transp., Inc.*, 13 Misc. 3d 1209(A), 1209A, 824 N.Y.S.2d 754 (Sup Ct., Suffolk Co. 2006).

25   *Western Elec. Co. v. Brenner*, 41 N.Y.2d 291, 295, 392 N.Y.S.2d 409 (1977).

26   *Onsite Cos., Inc. v. Comfort*, 21 A.D.3d 1306, 1307, 802 N.Y.S.2d 578 (4th Dep't 2005).

27   *Jakks Pacific, Inc. v. Wicked Cool Toys, LLC*, No. 159812/2015, 2017 N.Y. Slip Op. 30200(U), 2017 N.Y. Misc. LEXIS 332 at *8 (Sup. Ct., N.Y. Co. Jan. 31, 2017).

employer, and not in their own interest.[28] This includes the duty to render services with the required level of skill and care.[29] In addition—although it rarely happens—the New York courts have recognized an employer's common law right to sue its own employees for negligence.[30]

[8.7]   What is the employee's common law duty to protect confidential information?

While employed, employees may not use their employer's confidential information for their own benefit, or for the benefit of someone other than their employer.[31] This includes using or disclosing employer information, even if that information falls short of being entitled to trade secret protection.[32] An employee who has access to trade secrets must exercise a standard of conduct higher than that of employees who do not and must act with utmost good faith, loyalty, and honesty.[33] The duty to protect employer trade secrets and confidential information may extend beyond the termination of employment for so long as the information in question is still confidential.[34]

[8.8]   If an employee has not signed a confidentiality agreement, is the employer still protected against the disclosure of confidential information?

Yes. The common law duty to protect an employer's confidences arises when an employment relationship is created, whether or not any written contract of employment or confidentiality agreement exists.[35]

---

28   *Id.*

29   *See generally* Jeffery M. Judd, Note, *The Implied Covenant of Good Faith and Fair Dealing, Examining Employees' Good Faith Duties,* 39 Hastings L. J. 483, 498 (1988).

30   *Gabourel v. Bouchard Transp. Co., Inc.,* 901 F. Supp. 142, 144–45 (S.D.N.Y. 1995).

31   *Shalor Designs, Inc. v. NBA Props., Inc.,* 264 A.D.2d 686, 687–88, 696 N.Y.S.2d 32 (1st Dep't 1999).

32   *Town & Country House & Home Serv., Inc. v. Newbery,* 119 N.Y.S.2d 324, 325 (Sup. Ct., Nassau Co. 1952), *aff'd,* 3 N.Y.2d 554, 170 N.Y.S.2d 328 (1958).

33   *Schroeder v. Pinterest Inc.,* 133 A.D.3d 12, 22, 27, 17 N.Y.S.3d 678 (1st Dep't 2015).

34   *Town & Country House & Home Serv., Inc.,* 119 N.Y.S.2d at 325.

35   *Business Networks of New York Inc. v. Complete Network Solutions, Inc.,* Index No. 605463/98, 1999 N.Y. Misc. Lexis 718, *12, 1999 WL 126088 (Sup. Ct., N.Y. Co. Feb. 19, 1999).

[8.9]   Do all employees owe the same duties?

No. While all employees owe their employer a duty of loyalty, certain employees, by virtue of positions that require trust, also owe their employers a more demanding "fiduciary" duty. A fiduciary relationship creates a higher level of trust than normally is present in the marketplace.[36] The most famous formulation of this standard was set forth by New York Court of Appeals Judge Benjamin Cardozo in 1928:

> Many forms of conduct permissible in a workaday world for those acting at arm's length, are forbidden to those bound by fiduciary ties. A trustee is held to something stricter than the morals of the market place. Not honesty alone, but the punctilio of an honor the most sensitive, is then the standard of behavior.[37]

Parties may commit by agreement to a higher level of responsibility and fair dealing between them than what a typical arm's length transaction may require. Circumstances may also create a fiduciary relationship between the parties, particularly where one party is disadvantaged or less informed than the other.[38]

Further, some employment relationships create fiduciary obligations by their very nature. For example, the officers employed by a corporation are fiduciaries and owe that corporation a duty of utmost good faith in the discharge of their corporate duties.[39]

[8.10]   Can an employer require an employee to sign an employment agreement?

Yes, but with some limitations. An employer may condition initial or continuing employment on the acceptance of certain terms, including signing a written contract.[40] So long as the contract terms are lawful, the employer may refuse to employ anyone who does not agree to them. However, there are terms that an employer may not demand, including

---

36   *Lamdin v. Broadway Surface Adver. Corp.*, 272 N.Y. 133, 138 (1936).

37   *Meinhard v. Salmon*, 249 N.Y. 458, 464 (1928). Judge Cardozo finished his judicial career as a Justice of the United States Supreme Court.

38   *Pai v. Blue Man Grp. Publ., LLC*, No. 650427/2016, 2018 N.Y. Slip Op. 30454(U), 2018 N.Y. Misc. Lexis 893, *6–7 (Sup. Ct., N.Y. Co. Mar. 15, 2018).

39   *Busino v. Meachem*, 270 A.D.2d 606, 609, 704 N.Y.S.2d 690 (3d Dep't 2000).

40   *Taylor v. Blaylock & Partners, L.P.*, 240 A.D.2d 289, 290, 659 N.Y.S.2d 257 (1st Dep't 1997).

demands that an employee waive the right to claim workers' compensation benefits, or release the right to be paid minimum wage and overtime, or relinquish the right to work in a safe working environment that is compliant with federal, New York, and local safety standards.[41]

Additionally, while an initial employment agreement may include a covenant not to compete with the employer's business (or not to solicit the employer's employees or customers) for some period after his or her employment ends, an employer may not *later* impose such a covenant without some additional consideration to the employee (usually, a payment or a contract renewal) in exchange for the covenant. *See* Chapter 9 of this book, "Protecting the Employer's Business," for additional discussion of covenants not to compete

[8.11] Can an employee be required to arbitrate any employment disputes?

An employer may condition initial employment and continued employment on any lawful terms, including an agreement waiving access to the courts and compelling the use of arbitration to resolve workplace disputes.[42] *See also* § 2.21 of this book.

There have, however, been efforts to impose limitations on the scope of agreements to arbitrate. Effective October 11, 2019 the New York Civil Practice Law and Rules were amended to provide that an employment agreement cannot require an individual to submit claims of employment discrimination to mandatory arbitration.[43] However, the statute further provides that it does not apply where federal law or applicable collective bargaining agreement are inconsistent. In *Latif v. Morgan Stanley & Co. LLC*, the United States District Court for the Southern District of New York held that a provision of the New York Human Rights Law prohibiting mandatory arbitration of sexual harassment claims is inconsistent with the Federal Arbitration Act (FAA) and is therefore invalid. This holding suggests that an employer may be able to require employees to sign an agreement to submit employment discrimination and harassment claims to arbitration as well.[44]

---

41   *Harper v. Fredonia Seed Co.*, 275 A.D. 244, 245, 89 N.Y.S.2d 530 (4th Dep't 1949).

42   *Fletcher v. Kidder, Peabody & Co.*, 81 N.Y.2d 623, 641, 601 N.Y.S.2d 686, *cert. denied*, 510 U.S. 993 (1993).

43   CPLR 7515.

44   *Latif v. Morgan Stanley & Co. LLC*, No. 18-CV-11528, 2019 U.S. Dist. LEXIS 107020, 2019 WL 2610985 (S.D.N.Y. June 26, 2019).

[8.12]   What is the faithless servant doctrine?

Under the faithless servant doctrine, an employee who is faithless in the performance of his or her duties forfeits the right to compensation, whether in the form of commissions or salary. This includes the forfeiture of any amounts previously paid to the employee while he or she was acting in a faithless manner.[45]

Because forfeiture is a drastic remedy, the courts apply this rule narrowly.[46] Generally, such a claim "is available only where the employee has acted directly against the employer's interests—as in embezzlement, improperly competing with the current employer, or usurping business opportunities."[47] Thus, *intentional* wrongdoing is required to prove that an employee has been faithless. For example, a salesman compensated solely on commission does not breach either a duty of good faith or of loyalty by failing to zealously pursue sales.[48]

There is an additional discussion of the faithless servant doctrine in Chapter 9 of this book, "Protecting the Employer's Business."

[8.13]   Does an employee have an obligation to respond to an employer's work-related questions?

Yes. The duty to respond to work-related questions is part of the employee's common law duty of loyalty and good faith. It is implied in every employment relationship that the employee will obey the lawful and reasonable rules, orders, and instructions of the employer, which reasonably extends to an instruction to respond truthfully to the employer's questions.[49] In the private sector, there is no workplace right to remain silent even if an employee's answer might be incriminating.

---

45   *Feiger v. Iral Jewelry, Ltd.*, 41 N.Y.2d 928, 928, 394 N.Y.S.2d 626 (1977); *see also Murray v. Beard*, 102 N.Y. 505 (1886); *Beatty v. Guggenheim Exploration Co.*, 223 N.Y. 294 (1919); *Wendt v. Fischer*, 243 N.Y. 439 (1926).

46   *Linder v. Innovative Commercial Sys. LLC*, 41 Misc. 3d 1214(A), 981 N.Y.S.2d 636 (Sup. Ct., N.Y. Co. 2013), *aff'd*, 127 A.D.3d 670, 8 N.Y.S.3d 191 (1st Dep't 2015).

47   *Veritas Capital Mgmt., LLC v. Campbell*, 82 A.D.3d 529, 530, 918 N.Y.S.2d 448 (1st Dep't 2011); *accord Pozner v. Fox Broadcasting Co.*, 59 Misc. 3d 897, 900, 74 N.Y.S.3d 711 (Sup. Ct., N.Y. Co. 2018); *Soam Corp. v. Trane Co.*, 202 A.D.2d 162, 162, 608 N.Y.S.2d 177 (1st Dep't 1994) (employee promoted competitor's products over employer's); *In re Blumenthal (Kingsford)*, 40 A.D.3d 318, 318, 833 N.Y.S.2d 897 (1st Dep't 2007) (employee made systematic unauthorized transfers from business to himself and his wife).

48   *Linder*, 41 Misc. 3d 1214(A).

49   27 Am. Jur. 2d Employment Relationship § 155; 52 N.Y. Jur. Employment Relations § 228.

[8.14] **What information must an employer provide to employees in writing** *at the time of* **employment?**

To create an employment relationship, there must be a sufficiently precise and definite exchange of promises between an employer and a prospective employee to establish the terms of the employment.[50] Often, this exchange of information and promises will be verbal or even implied from past history and all the pertinent circumstances,[51] but New York law requires that certain information be disclosed in writing in English or in the new employee's primary language.[52] Specifically, the New York Wage Theft Prevention Act requires written disclosure of the following information at the time of hire:

- The rate or rates of pay and basis thereof, whether paid by the hour, shift, day, week, salary, piece, commission, or other;

- Allowances, if any, claimed as part of the minimum wage, including tip, meal, or lodging allowances;

- The regular pay day designated by the employer;

- The name of the employer and any "doing business as" names used by the employer;

- The physical address of the employer's main office or principal place of business and a mailing address if different; and

- The telephone number of the employer.[53]

New York law also requires disclosure of the employer's policy on sick leave, vacation, personal leave, holidays, and hours, either in writing or by public posting.[54] Various federal and New York laws also require employers to display informational postings at prominent places in the workplace.

This topic is also discussed in Chapters 1 and 3 of this book, "Recruitment and Hiring" and "Wages and Salary," at §§ 1.41 and 3.1, respectively.

---

50   Sulds, New York Employment Law, Ch. 1, § 1.02 (Matthew Bender).

51   *Id.*

52   Labor Law § 195(5).

53   Labor Law § 195(1); *see also* Chapter 1 of this book at § 1.4.1.

54   Labor Law § 195(5).

[8.15] **What information must an employer provide to employees** *during* **employment?**

Employers have disclosure obligations both to employees individually and to employees as a group.

[8.15.1] *Wage Statements*

An employer must provide a written wage statement every time an employee is paid.[55] The wage statement must contain the following information: (1) the dates of work covered by that payment of wages; (2) the name of the employee; (3) the name of the employer; (4) the address and phone number of the employer; (4) the rate or rates of pay and the basis for pay (whether paid by the hour, shift, day, week, salary, piece, commission, or other); (5) the employee's gross wages for the period; (6) any deductions taken against salary; (7) any allowances claimed as part of the minimum wage (e.g., tips, meals, and housing); and (8) the employee's net wages for the period.

For employees who are not exempt from overtime compensation, the wage statement must also include: (1) the regular hourly rate or rates of pay; (2) the overtime rate or rates of pay; (3) the number of regular hours worked, and (4) the number of overtime hours worked.

For employees paid a piece rate (payment of a fixed sum for service or production, as opposed to payment by the hour, week, or some other time increment), the statement must also include: (1) the applicable piece rate or rates of pay and (2) number of pieces completed at each piece rate.

Upon request by an employee, an employer must furnish an explanation in writing of how the employee's wages were computed. An employer must also notify employees in writing or by publicly posting its policies on sick leave, vacation, personal leave, holidays and hours.

[8.15.2] *Benefits Disclosures*

An employer that offers certain fringe benefits, such as pension, retirement benefits, health, life, or disability insurance, or other tax deferred benefits, must provide disclosures required by federal law (most notably, the Employee Retirement Income Security Act[56] (ERISA)) and New York law. Disclosures are also required for unpaid leave under the federal

---

55   Labor Law § 195(3).

56   29 U.S.C. §§ 1001–1461.

Family and Medical Leave Act (FMLA) and paid family leave under the New York Paid Family Leave Act.[57]

[8.15.3] *Workplace Posting Requirements*

Posting requirements are imposed by nearly all of the federal and New York statutes that regulate employment or the workplace generally. For example, mandatory posting requirements exist for the minimum wage and overtime laws, the workers' compensation and disability laws, the Family and Medical Leave Act, Law, the Polygraph Protection Act, the Employee Retirement Income Security Act, both federal and New York anti-discrimination laws, the Wage Theft Prevention Act, the New York Paid Family Leave Law, and the workplace safety laws, among others. Although the required postings may be obtained from the appropriate federal or New York oversight agencies, many employers prefer to purchase posters that consolidate all the mandatory postings into a single, very large, poster.[58]

[8.16] What information must an employer provide to employees *at the end* of employment?

An employer must inform a terminated employee, in writing and no later than five days after termination, of the exact date of termination and the exact date of cancellation of employee benefits.[59]

[8.17] What workplace records must an employer retain, and for how long?

Payroll records must be retained for at least six years,[60] but the general rule of thumb is to keep all employment records for at least six years.[61]

An employer may maintain and retain records in electronic form, but those records or certified copies of them need to be available upon request

---

57   *See* 29 C.F.R. § 825.300 (employer notice requirements under the Family Medical Leave Act); N.Y. Workers Comp. Law § 229 (employer notice requirements regarding New York paid family leave).

58   Comprehensive listings of the federal and New York posting requirements may be found on websites maintained by the United States and New York Departments of Labor, as follows: www.dol.gov/general/topics/posters/ and www.labor.ny.gov/workerprotection/laborstandards/employer/posters.shtm.

59   Labor Law § 195(6).

60   Labor Law § 195(4).

61   *See* Chapter 1 of this book, "Recruitment and Hiring," at §§ 1.6 and 1.18 for a discussion of retaining employment application records.

of the New York State Commissioner of Labor at the place of employment.[62] Similarly, employers may provide their employees' payroll information electronically, but employees need to be able to access that information and print it out if desired at the place of business.[63]

In Chapter 1 of this book, we recommend that employers retain employment *application* records for three years: *see* §§ 1.6 and 1.8.

[8.18] Are employers required to protect employee information from third parties?

An employer has a common law duty to take reasonable precautions to protect the personal identifying information (PII) that it collects from its employees. While there is not a bright-line standard as to what is "reasonable," courts will balance the level of risk, the burden and costs of the safeguards, and the relationship between the parties, among other things, in deciding the extent of the employer's obligation.[64]

The duty to protect PII is also codified in New York Labor Law making it illegal for an employer to "communicate an employee's personal identifying information to the general public."[65] Further, the statute provides that "[i]t shall be presumptive evidence that a violation . . . was knowing if the employer has not put in place policies or procedures to safeguard against" the disclosure of PII.[66]

There are additional requirements imposed by both federal and state law regarding breaches of cybersecurity, but these are beyond the scope of this book. When its electronic data systems have been breached, an employer should consult legal counsel as to its disclosure and remediation obligations.

---

62   12 N.Y.C.R.R. § 142-2.6(d).

63   N.Y. Department of Labor Opinion Letter RO-10-0072 (July 13, 2010), https://www.labor.ny.gov/legal/counsel/pdf/Wage%20Statements/RO-10-0072.pdf; *see also* N.Y. Department of Labor, *Wage Theft Prevention Act Frequently Asked Questions*, https://www.labor.ny.gov/workerprotection/laborstandards/PDFs/wage-theft-prevention-act-faq.pdf.

64   *Sackin v. Transperfect Glob., Inc.*, 278 F. Supp. 3d 739, 748 (S.D.N.Y. 2017). Emphasis will be placed on the fact that employers are in better positions to secure this information, and require it from their employees, so they should bear the burden of potential liability. In *Sackin*, the court held that erecting a digital firewall, conducting data security training, and adopting retention and destruction policies were all examples of reasonable precautions.

65   Labor Law § 203-d(1)(d).

66   Labor Law § 203-d(3).

[8.19] What ongoing documents and information must an employer provide to employees?

There are a number of federal and New York laws which impose a duty on an employer to disclose information to its employees. For example, the federal Occupational Safety and Health Act imposes obligations to disclose information about potential workplace hazards, safety precautions and procedures, and other disclosures that might protect employees or promote workplace safety.[67] The New York Wage Theft Prevention Act requires an employer to furnish an explanation in writing of how an employee's wages are computed.[68]

[8.20] Do employees have access to the contents of their personnel files?[69]

In New York, employees do not have the right to demand access to their own personnel files. These records are the property of the employer, which may decide whether and in what circumstances they may be disclosed or copied. Employers should be careful in deciding whether, and on what terms, to provide access.

It should be noted that in unionized workplaces, many union agreements give employees the right to review (and, in some instances, to annotate or copy) the contents of their personnel files.

As a practical matter, it is often advisable to share evaluative materials which are critical of an employee's job performance or workplace behavior; that way, in the event of a later dispute, the employee cannot claim that he or she was not notified of the deficiencies.

[8.21] What information must an employee provide to the employer?

Federal law requires that employers verify the identity of all employees via U.S. Citizenship and Immigration Services Form I-9, and also to collect their tax information on form W-2. Accordingly, an employee must furnish the employer with the information needed to complete those forms.

---

67   29 C.F.R. § 1904.35.

68   *See* §§ 8.14–8.15 above.

69   *See also* Chapter 12 of this book, "Miscellaneous Topics of Interest," at § 12.4.

An employer may also require employees to provide other information (such as emergency contact information, home e-mail addresses, mobile telephone numbers and the like) which is reasonably related to the employer's ability to conduct its business.

[8.22] Can an employer regulate an employee's off-premises political activities?

Generally, no.[70] Under most circumstances, employees are protected from employment discrimination based on their legal political activities. Labor Law § 201-d makes it unlawful for any employer to refuse to employ, discharge from employment, or otherwise discriminate against an individual in compensation, promotion, or terms, conditions, or privileges of employment because of an individual's legal political activities outside of working hours, off of the employer's premises, and without use of the employer's equipment or other property.

There are two minor exceptions to this general rule:

• The prohibition does not apply to a person employed as a professional journalist, which is defined in Civil Rights Law § 79-h(a)(6) to mean anyone

> who, for gain or livelihood, is engaged in gathering, preparing, collecting, writing, editing, filming, taping, or photographing of news intended for a newspaper, magazine, news agency, press association or wire service, or other professional medium or agency which has as one of its regular functions the processing and researching of news intended for dissemination to the public.

• The prohibition also does not apply to certain federal, state, or local officers or employees who would otherwise be prohibited from engaging in certain types of political activities under federal law.[71]

[8.23] What types of political activities are protected under New York Labor Law § 201-d?

Under Labor Law § 201-d, the term "political activities" is defined as: "(i) running for public office; (ii) campaigning for a candidate for public

---

70   *See also* Chapter 1 of this book, "Recruitment and Hiring," at §§ 1.8 and 1.29, and Chapter 10, "Discipline," at § 10.20 for further discussion of the Labor Law § 201-d protections.

71   Labor Law § 201-d(3).

office; or (iii) participating in fund-raising activities for the benefit of a candidate, political party, or political advocacy group."

[8.24] Can an employer regulate an employee's off-premises recreational activities?

No. Labor Law § 201-d makes it unlawful for any employer to refuse to employ, discharge from employment, or otherwise discriminate against an individual in compensation, promotion, or terms, conditions, or privileges of employment because of an individual's legal recreational activities outside work hours, off of the employer's premises, and without use of the employer's equipment or other property.

Under Labor Law § 201-d, the term "recreational activities" is defined as "any lawful, leisure-time activity, for which the employee receives no compensation and which is generally engaged in for recreational purposes, including but not limited to sports, games, hobbies, exercise, reading and the viewing of television, movies and similar material."

[8.25] Can an employer regulate an employee's off-premises romantic activities with another employee?

An employer can enforce a rule that employees should not engage in romantic or dating relationships with one another. Appellate courts that have addressed this issue have held that engaging in a romantic relationship with a co-worker is not a protected "recreational activity" under Labor Law § 201-d, even if the relationship only occurs outside of work hours and off the employer's premises.

In *State v. Wal-Mart Stores*, the Appellate Division, Third Department considered a case in which two employees were discharged for violating the employer's policy prohibiting a "dating relationship" between a married employee and a co-worker other than his or her own spouse.[72] The Third Department reversed the lower court's denial of the employer's motion to dismiss the claim under Labor Law § 201-d, stating: "To us, 'dating' is entirely distinct from and, in fact, bears little resemblance to 'recreational activity.'"[73]

Similarly, in *Hudson v. Goldman Sachs & Co.*, the Appellate Division, First Department, affirmed the dismissal of the plaintiff's claim that his employer violated Labor Law § 201-d by discharging him for having an

---

72   207 A.D.2d 150, 151, 621 N.Y.S.2d 158 (3d Dep't 1995).

73   *Id.* at 152.

extramarital affair with a co-worker. The First Department stated that "romantic relationships are not protected 'recreational activities' within the meaning of" Labor Law § 201-d. [74]

However, in *Manhattan Pizza Hut, Inc. v. New York State Human Rights Appeal Board*,[75] the New York Court of Appeals ruled that the prohibition of "marital status" discrimination found in the New York Human Rights Law[76] did not prevent an employer from enforcing its anti-nepotism law where one spouse was the direct supervisor of the other spouse.

[8.26] Can an employer take action against an applicant or employee because the individual smokes cigarettes or drinks alcoholic beverages outside of work hours?

No. Labor Law § 201-d makes it unlawful for any employer to refuse to employ, discharge from employment, or otherwise discriminate against an individual in compensation, promotion, or terms, conditions, or privileges of employment because of an individual's legal use of consumable products prior to the beginning or after the conclusion of the employee's work hours, off of the employer's premises, and without use of the employer's equipment or other property.[77]

Under Labor Law Section 201-d, the term "work hours" is defined as "all time, including paid and unpaid breaks and meal periods, that the employee is suffered, permitted or expected to be engaged in work, and all time the employee is actually engaged in work."

[8.27] Can an employer take action against an applicant or employee for pro-union activity?

No. Labor Law § 201-d makes it unlawful for any employer to refuse to employ, discharge from employment, or otherwise discriminate against an individual in compensation, promotion, or terms, conditions, or privileges of employment because of an individual's membership in a union or any exercise of rights granted under the National Labor Relations Act[78] (the federal law governing the right of private sector employees to engage

---

74   283 A.D.2d 246, 246–47, 725 N.Y.S.2d 318 (1st Dep't 2001),

75   51 N.Y.2d 506 (1980).

76   Executive Law § 296.

77   Again, *see* Chapters 1 and 10 of this book, at §§ 1.8, 1.29, and 10.20 for further discussion of the Labor Law § 201-d protections.

78   29 U.S.C. §§ 151–169.

in union activity) or the Taylor Law[79] (the New York law governing the right of public sector employees to engage in union activity).

[8.28] What remedies are available for violations of New York Labor Law § 201-d?

Under Labor Law § 201-d, the New York State Attorney General is authorized to apply for an order enjoining or restraining the commission or continuance of an alleged violation of the statute. If the Attorney General commences such a proceeding, a civil penalty in the amount of $300 can be imposed for the first violation and a civil penalty in the amount of $500 can be imposed for each subsequent violation.

In addition, an aggrieved individual can commence an action for equitable relief and damages under the statute. The equitable relief may include reinstatement to his or her employment. The monetary damages may include back pay for the time period when the individual otherwise would have been employed if the employer had not discriminated against the employee in violation of the statute. At least one court has held, however, that punitive damages, emotional distress damages, and reimbursement for attorneys' fees are not authorized under Labor Law § 201-d.[80]

[8.29] Can an employer maintain a policy restricting an employee's personal use of social media outside of work hours?[81]

During working hours, an employer has broad latitude to restrict employees' use of social media. Outside of working hours, an employer has a more limited scope.

There are a number of restrictions that an employer can place on an employee's personal use of social media outside of work hours. For example, an employer can and should restrict employees from engaging in sexual harassment or other types of harassment or discriminatory conduct against co-workers based on a protected characteristic[82] through personal social media accounts, even if such conduct occurs outside of working hours and

---

79   Civil Service Law §§ 200–215. Civil Service Law § 209-a also makes it unlawful to discriminate against any public employee by reason of protected union activity.

80   *McCavitt v. Swiss Reins. Am. Corp.*, 89 F. Supp. 2d 495 (S.D.N.Y. 2000).

81   This section addresses private sector employers only. While public sector employers may impose some regulations on use of social media, the permissible scope of those restrictions requires a First Amendment analysis which is beyond the scope of this book.

82   *See* Chapter 11 for a much more detailed description of protected characteristics and workplace discrimination and harassment issues.

without use of the employer's equipment or property. The model sexual harassment policy issued by the New York State Division of Human Rights provides that sexual harassment "is not limited to the physical workplace itself" and that "[c]alls, texts, e-mails, and social media usage by employees can constitute unlawful workplace harassment, even if they occur away from the workplace premises or during non-work hours."[83]

Similarly, an employer may impose: (1) a prohibition on engaging in rude, condescending, disparaging, or uncivil behavior toward other employees or other individuals with whom the employer does business (such as clients, customers, vendors, patients, etc.); (2) a prohibition on using the employer's logo or trademark without prior written approval from the employer; and (3) a prohibition on disclosing confidential or proprietary information about the employer, such as confidential financial data, customer information, or trade secrets.[84]

However, employers should be aware that the federal National Labor Relations Board has taken a very expansive view of the protections applicable to union organizing and other activity. An employer may not, under the National Labor Relations Act, promulgate a social media policy that includes any restrictions on an employee's right to form, join, or assist a labor organization, or to engage in other concerted activities for the purpose of collective bargaining or other mutual aid or protection.[85] For example, an employer may not prohibit employees from discussing their wages, benefits, working conditions, or other terms and conditions of employment with one another or with third parties through personal social media accounts.[86]

[8.30] Can an employer discharge or discipline an employee for inappropriate social media activity?

In general, yes, but an employer should approach these issues with caution.

If an at-will employee violates the employer's social media policy, the employer can take disciplinary action, but should be careful to do so in a manner that will not be considered discriminatory based on a protected

---

83   *See* N.Y. Division of Human Rights Model Sexual Harassment Policy, https://www.ny.gov/sites/ny.gov/files/atoms/files/StatewideSexualHarassment_PreventionPolicy.pdf.

84   *See* NLRB General Counsel Memo 18-04 (June 16, 2018).

85   29 U.S.C. § 157.

86   *See Long Is. Assoc. for AIDS Care, Inc.*, 364 NLRB No. 28, Slip Op. at 1 (June 14, 2016); *Schwan's Home Serv.*, 364 NLRB No. 20, Slip Op. at 17 (June 10, 2016).

characteristic. For example, if an employer discharges a male employee for a violation of its social media policy, but only issues a written warning to a similarly situated female employee who commits the same or a similar violation, the employer may potentially be subject to liability for sex discrimination.

If an employee is covered by a "just cause" provision in a collective bargaining agreement, or an individual contractual provision that affords the employee similar "just cause" protection, the employer can discharge or discipline the employee for a violation of the employer's social media policy, but the employee (or union) may have a right to challenge the discipline or discharge after it occurs. So, under these circumstances, an employer should be sure that the discipline or discharge meets the standard of "just cause" in order to be able to successfully defend itself against such a challenge. Arbitrators generally apply the following seven-factor test to determine if discipline or discharge is supported by just cause:

1. Whether the employee had notice of the possible or probable consequences of his or her misconduct;

2. Whether the employer's work rule was reasonably related to the orderly, efficient, and safe operation of the employer's business;

3. Whether the employer made an effort to determine if the employee violated the work rule;

4. Whether the employer's investigation was conducted fairly and objectively;

5. Whether there was substantial evidence of the employee's misconduct;

6. Whether the employer applied its rule evenhandedly and in a nondiscriminatory manner; and

7. Whether the degree of discipline is commensurate with the seriousness of the offense and the employee's prior work record.[87]

See Chapter 10 of this book, "Discipline," at § 10.6 for a more extended discussion of "just cause."

---

87   *See Engelhard Corp.*, 122 Lab. Arb. Rep. 81, 86–87 (Howell, 2006); *Atmos Energy Corp.*, 121 Lab. Arb. Rep. 908, 913 (Howell, 2005).

[8.31] Can an employer restrict employee use of workplace computers and electronic systems?

Yes.[88] There is no statutory or common law prohibition against an employer promulgating a policy that restricts an employee's use of workplace computers and electronic systems. Employees do not have an enforceable expectation of privacy arising from their use of employer computers, employer electronic mail, or internet access obtained through the employer's computers or networks. That said, it is prudent to inform employees to that effect, in order to avoid misunderstandings.

There are a number of restrictions that an employer may place on an employee's use of workplace computers and electronic systems. For example, an employer may include in its electronic systems policy:

- A prohibition on saving personal information and files on the employer's network;

- A prohibition on accessing, viewing, or downloading inappropriate content through the employer's electronic system;

- A prohibition on connecting personal devices to the employer's computers and electronic system without authorization from the employer;

- A prohibition against adding, deleting, or modifying software or applications on the employer's computers or network;

- A prohibition on using the employer's workplace computers and electronic systems to engage in any harassing conduct toward other employees or individuals with whom the employer does business (such as clients, customers, vendors, patients, etc.);

- A prohibition on using the employer's workplace computers and electronic system in a manner that violates copyright laws; and

- A prohibition on engaging in excessive personal use of the employer's workplace computers and electronic system that interferes with the employee's work duties or the work duties of other employees.[89]

---

88   *See also* Chapter 12 of this book, "Miscellaneous Topics of Interest," at § 12.12.

89   While an employer would be within its rights to prohibit all personal use of employer electronic systems, this is probably not realistic—and rules which are "more honored in the breach than the observance" can become difficult to enforce.

To some very limited extent, special protections may apply to protected union activity. In 2014, the National Labor Relations Board (NLRB), in *Purple Communications, Inc.*, held that employees have a presumptive right to use their employer's e-mail system during non-working time to communicate regarding union organizing and to engage in other protected concerted activities under Section 7 of the National Labor Relations Act.[90] However, that case was substantially overruled at the end of 2019 in *Caesars Entertainment d/b/a Rio All-Suites Hotel and Casino*. In the 2019 decision, the NLRB stated that unions have no right to use "employer-owned televisions, bulletin boards, copy machines, telephones or public address systems," and that access to employer e-mail systems would be required only in "those rare cases where an employer's email system furnishes the *only* reasonable means for employees to communicate with one another" (emphasis supplied).[91]

[8.32]   Can an employer discharge or discipline an employee for inappropriate use of workplace computers and electronic systems?

In general, yes; but see § 8.31 above for a discussion of precautions which should be considered.

[8.33]   Can an employer maintain a policy prohibiting employees from taking photographs or secretly recording conversations in the workplace?

There are no laws which generally prohibit employees from taking pictures or making sound or video recordings in the workplace.[92] However, under most circumstances, an employer can promulgate and maintain a

---

90   361 NLRB 1050 (2014).

91   368 NLRB 143 (2019) (internal citations omitted). Since the NLRB's membership changes each time the party of the President changes, future changes in the Board's current point of view are entirely possible.

92   Different considerations apply to setting up recording equipment to record conversations for which a person is not present. Under Article 250 of the New York Penal Law, a person is guilty of eavesdropping, a Class E felony, when he or she unlawfully engages in "mechanical overhearing of a conversation." N.Y. Penal Law § 250.05. The phrase "mechanical overhearing of a conversation" is defined in the statute as "the intentional overhearing or recording of a conversation or discussion, without the consent of at least one party thereto, by a person not present thereat, by means of any instrument, device, or equipment." N.Y. Penal Law § 250.00(2). So, for example, if an employee secretly placed a recording device in the employer's break room and recorded conversations between and among co-workers that occurred when the employee was not present in the break room, the employee would be guilty of eavesdropping.

policy prohibiting employees from taking photographs or making recordings (both audio and video) in the workplace. There are no New York statutory restrictions on an employer's right to promulgate such a policy.

The National Labor Relations Board has opined that employers may have legitimate reasons for prohibiting photographic or video recording in the workplace. In *The Boeing Co.*,[93] it ruled that an employer's policy prohibiting the use of camera-enabled devices to capture images or video in the workplace does not violate its employees' right to engage in protected concerted activity under Section 7 of the National Labor Relations Act. The NLRB found that such a policy, when reasonably interpreted, would have only a minimal potential effect on employees' exercise of their Section 7 rights, and that this effect was outweighed by the employer's legitimate business justifications for the promulgation of the policy. The employer's legitimate business justifications included: (1) compliance with security protocols; (2) protection of the employer's confidential and proprietary information; (3) protection of employees' personally identifiable information; and (4) prevention of disclosure of potential vulnerabilities that could create a risk of a terrorist attack.[94] The NLRB also stated that, although the justifications stated by the employer in *The Boeing Co.* case were especially compelling, a no-photography rule will generally be found to be lawful under most circumstances.

The issue of whether an employer can prohibit employees from secretly recording conversations with other individuals in the workplace is less clear. In *Whole Foods Market Group, Inc.*, the National Labor Relations Board ruled that an employer's policy prohibiting employees from recording conversations with a tape recorder or other recording device (including a cell phone or any other electronic device) violated Section 8(a)(1) of the NLRA because such a policy improperly restricted employees from engaging in activities protected by Section 7 of the NLRA.[95] In 2017, that decision was affirmed in an unpublished summary order issued by the U.S. Court of Appeals for the Second Circuit, which is the federal appellate court that has jurisdiction over appeals from cases brought in the U.S. District Courts in New York.

However, on June 6, 2018, the NLRB's General Counsel issued a memorandum to all NLRB Regional Directors, Officers-in-Charge, and Resi-

---

93   365 NLRB No. 154, Slip Op. at 17 (Dec. 14, 2017).

94   *Id.* at 18.

95   363 NLRB No. 87, Slip Op. at 4 (Dec. 24, 2015).

dent Officers providing guidance on employee handbook rules.[96] Citing the dissenting opinion of NLRB Member Philip Miscimarra in *Whole Foods Market Group, Inc.*, the General Counsel stated in the guidance that no-recording rules should be treated in the same manner as no-photography rules, and are generally lawful because the legitimate business justifications (i.e., encouraging open communications among employees without fear of being recorded) outweigh the minimal potential impact on employees' exercise of their Section 7 rights.[97] Although the General Counsel's memorandum does not have binding precedential effect on the NLRB or the federal courts, it is an indication that the *Whole Foods Market Group, Inc.* decision might be reversed if the issue of an employer's no-recording policy is considered by the NLRB again.

[8.34]   **Can an employer discharge or discipline an employee for taking photographs or secretly recording conversations in the workplace?**

In general, yes; but see §§ 8.31 and 8.33 above for a discussion of precautions which should be considered.

[8.35]   **Can an employer use an employee's name or likeness for advertising purposes or for the purposes of trade?**

Not without the employee's written consent.[98] Under New York Civil Rights Law § 50, a person, firm, or corporation that uses for advertising purposes, or for the purposes of trade, the name, portrait, or picture of any living person without having first obtained the written consent of that person is guilty of a misdemeanor.

Aside from the possibility of a criminal misdemeanor conviction (which is a somewhat remote possibility), an employer can also face a civil lawsuit from an employee whose name or likeness has been unlawfully used for advertising purposes or for the purposes of trade without the employee's consent in violation of New York Civil Rights Law § 50. The employee could obtain injunctive relief preventing the employer from engaging in further unlawful use of the employee's name or likeness and could recover damages for any injuries sustained as a result of the unlawful use of the employee's name or likeness.[99] If it is found that the employer knowingly

---

96   *See* NLRB General Counsel Memorandum 18-04 (June 6, 2018).

97   *Id.*

98   *See also* Chapter 12 of this book, "Miscellaneous Topics of Interest," at § 12.11.

99   Civil Rights Law § 51.

committed a violation of New York Civil Rights Law § 50, a jury may, in its discretion, award exemplary or punitive damages to the plaintiff.[100]

There is a one-year statute of limitations for filing a claim for a violation of New York Civil Rights Law § 50.[101] The statute of limitations begins to run from the time of the first publication or broadcast of the plaintiff's name or likeness for advertising purposes without the consent of the plaintiff.[102]

[8.36] Can an employer conduct video surveillance of employees?

Some surveillance is unlawful under any circumstances. The status of other surveillance equipment may depend on whether a workplace is unionized or non-unionized.

[8.36.1] *Forbidden Surveillance*

There are certain locations where the placement of hidden cameras is unlawful. Under New York General Business Law § 395-b, it is unlawful for an owner or manager of any premises knowingly to permit or allow a video recording device to be installed or maintained in or upon the premises for purpose of surreptitiously recording a visual image of the interior of any fitting room, restroom, toilet, bathroom, washroom, shower, or any other room assigned to guests or patrons in a motel, hotel, or inn.[103] A violation is a felony and is punishable by a term of imprisonment not to exceed 15 days, or by a fine of not more than $300, or by both imprisonment and a fine.[104]

In addition, New York Penal Law § 250.45 provides that any person who, for no legitimate purpose, intentionally uses or installs, or permits the utilization or installation of an imaging device to surreptitiously view, broadcast, or record a person in a bedroom, changing room, fitting room, restroom, toilet, bathroom, washroom, shower, or any room assigned to guests or patrons in a hotel, motel, or inn, without such person's knowledge or consent, is guilty of a class E felony of unlawful surveillance in

---

100 *Id.*

101 *See Comolli v. Huntington Learning Ctrs., Inc.*, 117 F. Supp. 3d 343, 350 (S.D.N.Y. 2015), *aff'd*, 683 Fed. Appx. 27 (2d Cir. 2017).

102 *Nussenzweig v. diCorcia*, 9 N.Y.3d 184, 188, 848 N.Y.S.2d 7 (2007).

103 General Business Law § 395-b(2-a).

104 General Business Law § 395-b(5).

the second degree. Under the statute, there is a rebuttable presumption that a person who installed a video camera or other recording device in these areas did so for no legitimate purpose.

Finally, it is unlawful to install video surveillance equipment which also records conversations: this would constitute the class E felony of eavesdropping. Under Article 250 of the New York Penal Law, a person is guilty of the felony of eavesdropping via the "mechanical overhearing of a conversation."[105] The phrase "mechanical overhearing of a conversation" is defined in the statute as "the intentional overhearing or recording of a conversation or discussion, without the consent of at least one party thereto, by a person not present thereat, by means of any instrument, device, or equipment."[106] So, the installation of a video camera in a work area that has an audio recording feature, without first obtaining the consent of employees whose conversations might be recorded, would be unlawful. The representatives of the employer who installed or permitted the installation of the audio recording device without employee consent could be found guilty of a class E felony.[107] However, at least one court has held that there is no civil cause of action available for an alleged violation of New York Penal Law § 250.05.[108]

[8.36.2]   *Non-Unionized Workplaces*

In a non-unionized workplace, an employer may unilaterally install visible or hidden surveillance cameras other than as prohibited by the provisions discussed in § 8.36.1 above. An employer is not required to notify employees or obtain employee consent in order to install either hidden or visible video surveillance cameras in the workplace.

[8.36.3]   *Unionized Workplaces*

In a unionized workplace—whether private sector or public sector—an employer generally may *not* install either hidden or visible video surveil-

---

105   Penal Law § 250.05.

106   Penal Law § 250.00(2).

107   Penal Law § 250.05.

108   *See Clark v. Elam Sand & Gravel, Inc.*, 4 Misc. 3d 294, 297, 777 N.Y.S.2d 624 (Sup. Ct., Ontario Co. 2004).

lance cameras in the workplace in order to monitor or investigate employee conduct without negotiating with the union.[109]

In the private sector, the National Labor Relations Board has held that the installation of video cameras in the workplace to monitor and investigate employee conduct is mandatorily negotiable, because the cameras could detect employee misconduct that could result in discipline.[110] The NLRB and the courts have generally not been receptive to an employer's position that requiring an employer to notify employees of the presence of hidden cameras and the negotiation over the placement of cameras would compromise the investigative purpose of installing the cameras.[111]

In the public sector, the New York State Public Employment Relations Board (PERB) has ruled that the decision by an employer to engage in videotape surveillance of a workplace for monitoring and investigating employees is generally mandatorily negotiable under the Taylor Law (the New York statute that governs unionization rights of public employees).[112] However, PERB has also created a limited exception to this general rule where the utilization of video surveillance is integral to the employer's core mission.[113]

Where negotiations with the union are required, any aspect of the installation of video surveillance cameras that affects the terms and conditions of employment of bargaining unit employees must be negotiated with the union. For example, some of the issues that will likely have to be negotiated include the work areas or locations where the surveillance cameras will be placed, the circumstances under which the cameras will be activated, and the extent to which the cameras will be used to monitor employee performance and conduct.[114]

---

109   This does *not* preclude an employer from installing surveillance cameras generally to protect its premises or chattels; what is addressed in this section is surveillance specifically intended to monitor or investigate employees.

110   *Colgate-Palmolive*, 323 NLRB 515 (1997) (employer's placement of hidden surveillance cameras in an exercise facility to catch suspected thieves was "plainly germane to the working environment" and was therefore mandatorily negotiable).

111   *See Nat'l Steel Corp. v. NLRB*, 324 F.3d 928 (7th Cir. 2003).

112   *Nanuet Union Free Sch. Dist.*, 45 PERB ¶ 3007 (2011).

113   In *Nanuet Union Free Sch. Dist.*, 45 PERB ¶ 3007 (2011), PERB provided the following example: "[I]n a correctional facility, unlike a civilian workplace, videotaping may be integral to the employer's core mission, and therefore the subject might be nonmandatory if the videotaping is necessary and proportional for meeting that mission."

114   *See Nat'l Steel Corp*, 324 F.3d 928; *Nanuet Union Free Sch. Dist.*, 45 PERB ¶ 3007.

Once video surveillance equipment has been installed in a manner consistent with the duty to bargain, an equipment upgrade which only changes the technology without changing the placement of cameras, the number of cameras, the purposes for which the cameras have been installed, or any other aspect of the system that impacts the terms and conditions of employment of bargaining unit employees, will probably not require negotiation with the union in order to make the upgrade. However, if the upgrade is likely to affect the terms and conditions of employment of bargaining unit employees in a manner that the prior video surveillance system did not, it is likely that the employer would be required to negotiate with the union over any such upgrades.

[8.37] How are "whistleblowers" protected?

New York law contains multiple provisions protecting employees from retaliation by their employers on account of protected "whistleblowing" activity. Those provisions are listed in Chapter 11 of this book, "Discrimination, Harassment and Retaliation," at § 11.61; and the considerations of proof in whistleblower cases are discussed in that chapter at §§ 11.62–11.65.

Broadly stated, New York law protects any employee from discharge from employment, from any other penalty, from threats, and from any other form of discrimination or retaliation under two different sets of circumstances: first, where the employee has acted (or is believed by the employer to have acted) to vindicate rights under the Labor Law; and second—and more generally—where the employee has complained of conduct which is unlawful for any reason, and which is *also* either a danger to the public health or safety, or constitutes health care fraud.

The actions that give rise to whistleblower protection involving Labor Law violations are set out in Labor Law § 215 as follows:

- *The employee has made a good-faith complaint* to the employer, to the Commissioner of Labor, to the New York State Attorney General, or to anyone else *that the employer has violated the Labor Law;*[115]

- *The employer believes* that the employee has made a protected complaint;[116]

---

115   Labor Law § 215(1)(a)(i).

116   Labor Law § 215(1)(a)(ii).

- The employee has taken legal action against the employer asserting a claim arising under the Labor Law;[117]

- *The employee has provided information* to the Commissioner of labor or the New York State Attorney General;[118]

- *The employee has testified, or is about to testify*, in a proceeding commenced under the Labor Law;[119]

- The employee has exercised any other rights under the Labor Law;[120]

- The Commissioner of Labor has made an adverse determination against the employer which involves the employee.[121]

In addition, employees are even more broadly protected by Labor Law § 740 if they disclose, or threaten to disclose, either to a supervisor in their place of work *or* to a public investigatory body, *any* action or practice of their employer "that is in violation of law, rule or regulation which violation presents a substantial or specific danger to the public health or safety, or which constitutes health care fraud."[122]

However, unlike the protections of Labor Law § 715, the protection under Labor Law § 740 for whistleblowing complaints by *employees of private-sector employers* applies *only* if the employee has, before taking a complaint to a public body, first brought the matter to the attention of a supervisor, and the employer has had "a reasonable opportunity" to correct the improper condition and has failed to do so.[123]

---

117   Labor Law § 215(1)(a)(iii)

118   Labor Law § 215(1)(a)(iv).

119   Labor Law § 215(1)(a)(v).

120   Labor Law § 215(1)(a)(vi).

121   Labor Law § 215(1)(a)(vii).

122   Labor Law § 740(2)(a). Additional specific prohibitions applicable to employers in the health care field are set forth in Labor Law § 741.

123   Labor Law § 740(3). However, the employee is protected *without* having first advised a supervisor if the employer retaliates because he or she has provided information to or testified before a public body with respect to the condition, or has objected or refused to participate in the activity giving rise to the condition, Labor Law § 740(2)(b)–(c).

Section 75-b of the Civil Service Law gives *employees of public-sector employers*[124] the same protections as are afforded by Labor Law § 740, and also, more generally, includes employee complaints of "improper governmental action."[125] In contrast to private-sector employees, there is no requirement that public-sector employees must first make an internal complaint in order to be protected.

[8.38]   What are the penalties for whistleblower violations?

A private-sector employer that discharges or otherwise penalizes an employee for whistleblowing activity protected by Labor Law § 215 (*see* § 8.37 of this chapter) is subject to two possible consequences: (a) proceedings by the Commissioner of Labor, or (b) a lawsuit by the employee. More specifically:

- The Commissioner of Labor may investigate any violations for a period going back six years; and upon finding a violation, may assess a fine of between $1,000 and $20,000; order a payment to the penalized employee of liquidated damages up to $20,000; order injunctive relief including rehiring or reinstatement; and order front pay and back pay as an alternative to reinstatement.[126]

- The employee may sue within two years after the prohibited conduct and request prospective injunctive relief to prevent future violations; request both court costs and reasonable attorneys' fees; and request for rehiring or reinstatement with no loss of seniority; and front pay and back pay.[127]

- If the employee has chosen to file a complaint with the Commissioner of Labor (but the employee does not have to file such a complaint in order to sue), the two-year period for the employee to bring suit does not begin to run until the earlier of: (a) the issuance

---

124   "Public employer" is defined in Civil Service Law § 75-b(1)(a) as

> (i) the state of New York, (ii) a county, city, town, village or any other political subdivision or civil division of the state, (iii) a school district or any governmental entity operating a public school, college or university, (iv) a public improvement or special district, (v) a public authority, commission or public benefit corporation, or (vi) any other public corporation, agency, instrumentality or unit of government which exercises governmental power under the laws of the state.

125   Civil Service Law § 75-b(2)(a).

126   Labor Law § 215(1)(b).

127   Labor Law § 215(2)(a).

of a compliance order by the Commissioner, or (b) notice from the Commissioner to the employee that the investigation has been concluded.[128]

- Employers and their agents (including corporate officers) who violate Labor Law § 215 may be prosecuted for Class B misdemeanors.[129]

- A private-sector employer that engages in "retaliatory personnel action" protected by Labor Law § 740 (*see* § 8.37 of this chapter) may be sued by the employee within one year after the retaliatory action (two years in the case of a health care employer), and may be subject to the same relief as is available under Labor Law § 215(2)(a).[130] It is worth noting, however, that if an employee brings such an action "without basis in law or in fact," the court may, in its discretion, award court costs and reasonable attorneys' fees to the prevailing employer.[131]

- A public-sector employer that discharges or otherwise penalizes an employee for whistleblowing activity protected by Civil Service Law § 75-b (*see* § 8.37 of this chapter) is subject to one of two alternative consequences:

  - If the employee is entitled to a hearing or other process prior to discharge or discipline, either by law or by a collective bargaining agreement, the employer's whistleblower violation is a defense to the disciplinary proceeding, and is a basis for reinstatement and back pay or other appropriate action if the employee has already been discharged or penalized.[132]

  - If the employee is *not* entitled to a hearing or other process prior to discharge or discipline, then the employee may sue and obtain the same relief as is provided under Labor Law § 740, described above.[133]

---

128   Labor Law § 215(2)(b).

129   Labor Law § 215(3).

130   Labor Law §§ 740(4)(a), 740(4)(d), 740(5).

131   Labor Law § 740(6).

132   Civil Service Law §§ 75-b(2), 75-b(3)(a).

133   Civil Service Law § 75-b(4).

PROTECTING THE EMPLOYER'S BUSINESS

Howard M. Miller
Candace J. Gomez

Edited by Jeffrey A. Kehl

CHAPTER OVERVIEW

In Chapter 8, "Employer and Employee Rights and Obligations," we review the general obligations which the law imposes on employers and employees, including the employee's general duty of loyalty (§ 8.5), the obligation to protect the employer's confidential information (§§ 8.7–8.8) and (briefly) the "faithless servant doctrine" (§ 8.12). In this chapter, we expand on the discussion of unfair competition and the ramifications of the faithless servant doctrine.

The law of unfair competition deserves a book of its own and a detailed analysis is beyond the scope of this volume. Cases involving unfair competition by employees are highly fact-specific, and no employer that wants to take action against an employee for unfair competition should do so without first consulting labor litigation counsel familiar with the law in this area. Accordingly, what is offered here is a general overview.

Unfair competition by an employee (or a former employee) can take one of two forms:

- Some conduct is prohibited by the common law as inherently inconsistent with the duties an employee owes to an employer. This conduct includes setting up a competing business while working for the employer, or using the employer's trade secrets or confidential information to the detriment of the employer, or to the benefit of some third party.

- Other forms of conduct are lawful in and of themselves, but may be restricted—within reason—by an agreement between the employer and an employee (often referred to as a "non-compete" agreement or a "restrictive covenant") to the effect that for some period of time following the end of his or her employment, the former employee will not compete with the former employer, and/or will not solicit the employees or customers of the former employer to do business with the former employee. While these covenants protect valid interests of the former employer, they also have the necessary effect of limiting the former employee's ability to earn a livelihood. Accordingly, courts will closely scrutinize these covenants to make sure that they are reasonable as to the scope of prohibited conduct, the duration (length) of the prohibition, and the geographic area encompassed by the prohibition.

The specific issues addressed below are as follows:

[9.1]   **May an employee make arrangements to compete with his or her employer while still employed?**

No. A classic example of what an employee may *not* do to his or her employer was described in a 1954 decision from New York's highest state court in *Duane Jones Company, Inc. v. Burke*.[1] In that case, a group of executives who worked for an advertising agency—apparently having decided that the head of the agency was behaving badly with respect to customers—advised him that if they could not buy out his interest, they would set up a competing advertising agency. He declined, and they resigned and immediately set up a competing agency, which almost immediately began to service the clients for whom the employees had worked before.

This result would not have been inherently unlawful but for the fact that, while still employed by their original employer, and while taking salary and putting in and being paid for expenses, they had made arrangements with the clients of their employer to join them in their new business. The New York Court of Appeals ruled as follows:

> [T]he individual defendants-appellants [*i.e.* the former employees], *while employees of plaintiff corporation*, determined upon a course of conduct which, when subsequently carried out, resulted in benefit to themselves through destruction of plaintiff's business, in violation of

---

1   306 N.Y. 172 (1954).

the fiduciary duties of good faith and fair dealing imposed on defendants by their close relationship with plaintiff corporation[2] (emphasis supplied).

Nor were the former employees successful in arguing that they did not actually compete with their former employer until after they had resigned, because having planned their course of action while working for the plaintiff, their competitive actions in the new business "were merely the results of a predetermined course of action."[3]

The lesson of *Duane Jones* is that while an employee may leave a job and go into competition with a former employer, he or she may engage in such competition while still an employee of the first employer. Thus, and employee may not, *while employed*, try to convince the employer's customers to leave the employer in favor of a competitor; may not, *while employed*, try to persuade other employees to join the competing enterprise; and may not, *while employed*, take or copy customer records which will confer an advantage on the competing enterprise.[4]

[9.2] How are trade secrets and or confidential information protected?

An important protection afforded to employers under the common law (in other words, an obligation which may be enforced without the need for an agreement specifically binding the employee) is the preservation of the employer's confidential information and trade secrets.

Separate and apart from any contractual obligation, New York law imposes a common law duty on employees and former employees not to use confidential information or trade secrets in competition with a current or former employer.[5] It is axiomatic that "[e]ven in the absence of a contract restriction, a former employee is not entitled to solicit customers by . . . the use of trade secrets, or confidential information."[6] This rule stems from the fiduciary duty owed by the employees to their employer, which continues even

---

2   *Id.* at 189.

3   *Id.*

4   For restrictions on what an employee may do *after* he or she has left employment, *see* §§ 9.3–9.6 below.

5   *See North Atlantic Instruments, Inc. v. Haber*, 188 F.3d 38, 47 (2d Cir. 1999); *P.S.C., Inc. v. Reiss*, 111 F. Supp. 2d 252, 255–56 (W.D.N.Y. 2000).

6   *Support Sys. Assocs., Inc. v. Tavollaci*, 135 A.D.2d 704, 522 N.Y.S.2d 604 (2d Dep't 1987) (citations omitted).

after the termination of the employment.[7] As stated by the Court of Appeals, "the duty of an agent or employee not to use confidential knowledge acquired in his employment in competition with his principal is implicit in the relationship. It exists as well after the employment is terminated as during its continuance. It is an absolute and not a relative duty."[8]

[9.3]   What qualifies as trade secrets or confidential information?

In its technical sense, a trade secret is defined as follows: "[A]ny formula, pattern, device or compilation of information which is used in one's business, and which gives [the owner] an opportunity to obtain an advantage over competitors who do not know or use it."[9]

However, New York has adopted a fairly broad definition of what is protected in the overall category of trade secrets and confidential information, and this includes customer and business information which might not technically qualify as a trade secret. Protected information includes: lists of customer prospects; the identity of contact persons at customers and prospective customers; customer preferences; knowledge of pricing, pricing methods and profit margins; revenue projections and product pricing strategies; and knowledge of future products and marketing strategies. All of these categories represent information that the employer has had to work to obtain for its specific business, and that should be protected against improper use by third parties.

The protection is not unlimited. Specifically, it does not extend to information that is generally known or generally ascertainable from public sources. An example of this could be the employee who leaves an employer which sells pet grooming aids, and either starts his or her own pet supply business or goes to work for a competitor. While the former employer's specific knowledge of its customers and prospects may be protected as confidential, the former employee will not be barred from making up lists of veterinarians, pet stores, and pet grooming businesses from printed or online business directories.

In determining what information is protected, an essential consideration is whether the information has been kept secret.[10] The owner of a trade

---

7   See *Arnold's Ice Cream Co. v. Carlson*, 330 F. Supp. 1185, 1188 (E.D.N.Y. 1971) and Chapter 8 of this book, "Employer and Employee Rights and Obligations," at § 8.7.

8   *Byrne v. Barnett*, 268 N.Y. 199 (1935) (citations omitted).

9   *North Atlantic Instruments, Inc. v. Haber*, 188 F.3d 38, 49 (2d Cir. 1999).

10   See *Lehman v. Dow Jones & Co.*, 783 F.2d 285, 298 (2d Cir. 1986).

secret or confidential information must take reasonable measures to protect its secrecy.

The following factors should be considered in determining whether information has been treated as a *bona fide* trade secret or confidential information:

- Has the information been kept under physical lock and key and password protected on the company's computers?

- Is access to the information, whether by hard copy or digitally, limited to those who need it for business purposes?

- Are the number of copies of sensitive information kept to a minimum?

- Is sensitive information marked "confidential" or some similar term?

- Is sensitive information left unattended or accessible electronically to those who are not authorized to receive it?

- Are appropriate measures to shield sensitive information taken when guests visit the facility?

- Are employees and third parties with access to sensitive information required to sign confidentiality agreements?

- Are employees instructed not to discuss confidential company plans or projects in the presence of visitors, especially suppliers and vendors?

While not all of the above factors must be present, they provide an overall guide to what may or may not be entitled to protection.

[9.4] What are the remedies for misuse of confidential information?

An employee who misappropriates confidential information or trade secrets may be enjoined (i.e. ordered) by a court not to use the information, in addition to an award of money damages for the financial harm caused to the employer:

> [A]n employee's use of an employer's trade secrets or
> confidential customer information can be enjoined even
> in the absence of a restrictive covenant when such con-
> duct violates a fiduciary duty owed by the former
> employee to his former employer.[11]

Injunctive relief can also include, for example, an order prohibiting the former employee from soliciting the employer's customers for a period of
months or years.[12]

[9.5]   What is a covenant not to compete?

In the employment context, a covenant not to compete is an employee's
agreement that following the end of his or her employment, the employee
will: (a) not compete at all with the former employer (whether as a direct
competitor or as an employee of a competing enterprise); and/or (b) not
solicit the employer's customers to come to a competing enterprise; and/or
(c) not solicit the employer's other employees to join a competing enterprise. The covenant will also typically include a specified period of time
that the prohibition will last, and will often state the geographic scope of
the prohibition (such as "will not work in the restaurant business in the
County of Rockland").

It is important to note that, unlike the common-law protections discussed
in §§ 9.1–9.4 above, the covenant not to compete is a creature of contract.
In other words, the employee *must affirmatively agree* to the restriction,
and the agreement embodying the restriction should be in writing.[13]

Further, there must be consideration (almost always, some new financial
benefit like a payment, a raise, a promotion, or an agreement to extend
employment) in order for a covenant not to compete to be binding on the

---

11   *Churchill Communications Corp. v. Demyanovich*, 668 F. Supp. 207, 211 (S.D.N.Y. 1987).

12   *Tour and Study v. Hepner*, 77 A.D.2d 843, 432 N.Y.S.2d 148 (1st Dep't 1980) (three-year injunction against solicitation of customers held to be proper despite absence of restrictive covenant); *see also Velo-Bind, Inc. v. Scheck*, 485 F. Supp. 102, 109 (S.D.N.Y. 1979) (granting
injunction where "[a]ppropriation of a former employer's customer list [violated] the fiduciary
obligation inherent to the employer/employee relationship").

13   It is not an absolute requirement that a covenant not to compete must be in writing, but there are
two compelling reasons why it should be. First, no party's interest is served by a dispute which
involves sorting out a "he said–she said" controversy. Second, the New York Statute of Frauds
(General Obligations Law § 5-701) requires that an agreement of this nature which cannot be
performed within one year is not enforceable unless it is memorialized in a signed writing. So,
for example, an agreement not to work in the restaurant business in Rockland County for a period
of 18 months would have to be in writing to be enforced.

employee. As often as not, a covenant is signed when an employee is first hired, and the commencement of employment is a benefit sufficient to constitute consideration. Similarly, if an employer conditions a raise, or a promotion, or the extension of a previously fixed term of employment upon agreement to a restrictive covenant, that new benefit will generally be sufficient. However, an employer which requires an employee who is already employed to sign a restrictive covenant without conferring some new benefit on the employee runs the serious risk that the covenant may not be enforceable.

[9.6] Are covenants not to compete enforceable?

Yes, but only within reasonable limits. On the one hand, a covenant not to compete protects the employer's business interests—but on the other hand, it may severely restrict the employee's ability to use the experience he or she has gained in working for that employer, and thus limit the employee's ability to earn a living.

New York courts will enforce non-compete agreements that are narrowly tailored to protect an employer from unfair competition from a former employee. To be enforceable, the agreement must not impose an undue hardship on the employee and must be reasonably limited in scope and duration.

The leading case in New York is *BDO Seidman v. Hirshberg*,[14] in which New York's highest court held that trade secrets and customer relationships are protectable interests that can serve the basis for a valid noncompete agreement. In that case, the Court ruled that customer relationships are a protectable asset, and recognized that certain employees, particularly those involved in sales, are often entrusted with being the sole or major contact with customers. The personal relationship developed between the employee and the customer—which the employer pays the employee to cultivate— belongs to the company. "The employer has a legitimate interest in preventing former employees from exploiting or appropriating the goodwill of a client or customer, which had been created and maintained at the employer's expense, to the employer's competitive detriment."[15]

---

14   93 N.Y.2d 382, 690 N.Y.S.2d 854 (1999).

15   *Id.* at 392. There is not, however, a similar employer interest in relationships that have nothing to do with the company's efforts. For example, when an employee brings in business from family members or personal friends, those relationships do not belong to the employer for the purposes of enforcing a non-compete or non-solicitation agreement.

At the same time, however, the *Seidman* court stressed that there are standards of reasonableness which must be applied in determining the validity of a restrictive covenant:

> The modern, prevailing common-law standard of reasonableness for employee agreements not to compete applies a three-pronged test. A restraint is reasonable only if it: (1) is no greater than is required for the protection of the legitimate interest of the employer, (2) does not impose undue hardship on the employee, and (3) is not injurious to the public. *A violation of any prong renders the covenant invalid.*

> New York has adopted this prevailing standard of reasonableness in determining the validity of employee agreements not to compete. In this context a restrictive covenant will only be subject to specific enforcement to the extent that it is reasonable in time and area, necessary to protect the employer's legitimate interests, not harmful to the general public and not unreasonably burdensome to the employee.[16]

The same reasonableness analysis applies to non-solicitation agreements. Particularly for lower level employees, courts are more likely to enforce an agreement that prohibits an employee from soliciting customers of the former employer with whom the employee dealt, rather than enforcing a broad non-compete prohibition that tries to prevent an employee from working for a competitor in any capacity.[17]

In assessing reasonableness, courts try to balance how much protection the employer really needs against the degree to which the covenant in question limits the former employee's ability to earn a livelihood.

---

16   *Id.* at 388–89 (citations omitted; emphasis supplied).

17   *See Ecolab v. K.P. Laundry Mach., Inc.*, 656 F. Supp. 894 (S.D.N.Y. 1987) (court issues preliminary injunction prohibiting former employees from contacting, soliciting, or accepting business from customers they serviced while employed by plaintiff); *Ecolab, Inc. v. Paolo*, 753 F. Supp. 1100, 1110 (E.D.N.Y. 1991) (enjoining defendants from servicing, selling, soliciting the sale of, or accepting orders for products or services competitive with those of plaintiff to or from customers of plaintiff with whom defendants Paolo or Elliott did business, whose accounts were assigned to either of them, or with regard to which either received commissions during the last 12 months of their employment with plaintiff, and from assisting others in such activities.).

So, for example, a non-compete covenant enjoining the sales manager of a commercial dairy outside Buffalo from working for a competing dairy anywhere in New York State will almost certainly be struck down as overbroad if the employer tries to enjoin the former employee from working for (or starting) a commercial dairy on Long Island. Inasmuch as dairies serve specific geographic areas, the employer simply is not harmed if the employee applies what he has learned about the dairy business at a dairy which does not compete for the same customers

By contrast, it might not be unreasonable for the customer relationships manager of a national advertising firm to be restricted from joining a competing advertising firm anywhere in the United States—provided that the duration of the restriction is not unreasonable.

The duration (length in time) of a covenant should be no greater than what is actually necessary to protect the employer's interest. For example, if a company wants to use non-compete agreements to protect confidential pricing, and that pricing information becomes "stale" after six months, the non-compete provision should only be in effect for six months. The same is true for customer relationships. If the employer needs only six months to re-establish costumer relationships with a replacement employee, then that should be the length of the non-solicitation agreement.

Similarly, an employer should narrow a non-solicitation agreement to prohibit solicitation of customers with whom the employee actually dealt. Trying to bar an employee from soliciting any and every customer of a large company, even when the employee had no contact with many of them, will likely be deemed by a court to be overly broad.

Finally, and especially in the case of high-level executives who may have agreed to broad non-compete agreements, an employer should anticipate that a reviewing court will look at whether the consideration (payment) for the agreement was sufficient to justify the extent of the restrictions.

[9.7] Is a seller of the good will in a business subject to an implied covenant not to compete after the sale?

No, there is no implied covenant not to compete from such a sale.

However, if a seller has also agreed to sell the "good will" of his or her business to the purchaser, then there is a New York common law doctrine known as the "Mohawk Doctrine," which prohibits the seller "from solic-

iting his former customers."[18] The Mohawk Doctrine is an implied covenant not to *solicit*, but it is not an implied covenant not to *compete*: the
seller can "accept the trade" from previous customers, but cannot, in per-
petuity, "directly solicit" the trade from former customers.[19]

[9.8]   What is the faithless servant doctrine?

As noted in chapter 8 of this book, "Employer and Employee Rights and
Obligations," at § 8.12, the faithless servant doctrine is a drastic remedy
which courts apply only in cases of serious, even egregious, acts of
employee disloyalty.

That said, the faithless servant doctrine is one of the most powerful weapons an employer can use against a disloyal employee, such as one who
starts a competing business while still employed. *It allows an employer to
recover the full amount compensation which the employer paid to an
employee during the period of disloyalty*, in addition to any other applicable damages.[20]

In other words, this doctrine, which is a sub-species of the more general
duty of loyalty and fiduciary duty, requires an employee to forfeit all of the
compensation he or she was paid from his or her first disloyal act going forward, without regard to any other damages that the employer can prove.
The forfeiture of compensation can include not just salary, but also the
value of benefits and deferred compensation such as stock options and
insurance in retirement. In addition to compensation forfeiture, a faithless
servant may be subject to punitive damages and reimbursement of the
employer's investigative costs, as well as disgorgement of profits. The policy behind this has been stated by New York's highest court as follows:

---

18   *Mohawk Maintenance Co. v. Kessler*, 52 N.Y. 2d 276 (1981).

19   What is meant by "directly solicit" and the parameters of the doctrine were explained by the New
York Court of Appeals, in *Bessemer Trust Co., N.A. v. Branin*, 16 N.Y. 3d 949 (2011).

20   *Feiger v. Iral Jewelry, Ltd.*, 41 N.Y.2d 928, 928–29, 394 N.Y.S.2d 626 (1977); *Phansalkar v. An-
dersen Weinroth & Co., L.P.*, 344 F.3d 184, 200 (2d Cir. 2003). *See also William Floyd Union
Free Sch. Dist. v. Wright*, 61 A.D.3d 856, 859, 877 N.Y.S.2d 395 (2d Dep't 2009) ("Where, as
here, defendants engaged in repeated acts of disloyalty, complete and permanent forfeiture of
compensation, deferred or otherwise, is warranted under the faithless servant doctrine."); *Long Island Network of Cmty Serv., Inc. v. Kinzer*, No. 19053-2012, 2013 N.Y. Slip Op. 33236(U), 2013
N.Y. Misc. LEXIS 6044 (Sup. Ct., Suffolk Co. Dec. 3, 2013) (applying "complete and permanent
forfeiture" against a chief financial officer who committed larceny); *In re Blumenthal*, 32 A.D.3d
767, 822 N.Y.S.2d 27 (1st Dep't 2006) (imposing forfeiture of all compensation where defendant
made systemic, unauthorized money transfers to himself and his wife: "[W]e decline the invita-
tion to abolish the faithless servant doctrine, which has long been the law of this State.").

> [T]he function [of a breach of fiduciary duty action], unlike an ordinary tort or contract case, is not merely to compensate the plaintiff for wrongs committed by the defendants but . . . to *prevent* them, by removing from agents and trustees all inducement to attempt dealing for their own benefit in matters which they have undertaken for others, or to which their agency or trust relates.[21]

The faithless servant doctrine has been applied to multiple types of employee misconduct, including unfair competition;[22] insider-trading;[23] theft;[24] diversion of business opportunities;[25] self-dealing in connection with the sale of high value art;[26] and off-duty sexual misconduct.[27]

---

21 *Diamond v. Oreamuno*, 24 N.Y.2d 494, 498, 301 N.Y.S.2d 78 (1969) (emphasis in original). *See also Astra USA Inc. v. Bildman*, 455 Mass. 116, 136 (2009) ("For New York . . . the harshness of the remedy is precisely the point").

22 *Maritime Fish Prods., Inc. v. World-Wide Fish Prods., Inc.*, 100 A.D.2d 81, 88, 474 N.Y.S.2d 281 (1st Dep't 1984).

23 *Morgan Stanley v. Skowron*, 989 F. Supp. 2d 356 (S.D.N.Y. 2013).

24 *William Floyd Union Free Sch. Dist. v. Wright*, 61 A.D.3d 856, 859, 877 N.Y.S.2d 395 (2d Dep't 2009); *City of Binghamton v. Whalen*, 141 A.D.3d 145, 32 N.Y.S.3d 727 (3d Dep't 2016).

25 *Art Capital Group, LLC v. Rose*, 149 A.D.3d 447, 52 N.Y.S.3d 85 (1st Dep't 2017).

26 *Schulhof v. Jacobs*, 54 N.Y.S.3d 613, 2017 N.Y. Misc. LEXIS 690 (Sup. Ct., N.Y. Co. 2017).

27 *Colliton v. Cravath, Swaine & Moore, LLP*, 2008 U.S.Dist. Lexis 74388, 2008 WL 4386764 (S.D.N.Y. 2008), *aff'd*, 356 Fed. Appx. 535 (2d Cir. 2009); *but see Pozner v. Fox Broadcasting Co.*, 59 Misc. 3d 897 (Sup. Ct., N.Y. Co. 2018) (declining to apply the faithless servant doctrine to sexual harassment).

CHAPTER TEN

DISCIPLINE

Louis P. DiLorenzo

Edited by Jeffrey A. Kehl

CHAPTER OVERVIEW

Employees sometimes engage in job-related misconduct; violate employer policies; engage in acts of dishonesty or disloyalty; may commit job-related crimes; or simply fail to perform their job duties in a satisfactory manner. The consequences of such acts can range from counseling, to disciplinary write-ups, to temporary suspensions with or without pay, to reassignment, to demotion, to reductions in salary, or to discharge.

In this chapter, we discuss the considerations which apply when developing and implementing disciplinary policies and procedures, as follows:

[10.1] Are employers required to have discipline policies?

[10.2] Why *should* an employer have a discipline policy?

[10.3] What are the basic elements of a discipline policy?

[10.4] Are there special rules for sexual harassment issues?

[10.5] What is "progressive discipline"?

[10.6] What is "just cause"?

[10.7] What are the general types and ranges of discipline that may be imposed?

[10.8] What is a Performance Improvement Plan?

[10.9] What is a "Last Chance Agreement"?

[10.10] Are job descriptions relevant to disciplinary decisions?

[10.11] What role do employee evaluations have in the disciplinary process?

[10.12] Can an employee be suspended pending an investigation of possible misconduct?

[10.13] May an employee be required to participate in an interview?

[10.14] Can an employee bring a representative to an interview?

[10.15] What considerations apply to investigations conducted by employer staff?

[10.16] When should an employer consider retaining an outside investigator?

[10.17] Should an employer's attorney(s) conduct a workplace investigation?

[10.18] What if a matter involves potential criminal conduct by an employee?

[10.19] What is "after-acquired evidence"?

[10.20] May an employee be disciplined for off-duty and/or off-premises conduct?

[10.21] May an employee be disciplined for social media activity?

[10.22] May an employee be disciplined because a customer or other third party demands it?

[10.23] May an employee be disciplined for poor attendance or lateness?

[10.1]   Are employers required to have discipline policies?

There is no requirement in New York law that a private-sector employer have any sort of discipline policy.[1] Unless otherwise required by a union collective bargaining agreement, by an individual employment contract, or by its own unilaterally adopted policy, a New York private-sector employer is free to discipline or terminate an employee, with or without notice, for any reason or for no reason (so long as the reason is not unlawful), and with any degree of process (or with no process at all).[2]

However, there are compelling reasons why employers should adopt and follow clear and fair discipline standards and procedures.

[10.2]   Why *should* an employer have a discipline policy?

There are a number of reasons why employers should consider implementing a formal discipline policy:

- *To encourage fairness and predictability.* Most employers and employees aspire to a workplace that is perceived as equitable and predictably run. This can be a significant factor in maintaining employee morale.

- *To improve performance.* A discipline policy can serve not just to penalize bad performance, but also as a mechanism to alert employees of their need to improve performance, and to give them a structured opportunity to do so. It can also serve to reinforce and encourage good performers to continue when they see that poor performance or misconduct is observed and addressed.

- *To provide guidance for managerial employees.* As is discussed elsewhere in this book (and especially in Chapter 11, "Discrimination, Harassment and Retaliation," at §§ 11.18–11.19 and 11.22),

---

1   By contrast, public-sector employers in New York are subject to numerous statutory and constitutional requirements setting forth the grounds on which disciplinary action may be taken, and the disciplinary processes which must be followed.

2   It goes without saying that when an employer disciplines or terminates an employee for reasons which are unlawfully discriminatory or retaliatory, or which violate other rights given to employees by law, there will be liability for taking the adverse action both in damages and in possible equitable relief such as reinstatement or front pay.

employers can be held liable for the improper actions of managerial employees and those same employees can be held individually liable. The existence of a discipline policy serves as guidance for, and a restraint on, managers who might otherwise take actions that would, whether through actual bad intent or mere lack of understanding, result in liability for the employer and/or themselves.

- *To provide a defense against claims by disciplined employees.* It happens with unfortunate frequency that a present or former employee sues his or her employer (or files an agency charge of discrimination), alleging that he or she was wrongfully denied a workplace opportunity, disciplined or discharged, or treated adversely in comparison to similarly situated employees, for an unlawful reason such as discrimination. In such cases the employer's defense will almost invariably be that its decisions were based upon the employee's poor performance or poor conduct. A consistently administered and appropriately documented disciplinary process can provide critical evidence to corroborate the employer's defense. In fact, the mere existence of the process may result in the avoidance of litigation if employees, or the lawyers with whom they consult, believe the employee was treated fairly and consistently.

- *To provide a defense against claims by third parties.* An employer may also be sued over employee misconduct allegedly committed against another employee, a customer, a supplier, or someone else who came in contact with the misbehaving employee during the course of the employer's business activities. These claims are most frequently predicated on an alleged lack of supervision or other forms of negligence by the employer; in other words, that the employer failed adequately to supervise the offending employee, and knew, or should have known, that it needed to take some action to protect third parties, and failed to do so. Again, the existence of a formal disciplinary process may be an important buttress for the employer's defense.

An effective discipline policy may also serve to correct or train employees in the hope it will prevent recurrence of the behavioral problems or concerns in question. Under the principle that we hope for the best but prepare for the worst, if the process does not correct the performance or conduct, then it will have established a documented process that was followed in order to reach the conclusions on which discipline was based. This record will include evidence of a proper investigation, an accurate record of the results of the investigation, and—where appropriate—communication of the results of the investigation to affected parties.

[10.3]   What are the basic elements of a discipline policy?

A discipline policy should set out the range of possible sanctions for disciplinary infractions, up to and including termination of the employment relationship. While it does not have to—and should not try to—establish some "pseudo-exact" correlation between itemized types of misconduct and particular penalties to be imposed, it should at least give examples, in a non-exhaustive manner, of the types of conduct and performance that are unacceptable. Further, the policy should make it clear that there is a range of penalties that may be imposed, taking into consideration the circumstances presented, including: the seriousness of the particular infraction; the likelihood and consequences of repeat conduct; and other factors such as an offending employee's past performance and disciplinary history.

The above said, it is generally recognized that it is simply not practical to attempt to itemize every possible type of conduct or behavior in which an employee might engage which could result in discipline or termination of employment or to develop a "formula" for determining appropriate discipline for such conduct or behavior.

[10.4]   Are there special rules for sexual harassment issues?

Yes. *See* Chapter 11 of this book, "Discrimination, Harassment and Retaliation," §§ 11.26–11.33 for the requirements in the New York Human Rights Law which apply to sexual harassment claims. These rules will impact employer action where discipline for sexual harassment is indicated.

[10.5]   What is "progressive discipline"?

"Progressive discipline" is a phrase often seen in union collective bargaining agreements and in labor arbitrators' interpretation of collective bargaining agreements. It is based on the principle that more severe penalties (such as termination of employment) should generally not be imposed until and unless more moderate means (such as counseling, a disciplinary write-up, or some other intermediate means of discipline) have been attempted, leaving more severe consequences for subsequent offenses.

As a concept, progressive discipline has much to recommend it, but there are employment situations that call for the immediate imposition of serious penalties, including dismissal (sometimes referred to as the "capital punishment" of the workplace). It may confidently be stated that few employers confronted with serious infractions (such as embezzlement by an employee, a serious assault by an employee in the workplace, or an intentional or reckless employee lapse resulting in bodily harm or some other serious loss) will be interested in anything other than termination of employment in the first instance.

Accordingly, while there is nothing wrong with adopting a progressive discipline policy, we strongly recommend that any such policy, in addition to *not* trying exhaustively to list offenses, or to "formulize" the level of discipline, should explicitly state: (a) that the policy is a non-binding guideline subject to change; (b) that the level of discipline imposed in any particular case may vary depending on the circumstances of the case; and (c) that in instances of serious misconduct, progressive discipline may not be applied at all.

Please see Chapter 2 of this book, "Terms of the Employment Relationship," at § 2.15. for an additional discussion of progressive discipline policies, and how to avoid turning a progressive discipline policy into a contractual obligation.

[10.6] What is "just cause"?

"Just cause" is a frequently used phrase which can, depending on who is using it and for what purpose, have varying connotations.

When found in union collective bargaining agreements, "just cause" has the meaning that has been ascribed to it over the years by labor arbitrators, and it is understood to mean a termination that is neither arbitrary nor capricious. Some arbitrators apply a seven-question test as described below (or some subset of those questions), which are intended to protect employees against arbitrary, capricious, or vindictive disciplinary actions on the part of their employers.

When used in an individual employment contract, "just cause" can be defined in the language of the contract. An example of such a contract provision might read as follows:

> *Employee's employment shall not be terminated prior to* [date] *except for 'just cause,' which shall be defined as (i) an act or acts of commission or omission of sufficient severity as to constitute a material failure of performance; (ii) the commission of a crime under applicable state or federal law which materially bears upon*

> *Employee's continued fitness to serve; (iii) material
> neglect of duty; (iv) a knowing and material departure
> from the norms of conduct or performance generally
> applicable to* [type of position in the relevant industry]*;
> or (v) physical or mental incapacity to perform the essen-
> tial functions of Employee's duties, with or without rea-
> sonable accommodation, which shall persist for a period
> of* [number] *calendar days.*

When a contract of employment is for a fixed term, New York law
implies as a matter of law that termination prior to the expiration of the
fixed term may *only* be for just cause. If there is a claim that this implied
requirement has been breached, and where the parties have not defined
what is meant by "just cause," a court will apply its own notions of what
would be equitable. Most of the time, the analysis will use some or all the
considerations in the seven-point arbitral standard described below.

The seven-point test was first articulated by Arbitrator Carroll R. Daugherty
in an arbitration case called *Greif Bros. Cooperage Corp.*,[3] and is as follows:

1. Did the employee have advance knowledge from the employer of
   the possible disciplinary consequences of the conduct?[4]

2. Was the prohibition of the conduct "reasonably related to the
   orderly, efficient and safe operation of the employer's business?"[5]

3. Did the employer, before taking disciplinary action, make an effort
   to find out whether the employee in fact committed the infraction?[6]

---

3   42 Lab. Arb. (BNA) 555, 557–59 (1964).

4   The employee's "knowledge" may be demonstrated by actual or constructive notice. It may be
     proven by communications from previous progressive discipline; by an employer handbook; or
     by a policy, or by directions given to an employer. It may also be imputed as a value common to
     members of a civilized community (e.g., conduct described in Ten Commandments or the New
     York Penal Code).

5   The more seriously the conduct or behavior impacts the mission of the business, the more serious
     may be the discipline to be imposed. For example, a waiter who is incredibly rude to a restaurant
     patron or an airline engine inspector who cuts corners on safety checks, violate rules clearly re-
     lated to orderly, efficient or safe operation of an employer's business.

6   This is why investigation of what happened—*before* taking disciplinary action—is important.

4.   Was the employer's investigation fair and objective?[7]

5.   Was there 'substantial evidence"[8] that the employee was guilty of the infraction?

6.   Has the employer "applied its rules, orders, and penalties even-handedly and without discrimination to all employees?"[9]

7.   Was the degree of discipline imposed reasonably related to the seriousness of what the employee did, and the employee's prior service record?[10]

The above criteria are not legal requirements, nor must each question be answered with a "Yes" for just cause to be found. It is, however, a useful checklist for employers to consider before making final disciplinary decisions. For example, a "No" to any of these questions does not mean disci-

---

7   This is the requirement that an investigation be carried out in a fair manner. Included in that process should be an effort to obtain the employee's version of what occurred. This is true, for several reasons, even if the evidence of guilt appears overwhelming at the time. First, the employee may be innocent and may have some explanation that is not apparent; it is better to discover that information sooner rather than later. Second, it is important to commit the employee to a version of events at a point in time where its veracity can be evaluated while evidence is still available. If an employee gives a plausible but untrue explanation weeks or months after an event, it may be much more difficult for the employer to ascertain—and later prove—the falsity of the account. Third, the employee may refuse to cooperate in the investigation, which will provide an additional basis for discipline and also provide a basis for the employer to rely on the available evidence gathered during the investigation. Fourth, the employee may provide false information when questioned, which is relevant to the imposition of discipline. Finally, the employee may admit the conduct (with or without an expression of remorse), and this establishes that the conduct occurred and should limit later arguments to the appropriate discipline for the proven and admitted conduct or behavior.

8   The concept of "substantial evidence" cannot be reduced to a formula. It will depend on the totality of the circumstances in any given case. However, it is important to remember that the employer's genuine and reasonable belief in the employee's guilt is critical in a subsequent review by a court or other tribunal. In New York law, the term "substantial evidence" has a specific meaning. The New York State Court of Appeals has defined "substantial evidence" as "proof within the whole record of such quality and quantity as to generate conviction in and persuade a fair and detached fact finder that, from that proof as a premise, a conclusion or ultimate fact may be extracted reasonably—probatively and logically." *Gramatan Avenue Associates v. State Division of Human Rights*, 45 N.Y.2d 176, 181, 408 N.Y.S.2d 54 (1978). Significantly, the standard for substantial evidence is "*less* than a preponderance of the evidence." *Id.* at 180 (emphasis supplied).

9   This rule is founded on the concept of "disparate treatment," which is discussed in Chapter 11 of this book, "Discrimination, Harassment and Retaliation," at § 11.20.

10   This step can be restated as, "Does the punishment fit the crime?" An employer that imposes a penalty disproportionate to the offense runs the risk of "shocking the conscience" of a fact finder, which may then refuse to sustain the employer's decision.

pline is inappropriate, but may lead the employer to modify the discipline, take steps to otherwise minimize the risk of a challenge to the decision or accept the risk and proceed.

When Arbitrator Daugherty set forth his seven points in 1964, concepts of accommodation and retaliation were virtually unknown in employment law. These concepts go beyond Mr. Daugherty's question of "even-handedness"; and if he were creating the list today, he would likely have added two more. which we call DiLorenzo's Corollaries (new factors 8 and 9):

8.   Is the employee entitled to reasonable accommodation for any reason, such as for religious beliefs or a disability, that might make discipline inappropriate?[11]

9.   Has the employee recently engaged in any protected activity from which it may be inferred by a trier of fact that retaliation for the employee's protected activity was the real motivation for the decision to discipline?[12]

Accordingly, even though: (a) an employer may not be subject to the "just cause" standards of a collective bargaining agreement or an individual employment agreement; and (b) these factors are not legal prerequisites to discipline, the checklist is a useful tool for identifying and assessing risks and weaknesses before making a final decision. This identification and risk assessment may lead to a modification of the decision or taking additional steps to strengthen defenses to a possible later attack in court or otherwise.

---

11   Assume for example, that an employer has a rule providing any employee who has not been actively employed for one year will be terminated. Assume further that several employees were not actively employed for one year due to layoff, and were terminated; but that an employee who was out on disability leave for a year asked for an extension of the one-year leave maximum as a "reasonable accommodation" for the disability. If the employer's inquiry is limited to a Step 6 inquiry about "even-handedness," the employer might conclude that the disabled employee may be terminated. However, the New York Human Rights Law requires more than nondiscrimination, it requires an analysis of whether this requested accommodation is reasonable and whether, because of the disability, the employee is entitled to modification of the rule previously consistently enforced. See Chapter 11 of this book, "Discrimination, Harassment and Retaliation," at §§ 11.35–11.43.

12   See Chapter 8 of this book, "Employer and Employee Rights and Obligations," at §§ 8.22–8.28 (protected activities) and Chapter 11, "Discrimination, Harassment and Retaliation," at §§ 11.61–11.64 (retaliation in general).

[10.7] What are the general types and ranges of discipline that may be imposed?

Depending on: (a) the nature and severity of employee misconduct (including any harm or dangers it may have posed); (b) the nature of the employee's position, duties and responsibilities, and length of service; (c) any relevant workplace training which the employee may have received; (d) the employee's prior disciplinary/performance history; (e) the employee's acceptance of responsibility for his or her acts or omissions; (f) the likelihood and possible consequences of a repeat violation; and (g) any extenuating circumstances; various disciplinary approaches and penalties may be appropriate. These may include:

- An oral warning;

- A written warning;

- A Performance Improvement Plan ("PIP");[13]

- The withholding of some discretionary benefit or opportunity;[14]

- Transfer to another position;

- Disciplinary probation;

- Suspension for some period of time;

- Demotion;

- A final warning;

- A "Last Chance Agreement";[15] or

- Termination of employment.

Unless otherwise required by a collective bargaining agreement or otherwise committed to by the employer (as, for example, in a stated policy or an employee handbook), the particular measure of discipline, and the

---

13 See § 10.8 below.

14 This might consist, for example, of withholding a discretionary raise or bonus; denying a requested promotion or reassignment; withholding a discretionary educational benefit; or denying discretionary time off. Needless to say, of course, there may be *non*-disciplinary reasons to deny an employee a raise or other benefit, or to transfer an employee to another position.

15 See § 10.9 below.

overall approach to be taken, are up to the discretion of management (pro-vided, of course, that the decisions are otherwise lawful). Nevertheless—and even though triers of fact are told not to substitute their judgment for the judgment of management—it is prudent to have an explanation for why one form of discipline was selected over others.

[10.8]   What is a Performance Improvement Plan?

A PIP can serve either or both of two purposes: (a) general guidance for the improvement of an employee's performance in a non-disciplinary con-text; and/or (b) an intermediate form of discipline which may lead to a more serious adverse consequence if there is not adequate improvement.

An effective PIP: (a) recites the acts or omissions that have created the need for the PIP; (b) establishes milestones, standards, or levels of behav-ior that the employee is expected to meet in order to address the earlier deficiencies; and (c) informs the employee of the consequences that may (or will) result from his or her failure to meet the terms of the PIP. It is recommended, in addition, that an effective PIP should:

- Identify the managerial employee who will be responsible for monitoring compliance;

- Set a time period for completion of the plan;

- Emphasize the continued level of performance that will be required following completion of the plan;

- Describe the consequences of a failure to achieve *and maintain* such level of performance; and

- When appropriate, offer assistance and feedback to the employee to help him or her improve.

We also recommend that an employer utilizing a PIP should identify interim and final review meetings, or some other stated process for evalu-ating and reviewing performance, during, and at the end of, the PIP.

In short, the PIP is designed to serve as a roadmap to improve performance, with the prospect of termination or some other adverse action if the required level of improvement is not achieved within the prescribed time period or maintained thereafter.[16]

Therefore, the more realistic the direction that is offered by the PIP, and the better defined are the milestones set forth to measure progress, the more the roadmap offered by the PIP will be perceived to be fair both by employees, by arbitrators, and by courts.

Where the need for correction is attributable to improper behavior or other improper conduct (which may include attendance and punctuality issues, failure or refusal to follow instructions, failure to follow employer policies, negligence, etc.), the PIP is designed to identify the misconduct and its severity, and to make it clear that serious consequences will follow in the absence of correction or improvement by the employee.

[10.9] What is a "Last Chance Agreement"?

A "Last Chance Agreement" is sometimes offered to an employee who has engaged in conduct which would otherwise warrant termination of employment or other serious discipline. It is the employee's agreement that further misconduct (or further failures of performance) *will* result in termination of employment.[17]

Reasons for such a Last Chance Agreement include: (a) the hope that there is still some possibility the employee, recognizing the gravity of the situation, may redeem him or herself; and (b) minimizing the litigation or legal risk of a challenge to the termination should the employee not fulfill the terms of the agreement. It is an extreme alternative and should set forth in a written document reciting (a) the employee's agreement with the relevant admissions, and (b) his or her understanding that a recurrence of the conduct in question (or any other serious breach on the part of the employee) will automatically result in his or her termination.

There is no "one-size-fits-all" for what terms should be included in a Last Chance Agreement: the agreement can, and should, be tailored to meet

---

16   Placement on a PIP may also be attributable not to improper behavior or conduct of a disciplinary nature, but rather to sub-par performance due to lack of ability, changes in the job, a poor hiring decision, or personal or other problems. In such instances, the PIP is not a form of discipline, but the fact remains that the employer has a business need to change the *status quo*.

17   In a unionized workplace, a union representative will almost always be involved in the negotiation of a Last Chance Agreement with a bargaining unit member,

the employer's specific circumstances. For example, if the employer would otherwise be subject to a grievance, arbitration or hearing process before taking further action, a Last Chance Agreement may provide (a) that the process will be waived altogether and the employer may move straight to termination; or (b) that the power of the decision-maker in an arbitration or discharge hearing will be limited to determining whether the employee committed the charged offense, with no discretion to change the automatic penalty of termination.

[10.10] Are job descriptions relevant to disciplinary decisions?

They can be. In evaluating the need for and appropriateness of disciplinary action, context often matters and, in that regard, a job description that is carefully drafted to reflect the employee's duties and responsibilities, may well help clarify, and support, the basis for the decision reached. Of course, job descriptions should, where appropriate and possible, broadly include all related duties and other assignments that may be directed by management.[18]

[10.11] What role do employee evaluations have in the disciplinary process?

Depending on the circumstances, an employee's previous performance evaluations may (or may not) be relevant.

For example, if an employee is found to have embezzled funds from his or her employer, or is found to have assaulted a co-worker, it will be substantially irrelevant that the employee's previous evaluations were generally (or even completely) positive.

However, if the employee is being terminated for poor productivity, or for excessive absenteeism or tardiness, it may very well be relevant whether previous evaluations made any reference to these problems. If, in such a case, the employee claims to have been disciplined or terminated for discriminatory reasons, the absence of a reference to these problems in earlier evaluations may be argued as evidence that the employer's stated

---

18   An example would be the statement, at the end of a specific list of responsibilities, "and such other duties and responsibilities as may be assigned from time to time."

reason for discipline was "pretextual."[19] For example, if the stated reason for discipline is absenteeism, and if prior evaluations state that the employee's attendance meets or exceeds expectations, a fact finder might conclude that the employer's stated reason for termination was pretextual. Evaluations also offer an opportunity to provide evidence of actual notice as described in Item 1 of the Seven Steps of Just Cause, and perhaps provide evidence of the reasonableness and importance of the job requirement, as described in Item 2 in the Seven Steps.

The employer's practice in evaluating other employees should also be considered. For example, an employee may claim that he or she was treated in a discriminatory manner because other employees who had similar (or even worse) performance evaluations were not disciplined or discharged.

There are three lessons to be derived from the foregoing:

- First, employee evaluations should not ignore performance problems, because the absence of any reference to the problems may have consequences in subsequent employment disputes.[20]

- Second, in evaluating proposed disciplinary action or disciplinary consequences against an employee, employers should review the employee's prior performance evaluations and the evaluations of other similarly situated employees.

- Third, fact finders give great weight to the existence—or nonexistence—of documents, such as evaluations which have been prepared before an employment dispute arises.

---

19 In Chapter 11 of this book, "Discrimination, Harassment and Retaliation," at § 11.1, we address the "shifting burdens" analysis applied in discrimination cases pursuant to the United States Supreme Court's decision in *McDonnell Douglas Corp. v. Green*, 411 U.S. 792 (1973). Under that analysis, an employee who brings an employment discrimination claim must make at least a "*prima facie* case" that he or she was discriminated against because of a protected status or category. If the employee has made a *prima facie* case, then the employer must come forward with a legitimate, non-discriminatory reason for the adverse personnel action. If the employer has articulated a legitimate and non-discriminatory reason, then, in order to pursue her claim further, the employee must demonstrate that the employer's stated reason was "pretextual" (false).

20 Such evaluations may also meet the test of advance notice to the employee of deficiencies and employer expectations.

[10.12] Can an employee be suspended pending an investigation of possible misconduct?

Yes, unless a collective bargaining agreement limits the ability to do so; and this is a prudent course of action in some cases. Where an allegation of misconduct is serious but there is a need for more facts to be developed before a determination of what happened can be made (and an appropriate response selected), the immediate removal of the employee from the premises may be appropriate.

An interim suspension is not inherently disciplinary but is instead imposed so that due diligence can take place. In such a case, it is more properly characterized as an interim "suspension pending investigation." Of course, it is entirely possible that discipline may follow when the facts have been investigated.

Depending upon the circumstances, and in the employer's discretion, the suspension pending investigation may be with or without pay. The pay determination does not have to be made at the time of suspension; retroactive pay can be provided, if appropriate, after the investigation is completed.[21]

While it is good practice for any investigation to be completed expeditiously, a hurried investigation has pitfalls of its own, and the suspension pending investigation can be an important option designed to avoid a hurried or abbreviated investigation that otherwise might lead to an erroneous or unsupported determination and unexpected liability.[22] A methodical investigation also demonstrates that the employer did not "rush to judgment" when serious misconduct was alleged or serious discipline was imposed. In addition, it forestalls a later argument that if the alleged conduct was so serious and detrimental to the employer's operations, why did the employer condone it by allowing the employee to continue in employment and perhaps remain on the premises?

[10.13] May an employee be required to participate in an interview?

Yes. An employer may require an employee to attend a meeting or interview for any legitimate reason, and this includes disciplinary investigations whether the employee is the subject of potential discipline or simply

---

21   Again, however, a collective bargaining agreement may impose other or different requirements.

22   In addition, an interim suspension eliminates or minimizes the possibility of further misconduct against other employees or third parties while the investigation is pending.

a witness. The failure to participate is insubordination, which may itself warrant discipline up to and including termination.

However, where the employee is the subject of potential discipline, and the workplace is unionized, the employee has so-called *Weingarten* rights under federal law and is entitled to advance notice of the interview and of the (general) matters to be discussed. *See* Chapter 12 of this book, "Miscellaneous Topics of Interest," at § 12.3 for a more extensive discussion of this topic.

[10.14] Can an employee bring a representative to an interview?

In a non-unionized workplace, employees have no right to bring a representative (including an attorney) to an interview. However, where the employee is the subject of potential discipline, and the workplace is unionized, the employee may bring a union representative to the interview.[23]

Even where the employee has no right to bring a representative, there may be times when an employer will find it advantageous to permit an employee to bring a representative, or even an attorney. Again, *see* Chapter 12 at § 12.3 for a more extensive discussion of this topic.

[10.15] What considerations apply to investigations conducted by employer staff?

The level of investigation needed should be determined on a case-by-case basis, and one size does not fit all.

Sometimes there is simply no question as to what an employee has done, and no uncertainty that there should be a disciplinary consequence. In such circumstances, a complicated or extensive investigation will not be warranted.

However, there are times when a formal investigation is appropriate to find out what actually happened, or to resolve conflicting accounts of what happened; and in these circumstances it is important that the investigation be conducted by a person whose objectivity is not compromised. This means that the investigator should not be a person who has been an object of the conduct to be investigated; should not be a subordinate either of (a) a person who has complained of the conduct or (b) the person about whom the complaint has been made; and, where feasible, should not be in the chain

---

23   Again, *see* Chapter 12 at § 12.3 for a further discussion of this topic.

of command for either a complaining employee or an accused employee. It should also be determined, before an investigation starts, whether there would be any basis for a claim that the investigator might be biased either against an accused employee or a complaining employee. This is important to minimize claims that the investigation was not fair and impartial.

It is customary for employers that want to conduct an in-house investigation, and are large enough to have a human resources department, to designate an HR person to lead an investigation.

As with the identification of the investigator(s), thought should be given as to who will serve as the decision maker regarding guilt or innocence, and (if guilt is found) what discipline should be imposed. If the decision is later challenged, this will be the person who has the primary burden of defending it. Relevant considerations involve whether a history exists between a disciplined employee and a decision-maker that might support an argument of personal bias or of a discriminatory or retaliatory motive.

However, the mere fact that someone now involved in the decision to discipline the employee was earlier involved in the hiring and/or promotion, favorable review, increased compensation and/or bonus, or other actions positively affecting the employee subject to discipline in question is not a disqualifier, and may actually be helpful. For example, a fact finder is permitted to draw an inference that if the "same actor" hired an employee, knowing they possessed a protected characteristic under the law, it is unlikely the same actor would fire them for having such a characteristic.[24]

[10.16] When should an employer consider retaining an outside investigator?

Not every employer has the in-house capability to conduct an effective investigation. Even where an employer has human resources personnel who have been trained in the relevant techniques, not every case can be resolved by an internal investigation without leaving doubts as to the fairness of the process.

Among the factors to be considered in this regard are: (a) the capabilities of internal personnel who would be asked to conduct an investigation; (b) the objectivity of the proposed investigator(s); (c) the nature, sensitivity, and gravity of the issues in question; (d) the likelihood the internal investigation findings or recommendations may be challenged; (e) the

---

24   For more information on the "same actor" doctrine, *see* Chapter 11 of this book, "Discrimination, Harassment and Retaliation," at § 11.20.

extent to which, under these circumstances, an internal investigation, and any of its findings or recommendations, if challenged, would be deemed impartial and credible; and (f) the cost of an external investigation.

[10.17] Should an employer's attorney(s) conduct a workplace investigation?

There are both pros and cons to having an attorney who already represents the employer (whether as in-house or outside counsel) conduct a work-place investigation.

The advantages of doing so are: (a) the enhanced ability of a lawyer to identify and address legal issues; (b) the likelihood that the lawyer will have familiarity with conducting investigations; (c) the fact that the law-yer (presumably) is already familiar with the employer's operations; and (d) the likelihood that the employer will accept the factual conclusions and recommendations proposed by a trusted advisor.

However, it should be borne in mind that at least parts of an attorney's investigative report are likely to be covered by the attorney-client privi-lege, and this is where a significant potential drawback arises.

In many instances, an investigative report may be important evidence to be used to refute a claim by an employee who sues the employer for dis-crimination, breach of contract, or the like. In such cases, the employer will want to waive any attorney-client privilege which might otherwise attach to the result of the investigation, and this may have two effects: first, that the investigating attorney may become a fact witness in the dis-pute; and second (as a consequence of the attorney's status as a witness), that the attorney may be disqualified from representing the employer before a tribunal hearing the facts, under what is called the "witness-advocate" rule.

In other words, if an attorney's investigation is going to be used affirma-tively to demonstrate that no wrongdoing occurred (or to show that if there was problematic conduct, that it was not condoned, and that it was addressed), then the employer should be prepared to waive any attorney-client privilege; with the attendant risk that the lawyer who did the inves-tigation cannot represent the employer to defend a challenge to the disci-plinary action.

On the other hand, if the investigation is intended simply to guide internal decision-making and there is no plan to share the results with third par-ties, thought must be given to preservation of the attorney client privilege.

There is no hard-and-fast rule as to how these issues should be resolved, but employers may resolve them by hiring external fact investigators who are separate from advice-giving attorneys.

[10.18] What if a matter involves potential criminal conduct by an employee?

In some cases, an employee's alleged misconduct may involve acts which, if proven, would be criminal, and may become the subject of a criminal investigation by a local, state or federal prosecutor. Alternatively, the criminal investigation may already exist (and may, indeed, have been the reason why the employer became aware of the employee's possible misconduct), or it may be initiated because the employer has decided to report a matter of concern to law enforcement authorities.[25]

Where a criminal investigation is in progress, the employer will have to choose whether to conduct its own concurrent investigation, or whether simply to suspend the employee and await the outcome of the criminal matter. Again, there is no hard-and-fast rule to determine the resolution of this question, but it is generally advisable for the employer to conduct its own investigation if the matter impacts the workplace. Factors to be considered include:

- *Time.* Prosecutors have many demands on their schedules, and some criminal matters can literally take years to work their way through an initial grand jury investigation and a subsequent criminal trial. This may be inconsistent with the employer's timetable for resolution.

- *Availability of information.* If a criminal case against an employee goes to trial, the trial record and the verdict will be available to the employer—and if the employee is convicted of committing *a crime in connection with his or her work*, the employer can terminate the employment relationship without further ado. However, prosecutors almost invariably decline to share information at any time before it comes out in a trial and will more than likely decline to do so if a matter is resolved by a guilty plea. In addition, since guilty pleas are often the result of plea negotiations in which the defendant agrees to plead to a lesser offense, the guilty plea may or may not be helpful to the employer.

---

25   In this regard, we note that an employer's recovery on an insurance policy or fidelity bond which covers employee misconduct resulting in financial loss to the employer may require that a timely report to law enforcement must be made.

- *The possibility of acquittal.* Not every criminal case ends in a conviction or a guilty plea: some defendants are acquitted; and in some cases charges may be dropped or dismissed. However, an acquittal is not necessarily a "finding of innocence"; rather, it is a finding that guilt has not been proved to the criminal standard of "beyond a reasonable doubt." By contrast, an employer's burden of proof to sustain the legitimacy of an adverse personnel decision is much lower. Technically, this means that the employer is still free to act; but as a practical matter, there will be problems of "appearance" where an employer takes action against an employee who argues that he or she has already been "found innocent."

- *Interference with criminal proceedings.* While the foregoing factors suggest that employers may not want to defer their own action until the conclusion of a criminal proceeding, it may also be that prosecutors will ask an employer to defer so as not to interfere with the criminal investigation. These requests are entitled to serious consideration: an employer may not wish to be accused of having taken actions which interfered with law enforcement.

[10.19] What is "after-acquired evidence"?

It happens with some frequency that an employer will take disciplinary action based on the facts known to it at the time, but that after the employee's termination, the employer learns of other evidence of inappropriate conduct by the employee during his or her employment. If the employer can establish that had this other evidence had been discovered during employment, it would have been an additional basis for the employee's termination, then any entitlement the employee might otherwise have had to reinstatement, or to back pay and front pay from the date of discovery of the information forward, is eliminated.[26]

[10.20] May an employee be disciplined for off-duty and/or off-premises conduct?

The answer to this question will depend on many factors. New York law protects employees with respect to their lawful activities when they are not

---

26 *See McKennon v. Nashville Banner Publ'g Co.*, 513 U.S. 352, 357 (1995); *Norris v. N.Y. City Coll. of Tech.*, Case No. 07-CV-853, 2009 U.S. Dist. Lexis 3186, 2009 WL 82556 (E.D.N.Y. Jan. 16, 2009) (Block. J.); *Vichare v. AMBAC Inc.*, 106 F.3d 457, 468 (2d Cir. 1996); *Altman v. New Rochelle Pub. Sch. Dist.*, No. 13-CV-3253, 2014 U.S. Dist. Lexis 84714, 2014 WL 2809134, *14–15 (S.D.N.Y. June 19 2014); *EEOC v. Rose Casual Dining, L.P.*, Civ. Action No. 02-7485, 2004 U.S. Dist. Lexis 4335, 2004 WL 614806, *10 (E.D.P.A. Mar. 5, 2004); *Jones v. Ravens, Inc.*, 108 F. Supp. 2d 803, 812 (N.D. Oh. 2000).

at work—so if the off-duty conduct is *lawful and is unrelated to work*—the answer is generally "No." *See* Chapter 8 of this book, "Employer and Employee Rights and Obligations," at §§ 8.22–8.26 for a discussion of off-premises conduct which is protected by law.

However, off-duty conduct which directly impacts the workplace may be grounds for discipline. Examples would include:

- Harassment of a co-worker away from the employer's premises and outside of working hours;

- Off-premises activity which violates the employee's duty of loyalty to the employer, or which fall within the "faithless servant" doctrine;[27]

- Unlawful off-premises conduct, if the unlawful activity bears on the employee's fitness to render service; and

- Other acts which impact workplace safety, efficiency or harmony, and which are not otherwise protected by law.

[10.21] May an employee be disciplined for social media activity?

In some cases, yes, but an employer should approach these issues with care. *See* Chapter 8 of this book*,* "Employer and Employee Rights and Obligations," at §§ 8.29 and 8.30 for a further discussion of this topic.

[10.22] May an employee be disciplined because a customer or other third party demands it?

Maybe, but care should be taken independently to verify the accuracy of the complaint and to ensure that the proposed disciplinary action is lawful and appropriate.

Customer relationships are important, and an employer is free to take adverse action against an employee who does not serve a customer well, or who cannot maintain a good relationship with the customer. At the same time, however, the mere fact that a customer has complained is, without further inquiry, a risky basis for discipline.

For example, customer preference is not generally recognized as a defense to a claim of discrimination.

---

27   *See* Chapter 8 of this book, "Employer and Employee Rights and Obligations," at § 8.5 and
        Chapter 9, "Protecting the Employer's Business."

If a customer were to demand that an employee be disciplined because he or she had refused the customer's sexual advances, there is little doubt that compliance with the demand would result in liability on the employer's part.

However, the customer in question might very well not state the actual reason as the reason for his demand; rather, the complaint might be presented in pretextual language along the lines of "I don't find that Ms. X is responsive and she doesn't get my projects completed on time." In this scenario, the employer which takes action without inquiry would very likely learn the real reason when the employee sues her employer on the basis that she was discharged because she refused to have sexual relations with the customer.

The lesson to be taken here is that—as in virtually all cases in which discipline is being contemplated—it is important to make inquiry to be sure that any disciplinary decision is informed and fact-based.

[10.23] May an employee be disciplined for poor attendance or lateness?

Yes. Good attendance and punctuality are important in almost every workplace.

However, there are times when an employee's absence or lateness is protected by law, as discussed in other portions of this book. These are addressed in Chapter 4, "Employee Time Off," and Chapter 11, "Discrimination, Harassment and Retaliation," of this book, and include:

- Required meal breaks;

- Lactation time;

- Jury service;

- Time to vote;

- Crime victim and crime witness leave;

- Blood donation;

- Bone marrow donation;

- Military service;

- Emergency responder leave;

- Domestic violence leave;

- Paid family leave;

- Statutory leave for serious personal illness;

- Statutory leave for the serious illness of an immediate family member;

- Statutory leave for pregnancy or to bond with a new child; and

- Leave or variable schedules to accommodate a disability.

CHAPTER ELEVEN

DISCRIMINATION, HARASSMENT AND RETALIATION

Robert A. LaBerge
Christa Richer Cook
Nicholas P. Jacobson

Edited by John Gaal

CHAPTER OVERVIEW

Laws addressing various forms of workplace discrimination and prohibiting retaliation have steadily evolved over the past several decades and are modified and expanded on an ongoing basis. This chapter provides a practical legal overview and guide concerning workplace discrimination by asking and answering a series of substantive and procedural questions related to this critical area of New York employment law.

Specific topics covered in this chapter are as follows:

I. GENERAL PRINCIPLES AND BACKGROUND

[11.9]   How soon must a discrimination claim be brought?

II.   HIRING, CONTINUED EMPLOYMENT, AND POST-EMPLOYMENT ISSUES

[11.10] Does the New York Human Rights Law apply to the hiring process?

[11.11] Can someone complain about discrimination even if he or she did not apply for a job?

[11.12] Can an employer *ever* consider a job applicant's protected status in making an employment decision?

[11.13] Can an employer consider prior arrests or criminal convictions during the hiring process?

[11.14] Can an employee complain about discriminatory conduct which was directed at someone else?

[11.15] Can someone who quit his or her job file a discrimination claim for wrongful discharge?

[11.16] Can an employer be sued for giving a negative reference?

III.   LIABILITY FOR WRONGFUL ACTS

[11.17] What types of damages and relief can be awarded to successful complainants?

[11.18] Can an owner or manager of an employer be personally liable for damages under the New York Human Rights Law?

[11.19] What is "aider or abettor" liability?

IV.   OVERVIEW OF DISCRIMINATION THEORIES AND CONCEPTS

[11.20] What is "disparate treatment" discrimination?

[11.21] What is "implicit bias"?

[11.22] What is "cat's paw" discrimination?

[11.23] What is a "mixed motive" discrimination case?

[11.24] What is "adverse impact" discrimination?

[11.25] What is compensation discrimination?

V.   SEXUAL AND OTHER PROHIBITED FORMS OF HARASSMENT

[11.26] What employers are covered by New York's prohibition of sexual harassment?

[11.27] What is the definition of sexual harassment?

[11.48] Is a mandatory retirement age permissible?

3.   Pregnancy

[11.49] How is pregnancy protected under New York law?
[11.50] How much leave is required for pregnancy-related conditions and childbirth?

4.   Sexual Orientation

[11.51] Is sexual orientation protected under the New York Human Rights Law?
[11.52] What are the protections for sexual orientation?

5.   Transgender Status

[11.53] Are transgender employees protected under the New York Human Rights Law?
[11.54] What accommodations must be granted to transgender employees?

6.   Religion

[11.55] How is religion protected under New York law?
[11.56] What accommodation must be made for religious observance?

7.   Marital, Familial, and Domestic Violence Victim Status

[11.57] What is marital status discrimination?
[11.58] What is familial status discrimination?
[11.59] What is domestic violence victim discrimination?

8.   Arrests and Convictions

[11.60] What is discrimination based upon criminal history or convictions?

VII. RETALIATION

[11.61] What is "retaliation"?
[11.62] What are the elements of a retaliation claim?
[11.63] What is an "adverse employment action" in the retaliation context?

[11.64] How does an employee prove the relationship between protected activity and an adverse action?

VIII. PROCEDURAL CONSIDERATIONS

[11.65] Does it really matter whether a discrimination claim is brought under federal, state or local law?

[11.66] Where can an administrative discrimination complaint be filed in New York?

[11.67] How much time does a person have to file an administrative discrimination complaint, or to sue, in New York?

[11.68] Which agency will take the lead when an administrative complaint is "cross-filed" under federal, state, and local laws?

[11.69] What happens when an agency finds "no probable cause"?

[11.70] What happens when an agency finds "probable cause"?

[11.71] Can an individual who has filed an administrative discrimination complaint still pursue a claim in court?

I. GENERAL PRINCIPLES AND BACKGROUND

[11.1] Overview of the anti-discrimination and anti-harassment laws applicable to New York State workplaces

Anti-discrimination and anti-retaliation laws come from a variety of sources: the United States Congress, the New York State Legislature, and the legislative bodies of local governments. In many respects, federal, state, and local enactments overlap, but in other respects they may differ from one another significantly.

These laws have carved out significant exceptions to, and have placed various limitations upon, the common law "employment at will" doctrine in New York State.[1] This was not always the case; in fact, until the ratification of the Thirteenth and Fourteenth Amendments to the United States Constitution and the enactment of various civil rights laws during the post-Civil War Reconstruction Era, no federal or state legislation prohibited *any*

---

1   The "employment at will" doctrine is discussed in Chapter 2 of this book.

form of discrimination in the workplace. Even after that, it took almost another 100 years for additional federal legislation to be passed specifically prohibiting certain types of discrimination in employment.[2]

By contrast, the past 50 years have witnessed the passage of hundreds of federal, state, and local anti-discrimination laws, along with major judicial developments. The current federal, state, and local employment discrimination laws create a labyrinth of rules and procedures applicable to actual or perceived discrimination in the workplace. All of these rules apply to people (or groups of people) who have been "adversely impacted" (disadvantaged) in the workplace because they are members of a group having protected category or status, or because they have engaged in a protected activity.

In general, unlawful discrimination takes two overall forms:

• **Intentional discrimination** is found where an employer has disfavored individuals or groups because the employer is hostile toward a particular protected category or status of persons (such as members of minority groups, women, disabled people, veterans, etc.). This type of discrimination may be proven by a showing of actual hostility on the part of the employer *or* by a showing that the employer treats different groups of job applicants or employees differently (i.e., "disparate treatment"), based upon their membership in a particular category or status.

• **"Disparate impact" discrimination** is found where the employer may not have intentionally discriminated, but has adopted policies, otherwise apparently neutral, which have a significant adverse effect on a protected category or status. An example of this would be a policy by a contract cleaning company that all of its cleaners must have at least a community college degree. While this requirement is neutral on its face (and perhaps even praiseworthy for encouraging an educated workforce), it will be found to be discriminatory where there is a showing that otherwise qualified minority job applicants are less likely to have been able to attend college, but can otherwise meet the requirements of the position.

---

2   On July 2, 1964, President Lyndon B. Johnson signed the Civil Rights Act of 1964, which makes it "an unlawful employment practice for an employer . . . to fail or refuse to hire or to discharge any individual, or otherwise to discriminate against any individual with respect to his compensation, terms, conditions, or privileges of employment, because of such individual's race, color, religion, sex or national origin." 42 U.S.C. § 2000e-2(a)(1).

Additionally, there is increasing discussion and debate among academics, employee advocates, judges, and litigants regarding the impact of, and potential theories of recovery for, "implicit" or "unconscious" bias in the workplace.[3] Some studies have shown that employers may be less likely to look at the résumés of job applicants who have "minority-sounding" first names, or will evaluate the same piece of written work differently when it is believed that the author is white or non-white.[4] It is virtually certain that the contours of "implicit bias" will be tested in the courts in coming years. Implicit bias is discussed further in § 11.21 *infra*.

A comprehensive description of the whole range of anti-discrimination and anti-retaliation laws would require an entire book and is beyond the scope and intent of this chapter. Accordingly, this chapter focuses specifically on New York State's employment discrimination laws.[5]

Virtually all state and federal courts and discrimination agencies evaluate discrimination claims, at least in the first instance, under the "shifting burdens" analysis first articulated by the United States Supreme Court in *McDonnell Douglas Corp. v. Green*.[6] All employers and employment law practitioners should be familiar with this analysis for two important reasons: first, because it will assist them in understanding how discrimination claims are reviewed; and second, because it may help them avoid significant potential pitfalls.

Under the *McDonnell Douglas* analysis, an employee who seeks to bring an employment discrimination claim must make at least a *"prima facie case"* by asserting that he or she was discriminated against because of a protected status or category: for example, "I applied for a promotion for which I am qualified, but my employer didn't promote me because I have

---

3   *See, e.g.,* Audrey J. Lee, *Unconscious Bias Theory in Employment Discrimination Litigation,* 40 Harv. C.R.–C.L. L. Rev. 481 (Summer 2005), and Khalil Smith, *You Can't Solve Inclusion with Unconscious Bias Training,* Forbes Magazine, April 3, 2019, https://www.forbes.com/sites/khalilsmith/2019/04/03/you-cant-solve-inclusion-with-unconscious-bias-training/#4115a6bf29ef.

4   *See, e.g.,* Arin N. Reeves, *Written in Black and White; Exploring Confirmation Bias in Racialized Perception of Writing Skills,* Nextions Yellow Paper Series, 2014, http://nextions.com/wp-content/uploads/2017/05/written-in-black-and-white-yellow-paper-series.pdf.

5   In fact, the New York State Human Rights Law (the NYHRL), and its predecessor legislation (which was known as the Ives-Quinn Anti-Discrimination Act), pre-dated the first significant federal anti-discrimination laws by some 20 years and was the first comprehensive state legislation in the United States to prohibit workplace discrimination.

6   411 U.S. 792 (1973).

a disability" (or, "because I am of Latvian national origin," or "because I am Muslim," or "because I am a Vietnam veteran," or "because I am a victim of domestic violence")."[7]

If the employee has made a *prima facie* case, then it is incumbent upon the employer to articulate *a legitimate, non-discriminatory reason* for the adverse personnel action. For example, in the case above, the employer's response might be: "Ms. X may have a disability, but that isn't why she did not get the promotion. She did not get the promotion because she comes to work late at least 60% of the time, and the position for which she applied requires punctuality."

If the employer has articulated a legitimate and non-discriminatory reason, then, in order to pursue her claim further, the employee must demonstrate that the employer's stated reason was *"pretextual"* (false). This can be shown in a number of ways:

- The employee's attendance records do not support the employer's claim, either because they show that the employee's punctuality was significantly better than the employer said it was, or because the employer does not even keep records of attendance and punctuality; or

- The person who was promoted was not disabled, and had a punctuality record which was no better, or even worse, than that of the complaining employee; or

- The job in question (e.g., counting inventory in a warehouse) does not need to be started at any particular time, and the complaining employee has always made up any time when she was late in the morning by working later in the afternoon.[8]

After the above rebuttals, if they are factual, an employer will have a very hard time defending against the employee's discrimination claim because

---

7   It should be emphasized that the employee must claim that he or she did not get the promotion *because* of the alleged discrimination, and not simply that he or she did not get the promotion *and* that he or she belongs to a protected category of persons. Many discrimination claimants do not understand this difference, and it is critically important.

8   "Pretext can be shown by such weaknesses, implausibilities, inconsistencies, incoherencies, or contradictions in the employer's proffered legitimate reasons for its action that a reasonable fact-finder could rationally find them unworthy of credence and hence infer that the employer did not act for the asserted non-discriminatory reasons." *Adamson v. Walgreens Co.*, 750 F.3d 73, 79 (1st Cir. 2014) (quoting *Gómez-González v. Rural Opportunities Inc.*, 626 F.3d 654, 662–63 (1st Cir. 2010)).

it will result in an inference that, having given a false reason for the action, the employer's true reason was discriminatory.

When the employer's stated reasons for a challenged employment decision shift, change, or "evolve," this provides strong circumstantial evidence that the real reason for the decision might be a prohibited one. However, this is not enough, on its own, to establish that the real reason was discriminatory. The complaining employee still must produce evidence sufficient for the factfinder to conclude that: (a) the employer's stated reason was false, and (b) the actual motivating factor for the challenged employment decision was discrimination.[9]

The lesson to be learned from *McDonnell Douglas* and its judicial progeny is that an employer that lies about, or exaggerates its reasons for, the action (or inaction) that gave rise to a discrimination claim leaves itself worse off than when it started.

[11.1.1] *What are the prohibited forms of discrimination?*

There are numerous federal and New York State laws which prohibit discrimination in the workplace. The following lists the most significant federal and state laws, with the prohibitions noted in **bold type**.

[11.1.1.1] *Federal laws*

1. *Title VII of the Civil Rights Act of 1964,* as amended ("Title VII"),[10] prohibits employment discrimination on the basis of an individual's **race, color, religion, sex (including pregnancy), or national origin**. Title VII also prohibits **retaliation** against individuals for "opposing" unlawful employment practices or "participating" in investigations, proceedings, or hearings conducted in accordance with rights provided under the statute.

2. The *Equal Pay Act of 1963,* as amended, requires "equal pay for equal work," prohibiting discrimination **on the basis of sex** with

---

9   *St. Mary's Honor Ctr. v. Hicks,* 509 U.S. 502, (1993); *see also* Jody H. Odell, *Between Pretext Only and Pretext Plus: Understanding St. Mary's Honor Center v. Hicks and Its Application to Summary Judgment,* 69 Notre Dame L. Rev. 1251 (1994).

10   *See* 42 U.S.C. §§ 2000e–2000e-17, and regulations promulgated pursuant to Title VII at 29 C.F.R. Part 1601.

respect to compensation for work requiring "equal skill, efforts, and responsibilities."[11]

3. The *Age Discrimination in Employment Act of 1967,* as amended (ADEA), prohibits discrimination in employment against **"individuals who are at least 40 years of age."**[12] Additionally, the ADEA, like Title VII, prohibits **retaliation** against individuals for "opposing" unlawful employment practices or "participating" in investigations, proceedings, or hearings conducted in accordance with the rights provided under the statute.

4. The *Americans with Disabilities Act of 1990,* as amended (ADA),[13] prohibits employment discrimination against "qualified individual[s] on the basis of **disability**." The ADA generally defines the term "disability" as "a physical or mental impairment that limits one or more major life activities . . . ."[14] The ADA requires employers to provide "reasonable accommodations" to "qualified individual[s]" who are able to perform the "essential functions" of the employment position or role involved, with or without such (reasonable) accommodations. Additionally, as do Title VII and the ADEA, the ADA prohibits **retaliation** against individuals who "oppose" unlawful acts or practices or "participate" in any investigations, proceedings, or hearings conducted in accordance with rights provided under the statute.

5. The *Genetic Information Non-Discrimination Act of 2008* (GINA) prohibits **employers** from **using an individual's genetic information** when making hiring, firing, promotional, and job placement decisions.[15] GINA also prohibits **health insurers** from **denying coverage** or **charging higher premiums** to a person based solely

---

11   *See* 29 U.S.C. § 206(d)(1) and regulations promulgated under the Equal Pay Act at 29 C.F.R. Parts 1620 and 1621. Employers can defend against claims brought under the Equal Pay Act by establishing that compensation differences are attributable to seniority, merit pay systems, quantity or quality of production, or "any other factor, other than sex."

12   *See* 29 U.S.C. §§ 621–634., and the regulations promulgated under the ADEA at 29 C.F.R. Part 1630. While the statute's prohibition against age discrimination extends to all terms and conditions of employment, the ADEA expressly permits employers to follow the terms of *bona fide* seniority systems and employee benefits plans subject to various restrictions set forth in the statute.

13   *See* 42 U.S.C. §§ 12101–12213.

14   The ADA's definition of "disability" also extends to individuals who have "a record of such an impairment" or who are "regarded as having such an impairment. *See* 42 U.S.C. § 12102(1).

15   122 Stat. 881 (2008). *See* 42 U.S.C. § 12111(8)–(9).

upon the person's genetic predisposition to develop a disease in the future. GINA further prohibits **retaliation** against any individual for "opposing" unlawful practices or "participating" in any proceeding held in connection with the statute.

6. The *Uniformed Services Employment and Reemployment Act,* as amended (USERRA), prohibits discrimination based upon an individual's **past, present, or future military service**, which includes all "uniformed service in the Army, Marine Corps, Navy, Coast Guard, Air Force, and Air National Guard, and Public Health Service Commissioned Corps.[16] USERRA, among other things, requires employers of all sizes to grant leaves for training and active service and to reemploy service members following their training or service into the same positions they previously held, without diminution of compensation benefits or other terms and privileges of employment.

[11.1.1.2]   *Federal executive orders and laws affecting federal government contractors and subcontractors*

1. *Executive Order 11246* ("E.O. 11246") establishes certain non-discrimination, affirmative action, and recordkeeping requirements for **contractors** and **subcontractors** of the U.S. Government. E.O. 11246 specifically prohibits first-tier contractors having business with federal departments or agencies of $10,000 or more and their subcontractors from discriminating against individuals on the basis of **race, color, religion, sex, or national origin**. It also requires covered contractors to engage in affirmative action with respect to minorities and females, and to develop affirmative action plans designed to assess and track their efforts and results in this regard.[17]

2. The *Rehabilitation Act of 1973,* as amended (the "Rehabilitation Act"), prohibits discrimination on the basis of **disability** in programs conducted or sponsored by U.S. government agencies.[18] In

---

16   *See* 38 U.S.C. §§ 4301–05.

17   President Lyndon B. Johnson signed E.O. 11246 on September 24, 1965. The requirements are monitored and enforced by the Office of Federal Contract Compliance Programs (the OFCCP), part of the U.S. Department of Labor created by Executive Order 12086 signed by President Jimmy Carter on October 5, 1978. *See* the regulations promulgated by the OFCCP setting forth the requirements for these federal contractor affirmative action plans at 41 C.F.R. §§ 60-1-2, 60-300.80, and 60-741.80.

18   *See* 29 U.S.C. § 701–718b, and the regulations promulgated thereunder by the OFCCP at 41 C.F.R. Part 60-741.

the employment area, the Rehabilitation Act requires covered contractors and subcontractors doing $10,000 or more in business with
federal government agencies to implement policies prohibiting
discrimination against, and promoting the employment of, qualified disabled individuals. Contractors with 50 or more employees
and government contracts of $50,000 or more are also required to
develop affirmative action programs and to establish placement
goals for qualified disabled applicants and employees.

3.   The *Vietnam Era Veterans Readjustment Assistance Act of 1974*, as
amended (VEVRAA), prohibits discrimination against military
veterans (with or without disabilities) by contractors or subcontractors of the federal government holding federal contracts of
$100,000 or more.[19] In addition to prohibiting discrimination, the
VEVRAA requires covered contractors to take affirmative steps
with respect to the recruitment, hiring, training, and retention of
covered veterans and disabled veterans.

[11.1.1.3]   *New York State laws*[20]

A.   *Article 15 of the New York Executive Law*[21] is known as the New
York Human Rights Law (NYHRL), and prohibits employers,
employment and licensing agencies, and labor organizations from
discriminating against any "individual" because of that individual's
**"age [18 years of age or older], race, creed, color, national ori-
gin, sexual orientation, gender identity or expression, military
status, sex, disability, predisposing genetic characteristics,
familial status, marital status, or status as a victim of domestic
violence."**[22] With respect to employment, the NYHRL prohibits all
"unlawful employment practices," including discriminatory decisions with respect to recruiting, hiring, training, retention, disci-

---

19   *See* 38 U.S.C. § 4212 and the regulations promulgated under the VEVRAA at 41 C.F.R. Part 60-300.

20   Equal employment opportunity is a recognized civil right in New York State and its protection
serves as the subject matter of many different laws. In addition to the New York statutes and executive orders summarized in this subsection, equal employment opportunity is addressed both
in the New York State Constitution and in several other statutes. The New York State Constitution, Article 1, Section 11, prohibits discrimination in employment on the basis of race and religion and provides equal protection against discriminatory state action on any basis. The New
York Public Authorities Law, Public Health Law, Judiciary Law, Elections Law, and Unconsol-
idated Laws similarly contain provisions prohibiting discrimination or retaliation in employment
for a myriad of reasons.

21   Exec. Law §§ 290–301.

22   *See* Exec. Law § 296(1)(a) and (b).

pline, discharge, and all other terms and conditions of employment. The NYHRL also expressly provides that it shall be an "unlawful discriminatory practice" for any person to **retaliate** against any individual "because he or she has opposed [unlawful practices] or because he or she has filed a complaint, testified, or assisted"[23] in any proceeding, or for any person "to aid, abet, incite, compel or coerce" any individual in any act forbidden by Article 15.[24]

B. *New York Labor Law § 194* sets forth New York's version of the federal Equal Pay Act. Like the Equal Pay Act, New York law historically prohibited gender-based **pay differentials for equivalent work**. With its amendment in 2019, the state law is much broader than the federal Equal Pay Act: specifically, New York now prohibits compensation discrimination on the basis of *any* **category or status protected under the NYHRL**. Additionally, and also unlike the federal Equal Pay Act, the affirmative defenses for employers to justify pay differences for equivalent work are somewhat more limited than those available under the federal law and can be overcome if it is shown that the basis for the pay difference has a disparate impact upon individuals in a protected category.[25]

C. *Article 23-A of the New York Correction Law*[26] prohibits denial of employment or licenses based upon an applicant's or employee's **criminal conviction record** if that conviction record does not have a "direct relationship" to the employment sought or held. The statute sets forth seven factors, including the public policy encouraging employment of individuals with conviction histories, which public and private employers must consider and assess before denying employment based upon a prior conviction.[27]

D. *New York Military Law §§ 242–43 and §§ 317–18* prohibit employers from discriminating against employees **because of their military service**.[28] In addition to the potential claims and

---

23   Exec. Law § 296(7).

24   Exec. Law § 296 (6).

25   *See* discussion of Labor Law § 194 at § 11.25 *infra*.

26   Corr. Law §§ 751–53.

27   For a discussion of how this law applies to hiring procedures and decisions, *see* Chapter 1 of this book, "The Hiring Process," at §§ 1.8–11.11 and §§ 1.24–1.26.

28   See Mil. Law §§ 242–43 for the provisions applicable to public employers, and §§ 317–18 for the provisions applicable to private employers.

remedies which may be available pursuant to the USERRA and the NYHRL, Military Law § 252 provides that denying employment to an individual because of his or her military service is a misdemeanor.

E. Article 15-A of the New York Executive Law and New York State Executive Orders and Regulations.

1. *Article 15-A of the Executive Law*[29] sets forth various requirements designed to encourage **New York State contractors** to provide equal employment opportunities for disadvantaged individuals and businesses. This statute, among other things, prohibits discrimination by state contractors on the basis of **race, creed, color, national origin, sex, age, disability, or marital status**. Article 15-A additionally requires state contractors to implement diversity practices intended to enhance opportunities for minority- and women-owned businesses and minority and female applicants and employees.

2. *New York State Executive Orders* have been issued over the years and empower various state executive branch agencies to establish affirmative action requirements for state contractors.[30] Other executive orders have been issued to establish special committees or task forces to study and implement initiatives designed to address various ongoing workplace problem areas, such as **sexual discrimination** and **harassment,** and **sexual orientation discrimination** and **harassment**.[31]

3. *New York State Agency Regulations* have been issued to clarify and supplement the equal employment opportunity and anti-discrimination requirements set forth in the New York Executive Law and other state statutes. The New York State Division of Human Rights (NYSDHR), for instance, has issued guidance or promulgated regulations addressing various issues, such as **permissible** and **impermissible questions** and inquiries in employment applications and interviews, the scope and extent of an employer's duty to provide **workplace accommodations**; and rules and procedures applicable to proceedings before the NYSDHR. The NYSDHR

---

29   Exec. Law §§ 310–18.

30   *See, e.g.,* N.Y. Executive Orders Nos. 5 & 6, 9 N.Y.C.R.R. §§ 4.5 & 4.6.

31   *See, e.g.,* N.Y. Executive Orders Nos. 7, 19 & 28, 9 N.Y.C.R.R. §§ 4.17, 4.19, 4.28.

and the New York State Department of Labor have also issued other guidance and regulations relating to: employer posting requirements; apprenticeship training requirements; sexual harassment prevention; and several other subjects.

[11.1.1.4] *Local laws*

Article 12-D of the New York General Municipal Law[32] authorizes county, city, village, and town governments to create their own human rights commissions and laws. The General Municipal Law gives these local commissions authority only to educate the general public on human rights issues and to study and inquire into incidents and tensions among racial, religious, and national origin groups; in other words, the statute makes a local commission's role secondary to that of the NYSDHR. However, the General Municipal Law contains an exception for New York City, and specifically provides that "[n]othing in this Article shall be deemed to limit or reduce the powers of the New York City commission on human rights . . . [which] . . . shall be deemed to be concurrent with the jurisdiction of the New York state division of human rights."[33] In other words, the New York City Commission on Human Rights (NYCCHR) has, as to discrimination in the City of New York, the same powers that the NYSDHR has elsewhere.

The *New York City Human Rights Law* (NYCHRL)[34] was enacted in 1965, and applies to employers and employees who work in, or whose work is sufficiently connected to, one of the five boroughs of New York City. The NYCHRL is administered and enforced by the NYCCHR. The NYCHRL currently prohibits discrimination on the same basis as does the NYHRL with respect to race, creed, color, national origin, gender, disability, marital status, partnership status, alienage, victim of domestic violence or stalking status, citizenship status, unemployment status, consumer credit history status, or internship status. In addition, with respect to age, the NYCHRL contains no minimum age threshold and thus provides protection even to individuals under 18 years of age. Like the NYHRL, the NYCHRL provides protections which are broader than those provided under the federal antidiscrimination laws, and NYCHRL claims are often analyzed and assessed separately from companion claims filed under other civil rights laws.

---

32   Gen. Mun. Law §§ 239-o–239-t.

33   *See* Gen. Mun. Law § 239-s.

34   This law is found at Title 8 of the Administrative Code of the City of New York.

In addition to New York City, various counties, towns, and cities in New York State have established their own human rights commissions pursuant to the authority granted to them by Article 12-D of the General Municipal law. Some, but not all, of these local governments have also enacted their own human rights laws to supplement the protections afforded under the NYHRL.

As of this writing, the following counties have established human rights commissions and/or enacted human rights laws:

> Nassau County, Suffolk County, Westchester County, Ulster County, Rockland County, Orange County, Schenectady County, Chemung County, Onondaga County, Tompkins County.

As of this writing, the following cities (in addition to New York City), towns, and villages have established human right commissions and/or enacted human rights laws:

> Yonkers, Rye, White Plains, Larchmont, Mamaroneck, Rockville Centre, Troy, Auburn, Wallkill, Freeport, Niagara Falls, Buffalo, Ithaca, Syracuse.

[11.1.2] *Are Federal and State Anti-Discrimination Laws the Same?*

For the most part, New York and federal anti-discrimination and anti-retaliation laws overlap and cover the same prohibitions. However, there are a number of significant differences. In addition, some local laws set forth additional prohibitions.

Age discrimination. The federal ADEA applies to and protects individuals who are age 40 or older, and has been interpreted and applied to permit only claims by older employees who allege that they were discriminated against in favor of younger employees. By contrast, the NYHRL (state) applies to anyone over 18 years of age, and the NYC HRL (New York City) has *no* minimum or maximum age limits for coverage. Thus, while the ADEA prohibits discrimination against older employees only, the NYHRL and the NYCHRL prohibit discrimination against younger employees as well.

Sexual orientation, gender expression, and gender identity. The coverage and application of the federal, state, and local laws to discrimination based upon sexual orientation, gender expression, and gender identity have historically differed significantly. While various New York state and local laws have prohibited discrimination on the basis of sexual orientation and gender expression and identity for some time, the protections available under the federal laws are far less clear and continue to change. The federal courts in different parts of the United States have reached varying conclusions over the years as to whether sexual orientation and gender expression and identify are covered by Title VII's prohibition of gender discrimination. In addition, while the EEOC under the Obama Administration took a more expansive interpretation of Title VII's protections through a series of administrative decisions and guidance issued between 2012 and 2015, the Trump administration has reversed many of these initiatives since 2017.

Other protections. The NYHRL provides protection to several categories not currently covered by the federal anti-discrimination laws, such as marital status, familial status, domestic violence victim status, use of service animals, internship status, and criminal arrest and conviction history status. And, as is expanded upon below, the NYCHRL expressly extends protection to partnership status, and alienage or citizenship status, which are not currently covered by the federal laws or the NYHRL.

[11.2] How do employers deal with the different federal, state, and local requirements?

The lack of uniformity in the substantive and procedural provisions of the federal, state, and local anti-discrimination and anti-retaliation laws creates enormous challenges for employers and employees alike, as well as for attorneys and others who advise employers regarding these subjects.

Among the challenges for employers are the practical difficulties associated with developing employment policies and programs that comply with all of the divergent federal, state, and local law standards. Employers therefore must: (1) identify prohibitions and requirements contained in all of the laws which extend to their organizations; and (2) develop and implement policies and programs that are consistent and in compliance with the *broadest* of the requirements applicable to their operations in all places in which they do business.

There are also significant procedural differences among federal, state, and local law such as: different statutes of limitations and filing periods applicable to claims under the different laws; different administrative agency filing prerequisites and procedures; and different remedies and relief available under the different laws. In light of these many differences, and in view of the filing prerequisites and options, employees and employee representatives often are challenged to find ways to join claims under different laws in a manner that is efficient and maximizes the potential relief they can obtain for discrimination and retaliation in the workplace.

[11.3] Who is protected by the New York Human Rights Law?

The NYHRL applies to all "employees." However, the statute specifically excludes coverage for "any individual employed by his or her parents, spouse or child, or in the domestic service . . . ."[35] Accordingly, family members and domestic workers are not normally entitled to the NYHRL's protections. However, as is discussed in § 11.3.3 *infra*, domestic workers *do* have protection under the NYHRL against sexual harassment.[36]

The NYHRL covers both job applicants and actual employees. To pursue a claim under the NYHRL, the person asserting the claim must be able to show that he or she is *also* an "aggrieved person" within the meaning of the statute. An "aggrieved person" is an individual who can demonstrate that he or she was personally impacted by the alleged discriminatory employment practice in some way.[37]

[11.3.1] *Are independent contractors protected by the NYHRL?*[38]

Typically, the NYHRL has been interpreted to protect only actual employees and applicants for employment, and its coverage historically has not been extended to individuals who are properly considered to be independent contractors.[39] However, in New York City, independent contractors are covered by the NYCHRL.

Employers should be careful about using the independent contractor designation, because courts and agencies will look past the label if the individual in question is actually an employee. A multi-factor common law agency test is often applied to determine whether a complaining party is an independent contractor or an employee for purposes of NYHRL cover-

---

35   Exec. Law § 292 (6).

36   Exec. Law § 296-b.

37   Exec. Law § 297(1); *see also Levine v. N.Y. State Div. of Human Rights,* Index No. 10220/2016 (Sup. Ct. Suffolk Co. Mar. 31, 2017) and cases cited therein.

38   The distinctions between employees and independent contractors is also discussed in Chapter 12 of this book.

39   *See Scott v. Mass Mutual Life Ins. Co.,* 86 N.Y.2d. 429, 633 N.Y.S.2d 754 (1995); *see also Eisenberg v. Advance Relocation Storage, Inc.,* 237 F.3d 111, 113–14 (2d Cir. 2000); *Metro. Pilots Assoc. v. Schlosberg,* 151 F. Supp. 2d 511 (D.N.J. 2001).

age. While no one factor is controlling, the courts and administrative agencies usually look to 13 factors, also known as the "Reid factors," to determine whether an individual is an independent contractor or an employee entitled to protection under the NYHRL and the federal employment statutes.[40] The most important of these factors often is the degree of control which the hiring party exercises over the hired party. The greater the control, the more probable it is that the hired party will be found to be an employee.[41]

[11.3.2] *Are unpaid interns protected by the NYHRL?*

In most instances, yes. While both federal law and the NYHRL historically required that individuals receive "significant remuneration" to be covered by the statutes, the NYHRL was amended in 2014 to extend antidiscrimination and anti-harassment protections to persons serving in unpaid training programs. NYHRL § 296-c now makes it an unlawful employment practice for employers to discriminate against unpaid interns on the basis of *any* protected category or status. [42] Interns covered by this new section are individuals who work without compensation, primarily for training and experience purposes, and without any commitment that the employer will hire them at the end of their training. The training provided must principally benefit the intern, rather than the employer, and the internship cannot result in the displacement of regular employees. The statute prohibits discrimination in the solicitation, recruitment, or classification of applicants for covered internships and provides additional specific protections for interns with respect to sexual harassment, pregnancy discrimination, and retaliation.[43]

---

40 These factors are: (1) the hiring party's right to control the manner and means by which the project is accomplished; (2) the skill required; (3) which party provides the tools and equipment for the work; (4) the location of the work; (5) the duration of the relationship between the parties; (6) whether the hiring party has the right to assign additional projects to the hired party; (7) the extent of the hired party's discretion over when and how long to work; (8) the method of payment; (9) the hired party's role in hiring and paying assistants; (10) whether the work is part of the regular business of the hiring party; (11) whether the hiring party is in business; (12) the provision of employee benefits; and (13) the tax treatment of the hired party.

41 It should also be noted that misclassifying an employee as an independent contractor can have serious federal and state tax consequences for the hiring party.

42 The NYCHRL was similarly amended in 2014 to cover unpaid interns.

43 These distinctions mirror the interpretation of the federal Fair Labor Standards Act, which determines the classes of workers who must be paid the federal minimum wage.

[11.3.3] *Are domestic workers protected by the NYHRL?*

Only with respect to sexual harassment. "Domestic workers" were completely excluded from the NYHRL definition of "employee" when the law was first enacted, so domestic workers historically had no protection under the statute.[44] However, the NYHRL was amended in 2010 to address this deficiency as it relates to sexual harassment, but *not* as to any other protected categories or types of prohibited conduct.

[11.4] What employers are covered by the New York Human Rights Law?

Until 2019, the NYHRL provided that in order to be considered an "employer" covered by the NYHRL, an organization generally had to employ at least four "individuals." The NYHRL was amended in 2019 to drop the four-employee requirement, and to state the following new definition: "The term 'private employer' as used in section two hundred ninety-seven of this article shall include any person, company, corporation, labor organization or association."

Thus, while a discrimination claimant must generally still be an "employee" in order to bring a claim of employment discrimination, an employee may now bring such a claim even if he or she is the *only* employee of the employer.

Courts and administrative agencies take a broad view as to whether owners, partners, shareholders, etc., should be counted as "employees," and may also treat related enterprises as a single employer if the related enterprises effectively function as a single employer.

[11.5] Are out-of-state employers covered by the NYHRL?

Yes. The NYHRL applies to out-of-state companies which do not maintain offices in New York State if their allegedly discriminatory employment decisions have a sufficient impact upon New York State residents or

---

44 Exec. Law § 292(6); *see also Thomas v. Dosberg,* 249 A.D.2d 999, 672 N.Y.S.2d 164 (4th Dep't 1989) (refusing to apply the NYHRL to a home health aide because an individual working in domestic service was not an "employee" entitled to protection).

inhabitants.[45] It also applies to New York State employers who commit discriminatory acts elsewhere in certain situations.[46]

[11.6]   Are religiously affiliated employers covered by the NYHRL?

In some respects, yes; in other respects, no.

While the NYHRL makes it an unlawful discriminatory practice for an employer to condition employment upon an individual's religious beliefs (or lack of religious beliefs),[47] it expressly exempts from this prohibition "any religious or denominational institution or organization . . . limiting . . . admission to or giving preferences to persons of the same religion or denomination."[48]

The exemption extends not only to churches, synagogues, temples, mosques, and other places of worship, but also to other types of institutions run by religious organizations, such as religious health care and educational institutions, even though they may have a partially secular purpose.[49] As this provision has been interpreted and applied, exempt religious organizations can give preference in their hiring and placement decisions to persons of the same faith, so long as those preferences are reasonably calculated to further the organization's religious mission.

However, the exemption does not permit religious organizations to discriminate on the basis of any other protected status; further, it does not allow religious organizations to discriminate on the basis of religion in any way other than in the hiring and placement of mission-related employees.

---

45   Exec. Law § 298-a; *see also Griffen v. Sirva, Inc.*, 29 N.Y. 3d 174, 54 N.Y.S.3d 360 (2017); (recognizing that the NYHRL and the NYCHRL apply to out-of-state companies who make employment decisions that impact upon "inhabitants" and "persons" within New York State and New York City, respectively).

46   *See Hoffman v. Parade Publications*, 15 N.Y.3d 285, 907 N.Y.S.2d 145 (2010) (recognizing that for an out-of-state resident to pursue a claim under the NYHRL or the NYCHRL, this individual must show that "the discriminatory conduct had an impact in New York," which requires more than just alleging that the decision was made in New York).

47   Exec. Law §§ 296(10)–(11).

48   Exec. Law § 296 (11).

49   *See Scheiber v. St. John's University*, 84 N.Y.2d 120, 615 N.Y.S.2d 332 (1994), and 1986 N.Y. Op. Atty. Gen. 29, WL 223127.

[11.7] What are employers prohibited from doing under the NYHRL?

An employer may not discriminate or retaliate against an employee who belongs to any category subject to the protections of the NYHRL as to the entire range of employment decisions, including (but not limited to):

- Hiring;

- Firing;

- Promotion, transfer or demotion;

- Work assignments;

- Shift or schedule changes

- Compensation;

- Employee benefits; or

- Discipline involving a loss of compensation, status, or future opportunities.

The NYHRL further prohibits sexual harassment and other types of harassment based upon an individual's protected category, characteristic, or status.[50] The statute also requires employers to take various affirmative steps to prevent and correct harassment in the workplace.[51]

The NYHRL further requires that employers must provide "reasonable accommodations" for employees with disabilities, with pregnancy-related conditions, and for religious practices and beliefs.[52] In these areas, the statute and its implementing regulations encourage employers to engage in an

---

50   *See* discussion regarding prohibited harassment at §§ 11.26–11.34 *infra*.

51   Employers' obligations to develop policies and training regarding sexual harassment, and to investigate and address internal complaints of prohibited workplace harassment is discussed in § 11.32 *infra*.

52   *See* discussion regarding an employer's duty to provide reasonable accommodations for disabilities in §§ 11.35–11.46 *infra;* for pregnancy-related conditions, in §§ 11.49–11.50. *infra*; and for religious practices and beliefs, in §§ 11.55–11.56 *infra*.

"interactive process" with individuals requesting accommodations, and require employers to provide such accommodations so long as they are (a) reasonable and (b) do not cause "undue hardship" for the employer.[53]

[11.8] Can a business participate in a boycott, "blacklist," or refusal to do business?

Not if the basis for the action is membership in a protected category. The NYHRL provides that it is an "unlawful discriminatory practice" for any person to "boycott" or "blacklist," or "to refuse to buy from, sell to, or trade with, or otherwise discriminate against, any person" because of one of the protected categories listed in the statute.[54]

[11.9] How soon must a discrimination claim be brought?

The NYHRL is subject to a three-year statute of limitations which applies to discrimination actions brought in state court; in other words, a claim first asserted in a New York state court lawsuit must be brought within three years after the conduct complained of took place.[55] Shorter periods apply to non-gender-based discrimination charges filed with the EEOC, the New York State Division of Human Rights, and the New York City Commission on Human Rights.[56]

A claim based upon a single act of discrimination (such as discharge, demotion, transfer, or failure to promote) must be brought within three years after the act took place; if this is not done, then the employer can

---

53   *See* Exec. Law §§ 292(21), 292(21-e), 292(21-f), 296(3), and 296(10), and 9 N.Y.C.R.R. § 466.11.

54   *See* Exec. Law § 296(13). However, this provision further states that the prohibitions do not apply to boycotts connected with labor disputes, § 296(13)(a), or to boycotts "to protest unlawful discriminatory practices" § 296(13)(b).

55   *See* CPLR 214(2).

56   In "deferral states," which includes New York, a federal administrative discrimination charge alleging Title VII-based claims must be filed, or cross-filed, within 300 days of the last act of alleged discrimination. 42 U.S.C. § 2000e–5(e)(1). Under the NYHRL and the NYCHRL, administrative complaints based upon non-gender discrimination allegations must be filed within one year of the alleged discrimination. With respect to administrative complaints filed with the NYCCHR based upon gender-based discrimination or harassment, the filing period is extended to three-years. The NYHRL was similarly amended in 2019 and the limitations period for administrative complaints under that statute based on gender-based complaints will be three years effective Aug. 23, 2020. While the administrative filing period under the NYHRL and the NYCHRL for non-gender based discrimination allegations remains just one year, individuals do not have to file an administrative complaint as a prerequisite to pursuing a claim in court under either statute; rather, as is noted above, individuals can file complaints under the NYHRL or the NYCHRL directly in court and have three years to do so under both statutes.

ask the court to dismiss the case as time-barred. However, where an employee had been subjected to ongoing discriminatory conduct (such as continuing harassment), New York courts will apply a "continuing violation" theory to include acts which took place more than three years before suit is brought, so long as at least *some* of the conduct took place within the three-year limitations period.

II.   HIRING, CONTINUED EMPLOYMENT, AND POST-EMPLOYMENT ISSUES

[11.10] Does the New York Human Rights Law apply to the hiring process?

Yes. The NYHRL covers job advertisements, job applications, applicant screening, job referral processes and procedures, and/or training programs as they relate to covered individuals.[57] *See also* Chapter 1 of this book, "The Hiring Process."

The NYHRL expressly states that it is an unlawful discriminatory practice for an employer or an employment agency "to print or circulate or cause to be printed or circulated any statement, advertisement or publication, or to use any form of application for employment or to make any inquiry in connection with prospective employment, which expresses directly or indirectly, any limitation, specification, or discrimination" on the basis of any of the protected categories.[58] The statute similarly provides that it is an unlawful discriminatory practice for labor organizations, employers, and employment agencies to deny or withhold participation in any apprenticeship program, on-the-job training program, executive training program, or other occupational training or retraining program because of any of the protected categories.[59]

The New York State Division of Human Rights will investigate discriminatory job solicitations and screening processes even if there is no individual complaining about them. In this situation, the Division proceeds with an agency-initiated complaint and investigation with respect to the responsible employer, employment agency, or labor organization.

---

57   *See* Exec. Law §§ 296(1)(d) and 296(1-a). The hiring process is discussed in greater detail in Chapter 1 of this book.

58   Exec. Law § 296(1)(d).

59   Exec. Law § 296(1-a).

[11.11] Can someone complain about discrimination even if he or she did not apply for a job?

In some circumstances, yes. The New York State Division of Human Rights has investigated numerous complaints of allegedly discriminatory job advertisements, even though the individual filing the complaint with the Division did not actually apply for the position in question.

In evaluating complaints about job advertisements, the Division first considers whether the solicitation would have "chilled" a job searcher from applying for the job. For instance, advertisements which include statements like "no felons," "no Haitians," "seeking female," or looking for "young persons," are discriminatory and will be presumed by the Division to have a "chilling effect" on some job searchers. In these cases, individuals excluded by the advertisement may bring a claim even though they never actually applied for the position.

On the other hand, the Division has ruled that job advertisements seeking "waitresses" or "hostesses," while not gender neutral, do not express a specific limitation or restriction that will be presumed to be discriminatory; in cases like these, the Division would require a male complainant to have applied for the job and to have been rejected for the position in order to pursue a claim.

In addition, of course, a claimant must show that he or she was: (a) actively seeking a job of the type in question; and (b) met the minimum legitimate qualifications for the position. This is referred to as having "standing" to bring a claim.

The fact that someone did not actually apply for a job with that particular employer will not defeat standing *if* it was apparent from an advertisement or application that he or she would not have been considered for an unlawful reason, for example, that the would-be applicant had only a high school diploma and thus did not apply for a job as a cleaner where the advertisement said that applicants must have at least a community college degree.[60]

---

60   *See, e.g., Hailes v. United Air Lines,* 464 F.2d 1006 (5th Cir. 1972) (holding that a person who had a "real, present interest in the type of employment advertised" has standing and can challenge a discriminatory job solicitation, even though he had not actually applied for job, when he can demonstrate that he was "effectively deterred by the improper ad from applying for such employment.").

[11.12] Can an employer *ever* consider a job applicant's protected status in making an employment decision?

Almost never. As an almost universal rule, employers may not base an employment decision upon an applicant's protected status, or on criteria that exclude applicants in protected categories. There is an extremely limited exception for what is called a *"bona fide* occupational qualification" or BFOQ.

For example, an employer that operates a moving company might legitimately require that job applicants for its moving crews show they can lift 150 pounds, even though this may exclude some disproportionate numbers of female, older and disabled applicants, because moving crews need to be able to pick up heavy items. However, a taxi company looking to hire drivers would have a virtually impossible time justifying the same requirement.

The United States Supreme Court has ruled that the BFOQ defense "provides only the narrowest of exceptions to the general rule requiring equality of employment opportunities," and that an employer seeking to prove such an exception bears a heavy burden to show that the BFOQ is actually necessary.[61] Examples of BFOQs are often found in the artistic world, where directors or photographers can seek candidates of particular genders or ages if essential to the authenticity of the role to be portrayed. Other examples of BFOQs can be found with respect to certain faith-based requirements (e.g., a rabbi needs to be Jewish, a priest needs to be Catholic, etc.) and certain age-based requirements, such as mandatory retirement ages for pilots, firefighters, or police officers for safety reasons.

---

61   *See Dothard v. Rawlinson*, 433 U.S. 321 (1977) (holding that the weight and height restrictions used for screening prison guard candidates had an adverse impact upon female applicants, and did not provide the basis for a valid BFOQ exception); and *United Auto Workers v. Johnson Controls, Inc.*, 499 U.S. 187 (1991) (examining employment policies prohibiting women from working in potentially hazardous occupations, including jobs which were dangerous to reproductive systems, and rejecting the employer's BFOQ defense based upon the business' alleged interest in protecting employees' unborn fetuses); *see also* Stephen F. Befort, *BFOQ Revisited: Johnson Controls Halts the Expansion of the Defense to Intentional Sex Discrimination*, 52 Ohio St. L.J. 5 (Winter 1991).

[11.13] Can an employer consider prior arrests or criminal convictions during the hiring process?

It is unlawful to ask about or consider a job applicant's prior arrest record under any circumstances.[62] It is less clear whether an employer may ask about *pending criminal charges*, although for a variety of reasons employers should be wary of asking such questions until and unless a decision to make a provisional offer of employment has been made.

A prospective employer *may* ask about *prior criminal convictions*, but may *not* be able to do so in an initial job application in counties or municipalities which have adopted so-called "ban-the-box" legislation. No matter at what point in the hiring process a prospective employer may make such inquiries, it may base a decision not to hire because of the conviction *only* after following a specific process to determine whether the conviction is relevant to the job for which the applicant has applied.

See Chapter 1 of this book, "The Hiring Process," at §§ 1.8–1.11 and §§ 1.24–1.26 for a detailed discussion of how criminal history may be considered in the hiring process.

[11.14] Can an employee complain about discriminatory conduct which was directed at someone else?

Yes, under some circumstances. The courts have recognized "associational discrimination" claims under the NYHRL. For example, in *Chiara v. Town of New Castle,* the plaintiff, who was not Jewish but was married to a Jewish woman, alleged that his co-workers repeatedly made anti-Semitic remarks in his presence and harassed him after he told them that his wife was Jewish. He also claimed that he was fired at least in part because of his wife's religion.[63] The court noted that claims under the

---

62   "Prior arrest record" means any arrest, which is not still pending (i.e., unresolved), that was: (a) resolved or dismissed in favor of the accused (Criminal Procedure Law § 160.50); *or* (b) resolved by a youthful offender adjudication (Criminal Procedure Law § 720.35); *or* (c) resulted in a sealed or conditionally sealed record (Criminal Procedure Law §§ 160.55 and 160.58). However, *after* an individual has been hired, the NYHRL does *not* prohibit an employer from making inquiries into, or taking adverse employment actions with respect to, *current* arrests—but in such cases. if an employee is not terminated while the charges are still pending *and* the arrest is subsequently resolved in favor of the employee, then the employee would be protected by NYHRL § 296(16).

63   *Chiara v. New Castle,* 126 A.D.3d 111, 2 N.Y.S.3d 132 (2d Dep't 2015); *see also Macchio v. Michaels Elec. Supply Corp.,* 149 A.D.3d 716, 51 N.Y.S.3d 134 (2d Dep't 2017) (plaintiff stated a cause of action for discrimination based upon his association with African-American individuals).

NYHRL are "analytically identical to claims brought under Title VII, and that several federal court decisions recognized associational discrimination claims under Title VII."

A specific prohibition against associational discrimination was added to the New York State Division of Human Rights' regulations in 2016 to protect persons with a known association with, or relationship to, a member of, a protected class.[64] In order to prove a claim of discrimination, a complainant must establish that he or she was subjected to an adverse employment action because of his or her known relationship to, or association with, a member or members of a protected class.

[11.15] Can someone who quit his or her job file a discrimination claim for wrongful termination?

Usually not. In most circumstances, an employee's decision to quit precludes a claim for wrongful discharge.

However, if the employee can show that discriminatory treatment made the workplace so intolerable that he or she was effectively *forced* to resign, then he or she may be able to pursue a claim for "constructive discharge." To prevail on such a claim, the employee must show that the employer "deliberately created working conditions so intolerable, difficult or unpleasant that a reasonable person would have felt compelled to resign" under the circumstances.[65]

Employers can assert a number of defenses to "constructive discharge" claims. For example, the employer can show that the employee was planning to quit anyway (perhaps for another job, or to relocate to another city), or that the working conditions, while less than ideal, fell short of being "intolerable."

Under federal law, an employer can also advance the so-called *Faragher/ Ellerth* affirmative defense to show that (1) the employer exercised reasonable care to prevent and correct discriminatory conduct; and (2) the employee failed to take advantage of preventative or corrective opportunities available under the employer's internal policies.[66] However, this

---

64   *See* 9 N.Y.C.R.R. § 466.14(c)(1).

65   *Mascola v. City University of New York*, 14 A.D.3d 409, 787 N.Y.S.2d 655, 656 (1st Dep't 2005).

66   *Faragher v. City of Boca Raton*, 524 U.S. 775 (1998) and *Burlington Industries, Inc. v. Ellerth*, 524 U.S. 742 (1998); *see also Ferraro v. Kellwood Co.*, 440 F. 3d 96, 101 (2d Cir. 2006).

defense has now been essentially eliminated under New York law (*see* discussion in § 11.29, *infra*).

[11.16] Can an employer be sued for giving a negative reference?

Yes, *if* the employee can show that the negative reference was given for some prohibited reason, such as racial animus, or in retaliation for the former employee's prior protected activities.

The United States Equal Employment Opportunity Commission's *Compliance Manual* makes it clear that unlawful discriminatory or retaliatory acts can occur even after the employer-employee relationship has ended. According to the *EEOC Manual*, a former employer acts unlawfully by "giving an unjustified negative job reference, refusing to provide a job reference, [or by] informing an individual's prospective employer about an individual's protected activity."[67]

Courts have found that a negative job reference (or a refusal to provide a reference) can constitute an "adverse employment action" if the negative reference (or refusal to provide a reference) is improperly designed to interfere with a former employee's ability to obtain new employment based upon a protected status or activity. For example, in at least one case, a New York court has held that truthful statements by a former employer concerning a former employee's "medical issues" and absences "may violate the anti-retaliation provisions of the ADA, FMLA, and NYHRL" when shown to have been made by the former employer with an improper motive.[68]

III. LIABILITY FOR WRONGFUL ACTS

[11.17] What types of damages and relief can be awarded to successful complainants?

Historically, there were significant differences in the damages and relief that successful complainants could be awarded depending on whether the claims were brought under federal, state, or local law. Although most of the laws afforded successful complainants the ability to receive back pay, front pay (in certain circumstances), and equitable relief (reinstatement, promotion, etc.), the ability to receive compensatory damages, punitive damages, and attorney's fees depended upon the particular law under which the complainant sued and prevailed.

---

67   *See EEOC Compliance Manual* § 8-11(D)(2) (May 20, 1998).

68   *See Male v. Tops Markets*, Civil Action No. 8-cv-6234, 2011 U.S. Dist. Lexis 63966, 2011 WL 2421224 (W.D.N.Y. June 13, 2011).

The federal employment discrimination laws have always given success-ful charging parties the right to collect attorney's fees; and following enactment of the Civil Rights Act of 1991, they could also recover com-pensatory and punitive damages, the maximum value of which was capped at various levels based upon their employer's size. The maximum combined values of the compensatory and punitive damages available to successful charging parties under federal law are: (i) $50,000 for employ-ers with 15 to 100 employees; (ii) $100,000 for employers with 101 to 200 employees; (iii) $200,000 for employees with 201 to 500 employees; and (iv) $300,000 for employers with more than 500 employees.

Until recently, punitive damages and attorney's fees were generally *unavailable* to successful complainants under the NYHRL. This was espe-cially true for those prevailing complainants who pursued their claims in administrative proceedings before the NYDHR. Typically, the Division would award compensatory damages to successful complainants in rela-tively modest amounts of between $5,000 and $50,000. Because the Divi-sion could not award punitive damages, it might also impose civil fines, again in relatively modest amounts, against employers in egregious cases.

However, amendments to the NYHRL that became effective on October 11, 2019, now permit the Division to award punitive damages and attor-ney's fees to successful complainants in cases brought against private (but not public-sector) employers. Because these amendments are so recent, their impact upon private sector employers in cases litigated or mediated before the Division has yet to be determined.

[11.18] Can an owner or managerial employee of an employer be personally liable for damages under the NYHRL?

Yes, under New York law. Under most federal discrimination laws, indi-viduals who are not the actual employer generally do *not* have personal liability for discriminatory actions. However, under the NYHRL, owners and managers who have sufficient authority to make final employment decisions on behalf of the employer may have direct personal liability as "employers" under NYHRL § 296(1) if they have in some way partici-pated in the prohibited discrimination.[69]

New York courts and administrative agencies have held that individual owners, managers, and supervisors who have the power to hire and fire,

---

69   *See Magnotti v. Crossroads Healthcare Management, LLC,* 126 F. Supp. 3d 301, 306 (E.D.N.Y. 2015).

establish work schedules, determine pay rates, or control other terms and conditions of employment, can be found to be "employers" subject to personal liability for violations of NYHRL § 296(1)(a).[70] Generally, if a manager or supervisor is a "decision-maker" and has any "power to do more than simply carry out the decisions made by others," he or she can be held personally liable.[71]

However, before personal liability will attach to an individual, the complaining party must *also* show that the individual had personal "culpability" for the unlawful conduct.[72] This generally requires a showing that the individual owner, manager, or supervisor personally participated in the discriminatory conduct, or at least condoned the improper conduct after being apprised of it and failed to take corrective measures to address the discrimination.

[11.19] What is "aider or abettor" liability?

In contrast to federal employment discrimination laws, the NYHRL can impose personal liability upon individuals who are not themselves "employers," but who have "aided" or "abetted" violations of the statute.[73]

Under the NYHRL's "aider and abettor" provision, an individual who is not an owner or decision-maker can be held liable if he or she "participates" in discriminatory acts.[74] This can happen if an individual incites,

---

70   *See Donovan v. Agnew.* 712 F.2d 1509, 1514 (1st Cir. 1983) (recognizing that corporate officers with a significant ownership interest were "employers" within the meaning of the statutes where they had operational control over the company's day-to-day functions, including the power to set employee compensation).

71   *Chamblee v. Harris & Harris, Inc.,* 154 F. Supp. 2d 670, 677 (S.D.N.Y. 2001), *citing Patrowitch v. Chem. Bank,* 63 N.Y.2d 541, 483 N.Y.S.2d 659 (1984) (holding that an employee who was a corporate officer and a manager or supervisor of a corporate division but who did *not* have an ownership interest or the authority to do more than carry out the decisions made by others, was not an "employer" subject to individual liability under NYHRL § 296(1)(a)).

72   *See Marchuk v. Faruqi & Faruqi,* 100 F. Supp. 3d 302, 309 (S.D.N.Y. 2015), and cases cited therein (recognizing that the complaining party "must prove at least some minimum culpability on the part of . . . the owner or decision-maker" before direct liability will attach under Exec. Law § 296(1)(a)).

73   *See* Exec. Law § 296(6), and *Torres v. New York Methodist Hospital,* No. 15 CV-1264, 2016 U.S. Dist. Lexis 2365 (E.D.N.Y. Jan. 7, 2016) (recognizing that "[t]he aider and abettor provisions of the NYSHRL and the NYCHRL create a broad source of personal liability that is not limited to employers").

74   *Barella v. Village of Freeport,* 16 F. Supp. 3d 144, 157 (E.D.N.Y. 2014), *citing Tomka v. Seiler Corp.,* 66 F.3d 1295, 1317 (2d Cir. 1995); *see also Lewis v. Triborough Bridge & Tunnel Auth.,* 77 F. Supp. 2d 376, 380–84 (S.D.N.Y. 1999).

coerces, compels, or assists another person to engage in unlawful discriminatory or retaliatory conduct. Thus, it is now recognized by the courts that managers or supervisors, even if they have not themselves engaged in unlawful harassment, may be held liable for "aiding and abetting" unlawful harassment if they were made aware of harassing conduct and failed to take adequate remedial measures.[75]

IV.   OVERVIEW OF DISCRIMINATION THEORIES AND CONCEPTS

[11.20] What is "disparate treatment" discrimination?

"Disparate treatment," which is prohibited under both state and federal law, is the *intentional* act of treating a person or group less favorably based upon their membership in a protected category.

To establish a disparate treatment claim, an employee or job applicant must show that he or she was discriminated against with respect to a "material" (significant) term or condition of employment. This generally requires proof that the employee or applicant was treated less favorably in connection with a significant term or condition of employment than were others who are not members of the same protected category, or who do not share the same characteristic or status; e.g., where an employer starts a foreign-born new hire at a lower salary than an American-born new hire. In addition, however, the employee or applicant must show that the disparate treatment took place *because* of his or her membership in the protected category. Thus, in the previous example, the employer could justify the disparate treatment if the American-born applicant had more relevant experience or more highly developed skills, so long as the reason given was real and not pretextual.[76]

In evaluating proof of discriminatory intent, courts and administrative agencies recognize that it can be difficult to prove an employer's state of mind. For example, in the previous example, the employer may never have overtly said, "I think that foreign-born employees aren't worth as much as American-born employees." This is where the three-part *McDonnell Douglas* test discussed in § 11.1 *supra* comes into play.[77] To make a case,

---

75   *See Triborough Bridge & Tunnel Auth.,* 77 F. Supp. 2d at 384 (holding that "the case law establishes beyond cavil that a supervisor's failure to take adequate remedial measures can rise to 'actual participation'" under the NYHRL).

76   *See* discussion in § 11.1 *supra.*

77   411 U.S. 792 (1973).

the foreign-born employee must first allege that she was hired at a lower salary than an American-born employee with comparable or inferior qualifications, *and* that the reason for the disparate treatment was her national origin. The employer can then defend its decision by offering, as a legitimate and non-discriminatory reason for its decision, that the American-born applicant had more relevant experience. However, if further inquiry reveals that this claim is untrue, then it can be inferred that the employer's decision was motivated by discriminatory intent.

In addition to comparability, the decision must be based upon factors which are relevant. An employer hiring unskilled labor will have a very hard time defending its requirement that all unskilled labor applicants must have a community college degree, if there is no reason for the requirement other than that most white applicants in the applicant pool have attended community college, and most non-white applicants have not.[78]

Of course, there is room, in many cases, for argument as to what constitutes comparable and relevant credentials or experience, so every outcome is determined by the particular facts of the case. However, the basic lesson here is that an employer who advances a false basis for an employment decision in a discrimination case is looking at significant potential liability.

As noted above, in order for a discrimination claim to succeed, the disparate treatment must be "materially adverse." There will often be some differences between the ways different employees or applicants are treated, and a difference will not give rise to a discrimination claim unless it is material. New York courts and administrative agencies recognize that there are no "bright line" rules to apply in determining which employment actions meet this "materially adverse" standard. Accordingly, determinations as to whether an employment decision or issue is actionable under the disparate treatment discrimination theory are usually made on a case-by-case basis.

---

78   In this example, it would constitute disparate treatment if it were shown, either through direct evidence or by legal inference, that the employer *intended* to favor white applicants over non-white applicants. However, on the same facts and in the *absence* of such intent, the disproportionate exclusion of non-white applicants without a job-related justification could make out a case of disparate *impact*; *see, e.g., Griggs v. Duke Power Co.*, 401 U.S. 424 (1971) (discussing the application of the disparate treatment and adverse impact discrimination theories in the context of a high school diploma requirement for employment in, or transfer to, certain positions within an electric generating plant); *see* § 11.21 *infra*.

Notwithstanding the proposition that every disparate treatment claim is analyzed on its own particular facts, there is guidance that can be derived from the case law relevant to this issue.

For example, it is well-settled that serious employment actions, such as decisions to fire, demote, or discipline an employee, with an accompanying loss of pay or benefits, or a decision not to hire or promote an individual, are all "materially adverse" employment actions.

On the other hand, not everything that makes an employee unhappy is sufficiently "adverse" to be actionable under the disparate treatment theory. For instance, New York State courts and administrative agencies have often found that a mere reassignment of job duties, a lateral transfer without diminished job title or responsibility, or verbal counseling or reprimand without monetary loss, are mere "slights," "inconveniences," or "annoyances" of the workplace, and are insufficient to satisfy the "materially adverse" standard.[79]

Disparate treatment cases are often established by comparison of the claimant alleging discrimination to other "similarly situated" employees or job applicants. A "similarly situated" employee or job applicant is one whose employment situation is comparable to that of the individual who is alleging discrimination in all important respects. Showing that an employer treated "similarly situated" employees differently than the employer treated the individual alleging discrimination is probably the most common way to create an inference of discrimination.[80]

However, the "similarly situated" employee concept is not the only analytical method which is used to evaluate disparate treatment claims, and some of these analytical methods can be used in *defense* of an employer.

The so-called "same actor" defense applies where the same person (or group of people) which took or recommended an adverse employment action was also involved in making earlier *positive* decisions with respect to the complaining employee. For instance, if the same manager who hired a protected group job applicant (assuming, of course, that the manager knew at the time of hiring about the employee's protected group status) later made the decision to take the adverse action against that same

---

79   *See, e.g., Joseph v. Leavitt*, 465 F.3d 87, 90 (2d Cir. 2006), *cert. denied*, 549 U.S. 1282 (2007).

80   *See e.g., Shumway v. UPS*, 118 F.3d 60, 64–65 (2d Cir. 1997); *see also* Ernest F. Lidge III, *The Courts' Misuse of the Similarly Situated Concept in Employment Discrimination Law*, 67 Mo. L. Rev. 831 (Fall 2002).

employee, courts and administrative agencies may infer that the reason provided for the challenged employment action was *not* a pretext for unlawful discrimination. The "same actor" inference has been applied in many types of discrimination cases. However, the more time that passes between the favorable employment decision and the unfavorable employment decision, the less weight the trier of fact will give to the "same actor" inference.[81]

New York courts and administrative agencies have also recognized that if the decision-maker is in the same protected class as the individual complaining of alleged discrimination, then an inference *against* discrimination can be drawn.[82]

The concept of "temporal proximity" has also been applied in disparate treatment cases, in two different ways.

If an employee is claiming retaliation for the exercise of a protected right, it is *less* likely that retaliation will be found if a significant period of time has elapsed between the employee's protected action and the employer's adverse action.[83]

Similarly, if an employer takes the adverse action within a short time after the employee commits a workplace transgression which was the reason

---

81   *See, e.g., Dickerson v. Health Management Corp. of America,* 21 A.D.3d 326, 800 N.Y.S.2d 391 (1st Dep't 2005), recognizing that "where the hirer and firer are the same individual and the termination of employment occurs within the relatively short time span following the hiring, a strong inference exists that discrimination was not a determining factor for the adverse employment action taken by the employer"; *compare Ramos v. Marriott Int'l, Inc.,* 134 F. Supp. 2d 328, 345–46 (S.D.N.Y. 2001) (refusing to apply the "same actor" inference where multiple individuals where involved in the employee's hiring and more than one year had passed between this employee's hiring and termination).

82   *See Drummond v. IPC Int'l., Inc.,* 400 F. Supp. 2d 521, 532 (E.D.N.Y. 2005) ("a well-recognized inference against discrimination exists where the person who participated in the allegedly adverse decision is also a member of the same protected class"). *See also Schnabel v. Abramson,* 232 F.3d 83, 91 (2d Cir. 2000) (where the decision-maker was 51 years of age at the time that he hired the individual complaining of age discrimination, who was 49 years of age at that time and the decision was made within five years of the hiring); *Toliver v. Comty. Action Comm'n,* 613 F. Supp. 1070, 1073–74 (S.D.N.Y. 1985) (an inference of discrimination "is, to say the least, attenuated" if the group that denied a minority employee a promotion and eventually terminated him was comprised of a majority of members of the same protected group).

83   *See* §§ 11.61–64 for a full discussion regarding retaliation; *see also Chang v. Horizons,* 254 Fed. Appx. 838 (2d Cir. 2007), and *Nicastro v. Runyan,* 60 F. Supp. 2d 181 (S.D.N.Y. 1999) (both finding that a one-or two-year gap between an employee's protected activity and the adverse employment action undermined claim of a causal connection and recognizing that "[c]laims of retaliation are routinely dismissed when as few as three months elapse between the protected EEO activity and the alleged act of retaliation.").

for the employer's adverse action (as, for example, firing the employee within days after she was found to have submitted falsified time sheets), then it is less likely that the employer's reason for taking action will be found to have been a "pretext" for a discriminatory act.

However, if a significant amount of time passes between the event which the employer states was its nondiscriminatory reason for its decision and the adverse action, the likelihood that the employer's proffered reason will be viewed as pretextual increases.

[11.21] What is "implicit bias"?

The concept of "implicit bias" refers to unconsciously held stereotypes about categories of people which may affect the manner in which they are treated—even if the decision-maker does not have a conscious intent to discriminate. This is a concept which is being widely discussed and is the subject of trainings in many workplaces, although it has yet to be reflected in any significant body of judicial decisions.

A frequently discussed example of implicit bias is a study in which a law firm analytical memorandum was deliberately created over the name of "Thomas Meyers," a fictitious third year litigation associate at a fictitious law firm, and was described as follows:

> We followed a simple Question Presented, Brief Answer, Facts, Discussion and Conclusion format for the memo, and we deliberately inserted 22 different errors, 7 of which were minor spelling/grammar errors, 6 of which were substantive technical writing errors, 5 of which were errors in fact, and 4 of which were errors in the analysis of the facts in the Discussion and Conclusion sections.[84]

The memorandum was then given to sixty different partners from twenty-two actual law firms, all of whom had agreed to participate in what had been presented to them as a "writing analysis study." All of the readers were given identical memoranda, with identical information about the

---

84   Arin N. Reeves, *Written in Black & White: Exploring Confirmation Bias in Racialized Perceptions of Writing Skills* (Nextions, 2014), http://nextions.com/wp-content/uploads/2017/05/written-in-black-and-white-yellow-paper-series.pdf.

author (including his name), except that half the readers were told that the "Thomas Meyer" was African-American and half were told that he was Caucasian.[85]

Rating the memos on a scale of 1 to 5, the readers gave the Caucasian "Thomas Meyer" a composite score of 4.1/5.0 and gave the African-American "Thomas Meyer" a composite score of 3.2/5.0. Even though the errors in both memoranda were identical, the readers found twice as many spelling and grammar errors in the work of the African-American "Thomas Meyer," and significantly more factual and technical writing errors. The readers' subjective comments reflected the same discrepancy.[86]

Studies like the above show that people bring implicit (or unconscious) bias to their evaluations of others. Notwithstanding, a mere discriminatory state of mind is not unlawful. As the Supreme Court has observed, the question is not whether an employer holds stereotypical views, but whether it *acted* on those views to the detriment of an employee in a protected category.[87] However, the Court also observed that proof of stereotypical views may be evidence of the *motive* for an adverse employment action.[88]

Since the ultimate question is whether someone has been treated differently because of a protected characteristic, cases involving implicit bias will almost certainly be decided by the courts based upon the "adverse impact" analysis discussed in § 11.24. That said, employers wishing to avoid workplace decisions that could create adverse impact may do well to consider implicit bias training for managers and decision-makers.

[11.22] What is "cat's paw" discrimination?

The "cat's paw" theory of liability may be applied in the context of employment actions where the person who decided to take the adverse employment action did not harbor any discriminatory animus, but relied upon information received from others, who unbeknownst to the decision-maker, *did* have improper intent.[89]

---

85   *Id.*

86   *Id.*

87   *Price Waterhouse v. Hopkins*, 490 U.S. 228, 251 (1989).

88   *Id.*

89   *See Staub v. Proctor Hospital,* 562 U.S. 411 (2011).

The "cat's paw" theory derives from the fable in which an unwitting cat burns its paw after being tricked into pulling chestnuts out of a fire by a manipulative monkey (which then takes all of the chestnuts for itself).[90] Courts have often applied this theory of liability to situations where "a biased subordinate who lacks decision-making power uses the formal decision-maker as a dupe in a deliberate scheme to trigger a discriminatory employment action."[91] This type of improper influence over the decision-maker has led to liability in a number of different contexts, such as when a biased subordinate provides unwarranted negative input into an employment evaluation, or inaccurately reports the circumstances surrounding a workplace incident, which ends up leading to the protected group employee's discharge by a higher ranking "duped" administrator.

To avoid "cat's paw" liability, the employer must demonstrate that it would have reached the same determination even without the biased input. This typically requires proof demonstrating that the biased input was "too remote" and "unconnected" to the employment decision to be considered a causal factor, such as by showing that the decision-making official relied upon other employment issues in reaching his decision, or conducted an independent and fair investigation into the incident before taking the challenged employment action.

[11.23] What is a "mixed motive" discrimination case?

A "mixed-motive" case arises when a discriminatory (unlawful) consideration is one among a number of factors which led to a challenged employment decision.[92] In these situations, in order to avoid liability, the employer must be able to demonstrate that it would have reached the same decision even in the absence of the improper consideration.[93]

[11.24] What is "adverse impact" discrimination?

Adverse impact claims (or disparate impact claims, as they are sometimes called) differ from disparate treatment claims, which involve differential treatment of two employees *for discriminatory reasons* (*see* § 11.20 *supra*).

---

90   *See* Jean de La Fontaine, The Fables of La Fontaine (Elizur Wright, trans., J.W.M. Gibbs, ed., Project Gutenberg ed. 2014) (1882), https://www.gutenberg.org/files/7241/7241-h/7241-h.htm.

91   *Woods v. Berwyn*, 803 F.3d 865, 869 (7th Cir. 2015), and cases cited therein.

92   *See Price Waterhouse v. Hopkins*, 490 U.S. 228 (1989).

93   *See Desert Palace Inc. v. Costa*, 539 U.S. 90 (2003); *Fakete v. Aetna Inc.*, 308 F.3d. 335 (3d Cir. 2002).

Adverse impact claims typically challenge employment policies, procedures, or practices which, while apparently ("facially") neutral, have a disproportionately negative impact upon a protected class of individuals.[94] An adverse impact claim may exist when an applicant or an employee can demonstrate that an employer's selection process or minimum qualification standard for hiring, promotion, or layoff (such as a minimum educational requirement, physical abilities test score, height or weight cut-off, evaluation score, etc.) excludes a disproportionate number of protected group members as compared to the rate of exclusion of non-protected group members.[95]

Adverse impact claims differ from disparate treatment claims in that there is no need to show that the employer had a discriminatory *motive* in order for liability to result. For this reason, adverse impact claims are sometimes referred to as "unintentional discrimination" cases. The courts will apply the adverse impact theory in appropriate situations, even where the challenged selection process or employment criteria include both objective elements (e.g. standardized tests) and subjective elements (e.g. personal interviews), if the process results in protected group members being treated less favorably than non-protected group members.[96]

To establish a *prima facie* case of adverse impact discrimination, an employee must identify the specific aspect of the employer's selection process or standards that screened out a disproportionate number of protected group members.[97] The federal employment enforcement agencies have developed the *Uniform Guidelines on Employee Selection Procedures,* which set forth the recognized processes for validating employment selection procedures and which contain a simplified process for determining when selection procedures provide a sufficient indication of adverse

---

94 *E.g., Watson v. Fort Worth Bank and Trust,* 487 U.S. 977, 986–88 (1988); *Schallop v. N.Y.S. Dep't of Law,* 20 F. Supp. 2d 384, 402–03 (N.D.N.Y. 1998).

95 In *Griggs v. Duke Power Company,* 401 U.S. 424 (1971), the Supreme Court found that the employer's use of general aptitude tests and a high school diploma requirement for promotion eligibility (even though facially neutral) provided the basis for an adverse impact claim because these selection criteria excluded a statistically disproportionate number of African-American workers.

96 *Watson,* 487 U.S. at 986–88; *see also* Audrey J. Lee, *Unconscious Bias Theory in Employment Discrimination Litigation,* 40 Harv. C.R.-C.L. L.Rev.481 (Summer 2005).

97 *See, e.g., Smith v. City of Jackson,* 544 U.S. 228 (2005) (recognizing that to establish a prima facie case of adverse impact discrimination, the applicant or employee is "responsible for isolating and identifying the specific employment practices that are allegedly responsible for any observed statistical disparities").

impact.[98] The *Uniform Guidelines* state that, if an employer's use of a selection process or employment standard results in "[a] selection rate for any race, sex, or ethnic group which is less than four-fifths (4/5) or eighty percent (80%) of the rate for the group with the highest rate," then this should be viewed as evidence of adverse impact.[99] Although this "80% rule" has been widely criticized by statistical analysis experts, it is commonly relied upon by federal and state enforcement agencies and many courts when making, or reviewing, an initial threshold showing of adverse impact.

When a *prima facie* showing of adverse impact has been made, then the burden of proof shifts to the employer to demonstrate that the challenged selection process is job-related and consistent with business necessity.[100] This is a high standard, generally requiring a showing of how the challenged standard is necessary for successful performance of the employer's required business functions. Even when the employer is able to make this showing, an employee can still prevail on the adverse impact claim by showing that an alternative employment standard that would have alleviated or reduced the adverse impact was available to, but not adopted by, the employer.[101]

[11.25] What is compensation discrimination?

Discrimination claims based upon differentials in compensation can be pursued under two different statutes and legal theories in New York: (1) as disparate treatment claims under the NYHRL; or (2) as equal pay claims under Labor Law § 194.[102]

The NYHRL prohibits discrimination with respect to *all* terms and conditions of employment, including all forms of compensation, such as base wages, overtime compensation, discretionary bonuses, and pay increases based upon merit-based pay programs. To establish a disparate treatment claim with respect to compensation, employees must generally show both

---

98   *Uniform Guidelines on Employee Selection Procedures*, 29 C.F.R. pt. 1607, which were developed, adopted, and promulgated by the Equal Employment Opportunity Commission, the Office of Federal Contract Compliance Programs, the Department of Justice, and the Federal Personnel Service.

99   29 C.F.R. § 1607.4(D).

100   *See Schallop v. N.Y.S. Dept. of Law*, 20 F. Supp. 2d 384, 403 (and cases cited therein).

101   *Id.*

102   Compensation discrimination claims may also be brought under the federal Equal Pay Act, 29 U.S.C § 206(d)(1), and the other federal employment discrimination statutes. *See* discussion at § 11.1.1.1, above.

---

that: (1) they were paid or received less in compensation than did similarly situated co-workers; and (2) the *reason* for the lower compensation was their protected status. Merely alleging that co-workers were paid more is generally insufficient to satisfy the "discriminatory intent" requirement for a disparate treatment claim under the NYHRL.[103]

By contrast, a showing of discriminatory intent is *not* required for an equal pay claim brought under New York Labor Law § 194. Rather, all that is needed to make a threshold showing for an equal pay claim is a demonstration that the employee who is questioning her or his wage rate belongs to a protected class and is being paid less than employees in another category who work in the same establishment under the same or similar working conditions, and who perform work requiring equal, or substantially similar, skill, effort, and responsibility. As used in Labor Law § 194, the term "wages" includes base wages and salary, as well as wage supplements and benefits.

In the past, equal pay claims under both federal and New York law were limited to gender-based compensation discrimination. However, Labor Law § 194 was amended in 2019, and its coverage has been expanded to prohibit pay differentials based upon membership in *any* class or group protected by the NYHRL. Thus, § 194 now prohibits compensation discrimination based upon, or derived from, age, race, creed, color, national origin, sexual orientation, gender identity or expression, military status, sex, disability, predisposing genetic characteristics, familial status, marital status, or domestic violence victim status.

Compensation discrimination claims under Labor Law § 194 differ from disparate treatment claims under the NYHRL in another significant respect. Under Labor Law § 194, courts do not apply the three-part *McDonnell Douglas* test and employees do not retain the ultimate burden of proof on their claims.

Instead, to establish a Labor Law § 194 claim, the employee need only demonstrate that a pay disparity exists among employees performing equal or substantially similar work in the same establishment. Once this has been established, the burden shifts to the employer to prove a legitimate non-discriminatory basis for the difference in pay. The statute provides that employees may be paid differently for similar work, but only if the difference is based upon: (i) a seniority system; (ii) a merit-based pay system; (iii) a system that measures earnings by quantity or quality of pro-

---

103   *See Tomka v. Seiler Corp.*, 66 F.3d 1295, 1312–13 (2d Cir. 1995).

duction; or (iv) a *bona fide* factor *other than* status within one of the protected groups, such as education, training, or experience. Labor Law § 194 further provides that this "*bona fide* factor" must be job-related and consistent with business necessity.

V.   SEXUAL AND OTHER PROHIBITED FORMS OF HARASSMENT

[11.26] What employers are covered by New York's prohibition of sexual harassment?

All "employers" are covered and even when there was a (now-repealed) four-employee requirement (repealed in 2019), the law's provisions prohibiting sexual harassment had applied to all employers, regardless of the number of employees, since 2015.

[11.27] What is the definition of sexual harassment?

Workplace sexual harassment comes in two forms: (a) "*quid pro quo*" sexual harassment; and (b) "hostile environment" sexual harassment. While these two types of harassment are prohibited by both federal and New York State law, it is important to note that New York generally applies broader definitions, thereby creating a legal environment more receptive to employee harassment claims.

Common to both definitions of sexual harassment is the concept that the conduct in question is *unwelcome*: in other words, the conduct is being imposed upon a victim or victims who have not invited it and do not want it.[104]

Generally, *quid pro quo* sexual harassment occurs when a person in authority tries to trade job benefits, or job protection, for sexual favors. *Quid pro quo* harassment consists of unwelcome sexual advances, requests for sexual favors, or other gender-based verbal or physical conduct where submission to, or rejection of, such conduct is used as a basis for employment decisions affecting the individual. *Quid pro quo* sexual harassment occurs when an employee's hiring, compensation, benefits, promotions, continued employment, or treatment at the job become contingent up on his or her participation in (or acceptance of) sexual conduct.

---

104   So, for example, a female employee who initiates or willingly participates in sexual "banter" with a supervisor or with co-workers would—at least in theory—be hard-pressed to claim that the interactions were unwelcome. That said, it would be a very unwise employer who would condone such conduct in the workplace, regardless of who initiated it.

"Hostile environment" sexual harassment occurs when unwelcome sexual advances, requests for sexual favors, or other gender-based verbal or physical conduct has the purpose or effect of unreasonably interfering with the individual's work performance or creates an intimidating, hostile, or offensive work environment. This may include actions specifically directed at one employee (as would be the case with *quid pro quo* harassment) or it may consist of a sexualized workplace which is generally offensive.

To establish a hostile environment sexual harassment claim, a complainant must show that he or she was subjected to discriminatory conduct "because of sex." Harassing conduct will be deemed to be "because of sex" where it is (a) overtly sexual in nature (e.g., expressing a desire to have sex with the victim or commenting on the victim's anatomy); (b) demonstrates hostility towards an individual's sex (e.g., the use of derogatory or gender-offensive terms) or (c) is facially sex-neutral, but results in disparate treatment of the sexes (e.g., treating of female employees less favorably than male employees).

A hostile work environment claim may be established by alleging harassment by individuals of the opposite sex (men harassing women, or women harassing men) or by individuals of the same sex (men harassing men or women harassing women).

Under federal law, a hostile environment claim, in order to succeed must demonstrate that the offensive actions are "severe or pervasive." This is not the case in New York, which applies a broader standard; *see* § 11.29 *infra*.

Conduct giving rise to a hostile environment can include unwanted touching (which may be on any part of the body and is not restricted to touching "private parts"), talking about sexual activities or desires, sexual innuendos, invitations to sexual conduct, obscene language, demeaning language about the characteristic of one gender, dirty jokes, the display of sexualized or pornographic materials, and sexualized gestures.

[11.28] What if the person accused of sexual harassment did not mean to offend?

Sexual harassment law focuses on the victim, not on the harasser. The state of mind (intent) of a person accused of workplace sexual harassment is irrelevant. If the conduct in question: (1) would be considered offensive and harassing by a reasonable person; and (2) was actually offensive to the victim or victims, then it is harassment.

A complaint or protest about sexual harassment which is made immediately or soon after the offensive conduct took place is strong evidence that conduct was unwelcome, but the fact that the victim did not complain at the time is not some sort of admission that the conduct was welcome. The courts recognize that merely enduring or tolerating offensive conduct over a period of time does not mean that the conduct is welcome.

[11.29] Can an employer be liable for sexual harassment in the workplace of which the employer was unaware?

It may depend upon the type of harassment. *Quid pro quo* and hostile environment harassment are treated somewhat differently where the employer was unaware of the offensive conduct.

Quid pro quo harassment involves a higher-level employee (a supervisor or manager) using his or her position to harass a lower-level employee. If the employer has given the supervisor or manager a sufficient degree of control over the lower-level employee and the harassment results in some tangible adverse employment action (for example, the employee is transferred or demoted after rejecting the supervisor's sexual advances), then the employer as a whole will be strictly liable even if higher management did not know what was going on.

Under federal law, "hostile environment" harassment does not give rise to legal redress unless the conduct complained of can be characterized as "severe or pervasive." In addition, under federal law, an employer may assert the defense that the complaining employee did not take advantage of internal complaint procedures made available by the employer.[105] However, on both of these important points, *New York law is now different.*

The New York Human Rights Law was amended in 2019 to make it clear that the "severe or pervasive" standard does not apply to claims under New York law. The new standard is that conduct which is more than what a reasonable person would consider to be "petty slights or trivial inconve-

---

105   This is the so-called *Faragher/Ellerth* affirmative defense discussed at § 11.15 *supra*. *See Faragher v. City of Boca Raton*, 524 U.S. 775 (1998); *Burlington Indus., Inc. v. Ellerth*, 524 U.S. 742 (1998).

niences" can create a hostile environment.[106] In addition, the 2019 amendments state explicitly that the argument that an employee did not complain about sexual harassment is not a defense to liability.

The full effect of the 2019 amendments to the NYHRL remains to be explored. Before these amendments, an employer was not automatically liable for a hostile environment created at lower levels of the organization (for example, in the mail room or duplicating department of a large company) unless management knew or should have known about the harassment and failed to take prompt and effective action to stop it. This may or may not be the case going forward, as the courts and the New York State Division of Human Rights consider the effect of the amendments.

[11.30] What if a complaining employee was a participant in the harassing conduct?

It depends on the factual circumstances. An essential element of a sexual harassment complaint is that the harassing conduct was *unwelcome*. If the individual complaining of harassment participated in the allegedly offensive conduct, that can be interpreted as evidence that the conduct was not unwelcome to that individual.

However, courts and administrative agencies recognize that initial willing participation in sexually-charged jokes or banter, or other conduct of a sexual nature, does not necessarily preclude a subsequent valid complaint about sexual harassment. If the nature of the offensive conduct significantly changed, or if the complainant initially willingly participated in sexual conduct, but later informed the harasser that his or her conduct was no longer welcome, then the continued offensive or sexual conduct was unwelcome. In these cases, a reviewing tribunal will consider the totality of the circumstances before making a final determination.

---

106   This amendment brought the NYHRL more closely in line with earlier amendments to the New York City Human Rights Law, under which a plaintiff must show that he or she was "treated less well" than other employees because of his or her inclusion in a protected category. To be actionable, it is no longer necessary to show that the harassment had "unreasonably interfered" with the victim's ability to work; rather, the victim now just has to demonstrate that the harassment lead to "inferior terms, conditions, or privileges of employment" compared to those who were not subject to harassment. The "severity" or the "pervasiveness" of the harassment now are relevant solely with respect to the damages for which the employer might be held liable.

[11.31] Can an employer be liable for sexual harassment of non-employees?

In some circumstances, yes. As of April 2018, it is unlawful under the NYHRL for employers to permit sexual harassment of a non-employee who is a contractor, subcontractor, vendor, consultant, or other person providing services pursuant to a contract in the workplace, or who is an employee of such an entity.[107] An employer will be held liable for sexual harassment of such non-employees when it, its agents, or its supervisors knew or should have known that the non-employee was subject to such harassment and did not take immediate and appropriate corrective action. The extent of the employer's control over the non-employee and other legal responsibility that the employer has with respect to the harasser will be considered.[108]

However, the law does not extend protections to non-employees who perform services at locations other than the employer's own workplace.

[11.32] Are employers required to adopt sexual harassment policies and train employees regarding sexual harassment?

Yes and yes.

New York legislation was passed in 2018 which explicitly requires all New York employers to adopt a formal sexual harassment policy. The policy may be either: (a) a model policy that was published by the New York State Division of Human Rights; or (b) the employer's own written sexual harassment policy, so long as it meets or exceeds the minimum standards of the model sexual harassment policy. The sexual harassment prevention policy must be provided to all employees in writing.[109]

Every employer policy must:

- Prohibit sexual harassment consistent with guidance issued by the Department of Labor in consultation with the Division of Human Rights;

---

107   *See* Exec. Law §§ 296-d and 292(4). Furthermore, effective October 11, 2019, the NYHRL's protections for non-employees was expanded to all forms of unlawful harassment based upon any protected characteristic.

108   Exec. Law § 296-d.

109   Labor Law § 201-g.

- Provide examples of prohibited conduct that would constitute unlawful sexual harassment;

- Include information as to the federal and state statutory provisions concerning sexual harassment, the remedies available to victims of sexual harassment, and a statement that there may be applicable local laws;

- Include a complaint form;

- Include a procedure for the timely and confidential investigation of complaints that ensures due process for all parties;

- Inform employees of their rights of redress and all available forums for adjudicating sexual harassment complaints administratively and judicially;

- Clearly state that sexual harassment is considered a form of employee misconduct and that sanctions will be enforced against individuals engaging in sexual harassment as well as against supervisory and managerial personnel who knowingly allow such behavior to continue; and

- Clearly state that retaliation against individuals who complain of sexual harassment or who testify or assist in any investigation or proceeding involving sexual harassment is unlawful.

In addition, the law requires employers to provide annual sexual harassment training by utilizing either the training program provided by the state or by establishing a training program that equals or exceeds the minimum standards set by the state.[110] The training (which may be either in-person or online) must have an interactive component, and, at a minimum, contain the following:

- An explanation of sexual harassment consistent with guidance issued by the Department of Labor in consultation with the Division of Human Rights;

- Examples of conduct that would constitute unlawful sexual harassment;

---

110   *See* Labor Law § 201-g.

- Information as to the federal and state statutory provisions concerning sexual harassment and remedies available to victims of sexual harassment; and

- Information as to employees' rights of redress and all available forums for adjudicating complaints, and information addressing conduct by supervisors and any additional responsibilities for such supervisors.[111]

The training must be provided in the language spoken by the employees, and the interactive component should ensure that the employees understand what the training is telling them.

Effective August 12, 2019, the NYHRL also requires employers to provide employees, at the time of hire and at every sexual harassment prevention training, with written notice containing the sexual harassment policy and the information presented at the employer's sexual harassment training, such as printed materials, PowerPoint slides, handouts, etc.[112]

[11.33] Can an employer resolve a sexual harassment claim on terms which are kept confidential?

Yes, but subject to specific conditions, and only to a limited extent.

Settlement agreements, or resolutions of any claim which involves sexual harassment, cannot include a confidentiality or nondisclosure provision that would prevent the disclosure of the underlying facts and circumstances of the sexual harassment claim, unless the confidentiality provision is something that the *complainant* requests. In addition, complainants must be given 21 days to consider whether to accept or refuse a nondisclosure provision and, if they agree to it, must be afforded at least seven days after signing to revoke the agreement.[113]

Effective October 11, 2019, the law was amended to expand this prohibition on confidentiality provisions to apply not only to sexual harassment claims but also to all claims of discrimination, harassment, and/or retaliation unless the complainant requests confidentiality and the individual is given at least 21 days to consider the nondisclosure provision and seven days to revoke it. In addition, any term or condition in a nondisclosure

---

111   *Id.*

112   *Id.*

113   *See* Gen. Oblig. Law § 5-336 and CPLR 5003-b.

agreement must be provided in writing to all parties in plain English and, if applicable, the primary language of the complainant. Lastly, a nondisclosure agreement will be deemed void if it prohibits or restricts the complainant from "initiating, testifying, assisting, complying with a subpoena from, or participating in any manner with an investigation conducted by the appropriate local, state, or federal agency" or filing or disclosing any facts necessary to receive public benefits to which the complainant is entitled including, but not limited to, unemployment insurance and Medicaid.[114]

Additionally, as of January 1, 2020, nondisclosure provisions must explicitly state that employees are not prohibited from "speaking with law enforcement, the Equal Employment Opportunity Commission, the State Division of Human Rights, a local commission on human rights, or an attorney retained by the employee or potential employee."

However, the law does not prohibit settlement agreement provisions which preclude the individual from disclosing the amount of the settlement payment provided for in the agreement.[115]

[11.34] Are there other forms of prohibited harassment?

Yes. While sexual harassment has some unique rules and definitions, the NYHRL also prohibits harassment based on age, race, creed, religion, color, sex, national origin, disability, familial status, marital status, sexual orientation, predisposing genetic characteristics, gender identity or expression, transgender status, gender dysphoria, military/veteran status, and status as a victim of domestic violence.[116]

---

114   *Id.*

115   *See* New York State, *Combating Sexual Harassment: Frequently Asked Questions*, www.ny.gov/ combating-sexual-harassment-workplace/combating-sexual-harassment-frequently-asked-questions#for-employers.

116   *See* Exec. Law § 296(1)(h).

VI.   SPECIAL CONSIDERATIONS RELATING TO SPECIFIC TYPES OF DISCRIMINATION

1. Disability and Genetic Characteristics

[11.35] What are the protections for persons with disabilities?

People with disabilities (including people who are perceived to have disabilities, even if they are not actually disabled) are protected from all forms of discrimination in the workplace.

An employer's obligation does not begin until the employer is on notice of the disability, either because it is obvious or because the employee has so informed the employer.

Further, not every disability is protected in every setting. A protected disability is one which does not prevent the disabled person from performing the essential functions of a job, with or without reasonable accommodation.

Thus, a baseball team does not have to hire a blind person applying for a job as shortstop, because no matter how much he or she may know about baseball, the ability to see, catch, and throw the ball is an essential function of the position. However, a blind person applying for a job as an office employee can perform the essential functions of the position, although he or she may need some accommodation in the form of a Braille keyboard or a text-to-speech computer program. The concept of reasonable accommodation is discussed in § 11.38 *infra*.

While it is the employee's obligation to *request* an accommodation, it is the employer's obligation to *provide* a reasonable accommodation which will enable the disabled employee to perform the essential functions of the position, unless the accommodation would impose an undue hardship on the employer.[117] However, the accommodation need not be the one initially requested by the employee, if a different accommodation would be sufficient.

When an employer is asked to provide reasonable accommodation for a disabled employee, the employer must engage in the "interactive process" discussed in § 11.38 *infra*.

---

117   It should be noted that the courts and administrative agencies have set a high standard for what constitutes "undue hardship" for an employer. Mere inconvenience is not enough; see further discussion at § 11.39 *infra*.

The regulations implementing the New York Human Rights Law *suggest*, but do not require, that employers provide applicants and new employees notice of their rights with regard to reasonable accommodation of disabilities, and the procedures to be followed in requesting reasonable accommodation.[118]

[11.36] What is a "disability"?

To state a claim of disability discrimination under the NYHRL, a plaintiff must establish, among other things, that he or she meets the definition of an individual with a "disability." The NYHRL defines "disability" as: (a) a physical, mental, or medical impairment resulting from anatomical, physiological, genetic, or neurological conditions that prevents the exercise of a normal bodily function, or that is demonstrable by medically accepted clinical or laboratory diagnostic techniques; (b) a record of such an impairment, or (c) a condition regarded by others as such an impairment. However, as noted above, the statute covers only those disabilities which, upon the provision of reasonable accommodations, do not prevent the individual from performing in a reasonable manner the activities involved in the job or occupation sought or held.[119]

The NYHRL's definition of a "disability" is broader than the definition of a disability under the federal ADA. Under the ADA, a "disability" is defined as: (1) a physical or mental impairment that substantially limits one or more major life activities; (2) a record of such impairment; or (3) being regarded as having such an impairment.[120] Notably missing from the NYHRL is the requirement that the impairment "must substantially limit one or more major life activities." Thus, a condition can constitute a disability under the NYHRL regardless of whether or not it limits any of the individual's major life activities.

[11.37] What does it mean to be "otherwise qualified to perform the essential functions of a job"?

In order for an individual to be entitled to protection against disability discrimination under the NYHRL, including an entitlement to reasonable

---

118 9 N.Y.C.R.R. § 466.11(j)(1). The New York State Division of Human Rights' suggestions and a sample procedure may be found at https://dhr.ny.gov/general-regulations#466.11-a.

119 *See* Exec. Law § 292(21).

120 *See* 42 U.S.C. § 12102(2).

accommodation, the disabled individual must be "otherwise qualified to perform the essential functions of the job."[121]

To meet the "otherwise qualified" criterion, the individual must have the requisite job qualifications (which may include appropriate licensing or certification requirements) as well as be able to do the work satisfactorily. The individual must be qualified for the job by education, skill, experience, and ability to the same extent that such education, skill, experience or ability are required as *bona fide* job qualifications for all other employees. The individual must be able, with or without accommodation, to attain "reasonable performance," which is not perfect performance, but performance at a level reasonably meeting the employer's needs to achieve its business goals.[122] The employer's judgment as to what is minimum acceptable performance will not be second-guessed, provided that standards for performance are applied equally to all employees in the same position.[123]

An individual must also be capable of doing the job in a safe and reliable manner. An individual who poses a risk to him or herself or others while performing the duties of his or her position is *not* considered to be "otherwise qualified." For example, in analyzing an individual's qualifications to perform a position as a police officer, it was found that the plaintiff's disability, which made him susceptible to catastrophic bleeding, rendered him unable to perform his duties without endangering himself or others and, therefore, he was not "otherwise qualified" under the NYHRL.[124]

An individual is not qualified for a job if he or she cannot comply with the employer's normal standards of conduct. The regulations governing the NYHRL expressly state that the law "does not require accommodation of behaviors that do not meet the employer's workplace behavior standards that are consistently applied to all similarly situated employees, even if

---

121   See 9 N.Y.C.R.R. § 466.11(f)(3) (the NYSDHR's regulations state that "[e]ssential functions are those fundamental to the position; a function is essential if not performing the function would fundamentally change the job or occupation" in question. The regulation further provides that "[w]hat is an essential function is a factual question" which should be resolved by looking at the employer's job description and/or labor contract; the frequency that the function is performed; the consequences of the function not being performed; and the availability of other individuals to perform the function.

122   *See* 9 N.Y.C.R.R. § 466.11(d).

123   *See* 9 N.Y.C.R.R. § 466.11(f).

124   *See Giordano v. City of New York,* 99 Civ. 3649 (AGS), 2001 U.S. Dist. LEXIS 2039 (S.D.N.Y. Mar. 1, 2001); *see also* 9 N.Y.C.R.R. § 466.11(g).

these behaviors are caused by a disability." The standards of conduct that may be expected of all individuals, including individuals with disabilities, include dress codes, time and attendance policies, conduct standards, and policies prohibiting theft or intoxication on the job.[125] An individual who engages in misconduct is not "otherwise qualified" even if the misconduct is a manifestation of the medical condition or disability. For example, in *Cameron v. Community Aid for Retarded Children, Inc.,* an employee who suffered from anxiety was found to be not "otherwise qualified" for her management position due to her abusive and intimidating conduct and participation in shouting matches with other employees.[126]

[11.38] When and how may an employer talk about disabilities with a prospective or current employee?

Some disabilities, particularly physical disabilities, may be obvious, while other disabilities, including mental illnesses, may not be readily apparent.

Employers may generally *not* inquire about disabilities until *after* the decision has been made to make a provisional job offer to a job applicant believed to have a disability. At that point, it is necessary to pursue an *interactive process* to determine whether the disability needs, and can be met by, a reasonable accommodation,

As a general rule, the burden of initiating the interactive accommodation process rests with the *employee*, who must request an accommodation. The duty to accommodate a disability arises only if the employer has notice of an employee's disability, as well as notice that the employee needs an accommodation.

However, if an employer becomes aware of an individual's disability at the pre-hire stage, either because it is obvious or because the applicant volunteers the information during the hiring process, then that notice may trigger the duty to initiate the interactive accommodation process if it is reasonable to question whether the disability might pose difficulties for the individual in performing a specific job task. The *employer* may then

---

125   *See* 9 N.Y.C.R.R. § 466.11(g).

126   335 F.3d 60 (2d Cir. 2003).

ask whether the applicant would need reasonable accommodation to perform the task, or ask the applicant to describe or demonstrate how he or she would perform the job, with or without reasonable accommodation.[127]

After an employee has been hired, an employer may only make inquiries about the employee's disability if the inquiries are job-related and consistent with business necessity. Inquiries are "job-related" when they are based upon objective evidence indicating that either an employee's ability to perform the essential job functions will be impaired by the condition or an employee poses a direct threat due to the condition.

If an employee or job applicant identifies a disability and requests reasonable accommodation, then the employer may request medical documentation of the existence and nature of the disability, including what accommodations might be recommended. The employee must provide the medical documentation in order to proceed with the accommodation request.[128]

It is important to emphasize that this process must be "interactive"; in other words, there must be sufficient back-and-forth communication with the job applicant or employee to demonstrate that the employer has made efforts to understand the condition and to address how it might be dealt with.

Any medical information received during the interactive accommodation process must be treated as confidential and maintained in a separate file.[129]

[11.39] When is an accommodation "reasonable"?

The term "reasonable accommodation" means one or more adjustments which permit an employee or prospective employee with a disability or a pregnancy-related condition to perform, in a reasonable manner, the essential activities involved in the job.[130] These may include the provision of a handicap-accessible work location, modification (or purchase) of

---

127   *See* U.S. Equal Employment Opportunity Commission, *EEOC Enforcement Guidance on Reasonable Accommodation and Undue Hardship under the Americans with Disability Act.* (October 17, 2002) at Question 12 and n. 40, https://www.eeoc.gov//policy/docs/accommodation.html#reasonable.

128   *Id.*, at Question 6 and n. 27.

129   *See* 9 N.Y.C.R.R. § 466.11(j).

130   *See* Exec. Law § 292 (21-e).

equipment, support services for persons with impaired hearing or vision, job restructuring, and modified work schedules, provided that such actions do not impose an undue hardship on the employer.

Examples of reasonable accommodations include such things as adaptive computer software for a clerical employee with impaired vision; modified work area lighting for an employee with a seizure disorder; air filtering for an employee with substance sensitivities; a work area accessible without using stairs for an employee with limited mobility; or assistance with moving heavy objects or retrieving objects from high shelves for an employee who cannot reach or carry heavy objects. However, the NYHRL does *not* require employers to provide personal care needs, such as a personal care assistant, or non-work-related aids, such as a personal hearing aid or a wheelchair.[131]

A proposed accommodation that would eliminate essential functions of the job is not "reasonable" under the NYHRL.[132] For example, if a keypunch operator needs to pick up heavy objects or retrieve objects from high shelves only occasionally, then help from another employee is a reasonable accommodation because lifting and carrying is not an essential function of a keypunch operator position. However, if the position in question were that of a furniture mover, then the ability to lift and carry heavy objects would be an essential function of the position, and the employer would have no obligation to provide a second employee to help out.

For a discussion of service animals, *see* § 11.44 *infra.*

While the employee may (and usually does) request a specific accommodation, the accommodation does not have to be the accommodation initially requested by the employee. As part of the interactive process, an employer may explore, and offer, alternative accommodations—and an alternative will be considered to be "reasonable" if it is effective.

Whether a requested accommodation is "reasonable" under the law is based upon a consideration of multiple factors, including: (a) the efficacy or benefit provided by the accommodation toward removing the impediments to performance caused by the disability; (b) the convenience of the accommodation for the employer, including its comparative convenience as opposed to other possible accommodations; and (c) the "hardships,"

---

131   *See* 9 N.Y.C.R.R. § 466.11(a).

132   *See Gill v. Maul,* 61 A.D.3d 1159, 876 N.Y.S.2d 751 (3d Dep't 2009); *Kibler v. New York State Dep't of Correctional Servs.,* 91 A.D.3d 1218, 937 N.Y.S.2d 447 (3d Dep't 2012).

costs, or problems it will cause for the employer, including issues that may be caused for other employees.[133] Although an employer must engage in an interactive dialogue with an employee regarding accommodations, it is ultimately the employer's right to select which reasonable accommodation will be provided, so long as the chosen accommodation is actually effective in meeting the employee's needs.[134]

Accommodations that pose an undue hardship for an employer (i.e., significant difficulty or expense) are not considered to be reasonable.[135] That being said, however, courts and discrimination agencies set a fairly high bar for a showing of hardship. In assessing whether an employer can meet the undue hardship test, courts will consider: the overall size of the company with respect to its employees, facilities and budget; the nature of the employer's operations, including the composition and structure of the workforce; and the nature and cost of the accommodation, taking into account any money available from other sources to assist the employer in paying the cost of the accommodation.[136] Moreover, even if an accommodation requested by an employee would pose an undue hardship, the employer is required to discuss alternative accommodation options and provide another accommodation if a reasonable accommodation is possible.

[11.40] Are "temporary" disabilities covered by the NYHRL?

Yes. An individual with a temporary disability will be protected during a recovery period if he or she can "satisfactorily perform the duties of the job after a reasonable accommodation in the form of *a reasonable time of recovery.*"[137] In 2016, the NYHRL was amended to require employers to treat pregnancy-related conditions as temporary disabilities.[138]

However, the NYHRL "requires no more than *de minimis* accommodations for temporary disabilities in the areas of worksite accessibility, acquisition or modification of equipment, job restructuring, or support services for persons with temporarily impaired hearing or vision."[139]

---

133   *See* 9 N.Y.C.R.R. § 466.11(b).

134   *See* 9 N.Y.C.R.R. § 466.11(j).

135   *See* Exec. Law § 296(3)(b).

136   *See* 9 N.Y.C.R.R. § 466.11(b)(2).

137   *See* 9 N.Y.C.R.R. § 466.11(i)(1) (emphasis supplied).

138   As to pregnancy-related conditions, *see* further discussion at § 11.49 *infra.*

139   *See* 9 N.Y.C.R.R. § 466.11(i)(1).

An employer may be required to provide accommodations for temporary disabilities by adjusting an employee's work schedule, by reassigning an employee to an available position or available light duty, or by modifying work schedules for a recovery period. Courts will consider the employer's past practice, pre-existing policies regarding leave time or light duty, specific workplace needs, the size and flexibility of the workforce, and the employee's overall attendance record in determining whether an accommodation is reasonable in this context.[140]

[11.41] Does an employer have to provide a "light duty" assignment?

The NYHRL does not require an employer to create a *new* position in order to accommodate a disability; and this means that an employer does not have to create a "light duty" position *if it does not already have one.*

However, if an employer already has light duty positions, then, to satisfy its obligation to consider alternative forms of accommodation, it may have to consider a transfer to a light duty position.

The New York State Division of Human Rights regulations state that a light duty assignment may be a reasonable accommodation for an employee with a *temporary* disability—but the law does not require an employer to make the light duty position permanent, even if the employee's temporary disability becomes permanent.[141]

[11.42] Does an employer have to transfer an employee with a disability to a new position?

Yes, but only if there is another *existing* and *vacant* position for which the employee can show that he or she is qualified.[142] The employer does not have to create a new position, and does not have to displace another

---

140   *See* 9 N.Y.C.R.R. § 466.11(i).

141   9 N.Y.C.R.R. § 466.11(i)(1); *see also Mair-Headley v. County of Westchester*, 41 A.D.3d 600, 837 N.Y.S.2d 347 (2d Dep't 2007) (employer not required to create a new light-duty position as a reasonable accommodation); *King v. Town of Wallkill*, 302 F. Supp. 2d 279 (S.D.N.Y. 2004) (employer not required under the ADA or the NYHRL to create a permanent light duty position for a disabled employee).

142   Exec. Law § 292(21-e), 9 N.Y.C.R.R. § 466.11(a)(1)–(2). *See Mair-Headley*, 41 A.D.3d 600; *Pimental v. Citibank, N.A.,* 29 A.D.3d 141, 148, 811 N.Y.S.2d 381 (1st Dep't 2006) (*citing Mitchell v. Washington Cent. Sch. Dist.,* 190 F.3d 1, 9 (2d Cir. 1999) (recognizing that New York courts have uniformly held that the duty to accommodate an employee with a disability "does not require an employer to find another job for the employee or to create the job, or to reassign if no position is open").

employee from his or her position in favor of the employee with a disability.[143]

[11.43] How much leave or time off can be required as an accommodation?

While it is clear that a leave of absence may constitute a reasonable accommodation, employers often struggle with determining how long that leave must be in order to satisfy the law's accommodation obligations. The duration of an employee with a disability's leave of absence generally requires an individualized analysis of a variety of surrounding circumstances, including the employee's specific medical condition; the nature of the employee's job; the nature of the employer's operations; the overall financial resources and size of the employer; and whether the employee's condition is likely to improve within a reasonably determinable period, or if the recovery period will continue to be uncertain. An employer must make a case-specific assessment and engage in an individualized interactive process in order to determine how much leave will be necessary to accommodate an employee.

Courts have consistently held that an open-ended or indefinite period of leave is not reasonable.[144] The requirement of a fixed date for an anticipated return from leave reflects the fact that a reasonable accommodation is one which will enable an employee to perform the essential functions of the job either immediately or in the near future.

It is not unusual for employers to receive successive leave requests, rather than a request for a single designated leave period, and determining the reasonableness of such requests is fact-intensive. Courts frequently note that the duty to provide a reasonable accommodation is an ongoing obligation; and this means that some extensions of leave periods may be required.

Neither the EEOC nor the courts have created a bright line rule identifying how many requests for multiple extensions of continuous leave are required to be granted to an employee before these reach the level of unreasonableness. Courts have generally been inclined to find that additional leave is unreasonable if the employee is still uncertain about the

---

143   Exec. Law § 292(21-e); *see also McBride v. BIC Consumer Prods. Mfg. Co.*, 583 F.3d 92 (2d Cir. 2009) (a plaintiff seeking to hold a New York employer liable for failure to make a transfer or reassignment as a reasonable accommodation has the burden of demonstrating that a vacant funded position exists and that plaintiff was qualified to fill that position.).

144   *See Phillips v. City of New York*, 66 A.D.3d 170, 884 N.Y.S.2d 369 (1st Dep't 2009); *Romanello v. Intesa Sanpaolo*, 22 N.Y.3d 881, 976 N.Y.S.2d 426 (2013).

duration of his or her medical condition after an employer has engaged in the interactive process and has already granted repeated requests for extensions of leave.[145] However, the courts have consistently noted as well that the reasonableness of repeated requests for leave extensions must be considered on a case-by-case basis.

Employers should also bear in mind that the federal Family Medical Leave Act (FMLA) requires that an employee who has worked for the employer for 1,250 hours or more during the previous year, and who works at a site with fifty or more employees, must be granted up to twelve weeks of unpaid leave if he or she has a serious health condition.[146] *The FMLA entitlement is not subject to or conditioned upon a reasonableness or undue hardship analysis, and the leave cannot be denied.* It is only after an employee has exhausted his or her 12 weeks of FMLA leave that the employer can consider whether additional leave is reasonable and appropriate. Further, when an employee with a disability needs some additional leave beyond the 12-week FMLA period, agencies and the courts are unsympathetic to employers who do not give such requests serious consideration.

[11.44] May an employee bring a service animal to work?

The New York Civil Rights Law provides that an employee may be accompanied by a "guide dog, hearing dog, or service dog" so long as the person can perform the essential functions of the position.[147] The terms "guide dog," "hearing dog," or "service dog" mean a dog which is properly harnessed and has been (or is being) trained by a qualified person, to aid and guide a person with a disability.[148]

In addition, the New York Human Rights Law broadly recognizes the right to "the use of an animal as a reasonable accommodation." Notably, the statute does not expressly limit the "animal" to a dog.[149] The questions of when and where individuals can assert the right to be accompa-

---

145   *See, e.g.,* U.S. Equal Employment Opportunity Commission, *Employer-Provided Leave and the Americans with Disability Act.* (May 9, 2016), www.eeoc.gov/eeoc/publications/ada-leave.cfm.

146   29 U.S.C. §§ 2611(2) and 2612. In order to qualify for the leave, the employee may (and should) be required to provide medical documentation. A form approved by the United States Department of Labor, Certification of Health Care Provider for Employee's Serious Health Condition (Form WH-380-E) may be downloaded from https://www.dol.gov/whd/forms/WH-380-E.pdf.

147   *See* Civ. Rights Law § 47-a.

148   *See* Civ. Rights Law § 47-b(4).

149   *See* Exec. Law § 296(14).

nied by a "comfort animal" or emotional support animal is a rapidly developing area of the law.

[11.45] Must an employer accommodate a certified medical marijuana patient?

Generally, yes, subject to two exceptions.

Under the New York Compassionate Care Act (CCA), individuals with severe, debilitating, or life-threatening medical conditions (such as cancer, amyotrophic lateral sclerosis, multiple sclerosis, epilepsy, inflammatory bowel disease, post-traumatic stress disorder, substance abuse, Parkinson's disease, and Huntington's disease), which are accompanied by a qualifying associate or complicating condition (such as cachexia disease, severe or chronic pain, severe nausea, seizures, or severe or persistent muscle spasms) may be provided access to medical marijuana under the supervision of a CCA-registered health care provider.[150] In order to become a "certified" patient, an individual must be a resident of New York State, have a severe, debilitating, or life-threatening medical condition accompanied by a qualifying associate or complicating condition, and obtain a certification issued by a physician registered with the New York State Department of Health's Medical Marijuana Program.

A certified medical marijuana patient is deemed to have a "disability" under the NYHRL and is, accordingly, protected from discrimination unless he or she cannot perform the essential functions of the position.[151]

The first exception is that the CCA does not protect a person who is "impaired" at work as a result of using medical marijuana.[152]

The second exception is that an employer is not required to do any act that would put it in violation of federal law, or that would cause it to lose a federal contract or federal funding.[153] Thus, for example, the United States Department of Transportation issued a directive in 2012 stating that

---

150   *See* Pub. Health Law § 3369.

151   Pub. Health Law § 3369(2) specifically provides that "[b]eing a certified [marijuana] patient shall be deemed to be having a 'disability' under article fifteen of the executive law (human rights law) . . ."

152   *See* Pub. Health Law § 3369(2). Unfortunately, the CCA does not explicitly define what it means to be "impaired," so employers should be careful to keep an anecdotal record of how an employee's impairment manifested itself in terms of job performance.

153   *See* Pub. Health Law § 3369(2).

the use of medical marijuana is unacceptable for any employee who is subject to drug testing under Department of Transportation regulations.[154] Under this directive, an employer may lawfully refuse to let a medical marijuana patient drive a truck which is subject to DOT regulation and drug-testing requirements.

The above being said, it is nonetheless prudent to assume that a certified medical marijuana patient should not be summarily fired, and that the employer should engage in the interactive process to determine if there is some other, non-safety-sensitive function the employee can reasonably perform without undue hardship to the employer.

[11.46] What is discrimination based upon predisposing genetic characteristics?

Under the NYHRL, a "predisposing genetic characteristic" is "any inherited gene or chromosome, or alteration thereof, and determined by a genetic test or inferred from information derived from an individual or family member that is scientifically or medically believed to predispose an individual or the offspring of that individual to a disease or disability, or to be associated with a statistically significant increased risk of development of a physical or mental disease or disability."[155]

A "genetic test" is "a test for determining the presence or absence of an inherited genetic characteristic in an individual, including tests of nucleic acids such as DNA, RNA and mitochondrial DNA, chromosomes or proteins in order to identify a predisposing genetic characteristic."[156]

In general, employers are prohibited from: (a) requiring or administering genetic testing as a condition of employment; (b) buying or otherwise acquiring an individual's genetic test results or other information (such as a family history from which his or her predisposing genetic characteristics can be determined); or (c) making an agreement with an individual to take a genetic test or provide genetic test results or other information regarding their predisposing genetic characteristics.[157]

---

154   *See* Department of Transportation, *DOT Office of Drug and Alcohol Policy and Compliance Notice*, https://www.transportation.gov/sites/dot.gov/files/docs/odapc-notice-recreational-mj.pdf.

155   Exec. Law § 292(21-a).

156   Exec. Law § 292(21-b).

157   *See* Exec. Law §§ 296(19)(a)(1) and (2).

However, employers *may* require genetic testing as a condition of employment where the specific type of testing is directly related to an occupation and work environment that may pose increased risk of disease to individuals with particular genetic anomalies.[158]

Genetic testing is also permitted in those cases in which an employee provides written consent *and* requests genetic testing in furtherance of a workers' compensation claim, civil litigation, or to determine his or her potential susceptibility to chemicals or substances found in the workplace. Upon receiving the results of the testing, the employer is prohibited from taking any adverse action against the employee based upon the test results.[159]

Whenever an employee consents to genetic testing for a permitted purpose, the employee must first sign an authorization form explicitly specifying the purpose, uses, and limitations of the genetic testing, and the specific traits or characteristics being tested.[160]

The provision of the NYHRL prohibiting discrimination based upon predisposing genetic conditions was added in 1996. Since then, courts have considered the provision in only a handful of cases. In one, an employee alleged that she was terminated from employment because she was shorter than her four co-workers. The court found that height, in and of itself, does not constitute a predisposing genetic characteristic because an adult employee who has achieved his or her full height is no longer genetically predisposed to becoming that height. Further, the court held that a termination based upon the employee's height could not have constituted discrimination as a result of a predisposing genetic characteristic, as the employer did not rely upon any genetic test results or family history indicating that the employee was likely to develop a disease or disability in the future.[161]

---

158   Exec. Law § 296(19)(b).

159   Exec. Law § 296(19)(c).

160   *Id.*

161   *Peterson v. City of New York*, 36 Misc. 3d 1225(A), 957 N.Y.S.2d 266 (Sup. Ct., N.Y. Co. 2012), *aff'd*, 120 A.D.3d 1328, 993 N.Y.S.2d 88 (2d Dep't 2014).

2. Age

[11.47] Who is protected against age discrimination under New York law?

The federal ADEA protects persons over the age of 40 years from discrimination in employment. However, the NYHRL protects anyone who is 18 years of age or older and the NYCHRL has no lower age limit.[162]

Federal law has been determined not to protect younger workers from "reverse discrimination"; that is, from policies or actions which favor older workers.[163] However, since New York law protects younger workers as well, it should be presumed that such a reverse discrimination claim is possible.

[11.48] Is a mandatory retirement age permissible?

Generally, no. However, the NYHRL contains a very limited exception permitting a private sector (non-public) employer to set mandatory retirement for an individual 65 years of age or older who meets the following additional criteria:

- He or she must be a *bona fide* executive or hold a high policy-making position;

- He or she must have held the position in question for at least two years preceding mandatory retirement;

- He or she must be entitled to an immediate and non-forfeitable pension, profit-sharing or deferred compensation plan with a value of at least $44,000.[164]

The NYHRL also provides a limited exception to the mandatory retirement prohibition to allow a non-public institution of higher education to impose a mandatory retirement upon employees 70 years of age or older who are serving under a contract or a similar arrangement providing for unlimited tenure.[165]

---

162   *See* §§ 11.1.1.1., 11.1.1.3, 11.1.1.4., and 11.1 *supra.*

163   *See Gen. Dynamics Land Sys., Inc. v. Cline,* 540 U.S. 581 (2004).

164   *See* Exec. Law § 296(3-a)(e). There is a similar exception in the federal ADEA; *see* 29 U.S.C. § 631(c)(1).

165   *See* Exec. Law § 296(3-a)(f).

3. Pregnancy

[11.49] How is pregnancy protected under New York law?

Pregnancy is protected under several different provisions of New York law.

The NYHRL's prohibition against sex discrimination includes protections for pregnant employees, including during pregnancy, after childbirth, and with respect to related medical conditions. It further prohibits employers from forcing a pregnant employee to take a leave of absence unless the condition of being pregnant prevents the employee from performing her job in a reasonable manner.[166]

Pregnancy discrimination can also be considered a form of familial status discrimination, inasmuch as the definition of familial status includes the status of being pregnant.[167]

Another source of protection is the NYHRL's provisions governing disability discrimination and accommodation. Since 2016, the NYHRL has required an employer to provide accommodations to employees with pregnancy-related conditions unless doing so would result in an undue hardship for the employer.[168] A pregnancy-related condition must be treated as a temporary disability.[169]

The term "pregnancy-related condition" means a medical condition related to pregnancy or childbirth that inhibits the exercise of a normal bodily function or is demonstrable by medically accepted clinical or laboratory diagnostic techniques.[170] As with other disability-related workplace accommodations, an employer may require a pregnant employee to provide medical documentation to support a requested accommodation.[171]

---

166   *See* Exec. Law § 296(1)(g).

167   *See* Exec. Law § 292(26)(a).

168   *See* Exec. Law §§ 296(3)(a)–(b) and 292(21-e).

169   *See* Exec. Law § 292(21-f); *see also* the discussion of temporary disabilities in § 11.40 *supra*.

170   *See* Exec. Law § 292(21-f).

171   *See* Exec. Law § 296(3)(c).

The New York State Division of Human Rights' guidance materials for employees and employers[172] explains that pregnancy-related conditions need not meet the definition of "disability" to trigger an employer's accommodation obligation under the law. Instead, *any* medically advised restrictions or needs related to pregnancy will trigger the need to accommodate.

The guidance also identifies some of the accommodations which employers may need to provide for pregnant employees, including such things as increased time for bathroom breaks and increased water intake. Reasonable accommodations may also include: making minor workplace modifications, such as letting a pregnant employee sit for a job normally done standing; reassigning the employee to another available position; reassigning the employee to an available light duty position; or transferring the employee away from hazardous duty. They may also include modified or adjusted work schedules for doctor visits or recovery from childbirth.

It is important to note that these accommodations are required *if the employee requests them*, and *not* because the employer unilaterally thinks that they might be a good idea. A pregnant employee may not be forced to accept a transfer to another position against her will.

The New York Labor Law was amended in 2019 to prohibit discrimination based upon an employee's or a dependent's "reproductive health decision making." This protection includes decisions about such matters as obtaining fertility-related medical procedures; using birth control drugs or contraceptive devices; or having an abortion.[173] The law also prohibits employers from accessing an employee's personal information regarding the employee's, or the employee's dependent's, reproductive health decision-making without the employee's prior informed affirmative written consent.

[11.50] How much leave is required for pregnancy-related conditions and childbirth?

Many employers and employees are under the impression that an employee is entitled to some fixed period of leave (usually believed to be six or eight weeks) once she has given birth. This is a misconception. Leaves for pregnancy and childbirth are to be treated the same way as are

---

172   *See* https://www.ny.gov/working-while-pregnant-know-your-rights/pregnancy-rights-employees-workplace and https://www.ny.gov/programs/pregnant-or-breastfeeding-workplace-know-your-rights.

173   *See* Labor Law § 203-e.

any other leaves for illness or disability, which are determined on an individual basis and with reference to medical documentation provided by the employee. This means that an employer should treat an employee who needs time off for pregnancy or childbirth the same way as it treats an employee who needs time off for a broken hip or pneumonia in terms of available paid and unpaid leave, benefits continuation during the leave, and restoration to the employee's position at the end of the leave.

In addition, there are statutory requirements which bear upon pregnancy, pregnancy-related conditions, and childbirth.

Under the federal Family Medical Leave Act (FMLA),[174] eligible employees (i.e., those who worked at least 1,250 hours during the preceding year and who work for an employer covered by FMLA) are entitled to up to 12 weeks of unpaid leave in any year: (a) for a serious personal health condition, or (b) for the serious health condition of a close family member; or (c) for the birth or adoption of a child. Such FMLA leave is available to both mothers and fathers, and requires both that any employer-provided health insurance must be continued for the FMLA leave period, and that, with narrowly limited exceptions, the employee must be restored to his or her position at the end of the leave.

Additionally, most New York employees are covered by the New York State Paid Family Leave Benefits Law (PFL), which took effect on January 1, 2018.[175] Under the PFL, both mothers and fathers who meet minimum hours of work are entitled to partially paid family leave for a number of reasons, including in order to bond with a newly born, adopted, or foster child. The paid leave is funded by deductions from employee pay, and is being phased in so that, by the year 2020, eligible employees will be able to take 12 weeks of paid family leave. Many employers will make PFL and FMLA leaves run concurrently with each other and with any other available employer-provided paid leave for illness or vacation.

For a more comprehensive discussion of PFL, *see* Chapter 4 of this book, "Employee Time Off," at §§ 4.65–4.80).

---

174   29 U.S.C. § 2601 and 29 C.F.R. pt. 825.

175   *See* WCL art. 9.

4. Sexual Orientation

[11.51] Is sexual orientation protected under the NYHRL?

Yes. Although express coverage against discrimination on the basis of sexual orientation was first proposed in the New York State Assembly in 1971, the Sexual Orientation Non-Discrimination Act (SONDA) was not passed and enacted until January 16, 2003.[176] SONDA amended the NYHRL to prohibit discrimination in employment, housing, public accommodation, education, credit, and the exercise of civil rights.

As this book was being finalized, the United States Supreme Court decided that sexual orientation is also protected under federal law.[177] The full implications of that decision remain to be explored.

[11.52] What are the protections for sexual orientation?

The NYHRL's prohibition against sexual orientation discrimination extends to all forms of discrimination, including disparate treatment (e.g., refusing to hire or promote or deciding to discipline or discharge),[178] adverse impact,[179] and unlawful workplace harassment (*quid pro quo*, hostile work environment, etc.).[180]

5. Transgender Status

[11.53] Are transgender employees protected under the NYHRL?

Yes. A transgender person is defined as an individual who has a gender identity different from the sex assigned to that individual at birth.[181]

In 2016, the New York State Division of Human Rights adopted regulations prohibiting discrimination and harassment based upon gender identity, transgender status, and gender dysphoria. Under the regulations, discrimination on the basis of gender identity and the status of being transgender is a form of sex discrimination. Further, discrimination on the basis of gender dysphoria, which is a recognized medical condition

---

176   2002 N.Y. Laws 2.

177   *Bostock v. Clayton County, Georgia,* ___ U.S. ___, No. 17–1618 (June 15, 2020).

178   *See* § 11.20 *supra.*

179   *See* § 11.24 *supra.*

180   *See* §§ 11.27 and 11.34 *supra.*

181   *See* 9 N.Y.C.R.R § 466.13(b)(2).

related to an individual having a gender identity different than the sex assigned at birth, is a form of disability discrimination.[182]

As this book was being finalized, the United States Supreme Court decided that transgender employees are also protected under federal law.[183] The full implications of that decision remain to be explored.

In 2019, the New York Legislature passed the Gender Expression Non-Discrimination Act (GENDA), which amends the NYHRL to prohibit discrimination on the basis of gender identity or gender expression, including a person's transgender status.[184] GENDA codifies the protections for transgender and gender non-conforming persons which had previously been adopted by regulation.

The term "gender identity or expression" is defined as a person's actual or perceived gender-related identity, appearance, behavior, expression, or other gender-related characteristic, regardless of the sex assigned to that person at birth.[185] Any form of discrimination or harassment based upon gender identity or transgender status is prohibited.[186] Additionally, the law extends disability and accommodation provisions to gender dysphoria, so it constitutes disability discrimination to fail to provide reasonable accommodation to, or to harass, an applicant or employee by reason of gender dysphoria.[187]

---

182 *See* 9 N.Y.C.R.R. § 466.13.

183 *Bostock v. Clayton County, Georgia*, ___ U.S. ___, No. 17–1618 (June 15, 2020).

184 See Exec. Law § 296(1)(a).

185 *See* Exec. Law § 292(35).

186 Notably, the New York City Commission on Human Rights issued guidance in 2015 regarding the prohibition of discrimination and harassment against transgender persons under the NY-CHR. *See* NYC Human Rights, *Gender Identity/Gender Expression: Legal Enforcement Guidance* (Feb. 15, 2019) https://www1.nyc.gov/site/cchr/law/legal-guidances-gender-identity-expression.page The Guidance provides that, when an employer engages in prohibited discrimination against, or harassment of, a transgender employee, the Commission can impose civil penalties of up to $125,000, and up to $250,000 for "willful, wanton or malicious conduct." The NYCHRL was amended in 2018 to strengthen the protections against discrimination for transgender employees and to broaden those protections by expanding the definitions related to gender identity and expression. The NYCHRL defines "gender" as "actual or perceived sex, gender identity and gender expression, including a person's actual or perceived gender-related self-image, appearance, behavior, expression or other gender-related characteristics, regardless of the sex assigned to that person at birth." N.Y.C. Admin. Code § 8-102.

187 *See* 9 N.Y.C.R.R. § 466.13.

Employers may request medical documentation from an employee who seeks workplace accommodations by reason of gender dysphoria. Such requested accommodations may include medical or personal leave or changes in work schedule. In such cases, the employer must engage in the interactive process described in §§ 11.38 and 11.39 *supra*.

[11.54] What accommodations must be granted to transgender employees?

The NYHRL protects the way a person expresses gender through speech, dress, and behavior. Thus, insisting that a transgender female (an individual who was assigned male at birth but identifies as female) comply with the company's male dress code would be unlawful. An employer's enforcement of a dress code requirement under such circumstances is unlawful sex stereotyping.

The New York State Division of Human Rights has also taken the position that employers must allow individuals to use the restroom that conforms with a transgender employee's gender identity.

One of the most common issues regarding gender-nonconforming employees arises when an employee requests to be referred to by a name and pronoun consistent with the individual's gender identity. For example, if an employee, Christopher, were to inform his employer of a name change to Christine to reflect her gender identity, then the employer would be required to refer to her as Christine and by female pronouns and titles. The employer would also be required to direct supervisors and co-workers to refer to her by using her preferred name and using female pronouns and titles (e.g., she, her, Ms., Mrs.), regardless of whether the employee had gone through the steps of obtaining a court-ordered or other legal name change. If Christine's co-workers begin to harass her at work based upon her transgender status, including calling her derogatory names and/or referring to her as "Christopher," could and would constitute harassment and the employer might be liable for the co-workers' harassing conduct if it does not take steps to end it.[188]

An employer may not require an individual to provide medical information or proof of having undergone medical procedures in order to use a preferred name, pronoun, or title. There are limited circumstances under which an employer would not be obligated to use a transgender

---

188   *See* N.Y. Division of Human Rights, *Protecting Against Gender Identity Discrimination under the New York State Human Rights Law*, https://dhr.ny.gov/sites/default/files/pdf/DHR-gender-identity-brochure.pdf.

employee's preferred name, such as where federal, state, or local law requires otherwise (e.g., to verify employment eligibility with the federal government).

6. Religion

[11.55] How is religion protected under New York law?

The NYHRL makes it unlawful for an employer to refuse to hire an applicant, to terminate an employee, or otherwise to discriminate against an employee in compensation or in other terms, conditions, or privileges of employment on the basis of that individual's "creed" (religion).[189] Employers may not retaliate against applicants or employees for reporting alleged religious discrimination in the workplace.

The law also prohibits employers from discriminating against an applicant or current employee because of his or her observance of any particular day as a sabbath or other holy day in accordance with the requirements of that person's religion.[190] The law was amended in 2019 expressly to prohibit discrimination against employees based upon their attire, clothing, or facial hair worn in accordance with the employees' religion. The employer will bear the burden of demonstrating that it cannot reasonably accommodate the employee's religious practice, such as wearing a yarmulke, headscarf, turban, burqa, or hijab, without undue hardship to the business.[191]

The NYHRL protects employees from harassment based upon their religion or religious practices. Religious harassment occurs when employees are forced to abandon, alter, or adopt a religious practice as a condition of employment, or are subjected to a hostile work environment based upon religion. The types of conduct that may create a hostile work environment based upon religion include: making offensive religious-based comments and displaying conduct concerning religious beliefs, practices, garb, etc.; joking about a person's religion; referring to people using derogatory names; creating religiously offensive symbols or graffiti; excluding a person from projects or advancements because of religion and treating a person based upon stereotypical assumptions related to their religion.

---

189   *See* Exec. Law § 296(1)(a).

190   *See* Exec. Law § 296(10)(a).

191   *Id.*

[11.56] What accommodation must be made for religious observance?

The prohibition against discrimination on the basis of religion includes an obligation on the part of employers to accommodate employees' religious practices, including prayer times, days of rest, grooming, and dress.

A reasonable religious accommodation is any adjustment to the work environment that will allow the employee to comply with his or her religious beliefs without creating an undue hardship for the employer. Some of the most common methods of religious accommodation include flexible scheduling, flexible arrival and departure times, flexible work breaks, designation of a work location for prayer during the workday, floating or optional holidays, lateral transfer or change of job assignment, modification of workplace practices and policies (such as by making exceptions to the company's dress code and grooming requirements that prohibit religious dress and grooming, such as a hijab, beard, skullcap or turban), and means to enable an employee to make up time lost due to the observance of religious practices.

Under both New York and federal law, an employer must make a reasonable accommodation to permit an employee to be absent from work for religious holidays or observances. The employer may require employees to make up work missed at another time, may charge time missed against paid leave (other than sick leave); or may require employees to take leave without pay for time not made up or charged to paid leave.[192]

An employee's religious beliefs are protected if they are *bona fide* and sincerely held. This is a broad standard, and employers should be cautioned against making assumptions either about religious requirements or about an individual employee's degree of religious commitment.[193] Religious beliefs must be accommodated unless the employer can demonstrate that providing the accommodation would result in an undue

---

192 *See* Exec. Law § 296(10)(b).

193 *See, e.g.,* U.S. Equal Employment Opportunity Commission, *Compliance Manual, Section 12: Religion Discrimination* (Jul. 22, 2008) https://www.eeoc.gov/policy/docs/religion.html (recognizing that "[b]ecause the definition of religion is broad and protects beliefs and practices with which the employer may be unfamiliar, the employer should ordinarily assume that an employee's request for religious accommodation is based on a sincerely-held religious belief . . . An employer also should not assume that an employee is insincere simply because some of his or her practices deviated from commonly followed tenets of his or her religion.").

hardship on the employer. Where there is more than one reasonable accommodation that will meet an employee's needs, the employer may choose which one to provide.

It is the employee's initial obligation to inform his or her employer of the need for an accommodation for his or her religious beliefs and the failure to do so constitutes a waiver of the employee's right to a religious accommodation.[194] Once an accommodation has been requested, the employer must make an accommodation; that burden cannot be shifted to the employee to arrange for the accommodation. For example, in one case, an employer was found to have discriminated against a Seventh Day Adventist by failing to accommodate her observance of the sabbath when it placed the burden upon the employee to find other workers willing to switch assignments with her so that she could observe the sabbath.[195]

In some circumstances, an employee's co-workers will complain about an accommodation granted to the employee for religious observance. Complaints of this nature do *not* constitute an "undue hardship" which could relieve the employer of its obligation to provide accommodation, unless the accommodation actually infringes upon the rights of the complaining co-workers. Further, were the co-workers to take out their frustration on the accommodated employee, then their behavior would likely constitute actionable harassment.

7. Marital, Familial, and Domestic Violence Victim Status

[11.57] What is marital status discrimination?

"Marital status" under the NYHRL means whether an individual is "single, married, separated, divorced or widowed."[196] Individuals are protected from an employer's refusal to hire them based upon their marital status, and from being terminated from employment, or otherwise discriminated against in the terms, conditions or privileges of employment, as a result of their marital status.[197]

---

194   *See State Div. of Human Rights ex rel. Campbell v. Rochester Prods. Div.,* 112 A.D.2d 785, 492 N.Y.S. 2d 282 (4th Dep't 1985); *Betz v. Memorial Sloan-Kettering Cancer Ctr.,* No. 95 Civ. 1156(RPP), 1996 U.S. Dist. LEXIS 10568, 1996 WL 422242 (S.D.N.Y. July 24, 1996).

195   *North Shore Univ. Hosp. v. State Human Rights Appeal Bd.,* 82 A.D.2d 799, 439 N.Y.S.2d 408 (2d Dep't 1981).

196   *Manhattan Pizza Hut, Inc. v. New York State Human Rights Appeal Bd.,* 51 N.Y.2d 506, 510, 434 N.Y.S.2d 961 (1980); *Pibouin v. CA, Inc.,* 867 F. Supp. 2d 315, 319 (E.D.N.Y. 2012).

197   *See* Exec. Law § 296(1)(a).

Under the NYHRL, employers are only prohibited from discriminating against an individual based upon the individual's marital *status* (i.e., whether he or she is single, married, divorced, separated, widowed, etc.); they are not prohibited from discriminating based upon the identity of the individual's *spouse*: "[T]here is no protection afforded under NYHRL regarding one's marriage to a particular person."[198]

Local laws may offer protections to individuals based upon the identity of their spouse. For example, the Appellate Division, First Department, has held that the NYCHRL's marital status protections could encompass discrimination based on the identity or occupation of an employee's spouse.[199] In *Morse*, the plaintiff alleged that his employer perceived that a female co-worker with whom he had two children was his spouse, and that his employer discriminated against him by terminating him when his perceived spouse left to work for a competitor. The First Department held that the plaintiff's allegations were sufficient to state a cause of action for marital status discrimination under the NYCHRL.

[11.58] What is familial status discrimination?

"Familial status" under the NYHRL refers to: a person who is pregnant; a person who has a child; a person who is in the process of securing legal custody of a minor; or a person under the age of 18 years who is living with a parent, a legal custodian, or the designee of such parent or legal custodian.[200]

It is unlawful for an employer to refuse to hire, to fire, or otherwise to discriminate in employment against any person by reason of his or her familial status[201].

[11.59] What is domestic violence victim discrimination?

A person is a "domestic violence victim" under the NYHRL if he or she is the "victim of an act which would constitute a family offense" pursuant to N.Y. Family Court Act § 812.[202] Such offenses include disorderly con-

---

198 *Pibouin*, 867 F. Supp. 2d 315.

199 *Morse v. Fidessa Corp.*, 165 A.D.3d 61, 68, 84 N.Y.S.3d 50 (1st Dep't 2018).

200 Exec. Law § 292(26).

201 Exec. Law § 296(1)(a); *see also* N.Y. Division of Human Rights, *Guidance on Familial Status Discrimination for Employers in New York State* https://dhr.ny.gov/sites/default/files/pdf/guidance-familial-status-employers.pdf.

202 Exec. Law § 292(34).

duct, harassment, sexual misconduct, forcible touching, sexual abuse, stalking, criminal mischief, menacing, reckless endangerment, criminal obstruction of breathing or blood circulation, strangulation, assault, attempted assault, identity theft, grand larceny, and coercion, occurring between spouses or former spouses, parents, parent and child, or between members of the same family or household.[203]

It is unlawful for an employer to refuse to hire, to fire, or to otherwise discriminate in employment against any person by reason of that person's status as a domestic violence victim.[204]

The NYHRL was recently amended to require employers to provide reasonable accommodations to employees who are victims of domestic violence or parents of children who are victims of domestic violence.[205] Employers must, unless it creates an "undue hardship," provide a reasonable amount of unpaid time off from work to enable the employee to do the following:

1. Seek medical attention for injuries caused by domestic violence (including for a child who is a victim of domestic violence, provided that the employee is not the perpetrator);

2. Obtain services from a domestic violence shelter, program, or rape crisis center as a result of domestic violence;

3. Obtain psychological counseling relating to domestic violence (including for a child who is a victim of domestic violence, provided that the employee is not the perpetrator);

4. Participate in safety planning and to take other actions to increase safety from future incidents of domestic violence, including temporary or permanent relocation; or

5. Obtain legal services in relation to domestic violence, to assist in the prosecution of a domestic violence offense, or to appear in court in relation to incidents of domestic violence.[206]

---

203   Family Court Act § 812.

204   Exec. Law § 296(1)(a).

205   Exec. Law § 296(22).

206   Exec. Law § 296(22)(c)(2).

In determining whether an "undue hardship" exists that would relieve the employer of the obligation to provide leave, the factors considered are:

1. The overall size of the business with respect to the number of employees, the number and types of facilities, and the size of the budget; and

2. The type of operation in which the business is engaged, including the composition and structure of the workforce.[207]

It should be noted that both courts and administrative agencies generally set a high standard of inconvenience before an employer can successfully assert a claim of undue hardship.

The employer does not have to pay an employee who takes domestic violence leave, but the employee can be required to use available paid leave. If no paid leave is available, then the leave may be treated as unpaid leave.[208]

An employee who plans to take domestic violence leave must give reasonable advance notice when it is feasible to do so.[209] If giving advance notice is not feasible, then the employer can require an employee who asks for leave as a reasonable accommodation to provide certification for the absence(s) in the form of:

1. A police report indicating that the employee or his or her child was a victim of domestic violence;

2. A court order protecting or separating the employee or his or her child from the perpetrator of domestic violence;

3. Evidence from a court or prosecuting attorney that the employee appeared in court; or

4. Documentation from a medical professional, domestic violence advocate, health care provider, or counselor that the employee or his or her child was undergoing treatment or counseling for physical or mental injuries resulting from domestic violence.[210]

---

207   Exec. Law § 296(22)(c)(3).

208   Exec. Law § 296(22)(c)(1).

209   Exec. Law § 296(22)(c)(4).

210   Exec. Law § 296(22)(c)(5).

Reasonable accommodation for the victims of domestic violence is also required by the NYCHRL.[211]

8. Arrests and Convictions

[11.60] **What is discrimination based upon criminal arrests or convictions?**

Simply stated, it is *always* unlawful to ask a job applicant about (or otherwise to discriminate against a job applicant because of) any past arrest record. *See* § 11.13 of this chapter.

There are also serious limitations on an employer's inquiries about, and decisions based upon, prior criminal convictions. *See* § 11.13 of this chapter, and Chapter 1 of this book, "The Hiring Process," at §§ 1.8–1.11 and §§ 1.24–1.26.

The NYHRL does not prohibit employers from asking about *pending* criminal charges brought *while the individual is an employee*. Thus, if an employee is arrested and/or accused of a crime during the course of his or her employment, then, while the charges are pending (open and unresolved), the employer is permitted to ask about, and take action as a result of, the arrest or criminal accusation.

However, if the employer does *not* take action while the charges are pending, and the charge is subsequently resolved in favor of the employee, then the employee becomes protected and the employer cannot later take action against the employee based upon the arrest or criminal accusation.[212]

We strongly recommend that any inquiry into a pending criminal charge be directed at the *conduct* with which the employee was charged, rather than at the mere fact of the arrest. An inquiry focused upon the conduct will reveal whether it was of such a nature that it should be of concern to the employer. For example, the action to be taken against an employee in a child care facility may be very different if the arrest was for child abuse than if it was for failure to answer a speeding ticket summons.

An employee's refusal to disclose the reason for which he or she was arrested, or to keep the employer informed of the status of criminal charges, may be an independent basis for taking an adverse personnel action.

---

211   N.Y.C. Admin. Code § 8-107.1.

212   N.Y. Department of Labor, *Employers*, https://www.labor.ny.gov/careerservices/ace/employers.shtm.

VII. RETALIATION

[11.61] What is "retaliation"?

The concept of "retaliation," which exists under both New York and federal law, is very important for employers to understand, because an employer may be found liable for retaliating against an employee who complains of discrimination *even if the underlying charge of discrimination lacks merit.*

The NYHRL prohibits employers from retaliating or discriminating against individuals because they opposed employment discrimination, or because they filed a complaint, testified, or otherwise assisted in an action commenced pursuant to the NYHRL.[213] In addition, many other New York laws prohibit retaliation, including the following:

- **Labor Law § 27-a** prohibits discrimination or retaliation against a public employee because the employee filed a complaint about, or provided information relating to, a health and safety complaint.

- **Labor Law § 215** prohibits retaliation against an employee who makes a complaint concerning a violation of the Labor Law, or otherwise providing information relating to such a complaint.

- **Labor Law § 736** prohibits retaliation against an employee for filing a complaint or providing information relating to a complaint that an employer required, requested, suggested, or knowingly permitted an employee to submit to a psychological stress evaluator examination.

- **Labor Law § 740** prohibits retaliation against an employee who discloses or threatens to disclose a policy or practice of the employer that is in violation of a law, rule, or regulation, and which presents a substantial and specific danger to public health or safety, or which constitutes health care fraud. It also prohibits retaliation against an employee who provides any information in an investigation or hearing regarding such a violation, or who refuses to participate in such activity in violation of the law.

- **Labor Law § 741** prohibits retaliation against a health care employee who discloses or threatens to disclose a policy or practice of the employer that the employee reasonably believes to con-

---

213   Exec. Law § 296(7).

stitute improper patient care, or who objects or refuses to participate in an activity which the employee believes to constitute improper patient care.

- **Labor Law § 861-f** prohibits retaliation against an employee for making a complaint regarding the employer's violation of the New York Construction Industry Fair Pay Act, or otherwise providing assistance with regard to such a complaint.

- **Labor Law § 862-e** prohibits retaliation against an employee for making a complaint regarding the employer's violation of the New York Commercial Goods Transportation Industry Fair Pay Act, or otherwise providing assistance with regard to such a complaint.

- **Labor Law § 880** prohibits retaliation against an employee for asserting his or her rights under the New York Toxic Substances Act.

- **Civil Service Law § 75-b** prohibits public employers from retaliating against an employee who discloses information to a public body regarding a violation of law that creates a substantial and specific danger to public health or safety, or which the employee reasonably believes to be the case and to constitute an improper governmental action.

- **Not-For-Profit Corporation Law § 715-b** requires not-for-profit corporations with twenty or more employees to adopt a whistleblower policy prohibiting the corporation from retaliating against employees who make good faith reports that the corporation has taken action that is illegal, fraudulent, or in violation of any policy adopted by the corporation.

- **Social Services Law § 460-d** prohibits retaliation against an employee of an adult care facility who files, or provides information relating to, a complaint of incorrect operation of the facility.

- **Education Law § 3028-d** prohibits retaliation against a school district, charter school, or Board of Cooperative Educational Services (BOCES) employee who makes a report regarding the employer's fiscal practices where they have reasonable cause to suspect that such practices violate local, state, or federal law.

- **Workers' Compensation Law § 120** prohibits employers from discriminating or retaliating against an employee because the employee has claimed or sought workers' compensation benefits or has provided information with regard to a workers' compensation claim.

[11.62] What are the elements of a retaliation claim?

To establish *a prima facie* claim of retaliation under the NYHRL, an employee must show that: (1) he or she engaged in protected activity, (2) the employer was aware that the employee engaged in protected activity, (3) the employee suffered an adverse employment action, and (4) there is a causal connection between the protected activity and the adverse action.[214]

If the employee has established a *prima facie* case, then the *McDonnell Douglas*[215] burden-shifting analysis (*see* § 11.1 *supra*) applies. The employer has the burden of articulating a legitimate, non-pretextual reason for the adverse employment action, following which the employee may attempt to show that the reason put forth by the employer is in fact pretextual, and that the employer's actions were truly retaliatory in nature.

Protected activity most often consists of an employee complaint about a discriminatory, or other improper, practice. The complaint need not be made to an outside agency: internal complaints are also protected. The United States Supreme Court has held that employees "virtually always" engage in protected activity by opposing unlawful discrimination when they communicate to their employer that they believe the employer engaged in employment discrimination.[216] Any activity resisting, contending against, or confronting unlawful discrimination constitutes protected activity in opposition to discrimination.[217]

An employee's complaint does not have to be valid for it to be protected. An employee's complaint or concern will constitute protected activity so long as

---

214 *Forrest v. Jewish Guild for the Blind,* 3 N.Y.3d 295, 312–13, 786 N.Y.S.2d 382 (2004).

215 411 U.S.792 (1973).

216 *Crawford v. Metro. Gov't of Nashville & Davidson Cnty.,* 555 U.S. 271, 276 (2009). Although that case concerned protected activity under Title VII, retaliation claims under Title VII and the NYHRL are evaluated under the same standards. *See Kodengada v. IBM,* No. 00-cv-7434, 2000 U.S. App. LEXIS 31322 at *6–7 (2d Cir. Dec. 4, 2000); *Maher v. Alliance Mortg. Banking Corp.,* 650 F. Supp. 2d 249, 259 (E.D.N.Y. 2009).

217 *Littlejohn v. City of New York,* 795 F.3d 297, 317 (2d Cir. 2015).

the employee had a good faith, reasonable belief that he or she was opposing unlawful employment discrimination.[218] The belief must be objectively reasonable; in other words, it needs to have a factual basis, and a merely subjective belief that the conduct opposed was unlawful is not sufficient.[219]

To constitute protected activity, an employee's discrimination complaint must be sufficiently specific to put the employer on notice that the employee is objecting to unlawful employment discrimination rather than just unfair, unkind, or improper treatment.[220] The objection must also be related specifically to employment discrimination; objections to other types of discrimination do not constitute protected activity.[221]

When employees engage in protected activity by testifying or otherwise assisting in an action commenced pursuant to the NYHRL, they do not need to establish that they had a good faith, reasonable belief that the complaint opposed unlawful conduct; in other words, these activities are automatically protected without regard to the participating employee's state of mind.[222]

Where an employee's participation in an internal investigation results in that employee's report of unlawful activity, that report can constitute protected activity. For example, where an employee who is being interviewed during the course of an internal investigation shares information about instances of harassment that she experienced personally, those statements have been found to be reports of harassment constituting protected opposition to discrimination.[223]

As discussed above, protected activity includes both opposition to unlawful employment discrimination and participation in NYHRL proceedings. Employees can engage in protected activity in opposition to unlawful

---

218   *Kelly v. Howard I. Shapiro & Assocs. Consulting Eng'rs, P.C.*, 716 F.3d 10, 14 (2d Cir. 2013); *Bd. of Educ. of New Paltz Cent. Sch. Dist. v. Donaldson*, 41 A.D.3d 1138, 1140 (3d Dep't 2007).

219   *Dottolo v. Byrne Dairy, Inc.*, No. 5:08-CV-0390, 2010 U.S. Dist. LEXIS 62132 at *20–21 (N.D.N.Y. June 22, 2010); *Sullivan-Weaver v. New York Power Auth.*, 114 F. Supp. 2d 240, 243 (S.D.N.Y. 2000); *Martin v. State Univ. of New York*, 704 F. Supp. 2d 202 (E.D.N.Y. 2010).

220   *See Krause v. Kelehan*, No. 6:17-cv-1045, 2018 U.S. Dist. LEXIS 70743 at * 16–17 (N.D.N.Y. Apr. 26, 2018).

221   *Kelly*, 716 F.3d at 15; *Wimmer v. Suffolk Cnty. Police Dep't.*, 176 F.3d 125, 134–35 (2d Cir. 1999) (complaints concerning racial slurs made by other police officers towards black citizens was not an objection to employment discrimination, and therefore did not constitute protected activity).

222   *Correa v. Mana Prods.*, 550 F. Supp. 2d 319, 329 (E.D.N.Y. 2008).

223   *Crawford v. Metro. Gov't of Nashville & Davidson Cnty.*, 555 U.S. 271 (2009).

employment discrimination by making informal complaints to management, writing critical letters to customers, or expressing support for co-workers who have filed claims. An employee can also oppose discrimination by refusing to participate in unlawful activity.

The above being said, the form of an employee's opposition must be reasonable for it to be protected. For example, the employee who slaps a co-worker for making discriminatory comments,[224] or who makes a complaint in a manner that is excessively disruptive or insubordinate, has not engaged in protected activity.[225]

Any type of participation in an administrative or legal proceeding under the NYHRL is protected. Participation in a proceeding brought by another employee, such as by agreeing to testify, constitutes protected activity.[226] A person who defends him or herself against a charge of discrimination has been found to have engaged in protected participatory activity.[227] However, mere participation in an internal investigation (unless the employee reports unlawful activity while participating) will not constitute protected activity.[228]

[11.63] What is an "adverse employment action" in the retaliation context?

The standard for finding an "adverse employment action" is significantly lower in the context of a retaliation claim than it is in the context of a discrimination claim. (*See* § 11.24 *supra* for a discussion of this concept in discrimination claims).

In the retaliation context, "an adverse employment action is one which might have dissuaded a reasonable worker from making or supporting a charge of discrimination."[229] For a retaliatory act to constitute an adverse action, it may involve actions not traditionally associated with the employer-employee relationship. Some examples of conduct which courts

---

224 *Cruz v. Coach Stores,* 202 F.3d 560, 566 (2d Cir. 2000).

225 *See Matima v. Celli,* 228 F.3d 68, 79 (2d Cir. 2000).

226 *Jute v. Hamilton Sundstrand Corp.,* 420 F.3d 166, 175 (2d Cir. 2005).

227 *Deravin v. Kerik,* 335 F.3d 195, 204 (2d Cir. 2003).

228 *VanDeWater v. Canandaigua Nat'l Bank,* 70 A.D.3d 1434, 1435, 893 N.Y.S.2d 916 (4th Dep't 2010).

229 *Keceli v. Yonkers Racing Corp.,* 155 A.D.3d 1014, 1016, 66 N.Y.S.3d 280 (2d Dep't 2017) (*citing Burlington N. & Santa Fe Ry. Co. v. White,* 548 U.S. 53, 68 (2006); *Arevalo v. Burg,* 129 A.D.3d 417, 10 N.Y.S.3d 231 (1st Dep't 2015).

have found could constitute an adverse action by an employer for retaliation purposes include filing counterclaims against an employee that could have had a negative impact on his reputation within the industry[230] filing a lawsuit against the employee in order to deter the employee from seeking legal redress;[231] and contesting an employee's application for unemployment insurance benefits.[232] A court even found that a former employee of an indoor cycling facility could have suffered an adverse action when the employer barred the former employee and his attorney from the premises.[233]

However, the mere fact that a complaining employee has "been given the cold shoulder" by co-workers does not constitute an adverse action that could serve as the basis for a retaliation claim. The United States Supreme Court has held that "petty slights, minor annoyances, and simple lack of good manners" are not sufficient to deter a reasonable employee from reporting or supporting a discrimination claim.[234] Thus, being yelled at in front of other co-workers by a supervisor, without further consequences, has been found not to be a materially adverse action sufficient to give rise to a retaliation claim.[235]

[11.64] How does an employee prove the relationship between protected activity and an adverse action?

Employees can establish a causal connection between protected activity and an adverse action by showing "temporal proximity" between the protected activity and the adverse action. To show this, the adverse action

---

230 *Kreinik v. Showbran Photo, Inc.,* No. 02 Civ. 1172, 2003 U.S. Dist. LEXIS 18276 at *23–24 (S.D.N.Y. Oct. 10, 2003).

231 *Mejia v. T.N. 888 Eighth Ave. LLC Co.,* No. 150228/2014, 2018 NY Slip Op. 30737, 2018 N.Y. Misc. LEXIS 1509 at *19 (Sup. Ct., N.Y. Co Apr. 24, 2018).

232 *Electchester Hous. Project, Inc. v. Rosa,* 225 A.D.2d 772, 773, 639 N.Y.S.2d 848 (2d Dep't 1996).

233 *Oram v. SoulCycle LLC,* 979 F. Supp. 2d 498, 511 (S.D.N.Y. 2013).

234 *Burlington N. & Santa Fe Ry. v. White,* 548 U.S. 53, 68 (2006); *see also Vito v. Bausch & Lomb, Inc.,* No. 07-cv-6500, 2010 U.S. Dist. LEXIS 16078 at *36 (W.D.N.Y. Feb. 23, 2010), *aff'd,* 403 Fed. Appx. 593 (2d Cir. 2010); *King v. New York City Health & Hosps. Corp.,* No. 107231/06, 2010 N.Y. Slip Op. 33967(U), 2010 N.Y. Misc. LEXIS 7001 at * 10 (Sup. Ct., Kings Co. Apr. 20, 2010), *aff'd,* 85 A.D.3d 631, 925 N.Y.S.2d 820 (1st Dep't. 2011).

235 *Ragin v. E. Ramapo Cent. Sch. Dist.,* No. 05 Civ. 6496, 2010 U.S. Dist. LEXIS 32576 at *57–58, 2010 WL 1326779 (E.D.N.Y. Mar. 31, 2010), *aff'd,* 417 Fed. Appx. 81 (2d Cir. 2011).

must be "very close" in time after the protected activity; as a general rule, causation will not be found where the protected activity and the alleged retaliation occur more than two months apart.[236]

The above being said, temporal proximity alone is not enough to establish that an employer's non-retaliatory reason for the action is actually a pretext for discrimination.[237] Further, the *absence* of temporal proximity is not fatal to a retaliation claim where there is other evidence supporting causation.[238] An employee can demonstrate that an action was retaliatory by showing direct proof of a retaliatory animus, or by showing that similarly situated co-workers who did not engage in protected activity were treated differently.[239]

Finally, it should be noted that employees who have engaged in protected activity are not shielded from discipline (including transfer, placement on leave or termination) simply because they have engaged in that activity. An employer can take an adverse action against an employee who has engaged in protected activity for a non-retaliatory reason, including poor performance,[240] misconduct by the employee,[241] or a legitimate business reason, such as a reorganization or layoff.[242]

Nevertheless, employers should remember that an inference of retaliation may be found where protected activity is closely followed by an adverse action.

---

236   See *Abram v. New York State Div. of Human Rights,* 71 A.D.3d 1471, 1475, 896 N.Y.S.2d 746 (4th Dep't 2010); *Parris v. New York City Dept. of Educ.,* 111 A.D.3d 528, 529, 975 N.Y.S.2d 42 (1st Dep't 2013) (five months between the protected activity and the adverse action is insufficient to establish a causal connection); *Knox v. Town of Southeast,* No. 11 Civ. 8763, 2014 U.S. Dist. LEXIS 45888 at *40, 2014 WL 1285654 (S.D.N.Y. Mar. 31, 2014) ("[M]any of the decisions in this Circuit . . . . have held that a passage of more than two months between the protected activity and the adverse employment action does not allow for an inference of causation."); *compare with Krebaum v. Capital One, N.A.,* 138 A.D.3d 528, 528–29, 29 N.Y.S.3d 351 (1st Dep't 2016) ("The temporal proximity of plaintiff's complaint and the termination of his employment one month later indirectly shows the requisite causal connection.").

237   *El Sayed v. Hilton Hotels Corp.,* 627 F.3d 931, 933 (2d Cir. 2010).

238   *Harrington v. City of New York,* 157 A.D.3d 582, 586, 70 N.Y.S.3d 177 (1st Dep't 2018).

239   *Baldwin v. Goddard Riverside Cmty. Ctr.,* 53 F. Supp. 3d 655, 669 (S.D.N.Y. 2014), *aff'd,* 615 Fed. Appx. 704 (2d Cir. 2015).

240   See *Sharpe v. Utica Mut. Ins. Co.,* 756 F. Supp. 2d 230, 252 (N.D.N.Y. 2010).

241   See *Richardson v. City of New York,* 285 F. Supp. 2d 303 (E.D.N.Y. 2003).

242   See *Mosley v. City of Rochester,* No. 10-cv-6415, 2012 U.S. Dist. LEXIS 178090 at *15, 2012 WL 6569400 (W.D.N.Y. Dec. 17, 2012), *aff'd,* 574 Fed. Appx. 41 (2d Cir. 2014).

VIII. PROCEDURAL CONSIDERATIONS

[11.65] Does it really matter whether a discrimination claim is brought under federal, state, or local law?

Yes, although by the time a claim gets to court, it is usually presented under all applicable laws—federal, state, and local.

The New York City Human Rights Law has historically provided the broadest protections and remedies to victims of employment discrimination, followed next by those afforded by the New York [State] Human Rights Law. Federal employment discrimination laws, by contrast, have traditionally extended coverage to fewer protected groups and have contained limits on the remedies available.

The NYCHRL and the NYHRL cover multiple categories of people and characteristics that are not protected under federal law. The federal discrimination laws, for instance, do not prohibit discrimination on the basis of "marital," "familial," or "victim of domestic violence" status; arrest or conviction history; and several other categories protected under the NYHRL and the NYCHRL. The NYCHRL also provides protection for credit history, caregiver status, and unemployment status, none of which are covered by the NYHRL. In addition, while successful litigants under the NYCHRL and the NYHRL can also recover unlimited compensatory and punitive damages in appropriate cases, the federal discrimination laws place statutory caps upon the combined value of compensatory and punitive damages that a successful claimant can recover.

Under New York law, it is no longer required that workplace harassment be "severe or pervasive" in order to be actionable (whereas, by contrast, the "severe and pervasive" standard is still applied under federal employment discrimination statutes). Additionally, the NYHRL and the NYCHRL, again unlike federal law, do not permit employers to avoid liability for co-worker harassment through asserting the *Faragher-Ellerth defense*[243] (i.e. a harassment victim's failure to utilize preventive or correctional opportunities afforded by the employer). Finally, the **state** and **city** laws now extend their protections to contractors, subcontractors, vendors, and other non-employees providing services in the workplace.

The most significant difference between the NYHRL and the NYCHRL lies in how the state and city provisions define "reasonable accommoda-

---

243   *Faragher v. City of Boca Raton*, 524 U.S. 775 (1998); *Burlington Indus., Inc., v. Ellerth*, 524 U.S. 742 (1998).

tion." Both laws require employers to provide "reasonable accommodation" for employees' disabilities, religious needs, pregnancy, or domestic violence victim status. However, while the NYHRL (like federal law) requires employers to engage in an "interactive process" with an individual requesting an accommodation, the NYCHRL mandates that employers engage in a "cooperative dialogue" with such an individual. This "cooperative dialogue" process is supposed to be more detailed and formal than the "interactive process" mandated by the NYHRL and federal law. The NYCHRL also provides an express private right of action against employers who fail to fulfill this "cooperative dialogue" mandate, *even if the accommodation was granted*. The NYCHRL's "cooperative dialogue" mandate requires that the employer engage in a written or oral dialogue with the individual who may be entitled to an accommodation; this dialogue should address: (a) the individual's needs; (b) potential alternative accommodations which might address those needs; and (c) any difficulties or constraints on the employer's ability to provide the potential accommodations. Additionally, the NYCHRL's "cooperative dialogue" process requires that the employer, at the end of the dialogue, provide the individual who requested the accommodation with a written determination identifying any accommodation that was granted or denied.

[11.66] Where can an administrative discrimination complaint be filed in New York?

In New York State, a victim of discrimination, harassment, or retaliation can file an administrative complaint with the federal Equal Employment Opportunity Commission (EEOC), *or* with the New York State Division of Human Rights (NYSDHR), *or* with one of the municipal or county fair employment enforcement agencies situated throughout the state, such as the New York City Commission on Human Rights (NYCCHR), provided that complainant lives or works in New York state and/or the particular county or municipality where the fair employment enforcement agency has jurisdiction. As to each agency, a complainant may ask that his or her complaint be "cross-filed" with the federal agency and the state or city agency.

The EEOC, the NYSDHR, and the NYCCHR have entered into "work sharing agreements" that allow these agencies to accept and to "cross-file" with one another complaints that potentially arise under federal, state, and local laws. As is explained below, these agencies typically cooperate with one another but are deferential to the processing of the complaint by the agency with which it was filed initially.

[11.67] How much time does a person have to file an administrative discrimination complaint, or to sue, in New York?

A discrimination charge filed with the EEOC must be filed within 300 days of the alleged discriminatory act.

Under the NYHRL and the NYCHRL, an administrative complaint generally must be filed with NYSDHR or NYCCHR within one year of the discriminatory act; however, a claim based upon gender discrimination can be filed up to three years after the discriminatory act occurred.

Complainants asserting New York State or New York City claims are, however, not required to start with an administrative complaint; claimants may, if they choose, go directly to suit in state court. These actions must be commenced within three years of the discriminatory act.

[11.68] Which agency will take the lead when an administrative complaint is "cross-filed" under federal, state, and local laws?

According to the terms of the agencies' work-sharing agreements, the EEOC is expected to delay processing a discrimination charge for sixty days to permit the NYSDHR or one of the local agencies to exercise jurisdiction over the charge for investigation. However, it is normally the case that the agency in which the discrimination charge or complaint was filed initially assumes the lead in processing the complaint.

If the discrimination charge is filed first with the EEOC, then the EEOC will often refer the charge to its voluntary mediation program before it commences an investigation into the complaint. If mediation is unsuccessful, or if the charge is not referred to mediation, then the EEOC will usually require the employer to provide a written position statement responding to each of the allegations in the discrimination charge. Depending upon its initial assessment of the validity and seriousness of the discrimination allegations, the EEOC may also ask the employer to provide a response to a detailed request for additional information.[244]

The NYSDHR and the NYCCHR take a similar approach to investigations. The employer is asked to provide a written position statement along with supporting information in response to the allegations in the discrimination complaint. The employer's position statement is then sent to the complainant, who is afforded an opportunity to submit a rebuttal statement. Depending upon the agency's assessment of the merits of the complaint following its review of these written submissions, as well as based upon the agency's caseload and local practice, the agency may then schedule an in-person fact-finding conference in connection with the complaint. The fact-finding conference can be conducted with either one or both of the parties to the complaint. The agency often follows the conference by requesting additional information from one or both of the parties before the agency issues a written determination based upon its investigation.[245]

[11.69] What happens when an agency finds "no probable cause"?

The consequences of an agency "no probable cause" determination are quite different as between the EEOC on the one hand and the NYSDHR and NYCCHR on the other.

If the EEOC finds insufficient evidence to support the charging party's allegations or some other deficiency in the discrimination charge, then it will issue a "Notice of Dismissal." The Notice of Dismissal essentially ends the administrative process, but it is always accompanied by the issuance of a "Notice of Rights" (sometimes called a "right-to-sue letter"), advising the charging party that he or she has 90 days to file a complaint in federal district court and pursue a *de novo* (independent) review of his or her discrimination claim(s).[246]

By contrast, complainants who file with NYSDHR or NYCCHR are deemed to have made an "election of remedies" to proceed with the administrative filing rather than to proceed with a lawsuit in court. If the NYSDHR or the NYCCHR finds insufficient evidence to support the discrimination allegations following its administrative investigation, then the agency will issue a "no probable cause" determination that not only ends

---

244 As part of its intake process, the EEOC assesses discrimination charges pursuant to its Priority Charge Handling Procedure and assigns the charge a ranking of "A," "B," or "C." "A" charges are given highest priority; they are charges which the agency believes contain particularly credible claims; involve allegations of class or systemic discrimination; or touch upon issues important to the agency's current enforcement initiatives. "C" charges, on the other hand, involve allegations that appear on their face to be untimely or otherwise unactionable. The majority of charges are assigned a "B" ranking upon intake. "B" charges are viewed by the EEOC as sufficient to warrant an investigation involving at least the agency's request for the employer's position statement. Typically, only "B" charges are referred to the EEOC's volunteer mediation process.

245 9 N.Y.C.R.R. § 465.6.

246 The EEOC will also dismiss a case as a matter of administrative convenience if it feels that it does not have the resources to process the claim expeditiously, or if the claimant requests an administrative dismissal. In both instances, the dismissal is accompanied by a "right-to-sue letter" permitting the complainant to file in federal court within 90 days.

the administrative process but also precludes the complainant from pursuing *de novo* review of the state or local law claim in court. The complainant can still try to challenge the agency's determination as "arbitrary and capricious" or "without a rational basis" through an CPLR Article 78 proceeding, but the courts will grant this relief only in extreme circumstances.

However, there is another way for a complainant who has filed with the NYSDHR or NYCCHR to bring an independent action in court. State law has been interpreted to allow the agencies to grant an "administrative convenience" dismissal at any point before the public hearing on the complaint. If such a dismissal is requested and granted, then the individual's prior "election of remedy" is rendered a nullity, and the complainant can then pursue his or her discrimination claims in court.

[11.70] What happens when an agency finds "probable cause"?

If the EEOC finds "probable cause" to support the discrimination allegations based upon its investigation, then it will schedule a conciliation session. The EEOC typically will expect the employer to agree during the conciliation process not only to provide a remedy for the alleged discrimination, but also to take steps to prevent a recurrence of the circumstances that gave rise to the discrimination charge. If a conciliation agreement is not reached, then the EEOC can either commence its own independent enforcement action against the employer, or issue a "right-to-sue" notice permitting the complainant or complainants to commence a federal court action on their own.

In all but what it regards as the most serious cases of discrimination, the EEOC issues a right to sue notice and leaves court action to the individual complainant.

The NYSDHR and the NYCCHR follow a different process after a "probable cause" determination is issued. Unlike the EEOC, both of these agencies have administrative enforcement processes. Pursuant to these processes, once a "probable cause" determination is issued, a settlement conference is scheduled before an administrative law judge. At the conference, the complainant has the opportunity to be represented by counsel employed by the agency. If the case is not resolved during that settlement conference, then the complaint is scheduled for a public hearing before another administrative law judge, at which the complainant can again be represented by counsel employed by the agency.

Following the public hearing, the presiding administrative law judge will issue recommended findings of fact and conclusions of law. The administrative law judge's recommended decision and order is then subject to review by the agency's commissioner, who will issue the agency's final decision and remedy in the case. This decision is subject to judicial review, by either the complainant or the employer, through an CPLR Article 78 proceeding.

[11.71] Can an individual who has filed an administrative discrimination complaint still pursue a claim in court?

Yes as to federal claims; and often as to state-law claims.

As is explained above, claimants who file claims with the EEOC receive "right-to-sue" notices allowing them to commence an action in federal court within ninety days of their receipt of the notice, whether the EEOC found any merit in their claims or not.

For claimants who file only with the NYSDHR or the NYCCHR, the "election of remedies" doctrine discussed in § 11.69 *supra* applies, but a claimant can sue if he or she requests an "administrative convenience" dismissal instead of waiting for a final agency determination.

When a claimant "cross-files" with both federal and state agencies pursuant to the work-sharing agreements between the EEOC and the NYSDHR and the NYCCHR, the agencies that did not take the lead in investigating the discrimination claims typically will adopt the findings of the agency which did take the lead, as long as those findings have a rational basis and are supported by information compiled during the investigation.

CHAPTER TWELVE

MISCELLANEOUS TOPICS OF INTEREST

James J. Rooney
Erin S. Torcello
Mary E. Aldridge

Edited by R. Daniel Bordoni

CHAPTER OVERVIEW

In this chapter, we consider a variety of topics which are: (a) pervasive issues in employment law (many of which are also discussed, at least to some extent, in other chapters of this book); (b) difficult to classify; or (c) can be characterized as labor law "myths" which need to be debunked.

[12.1] What is the difference between an employee and an independent contractor?[1]

An individual performing work for hire in New York state is typically classified either as an employee or an independent contractor. Throughout this book, the reader will find references to the different application of New York law to employees on the one hand, and independent contractors on the other. Almost none of the legal protections that are afforded to employees are extended to independent contractors, and the latter are protected only to the extent of the agreements by which their services are engaged.

It is crucial for employers to properly classify individuals working for them, because significant liability can arise where employees are misclassified as independent contractors.

Some of the most substantial risks faced by employers arise when payments to individuals who should have been classified as employees are improperly treated as payments to independent contractors: this results in liability for unpaid federal, state and local income tax withholdings and liability for Social Security and Medicare contributions, plus associated penalties, fines and interest. Other significant financial risks include unpaid unemployment insurance premiums, unpaid workers' compensation premiums, and unpaid overtime compensation and work-related benefits. These liabilities can be potentially devastating for employers. Another substantial risk is a claim of benefit entitlement by or on behalf of common law employees misclassified as independent contractors. Claims have been successfully brought by persons who should properly have been classified as employees for pension and profit-sharing benefits, medical benefits, and even stock options.

There is no single definition of the term "independent contractor" under New York law. To make this determination, the courts and governmental agencies apply a variety of factor-based tests. As a general rule, however, true independent contractors are generally free from supervision, direction and control in the performance of their duties.

---

1   The introductory text in this section is identical to § 2.20 of this book in Chapter 2, "Terms of the Employment Relationship." Sub-sections §§ 12.1.1–12.1.5 elaborate on that discussion.

Courts and administrative agencies often rely on the so-called "*Reid* factors"[2] to determine whether an individual is properly designated as an independent contractor. Those factors are as follows:

- The skill required to perform the work in question: an independent contractor (who might, for example, be an attorney, an electrician, or an accountant) will often have skills that the rest of the employer's workforce does not.

- Whether or not the hired party supplies his or her own tools and equipment: an independent contractor will generally supply his or her own tools and equipment.

- The location of the work: an independent contractor will generally have his or her own separate business location.

- The duration of the relationship between the parties: an independent contractor is usually engaged for a specific project and does not perform services for the employer every day.

- Whether the hiring party has the right to assign additional projects to the hired party: an independent contractor is free to turn down additional assignments.

- The extent of the hired party's discretion over when and how long to work: an independent contractor generally decides when, where, and how he or she will get the engagement done.

- The method of payment: an independent contractor generally bills for his or her work and is paid a gross amount without withholding.

- The responsibility for hiring and paying assistants: an independent contractor is usually responsible for hiring and paying his or her own staff.

- Whether the work is part of the regular business of the hiring party: an independent contractor generally has his or her own business and performs functions which the employer does not perform with its own forces.

- Whether the hiring party is in business.

---

2   *Community for Creative Non-Violence v. Reid*, 490 U.S. 730 (1989).

- Whether the hiring party provides benefits to the hired party.

- How the payments to the hired party are treated for tax purposes.

While no one factor is determinative, the overall degree of control that the hiring party exercises over the hired party is the determining criterion: the more control that is exercised over the hired party, the more likely a court or administrative agency is to find that there is an employer-employee relationship.

While independent contractors do not enjoy many of the legal protections afforded to employees, they are afforded protections under the New York City Human Rights Law[3] and are protected from sexual harassment under the N.Y. Executive Law §§ 292(5) and 296-d; *see also* Chapter 11 of this book, "Discrimination, Harassment and Retaliation," at §§ 11.3.1 and 11.31.

[12.1.1] *Workers' Compensation*[4]

Whether an individual is covered under the Workers' Compensation Law is a factual determination by the Workers' Compensation Board. In making this determination the Workers' Compensation Board will examine the following factors:[5]

- Who has the right to control the work? The degree of direction and control that a business exercises over an individual performing work for it is an essential issue in determining whether an employer-employee relationship exists. The greater the degree of control over the manner in which the work is to be performed, the more it is shown that an employer-employee relationship exists. By contrast, the more the individual controls the time and manner in which the work is to be done, the more he or she has the characteristics of an independent contractor. Additionally, an independent contractor generally works under his own operating permit, contract, or authority.

- Is the individual in the same line of work as the employer? An employee normally does work of the same nature as the primary

---

3   N.Y.C. Admin. Code., tit. 8.

4   *See also* Chapter 5 of this book at § 5.4.

5   *See* N.Y. State Workers' Compensation Board, *Workers Compensation*, http://www.wcb.ny.gov/content/main/Workers/Coverage_wc/worker_empDefinition.jsp.

work performed by the business. If the work done by an individual is different than the primary work of the business, this may indicate that the individual is an independent contractor.

- How is the individual paid for his or her services? A business which pays someone wages on a regular basis (hourly, daily, weekly, or monthly), withholds taxes, and/or provides other employee benefits shows the characteristics of an employer-employee relationship. By contrast, if a business pays an individual on a per-task basis, the individual may be an independent contractor.[6]

- Who furnishes equipment and materials for the work? Independent contractors generally furnish their own tools and materials. If these are provided by the business paying for the work, that is an indication that the individual is an employee.

- Who controls the manner in which the work will be done? An employer may tell an employee how, when, and by what means work is to be done, and may fire the employee for not following those instructions. While an independent contractor's services may be terminated if they do not meet contractual requirements, an independent contractor retains a degree of control over the time when the work is to be accomplished and is not subject to discharge by the hiring entity because of the method he or she chooses to use in performing the work.

Employers who misclassify their employees as independent contractors and fail to obtain workers' compensation coverage are subject both to criminal and civil penalties under Workers' Compensation Law § 52.

If an employer fails to secure coverage for five or fewer employees in a 12-month period, the employer may be convicted of a misdemeanor and fined between $1,000 and $5,000. If an employer fails to secure coverage for more than five employees in a 12-month period, the employer can be convicted of a class E felony and fined between $5,000 and $50,000. If the employer has previously been convicted of a failure to secure coverage within the past five years and does so again, that employer can be convicted of a class D felony and fined between $10,000 and $50,000.

---

6   Whether the individual is paid using a Form W-2 or a Form 1099 for tax reporting purposes is not, in and of itself, determinative of the individual's status.

If the employer is a corporation, the corporation's president, secretary, and treasurer may be held liable as individuals. In addition to criminal penalties outlined above, significant civil penalties can also be imposed on the employers for failure to secure workers' compensation coverage.

Finally, an employer that fails to secure workers' compensation insurance coverage for its employees is also subject to workers' compensation claims and civil tort actions by injured employees.

[12.1.2] *Unemployment Insurance*[7]

The Unemployment Insurance Law defines "employment" as "(a) any service under any contract of employment for hire, express or implied, written, or oral and (b) any service by a person for an employer."[8] The New York State Department of Labor addresses the differences between employees and independent contractors as follows:[9]

> Even if your employer hired you to work as an independent contractor, the law may still consider you an employee. This means you may qualify for unemployment insurance (UI) benefits.
>
> We consider whether there is an employer-employee relationship based on several things. These include how much supervision, direction and control your employer has over your work.
>
> **Who is an Employee?**
>
> The way you are paid is a sign of worker status. Employees usually earn:
>
> - A salary
>
> - An hourly rate of pay or
>
> - A draw against future commissions (with no need to repay unearned commissions)

---

7   *See also* Chapter 7 of this book at § 7.3.

8   Labor Law § 511.

9   https://www.labor.ny.gov/ui/claimantinfo/ui%20and%20independent%20contractors.shtm.

Employees also may get certain *fringe benefits*. For example: an allowance or repayment for business or travel expenses.

The *nature of the work done* also helps decide if a worker is an employee or an independent contractor.

Unskilled or casual workers are often employees because they work under supervision. However, even professionals such as doctors and lawyers (with much freedom to do their work) may be employees if they are subject to significant control.

Workers may be employees if the employer *controls key parts* of the work done, other than results and means.

For example, a referral agency usually does not directly supervise the people it refers for jobs. But, it could be their employer, if it controls:

- Client contact

- Wages

- Billing and collection from clients

Who is an Independent Contractor?

Independent contractors perform their duties free from:

- Supervision

- Direction

- Control

They are in business for themselves, as they *offer their services* to the public.

Signs of independent contractor status include a person who:

- Has an established business

- Advertises in the electronic and/or print media

- Buys an ad in the *Yellow Pages*

- Uses business cards, stationery and invoices

- Carries insurance

- Keeps a place of business and invests in facilities, equipment and supplies

- Pays their own expenses

- Assumes risk for profit or loss

- Sets their own schedule

- Sets or negotiates their own pay rate

- Offers services to other businesses (competitive or non-competitive)

- Is free to refuse work offers

- May choose to hire help

If an employer-employee relationship exists, it does not matter what the hiring party calls it.

For example, if your employer gives you a 1099 form rather than a W-2 form, you may still be an employee. You may be an employee under the law, even if:

- *Your employer makes you sign a statement that you are an independent contractor*

- *You waive any rights as an employee*

- *Your employer makes you obtain a DBA to work for them.*[10]

An employer that has misclassified employees as independent contractors and has failed to report earnings and pay contributions due on the earn-

---

10   Emphasis in original.

ings of employees may incur additional assessments and interest.[11] An employer may be assessed interest at the rate of 1% of the amount of unpaid contributions for each month the employer is in default. Employers that *willfully* fail to pay contributions for unemployment benefits may be found guilty of a misdemeanor and fined up to $500 and imprisoned for up to one year.[12]

If the employer is a corporation, the corporation's president, secretary, treasurer, or officers exercising corresponding functions may each be guilty of a misdemeanor.[13]

[12.1.3] *Construction and trucking industries*

Under the New York State Construction Industry Fair Play Act,[14] a construction worker is presumed to be an employee, and not an independent contractor, *unless* the worker is: (1) a separate business entity as defined by the law, *or* (2) the worker is:

- free from control and direction in performing the job, both under contract and in fact;

- performing services outside of the usual course of business for the company; and

- engaged in an independently established trade, occupation, or business that is similar to the service being performed on the construction project.[15]

Similarly, the Commercial Goods Transportation Industry Fair Play Act[16] is aimed at preventing the "misclassification" of drivers of commercial vehicles who transport goods as independent contractors as opposed to treating these individuals as employees. The statute presumes an employment relationship for certain drivers who provide "commercial goods transportation services for a commercial goods transportation contractor."

---

11   *Unemployment Insurance Division, Independent Contractors,* N.Y. Dep't of Labor (Aug. 2019), https://labor.ny.gov/formsdocs/ui/ia318.14.pdf. *See also* Chapter 5 of this book at § 5.11.

12   Labor Law §§ 630, 633.

13   Labor Law § 631.

14   Labor Law §§ 861–861-g.

15   Labor Law § 861-c.

16   Labor Law §§ 862–862-e.

A "commercial goods transportation contractor" is defined as any sole proprietor, partnership, firm, corporation, limited liability company, association, or other legal entity that compensates a driver who possesses a state driver's license and transports goods in New York using a commercial motor vehicle.

This presumption that a driver is an employee may only be rebutted if the driver's services are reported on a federal income tax form 1099 *and* the driver meets at least one of the following multi-factor tests:

- First, the business may demonstrate that the driver is a *bona fide* independent contractor under the law's so-called "A-B-C test." Under this test, a driver must be:

- free from control and direction in performing the job, both under contract and in fact;

- performing services outside of the usual course of business for the employer; and

- engaged in an independently-established trade, occupation, profession, or business that is similar to the service at issue. To be considered an independent contractor, drivers must also be transporting goods under their own bill of lading and under their own Department of Transportation Number.

- Alternatively, a driver can show that he or she constitutes a "separate business entity."[17]

The definition of "separate business entity" under both the Construction Industry Fair Play Act and the Commercial Goods Transportation Industry Fair Play Act requires that in order to be considered an independent contractor as opposed to being an employee, the individual:

- is performing the service free from the contracting party's direction or control over the means and manner of providing the service subject only to the right of the contractor to specify the desired result;

- does not automatically terminate the existence of the entity when his or her work with the contractor ends;

---

17   Labor Law § 862-b.

- has a substantial investment of capital in the entity beyond ordinary tools and equipment and a personal vehicle;

- owns the capital goods, gains the profits, and bears the losses of the entity;

- makes his or her services available to the general public or business community on a regular basis;

- includes the services provided on a federal income tax schedule as an independent business;

- performs the services under the separate business entity's name;

- obtains and pays for any required licenses or permits in the separate business entity's name;

- furnishes the tools and equipment necessary to provide the service;

- hires its own employees without contractor approval, pays the employees without reimbursement from the contractor, and reports the employees' income to the Internal Revenue Service;

- has the right to perform similar services for others on whatever basis and whenever it chooses; and

- is not held out as being an employee of the contractor.[18]

Employers are subject to penalties under both the New York State Construction Industry Fair Play Act and Commercial Goods Transportation Industry Fair Play Act which are in addition to other civil and criminal penalties for misclassification of employees.

Construction Industry. An employer that willfully violates the New York State Construction Industry Fair Play Act by failing to classify its employees properly is subject to civil penalties of up to a $2,500 fine per misclassified employee for a first violation and up to $5,000 for a second violation within a five-year period. In addition, employers may also be subject to criminal prosecution for a misdemeanor and imprisonment for up to 30 days or a fine up to $25,000 for a first offense, and imprisonment for up to 60 days or a fine up to $50,000 for a subsequent offense. Further, an employer that is convicted under the criminal provision is ineligible for

---

18   Labor Law §§ 861-c(2), 862-b(2).

any public works contracts for up to five years. An employer that is a corporation, or an officer or shareholder who owns or controls 10% or more of the corporation and who knowingly allows a violation of the law, may also be subject to civil and/or criminal liability.[19]

Trucking industry. Violations of the Commercial Goods Transportation Industry Fair Play Act which are deemed to be "willful" are punishable by substantial civil and criminal penalties: a willful violation is a violation where the employer "knew or should have known that his or her conduct was prohibited." Civil remedies include a penalty of $2,500 per misclassified worker for a first violation, and a penalty of $5,000 per misclassified worker for subsequent violations. Criminal penalties include up to 30 days imprisonment or a fine not to exceed $25,000 for the first violation and up to 60 days imprisonment or a fine not to exceed $50,000 for subsequent violations.[20]

[12.1.4] *The "gig economy"*[21]

As an increasing number of American workers participate, whether by choice or by necessity, in the so-called "gig economy," the distinction between employees and independent contractors (or "contract workers") is becoming a topic of heightened scrutiny by regulators in states across the country. Many state regulators and attorneys general are bringing enforcement actions against businesses on the theory that their "gig" workers should properly be classified as employees.

The COVID-19 pandemic, which has led to massive nationwide lockdowns and layoffs as this book is being completed, is likely to result in even more attention to this area. It should be anticipated that the law will rapidly evolve—although not necessarily on a consistent basis from state to state—over the coming months and years.

[12.1.5] *Coordination among agencies*

The New York State Department of Labor has joined an initiative to curb the misclassification of employees as independent contractors by agreeing

---

19   Labor Law § 861-e.

20   Labor Law § 862-d.

21   The "gig economy" has come to include a wide range of services in many industries including transportation, financial services, and technology. In some cases, the individuals participating in it are independent contractors by any traditional standard; but in others they show many, if not almost all, of the traditional characteristics of employees.

to share information and to coordinate enforcement efforts with the United States Department of Labor.[22] This agreement increases the likelihood that an employer under investigation by a federal or state agency for an alleged misclassification will also find the subject employee(s)' classification analyzed and examined by another agency, leading to potential penalties under a variety of state and federal laws.

New York State has also established a Joint Enforcement Task Force on Worker Exploitation and Employee Misclassification of Workers consisting of the New York State Workers' Compensation Board, the New York State Workers' Compensation Fraud Inspector General, the New York State Department of Taxation and Finance, the New York State Attorney General's Office, and the Comptroller of the City of New York.[23] These departments have agreed to share information among themselves about employers suspected of improperly classifying employees as independent contractors, increase the awareness of the harms inflicted by improper worker misclassifications, create hotlines for the public, and refer cases to prosecuting authorities as appropriate.

[12.2]   What is the difference between an employee and an intern?

Interns are exempt from minimum wage requirements under both federal and New York State, provided that the factors discussed below are met. They are, however, protected by state and local anti-discrimination laws; *see* Executive Law § 296, 296-c and Chapter 11 of this book, "Discrimination, Harassment and Retaliation," at § 11.3.2.

In addition to protecting interns from discrimination, harassment, and retaliation, the New York City Human Rights Law also requires employers to provide a reasonable accommodation to an unpaid intern if the accommodation is necessary to allow the intern to satisfy the essential requirements of the job, provided that the disability is known, or should have been known, by the employer.

---

22   Partnership Agreement Between the U.S. Department of Labor, Wage and Hour Division and Labor Bureau of New York State Office of Attorney General (Nov. 18, 2013), http://www.dol.gov/whd/workers/MOU/ny.pdf.

23   *See* New York State, *Joint Task Force on Worker Exploitation and Employee Misclassification*, https://www.ny.gov/end-worker-exploitation/task-force-combat-worker-exploitation and N.Y. Department of Labor, *Employer Misclassification of Workers*, https://www.labor.ny.gov/ui/employerinfo/employer-misclassification-of-workers.shtm.

Under federal law, for exemption from minimum wage requirements, courts consider the following factors, which are commonly referred to as the "primary beneficiary" test:

- The extent to which the intern and the employer clearly understand that there is no expectation of compensation. A promise of compensation, express or implied, suggests that the intern is an employee.

- The extent to which the internship provides training that would be similar to that which would be given in an educational environment, including the clinical and other hands-on training provided by educational institutions.

- The extent to which the internship is tied to the intern's formal education program by integrated coursework or the receipt of academic credit.

- The extent to which the internship accommodates the intern's academic commitments by corresponding to the academic calendar.

- The extent to which the internship's duration is limited to the period in which the internship provides the intern with beneficial learning.

- The extent to which the intern's work complements, rather than displaces, the work of paid employees while providing significant educational benefits to the intern.

- The extent to which the intern and the employer understand that the internship is conducted without entitlement to a paid job at the conclusion of the internship.[24]

The test for minimum wage exemption under New York law is quite similar, and considers the following as demonstrating a true internship:

- The intern's training is similar to training provided in an educational program.

- The training is for the benefit of the intern.

---

24   U.S. Department of Labor (Wage and Hour Division), *Fact Sheet #71: Internship Programs Under the FLSA* (Jan. 2018), https://www.dol.gov/sites/dolgov/files/WHD/legacy/files/whdfs71.pdf.

- The intern does not displace regular employees and works under close supervision.

- The activities of the intern do not provide an immediate advantage to the employer and may even sometimes impede operations.

- The intern is not necessarily entitled to a job at the conclusion of the training period and is free to take jobs elsewhere in the same field.

- The intern is informed in writing that he or she will not receive any wages and is not considered an employee for minimum wage purposes.

- Any clinical training is performed under the supervision and direction of people who are knowledgeable and experienced in the activity.

- The intern does not receive employee benefits.

- The training is general and qualifies trainees or students to work in any similar business (in other words, the training is not designed specifically for a job with the employer that offers the internship).

- The screening process for the internship program is not the same as employment and does not appear to be for that purpose. The screening only uses criteria relevant for admission to an independent educational program.

- Any advertisements, postings, or solicitations for the program clearly discuss education or training, rather than employment, although employers may indicate that qualified graduates may be considered for employment.[25]

[12.3] Can an employee insist upon bringing an attorney (or other representative) to a disciplinary meeting?

Generally not. Employers have many important reasons to meet with employees, including planning, giving directions, discussing how to address workplace issues, and giving performance feedback. Employees

---

25   N.Y.S. Labor Standards, *Wage Requirements for Interns in For-Profit Businesses Fact Sheet (P725)* (July 2016), https://labor.ny.gov/formsdocs/factsheets/pdfs/p725.pdf.

have no right to insist on bringing a representative to ordinary workplace interactions.[26]

In unionized workplaces, a different rule applies when it can reasonably be anticipated that the matters to be discussed at a meeting may lead to a disciplinary consequence for the employee. In these situations, the employee has the right to bring a union representative (but *not* the employee's personal attorney) to the meeting—and, of course, a collective bargaining agreement may include other situations as to which an employer and a union have agreed that employees may have union representation at a meeting.

The United States Supreme Court has held that a union member is entitled to union representation at an investigatory interview that the employee reasonably believes could lead to discipline; and this entitlement is generally referred to as *"Weingarten* rights."[27] Under the *Weingarten* rule, if an employee wishes to have a union representative present during the interview, he or she must make a *clear request* for representation before or during the interview. When an employee requests representation, the employer must choose from the following three options:

- To delay the interview by stopping questioning until a union representative arrives and has a chance to privately consult with the employee; or

- To end and reschedule the interview; or

- To give the employee the choice to either proceed without representation, or to end and reschedule the interview.

If the employer refuses to grant the request for union representation and continues to ask questions, the employee has a right to refuse to answer, and the employer has committed an unfair labor practice under the National Labor Relations Act, which can lead to proceedings before the National Labor Relations Board.

---

26   However, there may be times when an employer may decide to permit an attorney to accompany an employee at a meeting. Whether doing so is in the employer's interest depends on all of the surrounding circumstances. Among these considerations is whether the employer might later be viewed—in an arbitration or other forum—as having taken advantage of the employee or otherwise treated the employee unfairly by denying him or her a representative.

27   *NLRB v. J. Weingarten, Inc.*, 420 U.S. 251 (1975).

The National Labor Relations Board has periodically attempted to extend *Weingarten* rights to *non*-unionized employees; but as of this writing is not attempting to do so.

[12.4] Does an employee have the right to review his or her personnel file?[28]

Some states have laws granting employees access to their personnel records. However, New York does not have such a law. New York also does not have any law that regulates an employee's access to employment references. Accordingly, there is no general obligation in New York to give employees access to their personnel files.

However, a New York employer may create such access rights through an employee handbook, through a personnel policy, or by agreement with a union.

The above does *not* mean that employers should not maintain and retain personnel files, for a number of reasons, including the following:

- Work eligibility records must be maintained pursuant to federal law.

- If it is shown that a problem employee has falsified information in an employment application or other records, that falsified information can be an independent reason to discharge the employee.

- It is often helpful to retain references submitted with job applications. For example, if an employer used a negative reference as a basis for not hiring an individual, that reference could be relevant to a subsequent discrimination charge or lawsuit.

- If an employee has been disciplined or discharged for workplace misconduct or non-performance and later challenges the adverse job action as improper, the employer will want a record both of the events leading to the decision and of any prior workplace problems.

In addition, employment applications should be maintained for at least one, and preferably three years. *See* Chapter 1 of this book, "The Hiring Process," at § 1.18.

---

28 *See also* Chapter 8 of this book at § 8.20.

It should also be noted that there are ways in which employees may be able to access their personnel files even if the employer has not chosen to permit such access. These include the following:

- An employee who files a charge of discrimination with a state or federal agency (such as EEOC, NYSDHR or NYCCHR) can seek access to the personnel file information, which is almost invariably requested from the employer by the agency.

- Under the federal Occupational Safety and Health Act, an employee is permitted to access the log and summary of occupational injuries and illness at his or her work site. An employee is also permitted to access exposure records that could shed light on the nature and amount of toxic substances to which the employee may have been exposed on the job. OSHA also grants employees the right to access their own medical records. The employer may, however, limit access by deleting parts of the medical records that contain the identities of individuals who provided confidential information about the employee's health.

- The New York Labor Law grants present and former employees the right, upon written request, to information relating to toxic substances to which they may have been exposed. An employee may not be disciplined, discharged, or otherwise discriminated against for exercising the right to access information regarding toxic substances.

[12.5]   What obligations do employers have to protect employees' Social Security numbers?

Employers are required to request employees' Social Security numbers for income tax and FICA withholding purposes, and may also request an employee's Social Security number to administer a claim, benefit, or procedure relating to the individual's employment, retirement, workplace injury, or termination.

Otherwise, however, an employer cannot require employees to disclose their Social Security numbers.[29]

---

29   *See generally*, Gen. Bus. Law § 399-ddd.

As to Social Security numbers received for proper purposes, employers must comply with a set of restrictions on further dissemination of the information. An employer may *not*:

- Post or publicly display the employee's Social Security number;

- Print the employee's Social Security number on an employee badge;

- Disseminate the employee's Social Security number or other personal information such as home addresses or telephone numbers; or

- Use Social Security numbers as ID numbers for occupational licensing.[30]

[12.6] Is an employer obligated to pay employees for any unused vacation, personal leave, or sick leave at the end of employment?

This topic is addressed in Chapter 4 of this book, "Employee Time Off," at §§ 4.6–4.10.

[12.7] Are employees entitled to severance pay if their employment is discontinued?

No. Many people believe that there is some sort of automatic entitlement to severance pay (usually believed to be two weeks' pay) when an employer decides to discharge an employee. This is a labor law myth. Neither federal nor New York law requires an employer to provide severance pay at termination of employment.

However, if an employer agrees to provide severance pay by the terms of an employment contract, collective bargaining agreement, or employer-sponsored severance plan or policy, the employer is required to comply with those terms. Employers should also keep in mind that an oral promise to provide this type of benefit may create an implied contract that binds the employer.

---

30   Labor Law § 203-d.

[12.8] Do employees have the right to leave the workplace during meal breaks or other break periods?

New York law does not require employers to let employees leave work premises for meal periods. Instead, employers are merely required to ensure that employees are completely free of work-related duties during their meal breaks. An employee is not considered completely relieved from duties if he or she is required to perform *any* work responsibilities, whether active or inactive, during that period. Employees may choose to remain at their desks or workstations during meal breaks, but they must not perform any work while doing so. Generally, employees who are required to remain at their desks or workstations during meal periods are not considered to be completely relieved of their duties.[31]

Required meal breaks are discussed in Chapter 4 of this book, "Employee Time Off," at §§ 4.1–4.5.

[12.9] Must employees be provided with a space to smoke?

No. In 2003, New York State passed the Clean Indoor Air Act, which prohibits smoking in virtually all indoor areas, including workplaces. Although Labor Law § 201-d protects employees right to use lawful consumable products (such as cigarettes and alcohol) on their own time, employers do not have an obligation to designate a space, whether outdoors or indoors, for smoking.

If, however, an employer chooses to create a smoking area, it should make sure that the designated area complies with the Clean Indoor Air Act and with any local laws restricting smoking in public.

As noted above, however, an employer may not penalize an employee for engaging in lawful off-duty and off-premises activities, including but not limited to smoking and consuming alcohol.[32]

[12.10] Are undocumented workers (illegal aliens) entitled to job protection?

Even though an employer is legally prohibited from employing an undocumented worker, otherwise-illegal employees who are hired are entitled certain (albeit limited) labor law protections.

---

31   N.Y. Department of Labor, *Meal and Rest Periods Frequently Asked Questions*, https://www.labor.ny.gov/legal/counsel/pdf/meal-and-rest-periods-frequently-asked-questions.pdf.

32   *See* Chapter 8 of this book, "Employer and Employee Rights and Obligations," at §§ 8.22–8.27.

The New York Court of Appeals has ruled that an unauthorized alien may recover lost wages where he or she was injured in the workplace in violation of Labor Law §§ 240 and 241.[33]

Similarly, a plaintiff's status as an unauthorized alien does not preclude him or her from recovering wages under the New York State's Minimum Wage Act. As one court observed, the New York statute does not define "employee" to exclude aliens, nor does it indicate a legislative intent that it was intended to protect American workers only.[34]

Unauthorized aliens are generally able to pursue actions for unlawful discrimination under state and federal law. While they are not protected against employment decisions based upon their unlawful immigration status,[35] the EEOC and most courts that have addressed this issue have held that a plaintiff's status as an undocumented worker does not bar him or her from proceeding with a claim for discrimination based on any of the protected categories identified in Title VII of the Civil Rights Act of 1964.[36]

[12.11] Is an employer allowed to use photos of its employees in marketing materials without their consent?

No. *See* Chapter 8 of this book, "Employer and Employee Rights and Obligations," at § 8.35.

[12.12] Can an employer monitor employees' email and Internet use without their knowledge or consent?

Generally, yes. *See* Chapter 8 of this book, "Employer and Employee Rights and Obligations," at §§ 8.31–8.32.

---

33   *Balbuena v. IDR Realty LLC*, 6 N.Y.3d 338, 812 N.Y.S.2d 416 (2005). The Court went on, however, to opine that the employee's status as an illegal immigrant could be taken into account by a jury in determining front pay awards.

34   *Nizamuddowlah v. Bengal Cabaret, Inc.*, 69 A.D.2d 875, 876, 415 N.Y.S.2d 685 (2d Dep't 1979) (a national of Bangladesh was covered by the Minimum Wage Act even though he entered the United States on a tourist visa and subsequently worked without a "green card" for the employer).

35   *Espinoza v. Farah Mfg. Co.*, 414 U.S. 86 (1973).

36   2 U.S.C. § 1311.

[12.13] Can an employer monitor employees' telephone calls without their knowledge or consent?

Only if at least one of the people actually participating in the call has consented. Otherwise, this would constitute the crime of "eavesdropping," which is a Class E felony under N.Y. Penal Law § 250.05.[37]

[12.14] Can an employer require the use of a "biometric" time clock?

Not if the device utilizes an employee's fingerprints, but otherwise, yes.

New York Labor Law § 201-a provides that "Except as otherwise provided by law, no person, as a condition of securing employment or of continuing employment, shall be required to be fingerprinted." Accordingly, a time clock which interprets biometric information from an individual's fingerprints has been interpreted to violate this section the New York Labor Law.[38] However, the New York State Department of Labor has further opined that a device that merely measures the geometry of the hand is legal so long as it does not scan the surface details of the hand and/or fingers similar to the scanning of a fingerprint.[39]

Moreover, while employers may not *require* employees to use a fingerprint-based biometric time keeping system, it may do so long as its use is voluntary on the part of employees. This means, however, that an employer may not take an adverse employment action against an employee who does not wish to use a fingerprint-based system, nor may the employer coerce employees to "voluntarily" use such a system.[40]

[12.15] Once an employment contract has expired, does the employee become "at will"?

Not necessarily. Under New York common law, where an employer and employee have entered into an employment contract containing a definite

---

37   The statute defines eavesdropping as "the intentional overhearing or recording of a conversation or discussion without the consent of at least one party thereto, by a person not present thereat, by means of any instrument, device or equipment."

38   *See* N.Y. State D.O.L. Op. Ltr. No. RO-10-0024 (Apr. 22, 2010). The New York State Department of Labor has opined that the use of such a time clock is unlawful even if the device does not store employees' fingerprint data, since § 201-a prohibits the fingerprinting of employees, not the storage of the fingerprint data. *Id.*

39   *Id.*

40   *Id.*

term, and the parties continue to perform under that contract for a period beyond the expiration, the agreement may be deemed to have been renewed for an additional period of time, which will depend on the duration of the expired agreement.

For contracts with a duration of less than a year, the general rule is that there is no presumption that the parties agreed to a renewal of the contract in the event of a hold over. "Where a contract of hiring or employment is for a less term than a year, there is no presumption that the parties agreed to its renewal for the same period by reason of the continuance of the employment or holding over for a short time after the term ended."[41]

The rule is different, however, for employment contracts with a duration of one year or more. In those situations, New York courts have held that "where one enters the employment of another for a fixed period at a stated annual salary, and the employment continues beyond that period, the presumption is continuance of the relationship for another year at the same salary."[42] This presumption is rebuttable if there is evidence that the parties entered into a new agreement with new terms, or there is evidence that the parties did not intend for the contract to automatically renew. "[T]he common-law rule cannot be used to imply there was mutual and silent assent to automatic contract renewal when an agreement imposes an express obligation on the parties to enter into a new contract to extend the term of employment."[43]

If a contract is deemed to have been renewed under the common law rule above, it is deemed renewed on the same terms and conditions as the original one, including the same rate of pay, as well as all the "provisions and restrictions forming essential parts of the original contract, even though collateral to the employment itself."[44] However, the renewal (unless confirmed in a writing) is considered to be *for one-year terms only*, because the New York "Statute of Frauds" does not allow enforcement of oral agreements which cannot be fully performed within one year.[45]

---

41   *Moskowitz v. Mawhinney*, 137 N.Y.S. 903 (1st Dep't 1912).

42   *Shenn v. Fair-Tex Mills, Inc.*, 26 A.D.2d 282, 283, 273 N.Y.S.2d 876 (1st Dep't 1966).

43   *Goldman v. White Plains Ctr.*, 11 N.Y.3d 173, 178, 867 N.Y.S.2d 27 (2008).

44   *Borne Chemical Co. v. Dictrow*, 85 A.D.2d 646, 648, 445 N.Y.S.2d 406 (2d Dep't 1981).

45   *Id.; see* Gen. Oblig. Law § 5-701.

[12.16] What is a "day" for purposes of computing deadlines?

This question is significant for employers (and, for that matter, for any party which has to interact with courts or regulatory authorities) because when an act must be taken within a specified number of days, a failure to act in time may result in serious consequences. For example, it may happen that an employer is given a specified number of days to appeal an adverse determination, or to submit information or a response to a regulatory agency, and the failure to act on time may result in a default or other loss of opportunity.

The art of counting days is set out in the New York General Construction Law[46] at §§ 19–20 and 25-a. The following principles apply:

- When counting days, the first day is always the first day *after* the triggering event. In other words, if a party has, for example, "ten days from the date of this letter to submit your response," then the date of the letter is "Day Zero," and the following day is "Day One."

- "Day" means "calendar day," not "working day" (unless otherwise defined by agreement in a contract), except as noted below.

- If the period of time to act is two days or less, then any Saturday, Sunday or public holiday which comes within two days after Day Zero does not count as a "day." As an example, if a party had two days to act after a triggering event on the Friday before Memorial Day weekend, then the first day of the period would be the Tuesday immediately following the Monday on which Memorial Day falls.

- For periods of time longer than two days, Saturdays, Sundays and public holidays *are* counted as "days"; *however*, if the final day to act falls on a Saturday, a Sunday or a public holiday, then the period is extended to the next business day.

Please note: The foregoing is generally true for the computation of periods of time in both state and federal litigation, but any party contemplating litigation, or which is already a party to litigation, should have periods of time computed by an attorney.

---

46   The word "construction" in the title "General Construction Law" has nothing to do with the construction of buildings; rather, it refers wo how statutes are to be "construed" (interpreted).

CASES

STATUTES, RULES & REGULATIONS

FEDERAL

Code of Federal Regulations (C.F.R.)

Internal Revenue Code (I.R.C.)

United States Code (U.S.C.)

NEW YORK

Arts and Cultural Affairs Law

General Business Law

General Construction Law

General Municipal Law

General Obligations Law

N.Y. Comp. Codes R. & Regs. (N.Y.C.R.R.)

N.Y.C. Human Rights Law

ABOUT THE EDITORS

LOUIS P. DiLORENZO, ESQ.

Louis P. DiLorenzo has practiced labor and employment law with Bond, Schoeneck & King, PLLC since 1976. He is the Managing Member of Bond's New York City office (which he established for the firm in 2004) and is Chair of the firm's Labor and Employment, Employee Benefits and Immigration Group. He also served as the General Counsel and Secretary to Agway, Inc., a Fortune 500 company, from 2002-04. In addition to his extensive experience before numerous Federal (EEOC, OFCCP, NLRB, DOL, etc.), State (NYS Division of Human Rights, NYS Department of Labor, etc.) and local (NYC Commission on Human Rights) agencies, Mr. DiLorenzo is an experienced litigator, having tried multiple jury cases to verdict in state and federal courts.

Mr. DiLorenzo is a former Chair of both the New York State Young Lawyer's Section and the Labor and Employment Law Section (and still serves on its Executive Committee), and is a former Editor of the New York State Bar Journal. He currently serves as co-chair of the Employment and Labor Relations Committee of the New York State Bar Association's Commercial and Federal Litigation Section and recently was appointed to the Bar Association's Task Force on Covid-19 Immunity and Liability. Mr. DiLorenzo is a prolific speaker and writer, appearing regularly on labor and employment law panels and as a conference keynote speaker, and his writings have appeared in the Syracuse Law Review, Fordham Law Review, Journal of College and University Law, New York State Bar Association Bar Journal, and the Duke University Journal of Gender Law & Policy, among other publications. Two of his articles in the New York Bar Journal have been cited with approval by the Supreme Courts of South Carolina and Michigan. He also has co-authored a guide for business managers and HR professions (*What Every Business Manager and HR Professional Should Know About . . . Federal Labor and*

Employment Laws) and a two-volume treatise (*Corporate* Counseling). In 2020 Mr. DiLorenzo was recognized with the prestigious Burton Award for Distinguished Legal Writing. Mr. DiLorenzo is often quoted in various publications, including Forbes, Business Week, the ABA Journal, Bloomberg Law, and the Daily Record, among others, on labor and employment issues of import. He is a former adjunct professor in Syracuse University's Whitman School of Management and former co-chair of the St. John's University Law School's Employment Law Institute.

Mr. DiLorenzo has long been recognized by Chambers, Best Lawyers in America, and Super Lawyers, among others. He has been named to the Corporate Employment Lawyers Hall of Fame by Human Resource Executive and Lawdragon, included in HR Executive Magazine's list of "Top 10 Labor Lawyers," and named a Benchmark Litigation Labor & Employment Star. Corporate Legal Times has dubbed him "The Great Negotiator."

Mr. DiLorenzo is a Fellow of the College of Labor and Employment Lawyers, a Fellow of the New York State Bar Foundation, a Fellow of the Trial Lawyer Honorary Society and a Member of the Federation of Defense & Corporate Counsel.

Mr. DiLorenzo is a graduate of Syracuse University and the University at Buffalo School of Law.

JEFFREY A. KEHL, ESQ.

Jeffrey Kehl brings 47 years of experience in labor and employment law to this book, including day-to-day employer counseling, workplace investigations, development of policies and procedures, negotiations, litigation, arbitration, mediation, discrimination and harassment training and defense, and general training for managers. A major portion of his work has been for educational institutions, both private and public, from pre-school through graduate programs; but he has also represented a variety of commercial entities including a major publishing conglomerate, and also numerous non-profit social service providers. In 1983, he helped create, and has since continued to represent, a new and innovative multi-employer self-insured health benefits consortium. He joined Bond, Schoeneck & King as a member (partner) in 2014, when the law firm of which he was a name partner, specializing in the law of educational and non-profit institutions with a heavy emphasis on employment law, merged into Bond. A graduate of Princeton University (where he honed his editing and writing skills as an English major) and Columbia Law School, he first trained in labor and employment law at Kaye, Scholer, Fierman, Hays & Handler (now Arnold & Porter). He currently serves as President of the Board of Trustees of the Kneisel Hall Chamber Music School and Festival in Blue Hill, Maine.

CONTRIBUTORS

MARA D. AFZALI	MARY E. ALDRIDGE
JEFFREY F. ALLEN	CAITLIN A. ANDERSON
JOHN M. BAGYI	MONICA C. BARRETT
MICHAEL I. BERNSTEIN	MICHAEL D. BILLOK
ANDREW D. BOBREK	R. DANIEL BORDONI
PAUL J. BUEHLER, III	MALLORY A. CAMPBELL
BETHANY A. CENTRONE	MICHAEL P. COLLINS
CHRISTA RICHER COOK	STEPHEN C. DALEY
NICHOLAS J. D'AMBROSIO, JR.	JAMES D. DATI
SANJEEVE K. DESOYZA	LOUIS P. DILORENZO
MELINDA G. DISARE	SAMUEL G. DOBRE
THOMAS G. ERON	STEPHANIE H. FEDORKA
DAVID M. FERRARA	RICHARD S. FINKEL
DANIEL P. FORSYTH	BRITTANY FRANK
JOHN GAAL	JACQUELINE A. GIORDANO
JOHN C. GODSOE	CANDACE J. GOMEZ
LAURA H. HARSHBARGER	BRIAN K. HAYNES

MICHAEL E. HICKEY

EMILY E. IANNUCCI

PETER A. JONES

JEFFREY A. KEHL

CHRISTOPHER T. KURTZ

RIANE F. LAFFERTY

KERRY W. LANGAN

BARBARA A. LEE

THADDEUS J. LEWKOWICZ

LARRY P. MALFITANO

ADAM P. MASTROLEO

KATHERINE S. MCCLUNG

PATRICK V. MELFI

HOWARD M. MILLER

JESSICA C. MOLLER

DANIEL J. NUGENT

CRAIG L. OLIVO

LOUIS ORBACH

JAMES C. HOLAHAN

NICHOLAS P. JACOBSON

RICHARD G. KASS

SHELLEY SANDERS KEHL

ROBERT A. LABERGE

DENNIS A. LALLI

BRIAN LAUDADIO,

COLIN M. LEONARD

SARAH A. LUKE

ROBERT F. MANFREDO

AISLING M. MCALLISTER

GREGORY J. MCDONALD

MELISSA E. GERECCI MEYLER

MARK A. MOLDENHAUER

HILARY L. MOREIRA

RANDALL M. ODZA

TERRY O'NEIL

WILLIAM L. OWENS

RAYMOND J. PASCUCCI

AARON M. PIERCE

KSENIYA PREMO

KATE I. REID

SARA M. RICHMOND

THERESA E. RUSNAK

NIHLA F. SIKKANDER

JANE M. SOVERN

AYANNA Y. THOMAS

SUBHASH VISWANATHAN

RICHARD C. WHITE

ROBERT W. PATTERSON

SHARON M. PORCELLIO

HANNAH K. REDMOND

GREGORY B. REILLY

JAMES J. ROONEY

KATHERINE R. SCHAFER

JOANNA L. SILVER

ERNEST L. STOLZER

ERIN S. TORCELLO

CAROLINE M. WESTOVER

PETER H. WILTENBURG